'0—
hist

IRAQ'S DEMOCRATIC MOMENT

FOULATH HADID

Iraq's Democratic Moment

HURST & COMPANY, LONDON

First published in the United Kingdom in 2012 by
C. Hurst & Co. (Publishers) Ltd.,
41 Great Russell Street, London, WC1B 3PL
© Foulath Hadid, 2012
All rights reserved.
Printed in India

Distributed in the United States, Canada and Latin America by
Oxford University Press, 198 Madison Avenue, New York, NY 10016,
United States of America.

A Cataloguing-in-Publication data record for this book
is available from the British Library.

ISBN: 978-1-84904-218-5

This book is printed using paper from registered sustainable
and managed sources.

www.hurstpublishers.com

CONTENTS

I dedicate this book to my father, Mohamed Hadid, to by brother Haytham Hadid and to my sister, Zaha Hadid.

LIST OF ILLUSTRATIONS

(Between pages 34 and 35)

PROLOGUE

This book had its origins in a difference of opinion I had in August 2003 with a British historian specializing in Iraq. I was a mature student working on a doctoral dissertation at Oxford University, on the subject of the democratization movement in Iraq from 1921–1963. Barely a week after a hip replacement operation, I hobbled through the gates of Wadham College on crutches, to be examined by two scholars of international renown. To my astonishment they took exception to my use of words such as 'freedom', 'democracy' and the 'popular will'. What could such terms mean in the context of Iraq, they asked?

Such a question puzzled me. These terms certainly represented the struggle of Iraqis over several generations for independence and representative constitutional government. This I knew from family history, personal experience and extensive research on the subject. I had thrown myself at all that had been written on the democratic movement in my country. I read memoirs by Ottoman officers, Iraqi politicians, Arab nationalists and monarchists. I sifted through piles of period newspapers, archived and recent; studied Public Record documents in English, French and Arabic. I interviewed many of the surviving decision-makers of the period, both Iraqi and Arab, to seek their views on the painful—and unfinished—process of democratization in Iraq and in other parts of the Arab world.

During the editing of my father Mohammad Hadid's memoir, I had gained a unique insight into the democratic struggle in which he had been so deeply involved. This subject became my overriding passion, and not surprisingly perhaps. I had grown up in a political Iraqi family, many members of which had been exiled and jailed for their resistance to foreign occupation or local repression. My maternal grand-father Moustapha al-Sabounchi first was exiled—like his father Mohammed Pasha before him—by the Ottomans for his Arab nation-alist stand; and then again by the British, for having been one of the financial backers of the Iraq Revolution of 1920.[1] In the thirties, my father Mohammed Hadid had been one of the founders and leaders of Iraq's democracy movement. He and many of his compatriots had devoted entire lives and been imprisoned in order to implement the democratic ideal that had been promised by the country's constitution. I myself had witnessed firsthand not just the energy but also the vio-lence unleashed by revolutions (Iraq 1958) and coup d'état (Morocco 1971). In the latter, I was shot at close range by machine-gun fire, wounded and taken prisoner by the rebels.

The beginnings of the story I tell here are shrouded in colonial intrigue. The cast of characters, mainly British intelligence officers, operating out of the Arab Bureau in Cairo, the India Office or White-hall, dabbled breezily with the grave processes of Arab politics, with-out ever stopping to gauge the consequences that their actions might have in the long term—British romance with the Arab world turned out to be nothing but 'British imperialism with Arab headgear' as one academic put it.[2] The decision to create a monarchy and import it to rule over the Iraqi people could have succeeded only if the decision-makers had adhered to the principles of constitutional and representa-tive government.

Faisal I, a stranger to Iraq, was planted by Britain on its throne. He had to grapple with the task of governing an artificial country made up of provinces cobbled together from the ruins of the Ottoman Empire. He boasted an impeccable pedigree, claiming descent from the Prophet Mohammed, and was known for his nationalist views (he was reputed to have been a member of al-'Arabiyya al-Fattat, the secret nationalist society). In an ideal world, he might well have proved the necessary agent of change that this new country needed. But things were not to be so easy. Despite a brave effort to juggle the possible with the improbable, Faisal never managed to solve any of the country's intrin-sic problems. Towards the end of his reign, frustrated and downcast, he left a scathing confidential memorandum berating Iraq and its peo-ple for their ungovernable nature.[3] The men Faisal brought with him—ex-Ottoman army officers who had served in his Arab Army—were to become the perennial members of Iraq's consecutive governments—until the 1958 revolution brought an end to the monarchy.

I have tried to write this book as free of personal views concerning the personalities involved as was humanly possible. I nevertheless apologize in advance to any friend or acquaintance who might consider that I have cast relatives of theirs in an unforgiving light. To students and specialists on Iraq, I must also make clear that this work never pretends to be an academic one. It is my account of Iraq's missed opportunities to develop a democratic form of government as clearly promised in its constitution. It is the poignant story of painstaking attempts by a group of nationalist leaders—belonging to opposition parties—to overcome the draconian obstacles placed in their path. These obstacles consisted of a still-colonial Britain, doggedly pursuing its regional agenda; a newly-minted monarchy, desperate to find a middle road to guide the young country through its infant years; and a pro-British set of palace-approved politicians, some of whom believed that the future of the country should be inextricably embedded in the British schema for the area. Loathe to seeing opposition parties ever reaching power, such men resorted to election fraud, the bending of the rule of law, and to wholesale repression. In this manner, they believed they could stamp out the democratic voice and longings of the Iraqi people.

In the process, the country was shackled to onerous treaties and oil concessions, many of them quite breathtaking in their imperialist greed. One particularly ill-starred agreement, the Portsmouth Treaty of 1948, had to be discarded when the country rose up as a whole against it. The Regent 'Abdulillah was forced to announce Iraq's rejection of it, even as the ink was still drying on its signature in England. Indeed, the *Wathba*—as this uprising came to be known—remains a seminal event in Iraqi history. It is also one of the manifold inspirations for the Arab Spring uprisings that the world has seen in 2011. In a courageous and defiant expression of popular will, Arabs in country after country are ridding themselves of dictatorships, in favor of democratically elected and representative governments.

As the story of Iraq's quest for democracy that I have attempted to portray in this book shows, the Arab Spring is no sudden wake-up call for democracy, but a process that began almost 100 years ago, as recounted by George Antonius in his seminal book of 1939, *The Arab Awakening*.

My fervent hope is that the torch has been passed to a new generation of Arabs, who will succeed where our forebears and we ourselves could not.

INTRODUCTION

The land that became Iraq had, for a millennium, been at the mercy of the forces of fragmentation brought about by foreign intervention as well as by internecine strife. The people inhabiting the land showed little interest in social cohesion. During the five centuries of Ottoman rule, for example, they preferred to live in separate provinces. By the time the modern history of Iraq began in 1918, the land that had once glittered as the learned centre of a great Arab caliphate had been crushed by poverty and illiteracy. Its divided people had borne the weight of several centuries of consecutive invasions and occupation, which plundered the land for its natural riches and controlled it for its strategic location. Greeks, Romans, Sassanians, Seljuks, Tartars and Mongols were among those who left their imprint on this land.

The last struggle for supremacy was that of the Ottoman and Persian Empires, which was to leave an indelible mark on the land and its people until its 'invention' as a new country to be called 'Iraq' following World War I. The resultant Sunni-Shi'ite-Kurdish slicing that took place in that era still defies solution today. For centuries, the style of government had been authoritarian, which rendered it almost impossible for the new state to adjust easily to such new values as had been generated by European notions of nationalism, freedom and democracy. Nevertheless, it was being asked to adopt such values—in name only by the West and passionately by its own democrats.

Iraq, as schoolchildren are taught, was not without its glorious history. As ancient Babylon, it was the acknowledged cradle of human civilization. Its formidable King Nebuchadnezzar II (634–562 BC) left for posterity a system of urban life that came to be called 'The Urban Revolution' that led to city life as we know it today. Babylonians invented the alphabet and, under their King Hammurabi, gave the world its first codified set of laws. In so doing, they invented the first legal system. Because of Iraq's two great rivers, the Tigris and the Euphrates, the first agricultural system was also developed there. This system spread to Europe and elsewhere, accelerating the evolution of settled society.[1] Those two majestic rivers had always played a vital role in shaping Iraq's destiny and, up until World War I, even gave it its name: *Bilad al-Rafidain'* (Land of the Two Rivers) or Mesopotamia.

Baghdad was the jewel in the crown of the Arab Empire, until its pillage by Hulagu in 1258. Under the Abbasids, the cultural renaissance was no less important than that which transformed Europe in the sixteenth century. The caliphs established libraries and centres of teaching that vied with each other for excellence and achievement. By the end of the millennium, Baghdad stood at the cutting-edge of Islamic learning. Scientific breakthroughs enabled a multicultural society almost identical to the West's in our time to advance at a stunningly rapid rate. Science was applied to solving practical problems, very much in the way that technology is harnessed to serve society today. Algebra and geometry produced complex calculation systems. Musa al-Khawarizimi's outstanding contribution to mathematics—the introduction of the concept of zero—still stands today as unique, considering that Europe only began to understand and to use this concept 400 years later. Al-Khawarizimi's own name has since been immortalized in the mathematical term 'algorithm'. Knowledge became integral to a society eager to continue to push the frontiers of achievement. Scholars' names resonated widely, becoming the celebrities of their day: Khalil bin Ahmad, who wrote the first lexicographic work in history; or the translators—al-Hajjaj bin Mattar, Thabit bin Qurrah, Qusta bin Laqa—who were but a few of those discovering the manuscripts of ancient civilizations, such as that of Greece, centuries before Europe used their annotated works to understand Greek philosophy. Schools at Western Universities for the study of Arabic were set up in Cambridge (1633), Oxford (1636) and the Ecole Spéciale des Langues Orientales in Paris (1795), in no small way to learn the language of these extraordinary scholars in order to benefit from their erudition. It can be said that with the Abbasids the Arab Empire had reached its apex in both civilization and conquest. Philip Hitti, in his seminal *History of the Arabs*, wrote, 'Around the name of the Arabs gleams that halo which belongs to world conquerors. Within a century after their rise this people became the masters of an empire extending from the shores of the Atlantic Ocean to the confines of China, an empire greater than that of Rome at its zenith'. And Baghdad was the centre of that empire.

By the 1500s, the Ottomans came to govern Mesopotamia through their co-sectarian Sunnis, to avert any possible threat from their Shi'a rivals in Persia. With the much-later creation of the modern state of Iraq, Sunni dominance continued, with a Sunni king and his retinue of Sunni army officers. The British—who were by then the real rulers of Iraq—further promoted Sunni predominance, since they wished to deal a vengeful blow to the local Shi'a for having fought them so ferociously in the 1920 Iraq Revolution and inflicted heavy losses. Later still, only five of the fifty-nine cabinets before the 1958 Revolution were headed by Shi'a Iraqis. The Sunnis of Iraq happened to enjoy religious and cultural affinity with a huge section of the Arab world by virtue of their shared values of Arab nationalism, which was by and large a Sunni affair. The religious elite of the Shi'a of Iraq, who were the majority sect and could logically have formed their own country, retreated instead into a 'quietist' existence, composed mainly of textual study and spiritual observance. Their masses, however, suffered greatly from this isolation, both socially and economically. This gave them a noted persecution complex—which had its political bedrock in Shi'a history and mythology—that found its violent outlet after the fall of Saddam's mainly Sunni regime.[2]

Added to Sunni-Shi'ite-Kurdish divisions was the existence of another important social force. This was represented by the regional Bedouin tribes, who inhabited a world that was totally different from that of the townspeople. The tribes lived a marauding existence, often marked by raids upon each other (exactly as they had done in pre-Islamic times in Arabia), which nevertheless had a complex system of etiquette and social behaviour that became very much part of their lawless identity.

Such was the dawn to which the territory that was to become Iraq awoke following the collapse of the Ottoman Empire. British troops paraded the streets and invaded lives; Indian soldiers (who made up the bulk of the British army in that part of the world) made their apparition as well—so that one colonized people was put in charge of colonizing another.

The consensus among scholars writing about this period is that Iraqis—including their deputies in the Ottoman parliament—had been quite content to be part of an Islamic Empire, even though they and other Arabs aspired to and even agitated for an improvement in their increasingly second-class status within what was fast becoming a Turkified (rather than a pan-Muslim) empire. Memoirs of prominent Iraqis such as Sulaiman al-Faidi and Tawfiq al-Swaidi come to that conclusion, as do the works of scholars such as Albert Hourani, Sukru Hanioglu, Hassan Kayali and Phillip Khoury. This phenomenon of contentment or acquiescence was largely true of most Arabs living under Ottoman rule. Even the Sharif Hussain, who was to father the Arab Revolt, was undecided on which side to fight as late as 1916.[3] For Arabs, the accepting of Ottoman rule was not difficult since it was a matter of superimposing imperial authority over local authority; and later on, of replacing one Muslim caliphate for another. Even as late as 1920, 'Abd al-Rahman al-Naqib—the Naqib of the Ashraf in Bagh-dad—went on record saying that he would never accept the Sharif of the Hijaz or any of his offspring as kings of Iraq, in spite of their descent in common from the Prophet Mohammad's family. He went on to say that he preferred to see the return of the Turks a thousand times over rather than to tolerate an imposed kingship by the Sharif or his sons, whom he considered to be tainted by too close an association with the British. Ironically, this same Naqib went on to become prime minister under the new King Faisal, having been assured by Percy Cox, the British Civil Commissioner, that Faisal was going to be a constitu-tional monarch.[4] According to Hanna Batatu, 400 Iraqi notables signed a petition as late as July 1923, exhorting the Ottoman caliph to deliver the Iraqis from these foreigners; 'from Faisal and his father who came to dominate the Moslems by fighting in the ranks of the Allies and by disuniting the Moslems under the cloak of Arab Nationalism'.[5] To add insult to injury, until 1924, Friday prayers in mosques were said in the name of the Ottoman sultan/caliph, as both the spiritual and the temporal leader, despite King Faisal's protestations that he took this as a personal affront.

Iraqis were no great adherents to an independent Arab identity. They hardly took in much about the Arab nationalist movement, which was more of a Syrian affair. Many sat in the Ottoman parliament, but their record of having expressed nationalist sentiment was scant. In his mem-oir, Tawfiq al-Swaidi (a future prime minister) states that most deputies were drawn from the landed classes, and were there more to protect their interests than to make any political statements.[6] They seemed content to serve under an Islamic caliphate. Some memoirs of the period, including Swaidi's, do show a certain nationalist fervour, but they display no democratic leanings—apart, perhaps, from attempting to secure a better 'deal' for the Arabs within the empire. Sassoon Heskial, for example, a pillar of Iraq's Jewish community who went on to become Iraq's first finance minister and was such a perennial member of the Ottoman parliament that he laboured under the name of *Abu al-Barlaman* (father of parliament), was himself not a parliamentarian or democrat in the recognized sense of the word.

Nevertheless, there was a trickle-down effect from the nationalist movement taking shape in Syria, in the guise of various secret societies such as al-ʿArabiya al-Fatat and al-ʿAhd. Consensus thinking among the elite members that were touched by the movement was their concerns about Arabism, social progress, and liberty from the Turkish yoke. On Arabism, many educated people felt strongly about reviving the Arabic language to take its place proudly alongside the languages of Europe, especially since it had been the motor of a glorious civilization whose 'fire had been extinguished', as Swaidi put it. Many who joined the secret societies did so because of their concern to defend Arab culture and the Arabic language. The Arabs, T. E. Lawrence wrote, had lost their 'geographical sense, their racial and political and historical memories; but they clung the more tightly to their language, and erected it into almost a fatherland of its own'.[7] Their language evoked past glories (*Amjad*) and these occupied a prominent place in Arab folklore.[8] The language further united all races and religions in the area, especially Christians. The latter contributed vastly to Arab culture and to the Arab nationalist movement. Basically, anyone who claimed Arabic as their mother tongue was regarded as an Arab.[9] Arabism was a natural precursor to nationalism, as it drew deeply on Arab culture to infuse and arouse people to attain nationalist goals.

These ideas culminated in the Arab Conference in Paris in 1913. Ironically, the Sharif Hussain added to the Arab dilemma by reflecting contemporary Hijaz Bedouin hostile thinking to Arab nationalism. He sent a telegram to Istanbul, protesting the conference as an act of treason.[10] (A few years later, extraordinarily enough, he did a *volte face* and, with his sons, was to lead the Arab Revolt). From an Iraqi perspective, Tawfiq al-Swaidi, a twenty-year-old studying at the Sorbonne, ended up representing Iraq along with another Iraqi student. Not to distract from these two young Iraqis' sense of nationalism—or to forget that the conference had been organized by students—they could hardly have been considered to be experienced politicians. It is a reflection perhaps of Iraq's lack of political interest in the nationalist cause that more experienced leaders were not sent to the conference, as in the case of other Arab countries.

On the social level, the atrocious conditions prevailing in the three *vilayet* that were now Iraq simply beggared belief. Post was delivered far too slowly by sea, across the desert on camels or over the Anatolian mountains on horseback. Travel was fraught with danger and, whatever route one took, it required a minimum of thirty days to reach Istanbul. Although, historically, the Turks had looked kindly on Baghdad's grandeur ('No friend is better than an Arab friend and no place is better than Baghdad', a conventional Turkish saying went), they nevertheless treated the city as if it had become a place of exile, where all those who incurred the wrath of the sultan finished their days in obscurity. Unfortunately many exiled *wali* exploited the situation to their advantage, with minimal or no control from Istanbul. Exploitation became rampant, with the best lands expropriated and assets seized without recourse to their owners. Corruption became *de rigueur* among civil servants—who were only paid once or twice a year, if that, and were forced to supplement their meagre incomes somehow. The army fared no better. Its soldiers' uniforms, food, and weapons were pitiful. They, too, were rarely paid, and it was not uncommon to see a shivering soldier, wrapped in the worn blanket he slept in, guarding a government building.

As for public opinion, it was limited to a handful of clerics, or to a few reactionaries who could barely read or write. Amongst these, there infiltrated a class of opportunist that belonged to neither faction, but exploited the chaotic conditions prevailing to their advantage. Such people eventually rose to become the notables in their local society, and this social misdevelopment was yet another testament to Iraq's misfortunes. For these men did anything that furthered their greed. They could be pro-Arab, pro-Turkish and pro-British—taking up any and every position that suited them. Nationalism and democracy, sadly, stood absolutely no chance with such adventurers.

The Iraqi intelligentsia, diminutive as it was, was nevertheless influenced by the collective thinking emanating from Damascus and Cairo. However, wider dissemination of these ideas into Iraqi society remained limited. The extremely poor economic, social and educational conditions prevailing in Iraq at that time agitated against this intellectual glimmer ever evolving into a true cultural renaissance. Iraq simply did not enjoy the intellectual and political freedom that Cairo and Damascus enjoyed. Suppression was total and the free exchange of ideas rare.[11] Educated Iraqis tended to study at the military schools of Istanbul (as evidenced by the statistic that out of 1400 Iraqi students studying in Istanbul in the years 1872 to 1912, 1200 graduated as army officers). That became even more evident when the new Iraqi state was formed, and almost all government portfolios were quickly filled by the ex-army cohorts of Faisal. Furthermore, in this same time span, seventy Iraqis attended the American University of Beirut (AUB), but apart from the Christians among them, the majority did not demonstrate any particular penchant for intellectual thinking, as had their Syrian counterparts. Indeed, it was the Iraqi Shi'a who were the first to embrace nationalist ideas and call for a renewal of Arab political and cultural destiny. Being fiercely Arab in their outlook, they did not then assimilate with Persians, and rejected Turks because of their persecution of them. In general, they were loath to abandon the idea of Islam as a viable system of governance, or to allow Western ideas to infiltrate into that Islamic system.[12]

In perusing memoirs of this period, one reads about those Iraqis newly-arrived in Istanbul who joined the Arab literary clubs such as *Nadi al-Muntada*. They describe feeling woefully inadequate because of their demotic Arabic, which was a mixture of Arabic, Turkish and Persian; their lack of general knowledge and culture, and their inferiority complex *vis-à-vis* the Syrians.[13] The Iraqis came up short on Arab history, poetry, literature, and on more general goals and objectives. All Iraqis who have left memoirs agree that the first whispers they heard about Arab independence were heard in these clubs. Al-Rasafi describes the design of an Arab flag of black, white, green and red that was already being conceived, even though there was not yet a country established for it to represent! An Iraqi deputy, Jamil Sidqi al-Zahawi from Baghdad, was forced in 1901 to defend the Arabness of Baghdad against other Arab deputies who claimed that it was not Arab at all, but totally Ottoman.

Zeine Zeine, in his *The Emergence of Arab Nationalism*, traces the nationalist trail which led to the Arab Revolt under the Sharif Hussain. But he strongly makes the point that the vast majority of the inhabitants of the Arab Near East remained loyal to the Ottoman government. Only a small and not necessarily Muslim group—secularly enlightened and politically ambitious—actively thought of separation. Zeine unpacks the phrase 'Arab Awakening' and explains that it was an awakening to the abuses, corruption and despotism of the Turkish regime and to the desire for reform. The wish to establish an independent Arab state simply had not yet occurred to the vast majority of inhabitants of the Ottoman provinces. Much has been written about Christian intellectuals—especially the Syrian Christians amongst them—clamouring for political reform and independence. Arab Muslim intellectuals, on the whole, were calling rather for administrative reform within the empire and sometimes for a return to 'pristine' Islamic practices and institutions. Zeine describes such men as 'the apostles of pan-Islamism', chief amongst them Muhammad 'Abduh, 'Abd al-Rahman al-Kawakibi and Rashid Rida.

In the Ottoman parliament, as stated earlier, Iraqi deputies were known not for their ideological cohesion but for their diversity of opinion. In any event, the majority amongst them seemed more interested in protecting their material status than waving any political banners. The Lynch affair was a telling example of how Iraqi deputies sprang into action to block the concession, mainly because it went against their own economic interests.[14] However, it did serve as an early lesson in trenchant parliamentary debate.

But such ambiguity was in the nature of the beast. Even the proposed Arab state promised to the Sharif Hussain remained ill-defined and ill-conceived. Those who participated in the Arab Revolt, and those who joined the Arab cause after the Armistice, were motivated by personal and local ambition, rather than by any overwhelming and abstract national idea. Nevertheless, Arab leaders looked forward, naively perhaps, to an independent existence and control over their political future. But Great Britain entered into the Sykes-Picot Agreement with France, and agreed to the partition of the Ottoman Arab provinces into European spheres of influence. France would receive most of Lebanon and Syria; Britain would control Iraq, while Palestine would be placed under international control.[15] In addition, the Balfour Declaration of 1917 committed Britain to the establishment of a Jewish homeland in Arab Palestine.[16] British Foreign Secretary Arthur James Balfour, in his untiring quest to support Jewish designs on Palestine, was responsible for the blunder made by the then Emir Faisal (goaded on by T.E. Lawrence) to acknowledge the right to create the state of Israel. In 1918, Faisal was totally dependent on a British monthly subsidy of 150,000 pounds sterling and, probably against his wishes, was made to sign an agreement with the British Zionist Chaim Weizmann on 3 January 1919 that was to haunt him thereafter. Even today this document is quoted by Israelis as the Arabs' acceptance of the existence of the state of Israel. Faisal made a meek attempt to show his disagreement by insisting that a post-script be added below the signatures, that his support for the document was contingent on the Arabs receiving full independence as promised by the McMahon-Hussein agreement.[17] In his memoir, Mohammed Hadid cites a meeting he had with Muzahim al-Pachachi (Minister-Plenipotentiary at the Iraqi Embassy in London when Hadid was a student at the London School of Economics in 1929) at which Pachachi showed Hadid a copy of the Faisal-Weizmann Agreement (hitherto unknown in Iraq). A copy of this agreement that Pachachi took with him to Baghdad was leaked to the public, causing a major stir. Pachachi was immediately accused by the pro-government press of being the source of the leak and that his intent was to tarnish the reputation of King Faisal.[18]

With the end of the war, Faisal pleaded the case of the Arabs at Versailles, but France had already moved troops into Beirut, and Britain did the same in Iraq. The Arabs in British-occupied Damascus grew impatient waiting for their independence, especially as western Syria was being infiltrated by France in order to insure her share of the territorial handout. The San Remo Conference of April 1920 handed Britain a League of Nations mandate for all of Palestine and Iraq, and gave the mandate for Syria and Lebanon to France.[19] Incensed Arab nationalists in Damascus were divided on how to respond to this betrayal by their so-called allies. Indeed, it was this period that heightened widespread feelings of Arab consciousness and

attracted adherents representing a variety of backgrounds and interests. From Europe, from Istanbul and the Arab provinces of the Ottoman Empire came former members of the Committee for Union and Progress and other officials, demobilized soldiers and officers (many of whom were Iraqi) who had fought in Ottoman armies, as well as those who had been involved in the Arab revolt from its beginning.[20]

Prominent among these were ex-Ottoman officers such as Yasin and Taha al-Hashimi, Ja'far al-'Askari and Nuri al-Sa'id; the Damascene officer Yusuf al-'Azmeh; leaders like Hashim al-Atasi from Homs and Ihsan al-Jabiri from Aleppo, both from important patrician families;

noted Lebanese patriots like Riyad al-Sulh and Sa'id Haydar; and former Istanbul officials like the Syrian Sati' al-Husri who came to Damascus and made that city truly 'the *ka'abah* of every Arab patriot'.[21]

Faisal's short-lived reign in Syria did not go well. Considerable resentment against him was displayed by Damascene notables, who had been jostled aside, ignored and even insulted by the Emir's sometimes boorish cronies. His upstart Iraqi and Syrian army officers, disorderly Hijazi troops and squabbling civilian nationalists deliberately isolated him, so that Damascene notables would not come into contact with him. Indeed, this was made conspicuously evident by their total absence from his government. This situation did not bode well for the budding nationalist movement.

Shortly after the collapse of his reign in Syria, Faisal was forced to wait in the corridors of power while another job was found for him. By that time, Hussain's Arab dream was in tatters. Faisal had been ejected from Syria, and 'Abdallah—who had been promised the throne of Iraq—was also looking for a kingdom. It is no wonder therefore that each of the sons of Hussain decided to develop his own agenda and cooperate fully with the British, since they were the decision-making occupiers able to fulfil their dreams of kingship.

Faisal started his reign with the usual dilemmas common to rulers transplanted from other countries. In his case, there was the added complication that the country to be ruled had been artificially created. This new Iraq was inhabited by heterogeneous and communally-divided populations, with none of the social cohesiveness or sense of territorial nationalism common to nation-states. The situation was further aggravated by the absence of any political community based on mutually-binding obligations between ruler and ruled and the absence of a political system established by consent and governed by the rule of law. Although the notions of nationalism and the concept of the nation-state originated in Europe, they were nevertheless strongly hungered for by nationalist intellectuals in the region. Given the way the region looked forward to a democratic future, those notions would probably have worked if obstacles had not been placed in their path by the Western mandatory powers, and through them by their local allies, with the result that democracy was stifled at every turn.

Thus was the area poised on a knife's edge, awaiting a fate that was to be decided by the Great Powers. These powers were engaged in frenetic activity which started with the Paris Peace Conference in 1918 and continued to the accords of San Remo in 1920. But such frenetic activity was not restricted to the Western powers alone. The people inhabiting the territories recently separated from the Ottoman Empire were also busy trying to determine their own future. The ancient city of Damascus now became the hub of Arab activity. It was there that Faisal went to become king—albeit for a few short months—and there that army officers who had fought with him gathered, clamouring for lucrative government posts. Damascus became a listening post for events about to decide the Arabs' fate. That fate was principally tied to Arab hopes for a United Arabia, which they believed had been promised to them by the Hussain-McMahon Agreement.

Harold Nicholson writes in his book *Peacemaking 1919* that Britain's pledges to the Arabs were in direct conflict with the promises it had made to France in the Sykes-Picot Agreement. This produced a sticky situation between the British and the French on the one hand, and the American president, Woodrow Wilson, on the other. Nicholson says that the McMahon-Hussain letters

were shrouded in the ambiguity inseparable from all oriental correspondence, yet the impression left on the mind of King Hussein was that Great Britain had assured him support in the foundation of a united Arab Empire with its capital at Damascus. It is true that in the course of the correspondence the British government (who were bound by an understanding with France dating from 1912 to 'disinterest themselves' in Syria) had some vague reservation about Damascus. This reservation, however, had not been studiously precise and it is significant that the subsequent Sykes-Picot Agreement was not communicated by us to the Arabs, even as our pledges to King Hussein were not, until March of 1919, disclosed to the French.

Both the British and the French embarked on a process of dissimulation and double-dealing of such magnitude that the Arabs simply found themselves hung out to dry—stripped of all the pledges the West had made them. It has become a somewhat hackneyed historical cliché that T. E. Lawrence described the British government as double-faced and treacherous in its dealings with Hussain. This is certainly the view promulgated in *Seven Pillars of Wisdom*. In a letter to *The Times*, dated 11 September 1919, Lawrence gave a summary account of McMahon's famous letter 24 October 1915, which clearly laid out the promises that McMahon had made to Hussain as well as their subsequent withdrawal by the British.

Lawrence was by no means the only one to tell how Britain had gone back on the promises it had made to the Arabs. Many British officials, in memoirs and other publications, lent authority to this notion, now an established fact. Thus Sir Hugh Foot (later Lord Carrigan) who spent fifteen years as a British official in the Middle East, states in his memoirs: 'The Arabs who fought with Great Britain in the first world war to throw off the yoke of the Turkish Empire were led to believe that they were fighting for their freedom... the main responsibility was ours... by prevarication and procrastination and basically by the fundamental dishonesty of our original double dealing we had made disaster certain... In 1915 we supported King Faisal's desert rising. In 1917 we signed the Balfour Declaration'.[22]

Sir Lawrence Graffty-Smith, a diplomat who spent a whole career in the Middle East, reveals himself censorious of his country's actions. He states categorically that the behaviour of the British government towards Hussain was nothing short of immoral and that the Sykes-Picot Agreement and the Balfour Declaration had 'made nonsense' of McMahon's promises. The Sykes-Picot Agreement, according to Graffty-Smith, was kept secret because it was so disreputable. It was kept hidden so that 'even our High Commissioner in Cairo, responsible for the political side of the Arab Revolt, heard of it later, and only casually'.[23]

Elie Kedourie says that the McMahon-Hussain letters, sixty years on, left nothing but guilt, recrimination and a soiled relationship with the Arab world. Kedourie blames officials such as Clayton, Storrs, and McMahon, whom he accuses of having been over-eager, frivolous, incompetent and, worst of all, of having entrapped future generations of British officials hopelessly in the labyrinth that they left behind.[24] Perhaps Lloyd George put the Western case most honestly when he declared that the British 'are there by conquest and there we shall remain'.[25]

The whole area was now a volcano about to erupt, and Iraq was no exception. Even though it was not then a major player like Syria, when the final betrayal was dealt to the Arabs at San Remo, it was Iraq which was the first to explode.

1

THE 1920 REVOLUTION
(AND HOW IRAQ WAS INVENTED)

For many Arabs, 5 May 1920 is a day that will live on in infamy. On that day, the San Remo Agreement was signed and Arab anger against Western powers began.[1] It has been argued that this date fuelled much of the nationalist feeling in the areas that Britain and France controlled in the Arab world at the time. George Antonius, in *The Arab Awakening*, describes it as the moment when the Arabs realized that the San Remo decisions amounted to 'nothing short of betrayal'.[2]

In Arab eyes, the San Remo Conference reneged on all the promises made to them in return for their contribution to the victory of the Allies over the Ottoman Empire and equally reneged on the debt of honour owed to them as a consequence. From that date onward, Arab relations with both the British and the French were marked by suspicion and mistrust. Elizabeth Monroe, in her book *Britain's Moment in the Middle East*, called it a period of 'promises broken and friends betrayed'.

San Remo wreaked havoc on what the Arabs had envisioned for themselves as a nation. It very simply dismissed their political wishes and desires, arousing great resentment in the minds of Arab leaders, resentment that lingers on in Arab minds to this day. It would not be an exaggeration to say that today's radical Islamic movements may have their roots in that period. San Remo was regarded as a flagrantly imperialist act, which not only violated the promises made but also the very principles which Britain and France were supposed to help engender in the countries they controlled. Those Arab leaders who had believed in an Anglo-Arab partnership had to endure considerable public resentment, once the selfishly-driven motives of the two powers became apparent.

Arab public disillusion was complete, coupled with a feeling of contempt for the dissembling Western powers. There followed a wave of anger that soon turned to despair, venting itself in the wild upheavals that followed. The Arab world, and more specifically those lands formerly under Ottoman rule, went into a downward spiral following the foreign intervention.

For eighteen months after the Armistice that brought World War I to an end, those Arabs who had heeded the advice of the Emir Faisal (who had led the Arab Revolt against the Ottomans) waited in apprehension as they watched the machinations of the Allies as they debated their fate at the Peace Conference. Their verdict, when finally announced, was to Arabs nothing short of a sentence of servitude, imposed not for any guilt on their part, but for the disparity between European military and economic might and their own weakness. In their political despair, they rose up and fought their occupiers in a series of revolts, the most serious of which broke out in Iraq within a few weeks of the announcement of the San Remo decisions.

This is where this story begins.

In 1918, there was no country called Iraq. The territory was made up of three distinct provinces of the Ottoman Empire—Baghdad, Mosul and Basra. Furthermore, the people inhabiting this land had no sense of nationhood and no tradition of a 'melting pot' of identity. The three city-states (*vilayat*) were no more connected to each other than they were individually to other geographic areas in the region. Indeed, Mosul traded more with Aleppo, Basra with Iran and India, and Baghdad mostly with Istanbul. For decades, the inhabitants of these cities had been dormant within the Ottoman system. There was hardly an inkling of the political activism or the nationalist fervour pervading other parts of the region at the time. Ali al-Wardi, the noted Iraqi anthropologist, framed the Iraqi attitude at that time in the Iraqi expression, current even today, as '*hatha mou shughli*' ('this is none of my business'). There was no rational reason why these three city-states should be lumped suddenly together as one country or one nation-state.

So what exactly happened?

In 1918, Turkey lost the war, and the two provinces of Baghdad and Basra fell to the British. The fate of Mosul was left undecided, since the British and Turkish armies had stopped—with the declaration of the Armistice—on opposite sides of the city. Turkey and Britain both claimed Mosul, but its fate was not decided until 1925, when it was joined to the new state of Iraq, thanks to some artful negotiations by the British, who were well aware of its vast oil deposits. They then rushed the Iraqis into an onerously one-sided Oil Concession Agreement as a 'trade-off' for having gotten Mosul to join their newly-created kingdom.

At the 1918 Peace Conference in Paris, President Woodrow Wilson gave the world his famous Fourteen Points. The twelfth point specifically referred to Ottoman territories, stating that 'nationalities then under Turkish rule should be assured of undoubted security of life and an absolutely unmolested opportunity of development'. There is no doubting the impact of Wilson's words on the populace of the area, now liberated from Turkish rule. But it soon transpired, however, that President Wilson's vision of dispensing democratic largesse was not meant by him to apply to Arab lands liberated from the Turks. Margaret MacMillan, a noted historian of the period, states in her book *The Peacemakers* that Wilson's words were far more ambiguous and equivocal than many took them to be, especially when it came to the Middle East.[3] Moreover, neither Wilson nor any other Western statesman had a clear idea of the nature of the peoples and nations involved in the Middle East. In his book *Sowing Crisis*, Rashid Khalidi writes that it was the realization at that conjuncture in history, when decisions were made without regard to the wishes of the people concerned, that the Middle East veered towards an impasse that has led to the mess that it is in today.[4]

The people inhabiting the area that became Iraq were caught up in the frenzy of political rights and self-government generated by President Wilson's Twelfth Point. The British had appointed A. T. Wilson as the Acting Civil Commissioner of the territory, with an apparatus of government set up to report back to the India Office. The scheme was to impose direct rule on Iraq, with Wilson as viceroy. There was even a plan to populate the land with Indians, who would be brought in to grow cotton.[5]

However, the people of these former Ottoman provinces kept up such a clamour for independence that the British and French were obliged to issue a document known as the 'Anglo-French Declaration'. It gave assurances that the British and the French, 'far from wishing to impose themselves on the people there, would support governments which the people shall have adopted of their own free will'. The date of this document was 8 November 1919, some eleven months following Woodrow Wilson's Twelfth Point. It was to prove yet another example of the many unkept promises made to the Arabs.[6]

A. T. Wilson wrote that the Anglo-French Declaration would have placed 'a potent weapon in the hands of those least fitted to control a nation's destiny'.[7] He simply sat on the whole thing and did nothing, safe in the knowledge that with direct rule, he would be the obvious choice for the job of viceroy.

The Iraqis, of course, disagreed. Their desire for independence was the fuse that lit the 1920 Revolution. A ground swell began to build for the withdrawal of the British and for the independence of the country. This became a rallying point, around which Shi'a, Sunni and Kurdish fighters met, led by their notables and intellectuals, together with Iraqi officers returning from the war, some who had defected to join Faisal, and others who had remained in Ottoman ranks but were now all united under one banner. This grouping, which took on the shape of a national movement, boasted names drawn from Iraq's elite families that included Sunni, Shi'a and Kurdish notables such as Baban, al-Sadr, Swaidi, Abul-Timman, Chadirchi, Naqshbandi, Daftari, and Fattah Pasha—names still known to Iraqis today. At a meeting famous in Iraqi history, that took place in the Haydar Khana Mosque, fifteen of these notables were elected to conduct talks with the British authorities.

A few days later, a delegation of these notables, now known as the 'Mandubin' or the elected ones, met with A. T. Wilson when the following demands were made:

1. The establishment of an Assembly to represent the country and decide upon its future government.
2. Freedom of the press.
3. Freedom of speech.

This was a seminal moment in Iraq's history. That simple early plea for democracy, and its rejection by the British, sparked a great uprising, which became known as the Iraqi Revolution of 1920.[8]

On 30 June 1920, the first bullet was fired in the town of Rumaitha (or some say in Tal'afar) and from there, the revolution spread to battlefields at Abu Sukheir, Hillah, Samawa, Daghara, Kufa, and Muntafiq. Thousands fell in battle. Although the Arabs fought with inferior weapons, they did so with such consummate skill that the British, including their commanding officer, General Aylmer Haldane, were persuaded that the Arabs had Turkish officers helping with their battle plans. On 17 August 1920, Wilson felt obliged to calm the provinces now in revolt for fear the revolution might spread to other provinces. Using the pretext of a condolence note on the occasion of the death of Imam Shirazi (a leading Shi'a cleric), he declared that he wished to establish peaceful relations with the religious leaders and avoid unnecessary bloodshed. He urged Iraqis to put their trust in the British government, which had always acted on the basis of its 'three-pillared policy of mercy, justice and religious tolerance'. He reminded the Iraqis that they were on a losing trend, since they did not have the financial resources or the modern weaponry to combat the British, who had such assets in abundance. The end result would beyond doubt be in favour of the British: all that was happening was an unnecessary spilling of blood. Thousands of copies of Wilson's note were dropped from the air over cities and battlefields, in addition to being published in British-controlled government newspapers.

Wilson's note did have an effect on certain elements of the population that wanted to terminate the revolution with an honourable peace. Furthermore, the tribal leaders of the Euphrates were disaffected with their Tigris brethren, and also with nationalist leaders in Baghdad and elsewhere, since these had failed to ignite an urban resistance movement to run parallel to the revolution in the Euphrates.

In retrospect, it can be seen that the revolution was doomed to failure—irrespective of the size of its war chest, the services of the noble men who fought for it, and the great sacrifices made. To crush the revolution, Britain deployed all the destructive weapons in its arsenal, from armoured cars to warplanes, to naval fleets and soldiers armed with the latest weapons. However, the reply to Wilson's note came from Imam Isfahani, another leading Shi'a cleric in Najaf, who warned him that the Iraqis would first demand their rights in a peaceful manner, but that if the British continued their policy of suppression, then the Iraqis would have no choice but to fight. He also told Wilson that his claim that British policy was based on mercy, justice and tolerance was utterly hollow. The British had murdered and exiled national leaders who had dared ask for independence; they had shot and killed children with all manner of weapons; and had caused untold misery to hundreds of people. As for justice, he said, summary execution, exile or imprisonment were the fate of anybody who, on the slightest rumour, was suspected of seeking independence. As for religious tolerance, British warplanes and armoured cars had fired at mosques and killed worshipers, including women and children (British warplanes had indeed bombed a mosque in Kufa).

On 6 October 1920, 100 tribal leaders and city notables signed a statement entitled 'The Protest of the Iraqi Nation' that was delivered to several European countries with an interest in the area, detailing the atrocities which the British were perpetrating in Iraq. It reminded Europe of promises made by Britain and France to help nations achieve their independence and establish governments based on the will of the people. When Iraqis demanded independence, they were met by persecution and the suspension of their rights and freedoms. The British, who had supposedly conducted a referendum to assess what sort of government Iraqis wanted, were accused of having committed electoral fraud by showing illiterate tribal leaders and their followers pieces of paper written in English, which purported to be land deeds. The tribal leaders signed, not knowing that they were effectively giving the British custodianship of Iraq.

The revolutionaries quickly established competent civil government in areas they controlled (the Middle Euphrates). They also conducted the war according to international rules of warfare of the time. They collected taxes, ensured ease of communications, set up local administration, and established both a logistical support system and an information system that connected the various battlefields.

All in all, a large number of casualties fell on both sides. The British may have camouflaged their losses and manipulated the actual figures in order not to glorify the Iraqi revolutionaries. In his book, *Iraq*, Phillip Willard Ireland gives the figures of 426 British dead, 1,228 wounded and 615 missing or taken prisoner.[9] Among the Iraqis, there were 8,450 casualties. In his book *Insurrection in Mesopotamia*, General Haldane gives the following figures: out of a force of 12,000 British and 61,000 Indians, twenty-six officers died, and 100 were injured. Among the rank and file, 2,000 were dead or wounded. On the Iraqi side, Haldane suggests that 8,450 were either killed or wounded.

What did the revolution achieve? One can state with some conviction that for Iraqis, this was a battle for freedom impelled by a natural desire to evict a foreign occupier. The Allies had simply not kept their promise of Iraqi self-rule and democracy based on President Wilson's Fourteen Points and the Anglo-French Declaration, and they were made to bear the consequences. They had behaved in an unacceptable manner, surrounding themselves with complicit local allies prepared to do their bidding. British officers and men acted in an arrogant and disrespectful way towards local leaders, which only reinforced their will to rebel. The revolution failed because the British, though suffering casualties, deployed superior air power to which the Iraqi revolutionaries simply had no response. It is interesting to note that for the next several years, the British air bases first at Hineidi then at Habbaniya were a premier feature of British policy. Indeed the use of air power allowed the British to restrict the revolution to the Euphrates area. Although urban nationalist leaders had been equally involved in launching the revolution, their role was soon diminished because it was easier for the British to arrest them within the confines of a city, and ship them en masse into exile.

Several writers have conjectured as to the financial resources that funded the revolution. Figures like £100,000 have been bandied about, but 'Abd al-Razzaq al-Hassani, in his book, *al-'Iraq fi Daurai al-'Ihtilal wal 'Intidab*, vigorously refutes it. He claims that at the rate of expenditure the revolution was running at, that sum would have lasted a good twenty months, rather than the mere four months it did last.

For Iraqis, 1920 became a date forever embedded in the minds of future generations. As has been mentioned, the British crushed the revolution by the use of superior firepower from the air against an enemy without an air force or air defences. Napalm bombs incinerated entire villages with their men, women and children, in scenes as awful as Halabja.[10] Churchill even stated that the use of chemical weapons was 'morally acceptable' in order to subdue the enemy.[11] One can only imagine world reaction if Saddam had said the same words when he crushed the Kurds! The Iraqis fought valiantly and exacted a heavy toll in British blood and treasure, so much so that Churchill was obliged to replace Arnold Wilson with Percy Cox, a supposed friend of the Iraqis.

What of British designs on Iraq? Iraq was there for the taking: the British had won the war, and to the victor go the spoils. Britain had wanted to make of Iraq a French Algeria—i.e. imposing direct rule, with Arnold Wilson as viceroy. Britain's imperatives had to be protected, with protection of the route to India the supreme interest. Oil was another enormous factor in the colonial equation. The brew gets murkier still if one throws in the racist attitude of the British towards the Arabs, together with the Arabs' own underdevelopment, and the appointment of a Hashemite as king, whom the British could easily manipulate. This then was the doubtful pot from which modern Iraq was to emerge.

The dilemma facing the British (now sporting a black eye from the 1920 Revolution), was how to substitute an Iraqi puppet government for British direct rule.

Enter the mandate system. The idea was that the League of Nations would set up a commission which would allocate a mandate to the Allied power which had the most experience by virtue of its geographic interests. The formula would thus allow Woodrow Wilson's ideals and Anglo-French *realpolitik* to merge. The British may have concocted the formula, but how were they going to make it work in ruling this newly-created country?

Enter the second set of players in this story: the Hashemites and their followers. The Hashemites had fought with the British against the Ottomans and were promised a united Arabia under the Sharif Hussain of the Hijaz. But once the war was won, the British and the French, preoccupied with dividing up the spoils, abandoned all intention of honouring their promises to the Arabs. The Sykes-Picot Agreement was going to be implemented, and the Sharif pushed aside. Well before the end of the war, Hussain had known of the Sykes-Picot Agreement (a very clear negation of the promise already made to him), as well as of the Balfour Declaration, but chose to ignore them because of British assurances that they would deliver on their promise to him once the war was won.[12]

His sons, 'Abdallah and Faisal, now both jobless, were prepared to take any fragment of a kingdom that the British might throw their way. Far from responding to their requests, the British treated them as irritants. Public Record Office documents are rife with stories of their ill-treatment. When Faisal was installed as king of Syria, the French marched on the country with 90,000 troops and gave Faisal an ultimatum to pack his bags and leave within hours. He tried to bargain for time, but when that failed, he felt obliged to send in his vastly outnumbered army of 4,000 men into battle against a superior French force and into certain defeat. The two armies met at the now historic and landmark battle of Maysalun.[13] Faisal's ragtag army, led by his minister of defence Yusif al-Adhmeh, fought valiantly, but was annihilated in a matter of hours. Adhmeh, himself still in his thirties, died leading his poorly-equipped men into battle to save 'Arab honour', according to Faisal.[14]

Faisal was thus forced to depart, leaving in a train that didn't even know in which direction it was heading. So it simply parked for a month in the wilderness at Dera'a (a town situated on the Syria-Jordan border), with Faisal forced to suffer the further ignominy of living in the cramped space of the train. The British, who only months before had accompanied Faisal and his Arab army triumphantly into Damascus, now just stood by and watched.

When Faisal left Dera'a on 1 August 1920 to an uncertain future, Ronald Storrs, in his book *Orientations*, wrote that

when his train of exile passed through Lydd, Sir Herbert Samuel (the Civil Commissioner) decided that he should be received on Palestinian territory not as a defeated fugitive but as a respected friend… he ordered a guard of honour for him when his train arrived. Although there were tears in his eyes and he was wounded to the soul, Faisal carried himself with the dignity and the noble resignation of Islam… When Faisal saw the soldiers on the platform on his arrival, he thought they were there to arrest him, and under the strain of previous days, broke down in tears when he found they were a guard of honour.[15]

Thus it came to be that the same Faisal, who knew very little about Iraq or its people, was chosen by Churchill at the Cairo Conference of 1921 to become the king of this newly-created country, after a farcical election process in which mostly illiterate Iraqis were shown a piece of paper and asked to choose one of the five candidates whose names were written on it.[16]

In his book *The Heart of Arabia*, St John Philby, the great explorer and an authority on Iraq, wrote that by the time the British had offered him the throne of Iraq, Faisal had betrayed his brother Abdullah (who never forgave Faisal for the usurpation of the Iraqi throne that was promised him by the British and his father), developed his own agenda for kingship independent of his father in Hijaz, and decided to dance to the British tune.

Faisal, the would-be king, thus arrived unheralded on a British ship in the port of Basra, with only a handful of British officials to greet him quayside. In *Iraq: A Political History from Independence to Occupation*, Adeed Dawisha tells us: 'Faisal had hoped to be warmly embraced by the people. Instead, he felt reticence, even hostility'.[17] He knew nobody in Iraq except for the Sharifian officers that had fought with him in the Arab army. Those same officers were to go on to create the new power structure, which produced men like Nuri al-Sa'id, Iraq's perennial pro-British prime minister for the next thirty-seven years. Sir Henry Dobbs, in a lecture to the Royal Empire Society following his retirement as High Commissioner in Iraq in the twenties, described the army officers that had now become Faisal's ministers as 'adventurers', hinting that they were more driven by opportunism than anything else.[18]

Faisal was thus crowned king of Iraq on 23 August 1921. Sandra Mackey, in her book *The Reckoning*, describes the scene:

At six o'clock on the morning of 23 August 1921, which dawned hot and still, fifteen hundred dignitaries almost entirely British, gathered in the courtyard of the Serai, dressed in their best fineries, to witness Faisal's coronation as king. Faisal walked in dressed in a khaki military uniform and sporting a spiked helmet. He proceeded towards a dais holding some chairs and a hastily constructed throne, supposedly a rough reproduction of the British throne in Westminster. In a scene foretelling the tragi-comic future of Faisal, the throne that he sat on was nailed together from beer boxes that still carried the name of the product 'Asahi Beer'. When all the speeches were over, and Faisal stood ramrod straight to the accompaniment of a twenty-one-gun salute, the military band broke into an enthusiastic rendering of the British National Anthem, 'God save the King'. The tragi-comedy continued and the whole ceremony took a total of thirty minutes.[19]

It would be unfair not to give Faisal credit for at least trying to make a nation out of a disparate jumble consisting of two former Ottoman provinces, later to be joined by a third; a complex mix of ethno-sectarian, multi-religious and different-speaking peoples. It would be beyond the remit of this book to delve deeply into the Arab nationalist movement, but if Faisal had any ideological drive at all, it was certainly that of an Arab nationalist. It was even rumoured that he had joined one of the early nationalist Secret Societies, probably *al-'Arabiya al-Fatat*. Faisal was essentially a product of three influences. One: an intensive saturation in Ottomanism, both in education and as a member of the Ottoman parliament (*Majlis al-Mab'uthan*) representing the Hijaz. Two: a thirst for modernity and Westernization, then sweeping Turkey, with a trickle-down effect on all Arab lands, including Iraq. Three: the Arab nationalist movement that began in Syria, but was now influencing many of the elites in adjoining territories.

To add to Faisal's woes, conditions in the land that was then called Mesopotamia simply beggared belief. The area was a true hinterland, a distant and ignored entity. Its only contact with the outside world was either through Istanbul, or through India as a secondary source. It was deprived of the most elementary services of modern life. Education, social services and basic state infrastructure were minimal, if existent at all. Such was the kingdom that Faisal was given.

As the twenties progressed, the British set the style of government by maintaining total control over every aspect of political and administrative life. Little room was left for Faisal and his key aides to promote progress towards democratic government. There were no genuine political parties in Iraq during Faisal's reign. Although it adopted the trappings of a Western-style democracy, his regime was very much authoritarian and oligarchic.[20]

The first constitution established monarchical powers that allowed Faisal to intervene in every aspect of the country's political life. The king was given unprecedented prerogatives to meddle in affairs of State. These made him much more of an autocrat than a democrat. In collusion with the British, his extensive decision-making powers were built into the constitution. This was to satisfy the British desire to wield power through the king, indirectly through the High Commissioner as the king's 'adviser'. British records abound with such examples. Cox's letter to Churchill of 4 December 1921, stated: 'The more nominal power the king has, the easier it will be for the High Commissioner to influence the course of events'. In the minutes of the Middle East department of the foreign and commonwealth office, it was stated that 'it was necessary and desirable for the constitution to be so framed as to enable us to control the Iraqi parliament through the king in order to secure the fulfilment of Treaty relations'. The main aim was to use these prerogatives to ensure the smooth passage of future treaties and to overrule opposition forces in parliament or the cabinet. It is generally accepted that the Treaty of Alliance (i.e., the Anglo-Iraqi Treaty and its subsidiary agreements) was the means through which Great Britain protected her dominant position in Iraq. Indeed, the constitution ensured that those clauses of the treaty dealing with Britain's privileged position were guaranteed.

Iraq presented a perfect case study of the plight of the imperialist. Lord Cromer put it best: 'The imperialist is always striving to attain two ideals which are apt to be mutually destructive—one, the ideal of good government, which connotes the continuance of his supremacy, and, two, the ideal of self-government, which connotes the abdication of that supreme position'.[21] It was patently clear that the machinations practised by the British in Iraq were in flagrant contrast to their own parliamentary government in Britain.

Perhaps the most damning comment about Faisal came from Sir Percy Cox, the High Commissioner who had presided over Faisal's coronation and from whom Faisal effectively took his orders. He said: 'In Baghdad, Abdel Rahman al-Naqib, Sassoon (Heskiel) and others of that calibre, regard him with profound distrust. He is regarded by the populace with contempt and resentment and I continually feel ashamed when asked why we inflicted them with such a paltry character for their king'.[22] Prime Minister Naqib intimated to Gertrude Bell before accepting the job 'that he preferred the return of the Ottomans a thousand times to accepting the Sharif Hussain or any of his offspring to rule the country'.[23] Another prime minister, Abd al-Muhsin al-Sa'dun, committed suicide in 1928, leaving a suicide note stating that he could not tolerate the public perception of him as a stooge of the British. His death sent tremors through Iraqi society, causing a negative backlash against Faisal and the British.

In a not dissimilar way, democracy in America started by putting together diverse immigrants from all over the world and fighting off a foreign occupier, motivated by the simple but resonating ideas of liberty, freedom and justice. Reading the history of the American Revolution, one can extrapolate many parallels between the two situations. This is borne out by the overwhelming desire of the people of the former Ottoman provinces to have America as their mandatory power, rather than Britain or France. This fact was made patently clear to the King-Crane Commission, which duly reported it in its summing-up, which, alas, was never read in Washington. The report was shelved. Faisal himself stated on many occasions that his vision of an Arab entity was that of a United States of Arabia, federated on foundations similar to those of the United States of America. In his book *The Arabs*, Eugene Rogan states:

The Uprising of 1920, referred to in Iraq as the 'Revolution of 1920', has a special place in the nationalist mythology of the modern Iraqi state comparable to the American Revolution of 1776 in the United States. These were not social revolutions so much as popular uprisings against foreign occupiers, and they marked the starting point of nationalist movements in both countries.

Whereas most Westerners have no knowledge of the 1920 Uprising, generations of Iraqi schoolchildren have grown up learning how nationalist heroes
stood up against foreign armies and imperialism in towns like Faluja, Baquba,
and Najaf—the Iraqi equivalents of Lexington and Concord.[24]

Faisal started his reign with one hand tied behind his back. Initially,
he had to deal only with the British as the senior partner in the Iraq
equation. He did not know the country or its people; he did not even
understand the dialect that Iraqis spoke. It was therefore logical that
he should bring with him to Iraq army officers that had formed the
bulk of his staff during the Arab Revolt. This corps of army officers
had not gone back to their respective provinces in Mesopotamia after
the end of the First World War, but had chosen rather to stay with
Faisal when he became king of Syria and became known as the 'Sharifian' officers. They felt that they had helped the British and French win
the war but were then deprived of collecting the booty owed them by
both of those countries. After failing to 'collect' in Syria, they jumped
on Faisal's bandwagon when he moved to Iraq, in order to claim their
spoils of war there.[25] This they did by becoming the new power structure supporting the monarchy. *Parvenu* figures, with no income except
that derived from their government jobs, came to form the second
power-block of the Iraq equation. They used their privileged positions
to scramble for the spoils of state land. By the end of Faisal's reign, this
group had become significant members of the landed classes, extending its influence into Iraq's agrarian society. Faisal himself, who arrived
in Iraq without property, expropriated in 1932 and without compen-
sation, a vast orchard on the outskirts of Baghdad belonging to an
Armenian landowner. It was said to contain 40,000 trees. This
attracted a great deal of criticism.[26]

The meal that the British served up to the new Iraqi nation was a bitter one. It started with the signature of the Anglo-Iraqi Treaty of October 1922, by the new Prime Minister Abd al-Rahman al-Naqib. The
treaty incorporated the terms of the mandate and committed Iraq to a
period of servitude. Hopelessly, Faisal tried to fight it, but in the end
he knew that he had to submit to British demands. He had hoped that
the treaty would mean the abandonment of the hated mandate and signal the beginning of a new dawn in Anglo-Iraqi relations. He was also
hoping that the treaty would legitimize him as a true king and banish
talk of his being a British puppet. In the period leading to his coronation, Winston Churchill had insisted in a telegram to Percy Cox that

25

Faisal should in his coronation address make a solemn declaration of his subservience to the British.[27] Faisal refused to do this, and had almost to relinquish the throne of Iraq as a result. A compromise was later reached. Suffice it to say that the British went into Iraq intending to fulfil their imperialist needs by way of a compliant king. And they made sure that Faisal knew it.

The British wanted control of Iraqi oil, which they obtained by negotiating a one-sided oil concession with an Iraqi government too ill-equipped to handle an agreement of such complexity. The concession, signed by the Iraqi government on 14 March 1925, was a piece of masterful skulduggery. It was rushed through a mere six days before the promulgation of Iraq's constitution, to avoid it being debated in parliament before being voted for. Indeed, the constitution was deliberately held up by the British for nearly nine months, despite a clamour by the populace for its immediate application, precisely to ensure that the oil concession would be granted without the need for parliamentary approval.

The British knew very well that they were dealing the Iraqis a dud hand—one that would rank as one of history's great cases of state rape. The tragedy was that the Iraqis in government themselves knew that they were dealing their own country a mortal blow. There was overwhelming popular resentment at the signing of the concession with two ministers—Rashid 'Ali and Mohammed Rida al-Shabibi—out of a seven-man cabinet submitting their immediate resignations.

To soften the blow and as a trade-off, the British promised that if Iraq were to sign the Anglo-Iraqi Treaty and the oil concession, Mosul—whose fate had not yet been decided—would be made to join the new state.

Thus, Iraq got off to a most inauspicious start. The two major players on the new Iraqi political scene now settled into their unequal roles. The British were running the show, while the king and his supporters were relegated to a role of facilitators of British wishes.

As indicated earlier, Iraq in the early twentieth century was a true backwater. There was little, if any, nationalist sentiment; practically no trickle-down effect from the burgeoning Arab nationalist movement in Damascus. Instead, there was still strong support for Ottoman rule. The country was hopelessly divided, with the Kurds and Shi'a having only a minimal say in the running of affairs. Thus, the emergence of political parties following Faisal's installation as king, to contest and participate in government, was something of a cut-and-paste affair. The electorate, still mostly illiterate, voted essentially for its notables.

The High Commissioner and the king were wary of planting seeds of dissent. They feared that political parties might form a true democratic opposition to government. Many of the parties that were formed under Faisal's reign necessarily reflected a pro-palace position.

The start of Faisal's reign in such a young country should have ushered in an era of burgeoning democracy. But the hodgepodge that actually resulted was a far cry from anything remotely democratic. Faisal's reign began with the wounds inflicted by the 1920 Uprising still fresh in Iraqi memory. The uprising was undoubtedly a massive outburst of national sentiment, catapulting new leaders onto a still undefined political scene. The trickle-down effect of the momentum thus produced was still very much in evidence when Faisal mounted the throne in 1921.

Opposition to the British, and to the treaty they were foisting on to the Iraqis, was made clear to Faisal and the High Commissioner in two separate cables sent by two newly-created parties, the Iraqi National Party, established on 2 August 1922, and the Iraqi Renaissance Party, established on 19 August 1922. They demanded a rejection of the mandate, and of any treaty that did not take account of Iraq's needs and political aspirations.

On 23 August 1922, Sir Percy Cox, the High Commissioner, visited the palace to present his good wishes to the king on the first anniversary of his coronation. As he was making his way up the stairs in the palace, shouts of 'Down with the mandate, Down with England' were heard outside. Sir Percy demanded that the king take immediate punitive action. The latter—genuinely or not—suddenly underwent an appendix operation, thus ruling himself out of taking any action. Undaunted, Sir Percy simply took over the reigns of government. He shut down the two political parties that had just been licensed, exiling their leaders, one to the island of Hinjam, the other to the Persian Gulf, and closed their two newspapers. For good measure, he exiled their editors as well.

Baghdad seethed with anger at such draconian methods. The Middle Euphrates tribes, fierce combatants in the 1920 Uprising, continued their defiance. Sir Percy sent a squadron of British aircrafts to strafe the *al-Fatla* and the *al-Agra'a* tribes and bombard their villages. Homes were destroyed, agricultural fields scorched and many women and children killed.

Such was the frightful debut of Iraq's political life. What followed was nothing more than a merry-go-round of governments, usually composed of ministers playing musical chairs. Between 1920 and 1932, fourteen cabinets were formed, with an average of eleven months in office.[28] No leader or party emerged with any cohesive ideology or political aim. Matters descended into farce, with governments brought in to carry out specific imperialist aims, only to resign immediately afterwards. For instance, the Naqib government of 30 September 1922 was brought in to rush through the Anglo-Iraqi Treaty before the formation of a constitutional parliament, so that the treaty would not have to be debated in parliament. Naqib immediately formed 'The Free Party', and put his son Mahmoud at its head despite both the party and the Naqib government's deep unpopularity. The whole country knew they were a mere tool of the British. Naqib signed the treaty on 16 October 1922, and resigned immediately afterwards, when another government was formed under Abd al-Muhsin al-Sʻadun.

Sensing the unpopularity of the treaty and the possibility of another popular uprising, the British recalled Sir Percy to London where, on 30 April 1923, they signed a protocol shortening the treaty from twenty years to four years, thus appearing to give the Iraqis the opportunity to renegotiate it. On 26 November 1923, yet another government was formed, this time under Jaʻfar al-ʻAskari, to conduct elections and bring to birth the first parliament, which it did on 27 March 1924. Almost immediately, members of parliament began to procrastinate about approving the Anglo-Iraqi Treaty. This proved irksome to Whitehall and to the High Commissioner, who kept up the pressure on Faisal and his government to approve the treaty by a parliamentary vote. The High Commissioner then wrote to Faisal warning him that dire consequences would befall the country if the treaty were not approved immediately. To make sure the threat was publicized—thus going against Faisal's wish to keep it quiet—the High Commissioner authorized its publication in the *Baghdad Times*. Things came to a head in the celebrated 'Cinderella at Midnight' episode, as described by Gertrude Bell. It was contrived that out of one hundred members of parliament, sixty-eight were convoked just before midnight—many fetched out of their beds, with some thinking they were being arrested—and taken to the parliament building. Whoever plotted the scheme had already lined up thirty-seven members to approve the treaty. Thus out of the sixty-eight present, it was certain that the treaty would pass, which it duly did.

It was evident that the plotters included some in the highest echelons of the High Commission, the palace and the government—further proof, if any were necessary, of the blatant interference in Iraqi affairs. More blatant still, was the acquiescence of the Iraqis in government, who were no doubt helpless (and had the honesty to say so).

As if all this were not enough, another government arrived on the scene on 14 March 1925, led by Yassin al-Hashimi. Like its predecessors, it had to deal with the signing of the oil concession, which strongly favoured Britain and suppressed the rights of the Iraqis to share in the wealth of their country. The British threatened to exclude Mosul from joining the new Iraqi state, if the government did not sign the concession. The promulgation of the Basic Constitutional Law was deliberately delayed, so that the government could sign the concession without needing to have it approved by parliament. As stated earlier, two ministers, Rashid 'Ali (Justice) and Mohammed Rida al-Shabibi (Education), resigned in protest. The oil concession was signed on 14 March 1925, and the Basic Law was promulgated on 21 March 1925. Yet again, the government resigned soon after it had accomplished its mission, to be replaced on 26 June by a Sa'dun government.

The charade of governments coming and going continued. On 19 September 1929, Sa'dun formed his fourth government, only to commit suicide on 13 October that same year, leaving a heart-rending suicide note to his son 'Ali. As stated earlier, Sa'dun told of his unwillingness to live any longer with the perception of him by the Iraqi people as a British stooge, not the freedom fighter nor the scion of a great tribe that he was—forced to endure unspeakable humiliations poured on him and his country by the British.

There was a continuous high turnover of governments, almost always with the same ministers merely changing ministries. The composition of those ministries generally reflected the emerging power structure of the country, mostly composed of Sharifian officers, tribal leaders, Iraqi nationalists (often former leaders of the 1920 Uprising), the mandatory Shi'a (usually given nothing more sensitive than the portfolio of education), the mandatory Kurd, the odd Christian and the first Jewish finance minister (Sassoon Heskiel). The political parties which emerged in the twenties had no particular ideologies and most were built around the reputation of their leader. They came and went with the same rapidity as the governments.

Even before the reign of Faisal had begun, there was agitation in Iraq to form political parties. Several attempts were then made in the second half of 1921, but all failed in the face of resistance from the king and the high commissioner. Nevertheless, momentum generated by political leaders involved in the national movement prior to the monarchy kept moving things forward towards the formation of political parties. This momentum eventually forced the hand of the government to promulgate a law on 2 July 1922, authorizing the establishment of parties and societies. It can even be said that party politics were born in Iraq on that date.

In rapid succession, as has been mentioned, the National Iraqi Party and the Iraqi Nahda Party were formed respectively on 28 July 1922, and 19 August 1922. The former was under the leadership of Ja'far Abul-Timman (a Shi'a), together with other notables who had participated in the 1920 Uprising. Some of them may have also belonged to the 'Ahd Party and/or to *Haras al-Istiqlal*. Timman's Party enjoyed wide popular support, since it had adopted the banner of total independence from British interference. For this, its leaders were exiled to Hinjam Island on 26 August 1922.

Other parties began to emerge on the Iraqi political stage and those included the Free Iraqi Party; the Naqib Party, which ran out of steam by the end of 1922; and the 'Umma Party, which was licensed on 20 August 1924, and which drew most of its membership from the legal profession. Two other parties, the Iraq Istiqlal Party, and the National Defence Association, were Mosul-based and supported the drive for Mosul to join the new state. Both parties disappeared after Mosul officially joined Iraq.

Al-Taqadum Party was formed on 26 June 1925, and fielded a formidable line-up of members of parliament under the leadership of Abd al-Muhsin al-Sa'dun. It can be argued that it was Iraq's first majority party, whose leader was the prime minister. It created a newspaper, *al-Liwa'*, which published the party's manifesto. However, the whole thing came to grief when accusations of treason were levied at Sa'dun, which led to his suicide on 13 November 1929, and the eventual dissolution of the party.

The formation and dissolution of the parties in the twenties was in the end a rather aimless exercise. The reasons why this was so can be attributed to several factors, of which the most important were as follows:

1. Iraqi politics began to develop as a result of fissures in the system that the British and their Iraqi political allies had devised. Self-

enrichment allowed the new ruling class to climb up the social ladder, leaving behind those suffering from poverty and deprivation both in town and country. This feudal system produced a schism between the new landowners and those working the land, who suffered the worst forms of exploitation. The evolution of the Iraqi economy started with the realization that the British were exploiting the natural resources of the country, as well as its trade and commerce. Furthermore, the beginnings of a modest industrial base led to the emergence of a working class in the oil fields and the railways. Workers began demanding their rights, as well as memberships in trade unions which could represent their interests.

But the political opposition of the time was not able to mobilize all the forces that were crying out for social justice, equality and democracy under the constitution. Some individuals among the politicians who were loyal to national aims as stated in the constitution were unable to parlay their own personal qualities into a national identity through political parties, with which a growing number of disaffected people could associate.

2. Organized political party life was a new experience for many Iraqi leaders. The necessity of having grass-roots support did not dawn on them. In almost all cases, a demonstrable lack of organizational ability led to the eventual demise of one or other of these parties. It became endemic to party life that everything gravitated around the leader, who himself shared little with his subordinates, and whose actions would be taken impulsively, often in reaction to rapidly developing events.

3. The draconian conditions, geared to stifle democracy through authoritarian rule by the king, were deftly manipulated behind the scenes by leaders who had made politics their profession and their means of livelihood. As such, they could be persuaded by personal gain to quit one party and join another, or would casually abandon political life altogether when it did not benefit them.

4. A large number of parties and politicians would disappear from the national scene abruptly, either because the High Commissioner would demand it, or the party or the politician would become expendable after having executed the deed for which they were brought to power in the first place. In all cases, the hidden hand of imperialism would work to weaken the fibre of political life for fear that it might develop into organized dissent and produce a proper parliamentary opposition.

In sum, parliamentary life as experienced by more developed democracies was totally absent in the formative years of Iraqi political life, with the added damaging effect of Iraqis themselves collaborating to carry out imperialist wishes, and contributing further to weakening the evolution of a robust democratic life.

As the twenties drew to a close, however, the forces for democratic change began to take shape. Student activists organized huge demonstrations and it is from their ranks that the next generation of opposition leaders emerged in the thirties, to take up the struggle for democracy.

The decade had started ominously when the 1922 Treaty was supplanted with the signature of the Anglo-Iraqi Treaty of 1926. The years in between saw a series of incidents which provided opportunities for people to vent their anger and frustration, both at the rampant exploitation of Iraq by the British, and at the conduct of a succession of weak and compliant Iraqi governments.

The first of these incidents occurred when Mr Goodall, a British teacher of English in the central secondary school of Baghdad, launched into an attack in his classroom on those Iraqi nationalist leaders who had shown opposition to the 1922 Treaty and to the Oil Concession Agreement. The students went on strike, claiming that the teacher had conducted himself in a manner not befitting his duties. The strike was resolved by the transfer of the teacher to another secondary school in Mosul. The students considered this a victory for the resistance movement and for the forces of dissent. It also served the purpose of the nationalist leaders, as it sent a forceful message to the government and to its British 'advisers' that the new generation of Iraqis was not about to allow Britain to walk all over them, as it had done to their seniors.

This was closely followed by the 'Nsouli' incident, which related to a history teacher in the central secondary school in Baghdad. Anis Nsouli had written a book about the Umayyad state in Damascus which provoked a massive sectarian reaction, only resolved by his dismissal. As soon as news filtered out of Nsouli's dismissal, a storm of protest enveloped the student body. Massive demonstrations followed, with banners and slogans that Baghdad's streets had never seen before. The demand was for freedom of expression. The incident provoked a violent reaction from the government, which fired three other teachers and dismissed the student ringleaders. One of these was Hussain Jamil, who would go on to become one of the founders of al-'Ahali Group in the thirties.

Yet another incident concerned Sheikh Dhari and was related to the assassination of Colonel Leachman during the 1920 Uprising. Sheikh Dhari was accused of the killing, but fled and remained in hiding until he surrendered to the authorities, when he was immediately imprisoned. He died in prison in early 1928, and a huge crowd attended his funeral. The incident, like the previous two, became a political rallying cry against British colonialism and Iraqi complicity with it. The actual funeral became a march for political freedom.

Another incident that caused a public outcry, taking the form of a political demonstration, was the visit to Iraq of Alfred Mond, a Zionist leader. His purpose in visiting the Middle East—and specifically Iraq—was to conduct studies relating to extending a pipeline from Iraq to the Mediterranean. It is widely supposed that Mond came to Iraq at the invitation of King Faisal. The memoirs of Chaim Weizmann suggest that Mond had contacts with King Faisal, when the latter seemed sympathetic to the establishment of a national home for Jews in Palestine.

Once again, the banners and the slogans proclaimed a rejection of the Balfour Declaration, calling for the downfall of Zionism and the success of the Arab Nation. Yet again, huge demonstrations filled the streets. The government banished the student ringleaders, among them Yusuf Zeinal and the intrepid Hussein Jamil.

These incidents signalled the awakening of Iraq's political consciousness, and the demand by the people of Iraq for a government run on democratic principles. The student body instigated most of the demonstrations. Many of its leaders went on to become the driving-force behind the democracy movement, mostly represented by al-'Ahali Group.

Fig. 1: King Faisal I with Gertrude Bell on a picnic outside Baghdad, early 1920s. Gertrude Bell Collection.

Fig. 2: Portrait of Saiyyid Talib al-Naqib, 1924. Humphrey Bowman Collection.

Fig. 3: Sir A. Clark Kerr with Nuri al-Sa'id, Baghdad, 1936. Vivian Holt Collection.

Opening of "Noah's Ark" June 30th 1943.
General Sir H. Pownall. C-in-C. Paiforce.
H.M. King Feisal II, S.H.P.
H.R.H. the Regent at the table behind.

Fig. 4: King Faisal II, General Sir H. Pownall and 'Abdulillah at the opening of 'Noah's Ark', 1943. Stewart Perowne Collection.

Fig. 5: King Faisal II visiting Tilbury docks, 1945. Stewart Perowne Collection.

Fig. 6: Stewart Perowne with 'Abdulillah and Gerald de Gaury, Baghdad, 1940s. Stewart Perowne Collection.

Fig. 7: 'Abdulillah and Nuri al-Sa'id, Baghdad, 1934. Humphrey Bowman Collection.

Fig. 8: Portrait of Nuri al-Sa'id, Baghdad, 1942. Humphrey Bowman Collection.

Fig. 9: Portrait of King Faisal II, 20 October 1954.

Fig. 10: King Faisal II [second from left] visiting with his fiancée Princess Fazileh [immediately to his left] in 1958.

Fig. 11: Mohammed Hadid, Founding member of al-'Ahali Group.

Fig. 12: Hussain Jamil, Founding member of al-'Ahali Group.

Fig. 13: Kamel Chadirchi, who followed Ja'far Abu al-Timman as leader of the al-'Ahali Group and later led the National Democratic Party.

Fig. 14: Ja'far Abu al-Timman, first leader of the al-'Ahali Group.

Fig. 15: Hikmat Sulaiman, Prime Minister of the Bakr Sidqi government.

Fig. 16: General Bakr Sidqi, leader of the 1936 Coup.

Fig. 17: 'Abd al-Karim Qassem.

Fig. 18: Mohammed Hadid visiting with President Nasser.

Fig. 19: Demonstrations celebrating Iraq's withdrawal from the Baghdad Pact in March 1959.

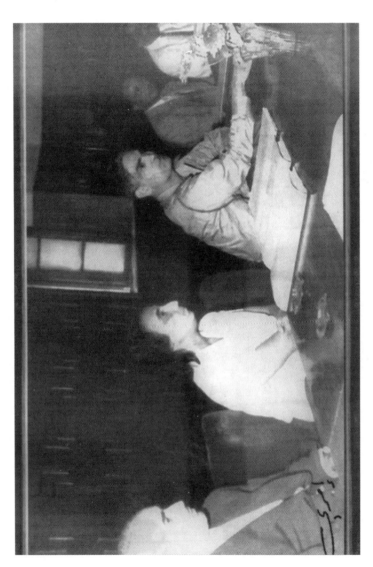

Fig. 20: 'Abd al-Karim Qassem, leader of the 1958 Revolution with Dr. Nuzaiha al-Dulaimi, the first woman cabinet minister in the Arab World.

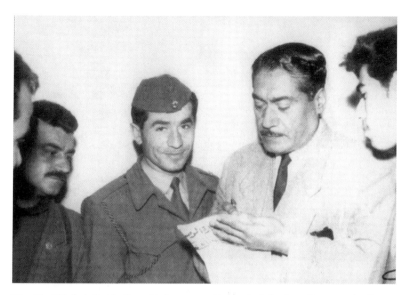

Fig. 21: 'Abd al-Qadir 'Isma'il, Secretary General of the Iraq Communist Party.

The End: From Baghdad Television, February, 9 1963

Fig. 22: Qassem's corpse following his summary trial and execution, 9 February 1963. From *Iraq Under Kassem* by Uriel Dann.

Paul Popper

Mahdāwī

Fig. 23: Colonel Fadhel 'Abbas al-Mahdawi, President of Mahkamat al-Sha'b, the notorious 'People's Court'. *From Iraq Under Kassem* by Uriel Dann.

2

THE ADVENT OF AL-'AHALI

The 1930s could not have gotten off to a worse start as far as Iraq was concerned. The decade opened with the signature of a new Anglo-Iraqi Treaty on 30 June 1930, by the government of Nuri al-Saʿid, who was purposely appointed by the British in that year to conclude the treaty. However, public opinion and the nationalist opposition parties quickly realized the heavy burden that the new treaty would impose on Iraq. Inter-party fighting erupted, leading to the resignation of one of the principal ministers, ʿAli Jawdat al-Ayyubi, who protested at Nuri's cavalier signing of the treaty in London, without bothering even to inform his colleagues in government.[1] Unperturbed by the commotion caused in the country by the treaty against which public opinion was dead set, as indeed were all opposition leaders, Nuri faithfully responded to King Faisal's request to sign it by saying: 'My colleagues and I shall attempt our utmost to fulfil Your Majesty's wishes of the nation by signing the new Anglo-Iraqi Treaty...'[2]

The cavalier attitude of Nuri in signing this crucial agreement without consulting his cabinet colleagues had a crushing impact on Iraq's prospects of establishing any semblance of genuine democratic rule. It set a template which successive Iraqi government leaders would copy. Nuri's style became standard practice in years to come by such leaders arrogating to themselves unconstitutional decision-making powers, often implemented by coercive police-state tactics. Indeed, this governmental style of dispensing with public opinion, and assuming dictatorial powers did become the norm for the duration of political life under the monarchy and thereafter in revolutionary Iraq.

In the run up to the signing of the 1930 Treaty, Nuri employed a system of 'bending' opposition leaders to his will, by offering them cabinet posts or other sweeteners. As an example, Nuri offered Muzahim Al-Pachachi a cabinet post in the government, which the latter accepted. Pachachi was a leading member of the National Party, and a vociferous critic of Nuri and the treaty. But in one fell swoop, Nuri 'turned' Pachachi, whose own party then proceeded to expel him. This happened on 7 December 1931, after which he went on to join Nuri's party, al-'Ahd. Three months later, Nuri resigned, only to form another government, which excluded al-Pachachi. The latter resigned immediately as a result from Nuri's party in order to salvage what was left of his reputation, only to find himself cast off in the political wilderness. Such was Nuri's hardball style of politics. Throughout his career, he practiced this style with great effect, and the list of personalities 'turned' like al-Pachachi reads like a startling Who's Who of Nuri's former political opponents, now turned ardent colleagues.[3]

On 2 June 1931, a Royal Decree ('*Irada*) was issued, authorizing the government to impose municipal taxes. These taxes incurred the wrath of a populace which was already seething from the repercussions of the 1930 Treaty, which contained highly onerous provisions that affected Iraqis economically. Relations between ruler and ruled were at their nadir. Despite the government's feeble attempts to explain the necessity of such new taxes, the loss of confidence became a major barrier for any possible popular compromise. A general strike was organized by the opposition parties—and especially by the National Party—which became the green shoot of dissent in what was an emerging democratic society. Popular will was being transformed into legitimate political action.

Surprisingly though, Muzahim al-Pachachi, the then interior minister in Nuri's government, and a noted nationalist, pursued these strike leaders with frightening zeal. Having once been a member of the opposition National Party, he had privileged knowledge of who they were, and proceeded to order their arrest.

The signature of the Anglo-Iraqi Treaty, the general strike, as well as the 'Nsouli' and Alfred Mond incidents, saw the birth of a new political movement. This was heir to the national movement of the twenties, which emerged from the small cracks in the system devised by the British for governing Iraq, which the king and his support team thought they could control and thus tolerate.

Unfortunately, the resultant political opposition of the twenties was not able to mobilize the national forces calling for social justice, equality and democracy that had been promised them by the constitution. This was in spite of the existence of leaders who had been loyal to national aims and had struggled for the implementation of peoples' rights under the constitution. Those leaders, despite their unimpeachable personal qualities, were unable to parlay those qualities into a national cause with which the growing number of disgruntled people could associate.

The emerging political movement, unable to integrate with the old style politicians and their parties, began its own activities with the publication of a newspaper by the name of *al-'Ahali*. The paper appeared on 2 January 1932, bearing the banner, 'Published by the Younger Generation' and carrying in its leading article the newspaper's vision to put 'the good of the people above all else'.

Al-'Ahali Group, which burst on the scene simultaneously with its newspaper, quickly gained credence for representing the first genuine democratic school of thought in Iraq. The birth of the group had its origins in the merger of two distinct groupings of young Iraqis that came to be known as the 'Baghdad Group' and the 'Beirut Group'.

The Baghdad Group owed its formation to Hussain Jamil. Jamil was born in 1908, of a father and grandfather who were both judges. By the time he went to law school in Baghdad, he had become quite aware of the nationalist movements erupting in his region, such as the Egyptian Uprising of 1919, the Iraqi Uprising of 1920, the Arab Revolt of the Sharif Hussain of the Hijaz and Mustafa Kemal's movement in Turkey. As a young student, Jamil joined student movements demanding freedom of speech and freedom of the press. His activism scored an early small triumph, in what was later called the 'Goodall Incident'. In 1926, Goodall was a teacher of English at a secondary school which Jamil attended. That period of the twenties had been made fraught by excessive British demands when negotiating the oil concession and the Anglo-Iraqi Treaty. Protest was rife at all levels of Iraqi society, resulting in attempts to assassinate two members of parliament, thought to be too compliant with British demands. In that period of great tension between the Iraqis and the British, Mr Goodall walked into his class (in which Jamil was a student), and stated that the Iraqis were ungrateful 'donkeys' (meaning idiots in Iraqi jargon), because of their opposition to the Anglo-Iraqi Treaty. He told students that Iraqis had failed to appreciate that Britain was there to civilize them, and help with their development.[4]

As soon as the class was over, the anger that permeated the classroom turned into a student strike. The students refused to attend any more of Goodall's classes, and persisted in their strike until the school was forced to transfer Mr Goodall to another school in Mosul, replacing him with another English teacher.

There is no doubt that this small success in student activism by Jamil instilled in him the idea that change could come about from organized dissent.[5] In the following scholastic year of 1926–7, another incident occurred in which the students (now led by Jamil) parlayed this new-found power of dissent, in what came to be known as the 'Nsouli Incident'. Anis Nsouli, a Lebanese graduate of the American University of Beirut (AUB), was a teacher of history who, with three other young graduates of AUB, had been brought over to Iraq by Sati'al-Husri, then Director of Education. Nsouli had written a history book that was thought to have ignited public sentiment because of alleged references to the Sunni-Shi'a divide. The publication of the book caused such a public outcry that the ministry of education felt obliged to fire Nsouli from his job and ban his book.

The incident became synonymous with constitutional issues such as freedom of speech and freedom of the press. Jamil immediately set upon organizing a strike by all students at the school. This started a contagion that spread to students at all levels of education, including the teachers. On Sunday 30 January 1927, a demonstration was organized in which hundreds of students gathered in one central location, and fiery speeches endorsing the freedom of speech were made. From there, the demonstration moved towards the ministry of education, to demand the reinstatement of Nsouli. The authorities called in the fire brigade to turn water hoses on the demonstrators. This led to a scuffle between firemen, policemen and demonstrators but, in the end, the police managed to disperse the crowd. That same evening, the police arrested the ringleaders, including Jamil who, with other student activists, was expelled from the school.

The incident, together with the expulsion of the students, became a major *cause célèbre* and engaged the attention of the king himself. The real issue became a test for the constitutional right of freedom of speech and thought. In the end, the government buckled and reinstated the expelled students. Although this was considered a triumph for freedom of speech, the order to dismiss Nsouli and his three teacher colleagues was not reversed, and all four had to leave the country.[6]

By 1928, Jamil, now joined by his cohort in the previous student incidents, 'Abd al-Qader Isma'il, a fellow student at the Law Faculty in Baghdad, heard it reported that Sir Alfred Mond, a leading British Zionist, was about to visit the city. Jamil and Isma'il quickly huddled to organize a demonstration against Mond's visit. Jamil moved to bring on board most student organizations to take part in the demonstration. Although the government kept Mond's date of arrival secret, Jamil managed to ascertain his means of transport and the actual time of his arrival. The student leaders had three days to organize, and printed banners calling for Palestine to remain Arab and for the downfall of Zionism, as well as the rejection of the Balfour Declaration.

On the day of Mond's arrival (8 February 1928), the demonstration began moving towards Baghdad's main thoroughfare, Rashid Street, to be joined by throngs of ordinary people who also wished to make their voice heard. It was not long before mounted police arrived on the scene and charged the demonstrators, who responded by throwing stones. They stood their ground despite severe police brutality, in order to be able to intercept Mond's arrival by means of the Nairn Bus Company. But the government, having foreseen this eventuality, diverted Mond's route, thus avoiding the possibility of a confrontation with his vehicle.

Jamil and his colleague Isma'il were both arrested, as were other student ringleaders. The incident was a close enough encounter for the government that it actually considered the option of opening fire on the demonstrators—luckily avoided this time. Nevertheless, and on the advice of the British advisor to the ministry of interior, Kinahan Cornwallis, many of the students who were arrested were whipped as punishment. On the day following the demonstration, a curfew was declared in Baghdad and further widespread arrests of students and other citizens were carried out.

Severe punishments were meted out and, in the case of Jamil and Isma'il, both were expelled indefinitely from the Law College of Baghdad. Both appealed against the decision but were turned down and were obliged to continue their studies elsewhere—in the case of Jamil, at Damascus University in Syria.

The Mond Incident was yet another opportunity for Iraqis to exercise their freedom of speech and, in this particular case, take on the further dimension of an anti-British demonstration. The demonstrators enjoyed unparalleled support among the populace, as evidenced by favourable articles in the local press. The exception was the government-owned *Baghdad Times*, which was published in English.

By the time the thirties dawned on Iraq, Jamil and Isma'il had become seasoned campaigners, well-versed in the politics of their new country. They were not aware that a very similar Iraqi student grouping, with socially conscious liberal and progressive ideas, had formed in Beirut. What came to be known as 'The Beirut Group' came about when Iraqi and other students from Arab countries, who were studying at the American University of Beirut (AUB), became enthused by the atmosphere prevailing at that university, which seethed with anti-British and anti-French sentiments. They were also strongly motivated by the ideas popular at the time, calling for Arab countries to become free and independent.

The Iraqi students at the AUB formed their own national grouping, whose philosophy was given the name al-Sha'biyya. This was a social-political movement, freedom-oriented, reformist in its thinking, dedicated to raising the standard of living for people, committed to the spread of education, and committed to public service, as well as the fight against corruption. The founding members were 'Abd al-Fattah'Ibrahim, Mohammed Hadid, 'Ali Haidar Sulaiman, 'Abdallah Bakr, Nuri Rufa'il, Darwish al-Haidary, and Ibrahim Baithoun. The leader of the group was undoubtedly 'Abd al-Fattah'Ibrahim, who, in addition to his forceful personality, enjoyed a particular skill for taking initiatives and for decision-making. He was also older and more experienced than the others, and in a more senior year at the AUB. None of the members ever imagined that their grouping would one day become 'al-'Ahali Group', and that the Sha'biyya' philosophy would remain its credo.[7]

The three most prominent members of the 'Beirut Group'—'Abd al-Fattah'Ibrahim, Mohammed Hadid and 'Ali Haidar Sulaiman—all went on to Western universities, putting the Sha'biyya ideas on a back burner. Ibrahim had read Parker Thomas Moon's book, *Imperialism and World Politics*, after graduating from the AUB and was much influenced by it. He chose to go to Columbia University for a Master's degree, in order to study under Professor Moon.[8]

At the AUB, as mentioned, Ibrahim was acknowledged as the leader and ideologue of the Sha'biyya grouping. While most of the aforementioned members were still students there, Ibrahim organized and then became president of a social club known as the 'The Young Iraqis' Club' (*Nadi al-Nash'a al-Iraqi*). Many Sha'biyya members joined the club, as did many apolitical Iraqis, who joined for social reasons.

Cracks soon appeared in the club's intermix of members, as Iraqis of different social classes joined and social differences manifested themselves. One noteworthy incident was a clash between Ibrahim and a member of the socially prominent and conservative Gailani family. Gailani considered himself of a higher social class than Ibrahim, and treated him with something close to disdain. This in spite of the fact that, academically, Ibrahim far outshone Gailani, had a much stronger personality, and possessed leadership qualities that distinguished him from the others. This was only a microcosm of the factional divide that would reappear again in the thirties, when Gailani and his ilk became supporters of the government, while Ibrahim, Hadid and others—many equal, if not of a higher social standing than Gailani—went into the opposition.

Ibrahim studied History at the AUB, where he took a course in Modern European History. When his professor asked the students to submit a research project, Ibrahim chose the Russian Revolution of 1917, perhaps attracted more by the word 'revolution' than by the ideology that lay behind it. His readings were also influenced by writings on leaders such as Bismarck and Napoleon. The academic atmosphere at the AUB inspired students to engage with liberal thought.[9]

Whatever influence such readings had on Ibrahim, they remained dormant when he returned to Baghdad in 1928, where he worked as a teacher. Soon afterwards, his academic ambition encouraged him to pursue graduate studies. But as his family's financial means were limited, he began to save from his teacher's salary so as to be able to afford to go to Columbia University. He finally did so in 1930, and was advised by Professor Moon to choose Britain's relationship with Iraq as the topic for his thesis. In 1931, he had to abandon his studies and return to Iraq, possibly for financial reasons. In 1932, he finished writing his thesis, and published it in January 1932, under a pseudonym. By the time Ibrahim had started forging a career in Iraq, his journey, which started at the American University of Beirut and finished at Columbia University, had opened up new horizons for him from these multicultural sources. This resulted in a particular mindset for relaunching the Sha'biyya in Iraq, this time under a different guise, which was that of al-'Ahali Group.

Mohammed Hadid, who had been a leading member of the Sha'biyya Group while at the AUB, had gone on to the London School of Economics (LSE) for his undergraduate studies. He was born in 1907 in Mosul, and was descended from a mercantile family that could trace its history to two centuries of trading in agricultural products in the Ottoman Empire. The family's business interests had expanded into property and, by the time Mohammed Hadid was born, his father, Hajj Hussain Hadid, was considered to be one of the wealthiest men in Iraq. He became mayor of Mosul at a time when that post was still given to distinguished citizens of the town, on an honorary basis, as recognition of their distinction. Hajj Hussain was active in Mosul politics, especially in the run-up to its joining the new Iraqi state during the struggle between Turkey and Britain over Mosul's future. Hadid's mother was descended from an equally distinguished family, al-Dabbagh, which had wide commercial interests, including some in European countries. The family had held positions of public service in the Ottoman Empire, and thereafter in the new Iraqi state. Hadid's maternal uncle had previously occupied the distinguished and honorary post of mayor in 1912–13, exactly as Hadid's own father had.

In 1924, Mohammed Hadid went to Beirut to finish his high school education with his cousin, Najib Sabounchi, who was also going there to study. They travelled overland by car, on unpaved roads, often in the wilderness, spending nights with tribal chiefs who were friends of both their fathers. To protect the boys against highway robbers, the chiefs would often send out armed outriders with the car, until it reached its next destination. Both Hadid and his cousin enrolled in the Preparatory School of the AUB (later to become known as the International College), where Hadid excelled. In an extraordinary result for one exam, for example, he managed to score 104 per cent in mathematics. Hadid was immensely influenced by his academic experience at the AUB. He was surprised to learn that the original site chosen to locate the AUB had been no other than his own hometown of Mosul. The project had failed, however, due to the conservative nature of Mosul's people, coupled with a lack of encouragement from the Ottoman authorities of the time.

Like most of the newly-arrived students, Hadid was swept into the political atmosphere that pervaded the AUB at that time. Sentiment ran high against the British and French occupations; the atmosphere was pregnant with nationalist feelings desiring the independence of Arab countries. The magnetic pull of the AUB to Arab students from Iraq, Palestine and Syria, in addition to the local Lebanese, added to the university's reputation of being at the forefront of liberal thought.

In early 1926, Hadid attended his first student political meeting, in protest at the signature of the Anglo-Iraqi Treaty. It was at that meeting that he got to know several of the student leaders, especially those from Iraq. The meeting ended with the dispatch of a telegram to King Faisal and his prime minister, protesting against the signature of the treaty. Hadid went on to join the aforementioned Sha'biyya Group, which included 'Abd al-Fattah'Ibrahim and 'Ali Haidar Sulaiman. He also joined the 'Young Iraqis' Club' (*Nadi al-Nash'a al-'Iraqi*) and was elected to its committee as treasurer.

While at the AUB, Hadid devoured the Arabic press, mostly articles written by Egyptian scholars and journalists, such as the eminent Mohammed Hussain Pasha Haikal, editor of *al-Siyassa*, which influenced his thinking a great deal. His English was not yet up to reading the British press, which he began to do later when he attended the London School of Economics (LSE).

Hadid graduated from the AUB at the top of his class, with exceptional marks in mathematics. This prompted him to do undergraduate studies at the LSE. Indeed, Hadid was to find his spiritual home at that institution. He had been aware of the politics of the area from the age of thirteen, when he had sat in his father's weekly *salon* or *diwaniyya*, where the town notables came to discuss the issues of the day. This was the period of the Iraqi Revolution of 1920, and army officers would attend these weekly meetings to give accounts of the news from the front. It was also a time when the wisdom of importing the Emir Faisal to the throne of Iraq was the major discussion point in Iraqi cities and social gatherings. Another issue was the necessity of establishing a national government on solid constitutional grounds, to guarantee personal freedoms as well as those of speech and press.

Having developed politically at the AUB at a young age, Hadid arrived at the LSE ready to become a political adult. The LSE of the thirties was a beehive of cutting-edge political and economic thought. The institution was brimming with star academics such as Hugh Dalton (who was to become Chancellor of the Exchequer in the first Labour government), Harold Laski (the great economist, political thinker, and leading member of the Labour Party), Lee Smith, another member of the Labour government, and Sidney Webb, founder of the LSE with his wife Beatrice Webb. Among those LSE academics that taught Hadid, he was most influenced by Richard Tawney, author of *The Acquisitive Society*. It was a work that Hadid claimed informed his thinking until the very end of his life.[10]

It would have been difficult for Hadid, like everyone then at the LSE, not to have been excited by the intellectual vigour of the place. The presence of 'Bloomsbury Set' members, such as John Maynard Keynes and Lytton Strachey, added to the institution's prestige.[11] Hadid remained forever influenced by his LSE experience so that, even in his twilight years, he would return to Bloomsbury to rummage through its bookshops. The LSE did not only possess teachers of liberal or social-ist thinking, it also had outstanding professors of conservative thought, such as Lionel Robbins (later Lord Robbins) who headed the econom-ics department and would become an economic advisor to Winston Churchill's government. Robbins later became chairman of the *Finan-cial Times*. Others included Eileen Power and William Beverage, who played a critical role in Britain's modern social transformation with his eponymous report, which laid the foundations of the welfare state.

As well as immersing himself in the full LSE curriculum of lectures and books, Hadid loved reading publications such as *The New States-man, The Economist, The Spectator*, and *The Tribune*—the latter being the mouthpiece of the Independent Labour Party, which stood to the left of the Labour Party. *The New Statesman* became his must-read weekly, as it carried regular columns by LSE professors such as Laski, Webb and G. D. H. Cole.

In his memoir, Mohammed Hadid speaks of the LSE's great impact on him. He writes of the progressive democratic direction that the col-lege advocated, which was most evident in its teaching and in its choice of books for its students that sought to reinforce such thinking. The LSE further stressed the necessity of seeking to eliminate economic bar-riers between social classes, as well as the importance of social justice. These principles were held by Hadid for the rest of his life.[12]

Another Sha'biyya member from the AUB was 'Ali Haidar Sulaiman, who became the president of both the Iraqi Society and the Young Ira-qis' Club after the departure of 'Abd al-Fattah'Ibrahim. He too had chosen history and had graduated at the top of his class. He was selected by the AUB to go to Switzerland to participate in a conference on Palestine. In 1930, Sulaiman returned to Iraq after his graduation and was appointed instructor at the Teachers College. Sulaiman was also deeply affected by the liberal teaching and atmosphere prevailing at the AUB, and went on to write *The History of European Civilization*. On its publication, it aroused the ire of the authorities in Baghdad, since they considered the book to have a worrying revolutionary slant. He was promptly removed from his teaching position and given the job of an inspector of schools—a mere administrative position—to eliminate any contact he might have with students, and avoid the spreading of his 'dangerous' thinking in classrooms. Like the other members of the Sha'biyya, he returned to Iraq saturated with Western culture, history and civilization. Like them, he looked towards a vigorous new society developing in Iraq, hopeful that it would model itself on the Western example.

Although they were not known as such when these students were studying in Baghdad or in Beirut, the two groups acquired the names of the Baghdad Group and the Beirut Group in later political literature. The two entities knew of each other as individuals, but when all the non-Baghdad Group students started returning home after studies in Western universities, it became inevitable that they would meet. This happened when 'Abd al-Fattah'Ibrahim (who would visit his relative 'Abd al-Qader Isma'il whenever he returned from the AUB for holidays in Baghdad) met Hussain Jamil, Isma'il's student collaborator. The three found much in common in their thinking. They discussed the necessity of reform in the country and the synergy that could result from communal work. Isma'il and Jamil hit upon the idea of starting a newspaper, which would become the mouthpiece of their ideology. They brought Ibrahim around to the idea with the promise that he could bring in his friends in the Beirut Group. Others, who had nothing to do with the two groups per se, but were young graduates sharing the same ideals, also joined the 'newspaper' project which was licensed to appear on 3 July 1931. In the autumn of 1931, Mohammed Hadid returned from London, and Ibrahim was charged with asking him to join the group, which he duly did. The newspaper was given the name *al-'Ahali*, which derived its meaning from the word 'The People' and reflected the desire of the founding group to represent popular interests. The name may have been modelled on Egypt's Wafd Party newspaper, also called *al-'Ahali*. It can be said that with Mohammed Hadid's joining, the Baghdad Group and the Beirut Group were linked as one entity, known thereafter as al-'Ahali Group.

Within six months of receiving its license, and only days before its license was about to expire, the al-'Ahali newspaper appeared on the stands on 2 January 1932. It carried under its title the banner 'A Newspaper Published by the Young Generation' and had a flaming torch as its emblem. The first leading article, written by 'Abd al-Fattah'Ibrahim, was entitled 'The Good of the People is Paramount'. It stated, *inter alia*: 'Our newspaper is a populist newspaper that seeks to put the good of the people above all else, calling for the improvement in standards of living, the guarantee of material and personal welfare, building a sound political and economic system for the country, developing its human and natural resources by the most effective means, etc.' The article further stated that it was neutral in its stand and did not support any of the existing political parties of the day.

The articles appearing in al-'Ahali now came thick and fast. Mohammed Hadid tackled economic issues in a thoughtful and analytical manner. 'Abd al-Fattah'Ibrahim wrote about political developments in countries struggling for their independence, drawing one example from India. Others wrote about European literature; or made translations from French and Russian sources. Soon, outsiders to the founding group began to contribute articles on the multitude of problems facing a young generation; on developments in the Arab world; on the difficulties of those in the labour force; as well as issues faced by the women of Iraq.

In an attempt to assemble all these founding ideas, in 1932 the al-'Ahali newspaper published a booklet that was called al-Sha'biyya: The principles that al-'Ahali aims to achieve. The booklet outlined al-'Ahali's programme for tackling the problems facing Iraq's newly-established society.

By the end of its first year, al-'Ahali had become the most important and popular newspaper of its day, read by people of all ages and walks of life. Among those taken with al-'Ahali was Kamel Chadirchi, who was to embark on a lifetime journey with the group just formed, and was soon to become one of its leaders.

There are many versions of how Chadirchi came to join the fledgling group of young, newly-returned graduates that formed the core of al-'Ahali. According to his own writings, Chadirchi himself was first attracted by reading their newspaper on a daily basis. He was struck by the similarity of its views with his own. He took the initiative of contacting 'Abd al-Fattah'Ibrahim and later Abd al-Qader Isma'il.

Both quickly recognized the synergic benefits that could accrue from a continued dialogue with him. The relationship strengthened when meetings began to include more members of al-'Ahali Group, such as Mohammed Hadid and 'Ali Haidar Sulaiman. Chadirchi was on average a good ten years older than most of al-'Ahali founding members and was thus looked upon by them as a more seasoned political figure. He had resigned on 7 November 1933 from the al-Ikha'a Party, where he had been the editor of the party newspaper and a leading member of the party's executive committee. Prior to his resignation, Chadirchi had planned to open a law practice. He consulted 'Abd al-Fattah' Ibrahim, who in turn sought advice from Hussain Jamil (who was himself a practising lawyer) on how Chadirchi should proceed. This resulted in Chadirchi taking an office adjacent to Jamil's, in the same building in Souk Daniel in Baghdad.

Since the founding members of al-'Ahali were in the habit of meeting at Jamil's office, and since Chadirchi had become aware of the closeness of their views to his own, he suggested that they may wish to meet in his large and comfortable home. Chadirchi, at that point in time, was unaware of the existence of the Sha'biyya Society.

Another version of how Chadirchi came to join al-'Ahali has been given by Majid Khadduri, the noted Iraqi historian. Khadduri writes correctly that when Chadirchi initiated his contact with the al-'Ahali Group and began meeting with them on a regular basis, he was still a leading member of the al-Ikha'a al-Watani Party, editor of its paper and member of its executive committee. He was also a close confidante of the leader of the party, Yassin al-Hashemi.[13] Khadduri does not suggest a compromise of ideals on Chadirchi's part but attributes his motives to having recognized an opportunity where he could assume the leadership of a younger, up-and-coming group rather than remaining stuck in his own party of older politicians, where there was little chance of advancement.[14]

A more likely version of Chadirchi's interest in al-'Ahali Group is provided by Mohammed Hadid in his memoir. He writes that Ibrahim Kamal (a high functionary in the ministry of finance—Hadid's head of department and colleague—and a close collaborator of Yasin al-Hashemi, then minister of finance) had intimated to Hadid that Chadirchi, who himself was close to Hashemi and a leading member of his party, may have been asked by him to penetrate the al-'Ahali Group, with the objective of recruiting members to Hashemi's own party in spite of al-'Ahali's strong opposition to the government in which Hashemi was a minister. As things turned out, Chadirchi abandoned Hashemi and realigned himself with al-'Ahali, after having resigned from his own party. This had a *déjà vu* element to it, as Chadirchi's father, Rif'at, who had been sent by the Ottoman authorities to quell a rebellion in Hilla, turned instead and joined the rebels, believing in their cause against Ottoman authority.[15]

Whichever version is most correct for Chadirchi's decision to join al-'Ahali—whether because of the similarity of their viewpoints, or his deliberate infiltration of the group in order to recruit them to al-Ikha'a Party, or as an attempt to assume the leadership of a fledgling but highly promising group of young politicians—the fact remains that his joining the group was a boon to its rising fortunes. Hadid, nevertheless, believed that despite the added value of Chaderchi's joining, the momentum already generated by the collective talents of its individual members would have led to the group's success, with or without Chadirchi.[16]

Kamel Chadirchi was born in 1897 in Baghdad to a wealthy patrician family of landowners. His father, Rif'at Chadirchi, who had notable stands as a nationalist, had served as mayor of Baghdad on several occasions under the Ottomans. Chadirchi's early education was uneven: he hesitated between medicine, which he began studying in Istanbul, and law, which he then pursued at the Law College of Baghdad. He followed his inner sense of curiosity by reading widely, especially books published in Cairo and Beirut, then the centres of Arab publishing, taking a particular interest in the French Revolution, the principles of which informed his future thinking. His little knowledge of English weighed him down as he struggled to master the rudiments of the language.[17] This hampered his ability to read the literature on matters of great interest to him, such as the Fabians, and generally to follow the progress and publications of the British Labour Party, on which the future National Democratic Party (NDP) was modelled, and which he was later to lead.

Chadirchi was to become a dominant presence in Iraqi politics as leader of al-'Ahali and later of the NDP. Indeed, he and Mohammed Hadid have been described as the Gandhi and the Nehru of Iraq of that era: Chadirchi for spending years in confinement for his memorable stand in the defence of the principles of his party and democracy, and Hadid for being the ideologue of the group and the person who gave it its intellectual ballast and its Fabian ideology.[18]

In his memoir, Chadirchi speaks at the very outset—even when still a member of the National Ikha'a Party—in the collective 'we' (meaning he and the founding members of al-'Ahali) when referring to the positions of al-'Ahali on the topics of the day, and its attacks mounted against the government, attacks which became more vehement as al-'Ahali became the voice of dissent in the country.[19] Chadirchi writes that those in government were not fully aware of the effect these articles were having on public opinion. The paper would have been closed down had it not been for the minister of justice, Mohammed Zaki, who was a supporter of al-'Ahali (without being a member) and who stood up for it when it was discussed in cabinet. Furthermore, this was a time in Iraq when King Faisal and many of the Ikha'a members in government tolerated a degree of freedom of speech and of the practice of democratic principles, sadly unknown in the Arab world today.[20]

What gave al-'Ahali a rocket-like boost in popularity was the position the group took on the Assyrian question, which made the government suspend the paper for ten days, bowing to the British embassy's strong protest against it. Al-'Ahali had suggested that the British should shoulder responsibility for the Assyrian issue, as it was of their own making. Apart from its historical importance in Iraqi history, the Assyrian Affair played a significant role in triggering a series of events that few historians have adequately alluded to and which were halted, if only temporarily, with the conclusion of the Anglo-Iraqi War of 1941.[21] It is beyond the scope of this book to detail the Assyrian tragedy in full. Suffice to say that the British ignored the promise they had made to the Assyrians of a national homeland (in what then became the North of Iraq) once the negotiations about Mosul were settled in favour of its joining the new country of Iraq.[22] When the British signed the Anglo-Iraqi Treaty of 1930 with the prospect of Iraq joining the League of Nations in 1932, they made no mention of the Assyrians or indeed of the promise they had made to them. Realizing the treachery that was about to engulf them, the Assyrians mounted a vigorous international campaign to alert the world to their cause, including submitting a petition to the League of Nations. They demanded either to be repatriated from Iraq or for Iraq to continue under British mandate rather than become independent. However, in its resolution of 14 January 1932, the League of Nations categorically turned down the Assyrian request for autonomous rule and delegated the responsibility for their settlement to the Iraqi government.

In an effort to endear themselves to Britain, many Assyrians—possibly making an early case for their homeland—had joined the British army prior to the Armistice which ended World War I. Totalling 4,500 soldiers, they made up what was known as the 'Levy', an auxiliary force commanded by British officers. The British, possibly trusting them in such a role because they were Christian, used them as a counterweight to the newly-formed Iraqi army. With cunning, the British deliberately relocated the Assyrians to Northern Iraq, to serve as their eyes and ears there, and gave them added control over Mosul's oil.[23]

The Assyrians did not endear themselves to Iraqi Arabs by exhibiting some of the same disdain that the British showed Iraqis, their government and their army. Furthermore, they refused Iraqi citizenship when it was offered them by the Iraqi government, preferring to settle such matters with the British mandate authority and its High Commissioner. On two occasions, in 1923 in Mosul and 1924 in Kirkuk, the Levy Assyrian forces committed acts of violence against the towns' citizens. These resulted in several casualties and fatalities.

There was certainly no love lost between most Iraqi Arabs and Assyrians. In fact, the majority were indignant at the high-handed jinks of Assyrian troops. Al-'Ahali Group and their newspaper led a relentless attack, with several articles reflecting the angry public mood building up against them, and describing the increasing intransigence of their spiritual leader, Mar Sham'un.[24] Matters came to a head when 1,000 Assyrian fighters, under their young leader Yaqu, attacked an Iraqi army outpost as the Assyrians tried to cross the border with Syria to see if they could establish a homeland there. This resulted in the death of thirty Iraqi soldiers and the wounding of many more. The Iraqi government could not tolerate such open defiance of its authority, and knew that it would lose political face if it did not mount a suitable response. This it did by sending a military force under the command of General Bakr Sidqi to suppress the Assyrian rebels, which it successfully did. Rashid 'Ali and his minister of interior, Hikmat Sulaiman, with the unqualified support of Crown Prince Ghazi who was acting as king in the absence of his father, King Faisal, in Europe, made this decision. It was met with hugely enthusiastic support by the populace, showing up both the popularity of the government and that of the crown prince. Faisal came back to Baghdad to deal with the worsening situation but found that matters had moved well beyond his control; the people were now totally behind the government, and his son Ghazi had achieved unprecedented popularity—what Faisal him-self had long coveted but had been unable to achieve.[25] He therefore returned to Switzerland, from whence he had come, and died there a week later in 1933. *Al-'Ahali* lauded the stance of the new King Ghazi in a leading article. It was addressed to 'Young King Ghazi the First', and did not even include an obituary of the deceased King Faisal. The latter's supporters stoned the paper and attempted to set its offices on fire. A major casualty for al-'Ahali, though, was the resignation of one of its founding members, 'Ali Haidar Sulaiman, because of the refusal of the group to publish his obituary of Faisal.[26]

The Assyrian Affair has not been given the importance it deserves by histories of the period nor, indeed, by Iraqi political biographies. It triggered a chain of events that brought about a union between Hik-mat Sulaiman, General Bakr Sidqi and al-'Ahali Group, which led in turn to the 1936 coup d'état, to the significant entry into politics of the military, and to the knock-on effect that resulted in the Anglo-Iraqi War of 1941. It was also to result in the Iraqi Revolution of 1958.

The year 1933 saw many events that affected al-'Ahali's accelerating fortunes. Kamel Chadirchi had added political ballast by joining the group. Al-'Ahali also managed to entice Ja'far Abul-Timman, one of Iraq's most eminent nationalist leaders, into its ranks, in the hope that he would become its leader. Those were heady days for al-'Ahali, as they further extended their reach to Hikmat Sulaiman (through Kamel Chadirchi). Sulaiman was another eminent nationalist leader, now bask-ing in the glow of the successful campaign against the Assyrians, as one of the architects of that campaign. He joined the group, and was later to bring in General Bakr Sidqi, with fateful results, as will later be seen. In the space of a year, al-'Ahali could boast a stellar line-up of eminent leaders in Abul-Timman and Sulaiman (although the latter didn't offi-cially join till early 1934), as well as a leader of the new generation in Chadirchi, who was ten years younger, as well as the host of brilliant young politicians who were the founding members of the group.

Unlike the old-style politicians (mostly ex-army officers) around King Faisal, selected for their willingness to please both the palace and the British, Ja'far Abul-Timman was the quintessential patriot. He had never flinched from fighting for his cause, whatever the consequences for him personally. He was born in 1881 to a wealthy patrician Shi'a family well-known for its charitable work. When the British arrived after the fall of Baghdad during World War I, they tried hard to recruit

Abul-Timman as an advisor, but he flatly turned them down. He rose to national prominence when he became a central figure in the 1920 Iraqi Revolution. He was the go-between and coordinator between the tribal and urban leaders. He was also one of the fifteen *Mandubin* (elected delegates) in the famous Haidar Khana meeting. The British had ordered his arrest, along with other delegates, to halt the spread of the revolution to urban areas. He became minister in the first Iraqi cabinet, but resigned immediately to signal his total rejection of the highly onerous Anglo-Iraqi Treaty, which was about to be foisted on his unsuspecting nation. He became leader of the Iraqi National Party and, in an attempt to foil yet another onerous Anglo-Iraqi Treaty in 1930, joined ranks with Yassin Hashemi's National Ikha'a Party to achieve that goal. By 1933, Abul-Timman realized that his partnership with Hashemi and his party was fruitless, since they had veered from a pledged goal not to support the treaty. He decided to quit politics altogether, and return to private life.

It was at this conjunction in Abul-Timman's life that he was approached by al-'Ahali. He joined and chaired a committee that al-'Ahali formed to eliminate illiteracy in the country (*Jam'iyat al-Sa'i li Mukafahat al'-Umiyya*). The committee included al-'Ahali members (Chadirchi, Hadid, Ibrahim, Sulaiman), as well as other prominent figures such as Nasrat Farisi and Fadhil Jamali. He then joined The Baghdad Club (*Nadi Baghdad*), another initiative by al-'Ahali to bring together the educated youth of the country in an intellectual-cum-social atmosphere, so as to discuss the issues of the day in an open manner. Al-'Ahali Group was always conscious of its mission to reach the youth of the country, especially through its newspaper devoted to the 'younger generation', as its logo stated. The Club was an immediate success, and became something of a meeting place for Iraqi graduates, mostly from the AUB. Older generation politicians joined as well, as in the case of Abul-Timman, Chadirchi, Naji al-'Asil, etc., thus providing an exciting forum of interaction between two generations.

It was not long before Abul-Timman was drawn further into the activities of al-'Ahali, such as their initiative to form a secret society based on the principles of al-Sha'biyya. Abul-Timman read the manifesto that al-'Ahali had prepared, and found it consistent with his own political beliefs. The socialist principles underlying the manifesto, he felt, did not conflict in any way with his belief in Islamic principles— as a pioneering example of democracy wedding itself to liberal Islam.

Like countless liberal-minded Muslims before and after him, he believed deeply that Islam was actually based on a working fusion of both democracy and socialism.

With Ja'far Abul-Timman now on board, the members of al-Sha'biyya Society now consisted of himself, Kamel Chadirchi, Mohammed Hadid, Hussain Jamil, and Abd al-Qader Isma'il.

Towards the end of 1933, al-'Ahali's attention turned to Hikmat Sulaiman as another possible candidate to join their society. Sulaiman was born in Baghdad in 1886 and was descended from a family of Turkish (*Kolmandi*) origin. His father was Turkish and his mother from the Caucasus. His brother, Mahmoud Shawkat Pasha, was a high-ranking army officer in the Ottoman army, and was one of the chief organizers of the Turkish coup d'état of 1908. He became the coup's leader and the country's prime minister. Hikmat, who was studying in Istanbul at that time and living with his brother, was immensely influenced by the movement created by the coup leaders in the Committee of Union and Progress (CUP), and soon became a CUP member himself. He remained an admirer of the way Turkey developed under Mustafa Kemal, and always regretted that Iraq had not followed the Kemalist example.

Sulaiman returned to Iraq after his education in Turkey (which was said to have been undistinguished, since he remained uninterested in books for the rest of his life). He followed his family into the management of their vast agricultural holdings, so much so that it was amusing to note that his accent when speaking Arabic was affected by the lilt of the countryside, mixed with a hint of Turkish. He continued to vacillate between being pro-British and pro-German and never decided which of the two positions best reflected his worldview. He said he admired the Germans because of their military precision and discipline, and the British for their diplomatic skills, as well as their imperialist reach and power.

In the post-war period after Germany's defeat, Sulaiman began cosying up in earnest to the British and came to occupy several administrative posts under them. He then advanced to cabinet posts in the game of musical-chairs that Faisal and the British were playing at that time. By then, he was torn between his pro-British, pro-palace stance and the core beliefs inherited from his father and gleaned from his brother, of being a revolutionary opposed to a colonial situation in Iraq. With the triumph of the Nazis in Germany, his pro-German instincts were rekindled. This probably influenced his role in the repression of the Assyrians. It also explains his increasingly close liaison with the army (he was the minister of interior at the time), and particularly with General Bakr Sidqi, who actually led the campaign. Sulaiman's cosy relations with the British suffered a serious setback as a result.

This then was Sulaiman's frame of mind when Kamel Chadirchi approached him on behalf of al-'Ahali to join their ranks. Sulaiman was unaware of the secret al-Sha'biyya Society or of the fact that Abul-Timman had joined it. When Chadirchi hinted that there could be a possibility of working with Abul-Timman in a new political grouping, Sulaiman showed great interest. He soon met with Abul-Timman at Chadirchi's house to discuss the matter in depth.[27]

Despite reservations on account of his variable political convictions, Hikmat Sulaiman was now on board. The line-up of al-'Ahali was complete. Its members were ready to assume their role in shaping Iraq's modern history.[28]

3

AL-'AHALI AND THE 1936 BAKR SIDQI COUP

In the period 1933–6, events agitated in such a manner as to set many of the political actors on the Iraqi stage on a collision course. Political allies became political enemies, and army officers plotted to remove their leaders by force. It was tantamount to chaos. Both Kamel Chadirchi and Hikmat Sulaiman conducted a courtship with al-'Ahali Group while still members of al-Ikha'a Party, as well as close confidantes of its leader, Yassin al-Hashemi. By 1934, both had divorced al-Ikha'a and had become betrothed to al-'Ahali. Ja'far Abul-Timman, a leader of the Nationalist Party, had helped it merge with that of Yassin to form the National al-Ta'akhi Party. Soon disenchanted with Yassin, Abul-Timman dissolved that union too and retired from politics, only to be pulled back once more by the lure of al-'Ahali, of which he became leader.

The Assyrian Affair also brought to prominence General Bakr Sidqi, considered by many a war hero. He himself was brought into al-'Ahali's orbit by his now close friend and collaborator, Hikmat Sulaiman. The plot further thickened when the whole political stage turned against the Yassin Hashemi-Rashid'Ali axis of government. If ever more turns to the plot were needed, the death of King Faisal and the coronation of a young, pro-nationalist, pro-army king, himself anti-Yassin, provided ample reason for what was about to unfold.

The sequence of events started with the Sulaikh Conferences.[1] Sulaikh was a suburb in North Baghdad where both Rashid 'Ali and

Hikmat Sulaiman happened to live. Hikmat, being from a family with vast agricultural interests, was very closely connected to the tribal chiefs in his area. He gave a series of dinners (as did Rashid 'Ali) to which he invited these tribal leaders, some of whom were disgruntled at not having been elected (by government manipulation) to parliament. At the same time, opposition to the government was mounting, first towards the government headed by 'Ali Jawdat al-'Ayyubi as prime minister, and then to the one that followed it led by Jamil al-Madfa'i. Such opposition came mostly from the Ikha'a politicians, Hikmat and Rashid 'Ali, now aided and abetted by Yassin al-Hashemi. The two blocs came together in the Sulaikh Conferences to plot their move against the government. This resulted in a plan for the tribes to mutiny in the hope of toppling the government. Bakr Sidqi, the man who had crushed the Assyrian Uprising to much popular acclaim now joined the Sulaikh talks, as did 'Abd al-Wahid al-Haj Sukkar, head of al-Fitla tribe.

Accordingly, al-Fitla—under the leadership of Sukkar—mounted an armed mutiny on 9 March 1935, a mere five days after al-Madfa'i had chosen his cabinet. Matters came to a head when parliament flatly refused to vote the legislation proposed by the government into law. Al-'Ahali became tangentially involved in the ensuing *mêlée*, since they had already mounted a virulent attack on the government, resulting in the government's shutting down the paper that had carried their attack, *al-Mabda'*, which belonged to Abul-Timman. This inferred that the attacks signified that the paper itself had adopted a pro-mutiny stand. The conjuncture of these events, coupled with Hikmat and Abul-Timman's involvement, gave rise to further speculation that al-'Ahali Group was implicated. But this was strongly rejected by Mohammed Hadid in his memoir, in which he gives an account of al-'Ahali's position. He writes that this had far less to do with the tribal mutiny than with the consistent critical position *al-Mabda'* had taken *vis-à-vis* the ineffectual comings and goings of various governments, which had failed to maintain agreed reformist programmes.[2]

With the resignation of the Madfa'i government, the king appointed Yassin Hashemi to form a cabinet. On 17 March, the cabinet took office, but trouble erupted immediately. Two appointees—Hikmat and Rashid 'Ali—both coveted the same post of minister of interior. Hikmat saw himself as far more deserving of the post since he believed he had masterminded the suppression of the Assyrian revolt, followed by his authoring of the Sulaikh resolutions. Yassin, well aware of Hikmat's relations with al-'Ahali, was reluctant to give the group such latitude in their demands for a free press, as well as the release of political detainees, and preferred that Hikmat should be given Finance as a portfolio.[3] Hikmat flatly declined this post, which may have resulted in Hashemi's 'Waterloo', since this one action led to Hikmat's plotting Hashemi's downfall.

Following the formation of his cabinet, Hashemi attempted to disarm the tribes. He asked them to lay down their weapons and trust in the law of the land. He correctly stressed that they should leave the settling of disputes to the constitutional judiciary system. Abdel-Wahid Sukkar's response was to parade in the streets of Baghdad with his tribal cohorts in a show of strength, to remind Hashemi that the latter was in power thanks to him. Other tribal leaders, however, soon began to see that Sukkar's position was more about grandstanding than genuinely caring for the welfare of the tribes. By May, the tribes had risen again, this time under Sheikh Khawwam in Rumaitha. There then followed another series of tribal uprisings, culminating in a revolt by Sheikh Sha'lan al-'Attiyya in June 1936. The government promptly dispatched General Bakr Sidqi to suppress that rebellion. This he did with devastating results, which seemed to appeal to public opinion. It further enhanced his legend as a war hero and, in an Iraqi equivalent of a ticker-tape parade on his triumphant return to Baghdad, Sidqi was hailed by the citizens as he drove through the streets of the city.

The government, instead of relaxing its grip on civil liberties, decided to do the opposite by strangling the freedom of the press and carrying out a draconian programme of shutting down several newspapers. Al-'Ahali members were keen to attack the government for its autocratic ways, but they were held back by Hikmat, who persuaded them to moderate their attitude and give the government some leeway, at least until its programme became clear. Indeed, Ja'far Abul-Timman, another ex-ally of al-Ikha'a, wrote an article in *Sawt al-'Ahali* on 18 April 1935 (edition No. 55), the group's then mouthpiece, in which he suggested the adoption of a wait-and-see policy.

However, this was not to last. *Al-'Ahali* returned to a spirited attack on the government, amidst a general worsening of the latter's popularity, caused by a decline in living standards and a faltering economy, as well as the suspension of Hashemi's al-Ikha'a party's activities. To al-'Ahali, this signalled an ominous move towards one-party rule, and an actual end of contestation in party life.[4] On 2 May 1935, *al-'Ahali* came out with a blistering attack, warning the citizenry of the looming loss of freedom of speech and of parliamentary plurality. On 10 May 1935, *al-'Ahali* unleashed another furious attack on the government for the excessive force it had deployed in putting down the tribal uprisings. It suggested that the way to deal with complaints by the tribes was to end feudalism, and introduce a land reform act more befitting a modern state. This proved too much for the government, which shut down *al-'Ahali* again for the rest of 1935.

In April 1936, the government signed an agreement with Britain for the management and operation of the Iraq railway system. This was accompanied by a secret addendum, stating that all acquisitions of rolling stock (engines, train-cars, spare-parts, etc.) had to be purchased from Britain. The deal was another product of the 1930 Anglo-Iraqi Treaty, which had distinguished itself only by its further exploitation of Iraq by the British.

The al-'Ahali Group met at Hikmat Sulaiman's house to discuss their response to the railway deal. Seeing that their newspaper, *al-'Ahali*, had been shut down by the government, Hikmat volunteered to publish a special edition of his own newspaper, *al-Bayan*, for which he had a license, in order specifically to give *al-'Ahali's* opinion on the agreement. The task of writing this leader was allocated to Mohammed Hadid (the economist in the group), and it was published the next day (4 April 1936) under the title, 'Iraq's Economy under the Mandate for another 20 Years'. Hadid exposed the inequities of the agreement in detail, as well as the collaboration of leading government figures—facts that the populace agreed with and were outraged by. The article exposed the agreement as showing nothing but a blatant disregard for Iraq's sovereign right to act freely in making such important economic choices.

The article critically signalled the first sign of a fissure between Hikmat and Hashemi, the latter being quick to suspend *al-Bayan* for a month. The government's repressive attitude worsened when further tribal uprisings occurred, firstly in Rumaitha on 21 April 1936, followed by the Agra tribe's revolt in June 1936, under its leader, Sha'lan al-'Attiyya. Dissent was rife throughout the country, as farmers rebelled against the allocation of state land to top government officials, who flagrantly enriched themselves in this manner, while the farmers continued to be forced to eke out a miserable existence.[5] Workers and small business owners were also up in arms at the deteriorating economic conditions that were affecting their lives, as the government laid off thousands of workers and minor government officials, sending unemployment soaring. The government's response was to persist in increasing its autocratic hold on power, stifling opposition and shutting down newspapers. As an example, when the government got wind that Hikmat was about to re-publish *al-Bayan* on 16 May 1936, it took immediate measures to have the police force surround the paper's offices and to seize the edition of that day before it could be distributed. Hikmat and Ja'far Abul-Timman immediately presented a memorandum to the king, decrying this act of abuse of the constitution by the police.

Hashemi then went on—in a speech delivered in Basra on 29 August 1936—to declare that he wished to stay in power for a further ten years in order to accomplish his goals.[6] This certainly must have tipped the scales as far as the opposition was concerned, proving to be the last straw and prompting Hikmat to begin his dialogue with Bakr Sidqi, and other army officers, to explore means of ejecting the government by force. This resulted in the Bakr Sidqi coup of 1936—the first of many coup d'états in Iraq and in the wider Arab world.[7]

The details of the coup have been described in several excellent works on the topic. But what is germane to this narrative is the interaction of al-'Ahali, the coup leaders, the palace and the British establishment in Iraq. Understanding how al-'Ahali and the military came together is critical to understanding this defining juncture in Iraqi history.

It will be remembered that Hikmat had recruited Sidqi to join al-'Ahali Group. Both men had no ideological affinity with the liberal socialism of al-'Ahali, but both had strong reformist ideas. This was fully known to al-'Ahali, who accepted that they only shared a reformist outlook. But Hikmat was a reformist in the Kemalist mould. He had been much taken by Mustafa Kemal, whom he had known as chief of staff to his brother, Mahmoud Shawkat Pasha, who led the coup d'état against the sultan in Turkey in 1909. Hikmat, who hero-worshipped his brother, developed his own agenda for effecting change by force, and through a close liaison with the military. He saw himself as the architect of both the military campaign that ended the Assyrian rebellion as well as that of the tribes. He was immensely impressed by what Kemalist Turkey and Reda Pahlavi's Iran had managed to achieve, and was not averse to a similar course being taken by Iraq.[8] In

fairness, such sentiments were common to a vast number of army officers and politicians at the time, aware of what the 1909 coup had
achieved in Turkey in terms of liberties and constitutional life. Al-
'Ahali Group's involvement in the 1936 Sidqi coup was a direct result
of these kinds of sentiments.[9]

Sidqi, who shared Hikmat's views of Kemalist Turkey, emerged as a
war hero following his daring, but ruthless, subjugation of the Assyrians. Hikmat was minister of interior at the time, and advised Sidqi on
how to handle the Assyrian campaign. A close relationship grew
between the two men, so much so that they became each other's confi-
dants.[10] Sidqi began to hint at the possibility of the army's intervention
in politics so as to fulfil Iraq's aspirations. But the Hikmat/Sidqi axis,
though intimate enough, remained one of cautious exploration on how
to strengthen the army along the lines of the Turkish model. There was
no hint at the time of any direct role the army could play in politics.
Indeed, Sidqi simply obeyed the government's order to subdue the
tribal mutiny in the Middle Euphrates. Having succeeded brilliantly in
that task, he began to see himself in the higher role of Chief of the
General Staff, instead of being content with his role as Deputy Chief.
It did not help that the actual chief, Taha al-Hashemi, was Yassin's
brother and was not likely to be retired in Sidqi's favour. Sidqi must
have thought also that, just like Mustafa Kemal and Reza Pehlavi,
coming from a humble background was no barrier to the top job, if
one was buttressed by a supportive populace believing in a reformist
agenda.[11] Sidqi and his friends in the army who shared his ambitions
very likely entertained the idea that, with Hikmat as prime minister,
those ambitions could and would be actualized.

It is more complex to comprehend the involvement of al-'Ahali in
such a scheme. Whatever explanation offered by the individual memoirs of the principals concerned, this uncharacteristic involvement by
al-'Ahali in what was in effect a military coup represented a strategic
turning-point in their political programme. A momentous decision
such as joining a government brought to being by military means was
not one that was arrived at lightly by al-'Ahali. By 1936, several of the
original founder members of al-'Ahali had left the group for one reason or another. 'Abd al-Fattah'Ibrahim had had ideological and personal differences with Chadirchi, and had stopped attending al-'Ahali
meetings before quitting altogether. Hussain Jamil was working away
from the capital as a judge and was giving priority to his legal career.

Ibrahim had been dead-set against al-'Ahali's involvement, and had made his feelings known. In fact, when al-'Ahali found itself later having to withdraw from government, Ibrahim's position was one of 'I told you so'.

The decision was then left to Ja'far Abul-Timman, Hikmat Sulaiman, Kamel Chadirchi and Mohammed Hadid, the latter being the only person left from al-'Ahali's original founding members. Hadid and Chadirchi shared an ideological worldview that gave their relationship a longevity that endured until 1958, when another strategic turning-point was to affect the fortunes of the group. Hikmat joined al-'Ahali because of his Kemalist reformist beliefs, and not because he believed in the group's particular ideology. Abul-Timman joined because he believed in their ideology, but his mental make-up was that of the older-style Iraqi politician, well-used to a certain way of conducting Iraqi affairs. Chadirchi and Hadid were instinctively against the coup, but were persuaded by Hikmat that the army would return to its barracks, and constitutional life would be restored along the lines that al-'Ahali advocated. This was an opportunity not to be missed, he insisted, being resolved on carrying out the coup. He preferred to do this with the support of al-'Ahali. If not, he would enlist the support of another group if need be.

Both Hadid and Chadirchi, the only two al-'Ahali principals who left memoirs, are strangely silent on the topic of why the group went along with the Hikmat/Sidqi scheme. It should not be forgotten that Chadirchi had been a close confidante of Hashemi's. Hikmat had been the latter's political ally, as was Abul-Timman. Hashemi was a respected nationalist with memorable stands, who was well-regarded in the Arab world for espousing the Arab nationalist cause.[12] Bakr Sidqi was ostensibly loyal to Hashemi, and had just executed the latter's orders to subdue the tribal mutiny led by Sha'lan al-'Attiyya. Hashemi admitted that his government had let the country down and was prepared to resign, which should have eliminated the need for a coup. Hikmat himself had urged al-'Ahali to moderate its attacks on Hashemi's government in its paper, despite Hashemi's denying Hikmat the position the latter coveted as minister of interior. In the incident recounted earlier of Hikmat's visit to Ra'uf Chadirchi's house on the day of the coup, Hashemi had just left Chadirchi's house prior to Hikmat's arrival. Ra'uf had been trying to broker a reconciliation between the two antagonists (he was a close friend of both parties) but had failed to do so.

The role of the king and the assassination of Ja'far Pasha al-'Askari, the minister of defence and the 'father' of the modern Iraqi army, a much-admired figure in the region, added another twist to the story. One must also not forget the ever-vigilant British, observing events close-up.

King Ghazi's relationship with Yassin Hashemi was an uneasy one to say the least. Ghazi enjoyed huge popularity amongst the people for his nationalist stands. Furthermore, the young army officers were devoted to him, and he spent most evenings in their company. He was prone to irk his family and senior aides by taking hazardous risks with high-speed driving and other 'childish' activities, as some critics described it. One such critic was Hashemi, who had given himself the role of Ghazi's 'guardian' from the time he went to study in England. Hashemi, most likely to protect him, had denied his request to purchase a car while still a student for fear of an accident. This did not endear Hashemi to Ghazi.

To make matters worse, Ghazi's sister, 'Azza, chose to elope with a Greek waiter with the unfortunate name of Anastas Charalambo.[13] This caused a huge royal scandal which demanded addressing by Hashemi's government. This was done on 16 June 1936, with the issuing of a decree banning any future marriage of a royal person without the king's consent. The king would reserve the right to deprive privileges due to a royal, including stripping them of their title. Hashemi, who had by now tired of the king's antics, used this incident to rope him in and place him and other royals under government surveillance. By this time, Ghazi could not tolerate Hashemi any longer and declared that he had no more need for the 'advice of Pashas'—referring tartly to Hashemi, Nuri and Ja'far, the latter two agreeing by now with Hashemi's measures to curb Ghazi.[14]

Did Ghazi know about the coup before it happened? There are several theories that have been offered by historians and memoir writers. One theory is tied with the mysterious decision by Ja'far al-'Askari to attempt to intercept Sidqi, and persuade him to abandon the coup. There are no sources that give the exact details of how the decision to send Ja'far was arrived at. Most historians have suggested that Ja'far volunteered to go himself, without actually questioning his rationale for choosing to do so. Ja'far did not see eye to eye with Hashemi and, if the sources cited below are to be believed, was planning a coup himself to force Hashemi out of government. Askari feared that the latter had begun to believe his own myth about being the 'Bismarck of Iraq' and would soon declare dictatorial rule.[15] After all, his declaration that he would rule for another ten years—coupled with his obsessive admiration for Mustafa Kemal and for Reza Pahlavi—did not dispel fears of such an eventuality taking hold.[16] To add more authenticity to Ghazi's possible complicit role in the coup, Muzahim al-Pachachi, the former prime minister, in a biography written by his son, Adnan al-Pachachi, confirms Ghazi's actual involvement. Muzahim, while serving as minister in the Rome embassy, seems to have intercepted a letter destined for Muwaffaq al-'Alusi. Alusi was a close associate of Nuri's, and the latter had sent the letter in 1937 while still a political refugee in Cairo, following the Sidqi coup. It is clear from it that Nuri believed that Ghazi was complicit in the coup, and that he should be gotten rid of by offering the Iraqi monarchy to Ibn Sa'ud, who could then become king of a joint Iraq and Saudi Arabia. In the letter, Nuri strongly hints at his readiness to broach the topic with the British, who similarly disliked Ghazi for his nationalist leaning. In a diary note dated 17 March 1951, Muzahim noted:

while visiting Kamel Chadirchi, I was informed by the latter, who quoted a high and reliable source, that while Nuri was in Cairo 1936–1937, he had presented a project to the British to combine Iraq and Saudi Arabia under one kingdom that would sign an alliance treaty with Great Britain similar to the Anglo-Iraq Treaty of 1930. He further outlined to the British the dangers affecting their interests in Iraq resulting from Ghazi's continued presence as king surrounded by the then present crop of supporters in government.

Muzahim goes on to state that in his opinion, Ghazi's anti-British stand, the contents of the intercepted letter, and the information gleaned from Chadirchi, left no doubt in his mind that Ghazi's death was no mere accident, but a planned murder.[17]

For Ja'far al-'Askari', however, it would have been sheer folly as minister of defence to have gone to join an army unit intent on toppling a government he was a part of. Ostensibly, he was simply carrying a letter from the king to Sidqi, a task that could have been delegated to a senior army officer, if indeed an army officer was needed at all. It is true that 'Askari was perceived as the 'Father of the Army', and passionately believed in that sobriquet himself, but he had already spoken to Sidqi by phone, as had the king and Hashemi. Sidqi assured the king of his and the army's loyalty to him and to the Crown. This calmed the king's fears who, it was said, had been planning to escape in a waiting private plane to Amman.[18] The most likely theory is that 'Askari was asked by Hashemi and Nuri to deliver Ghazi's message to Sidqi in person. All three, together with Ghazi, were at a meeting in the palace and had agreed that if anyone could pull off deterring Sidqi from marching on Baghdad, it was Ja'far al-'Askari. Hashemi had agreed to resign anyway, thus leaving no sense for Sidqi to go ahead with the coup as planned. The text of the letter is most telling and confirms this rationale:

19 October 1936

Dear Bakr Sidqi,

This letter [will be] handed over to you by Sayyid Ja'far al-'Askari who in coming to you in this special manner, will discuss [with you] the situation. I have just been informed that three bombs have been dropped [on Baghdad] by some aeroplanes; I was much surprised at this new action since I had already informed you by telephone of the necessity of stopping any further action until I [could] deal with the present position. Any further movement [on the part of the army] would inevitably have the worst effects on the future of the country and the reputation of the army, for there is absolutely no necessity for such action. Further details will be given to you by Ja'far.[19]

Ghazi, Commander-in-Chief

Whatever did transpire, 'Askari went to meet Sidqi, was intercepted en route and shot by four army officers sent by Sidqi. Ja'far's assassination was a seminal event in the planning of the coup, which had shocking and negative effects that no one had counted on. Sidqi had assured Hikmat and al-'Ahali Group that the coup would be a 'white' one. It was the condition that al-'Ahali insisted upon if they were to enter the coup government. In fact, when Hikmat learned of 'Askari's assassination, he and the other al-'Ahali members were reluctant to form the government and did not do so until very late in the day, when they realized that it was now too late to withdraw.[20] Furthermore, it has been reported in various books that the coup planners had wanted 'Askari to occupy the portfolio of defence, and Nuri al-Sa'id that of foreign affairs in the new government.[21] The choice of Ja'far made sense if one believed his anti-Hashemi sentiments and his desire for change. The choice of Nuri, however, seems less understandable, since he was the architect of the 1930 Anglo-Iraqi Treaty, and considered to be Britain's man in Iraq. Giving him the portfolio would have supposedly guaranteed British approval for the coup, but more reliable eyewitnesses who partook in discussions regarding the choice of ministers for the coup government discount Nuri ever having been a candidate. In any case, Nuri would have almost certainly turned the appointment down after Ja'far's assassination since they were brothers-in-law. Nuri, understandably, was now filled with an even greater desire for revenge, rather than for cooperating with any future coup government.[22]

As for Ghazi, an enigma continues to surround his role in the coup. The most likely version—even though no one version is supported by proper evidence anywhere—is that Ghazi did know about the coup. He spent his time drinking with his army officer friends, who knew full well his dislike of Hashemi. The latter's government was in any event hugely unpopular, a fact surely reported to Ghazi by his army companions. There was a meeting in the palace on the day of the coup, attended by Ghazi, Hashemi, Nuri and 'Askari, as well as by the British ambassador, Archibald Clark Kerr. The latter—accompanied by his deputy, Major Young, and by his ADC, Captain Holt,—advised the king that he must try by all means to stop the coup leaders and the army from reaching Baghdad. Hashemi remained calm throughout, but nevertheless suggested that he could mount a force that would resist and repel the advancing army. He nevertheless accused the king of being implicated in the coup, although Ghazi vehemently denied any knowledge of it.[23] As stated, Hashemi remained calm and dignified throughout and docilely offered his resignation to the king when news that the air force had bombed some government buildings reached their assembled group. The king accepted Hashemi's resignation immediately, without negotiation.

The British role in this unfolding drama is another enigma. One oft-repeated theory holds that on the eve of the coup, Hikmat contacted his close acquaintance, C. J. Edmonds, an advisor at the ministry of interior and a collaborator of Hikmat's, when the latter was minister during the Assyrian Affair. He wished to acquaint him in advance with the serious events about to happen if Hashemi remained in government so that he, in turn, would persuade the British ambassador to apply pressure on Hashemi to go, thus avoiding the necessity of any action to force him to do so. But this theory is discounted by Mohammed Hadid in his memoir as being highly unlikely. He wrote that he (Hadid) had participated in all the discussions preceding the coup and did not hear Hikmat intimate anything of the sort; nor did he hear it from Abul-Timman or from Chadirchi, who were also present. Furthermore, Hadid cast doubt on any such reckless action by Hikmat, with its attendant risk of exposure of the plot. The British would have certainly revealed it to the king and to the government, with dire consequences for Hikmat and everyone else involved.[24]

The planners of the coup certainly considered what actions the British might take. One would have been overt action to quell the coup. Thus, Nuri's intended inclusion in the cabinet was one way of assuring the British of the friendly intent of the new government towards maintaining its relationship with them. Ja'far's assassination, however, must have eviscerated that option. The British did indeed put their forces on alert in Egypt, as well as their forces in-country in Habbaniyya and Shu'aiba in the event that they were needed to foil the coup. After all, the British had enjoyed a very good working relationship with Hashemi's government, and were wary of Sidqi because of his anti-British attitude in the Assyrian Affair. Furthermore, the British were caught completely off guard by the lightning strike of the coup, the masterly manner of its execution and the failure of their own intelligence in predicting it and having to place their forces on alert.[25]

Hikmat, aware of these British preparations, went into top gear to allay British fears. He leant on his acquaintance, C. J. Edmonds, to act as intermediary with the British embassy. As a result, Hikmat met with the British ambassador. The latter must have been impressed, as he fired off three reports to the Foreign Office, in which he admitted that he went to the meeting prejudiced against the new prime minister, only to be surprised by his commitment to the Anglo-British 'friendship'. He further reported that the prime minister had asked for British help and counsel, and that the government was committed to honouring the terms of the 1930 Treaty, the Railway Accords and all other Anglo-Iraqi agreements that were already in existence. The tone of the ambassador's reports was even laudatory. Fearing that Sidqi might deal out a similar fate to other leaders of the outgoing government as he had done to Ja'far al-'Askari, the ambassador asked for safe passage for Yassin and Rashid 'Ali, who left the country to go to Lebanon and for Nuri, who had taken refuge in the British embassy, in order to fly out to Egypt on a British plane. The prime minister acceded to these requests.

Why the British chose to back the coup on the very first day rather than activate their plans to put it down in support of the Hashemi government has never been satisfactorily explained. The British ambassador was at the palace meeting when Ghazi and his ministers were discussing a response to the coup-to-be. He certainly could have given support to Hashemi's plan to meet the advancing force and resist it, but no such offer came from him. Was he aware of Hashemi's plan to declare a republic, and install himself as the Iraqi Atatürk? Britain would have risked losing the monarchy then, a pliable tool which they had successfully developed to govern Iraq from behind the scenes. The ambassador certainly must have been aware of Ghazi's intimate relationship with the army, and the latter's animosity towards Hashemi. He would have learned that, in a telephone conversation with the king followed by pamphlets dropped from the air over Baghdad, Sidqi had vouched loyalty to the Crown. The ambassador urged Ghazi to try and stop Sidqi from advancing on Baghdad, thus allowing himself time to interrogate the intentions of the incoming government as far as British interests in Iraq were concerned. When he met with Hikmat and was given calming assurances, he gave his superiors in London the green light to accept the situation, safe in the knowledge that not much would change as far as Britain was concerned.

4

AL-'AHALI IN GOVERNMENT

The shocking setback of Ja'far 'Askari's assassination apart, the coup was carried out with remarkable precision and in the utmost secrecy. Since it was the first coup d'état in the Arab world, its novelty factor came as a surprise to the general public. Majid Khadduri described it thus: 'The novelty of the procedure, and the masterly fashion in which it was carried out, brought to power a government of unprecedented popularity and prestige'.[1] It was quite remarkable that al-'Ahali Group would experience such a meteoric rise in their fortunes having hardly been in existence five years. They effectively became the civilian government of the coup.

However, it cannot be said that the coup leaders' philosophy, if they had any, was representative of the Sha'biyyia principles that al-'Ahali espoused. Sidqi had joined al-'Ahali because of the reformist ideas that he shared with Hikmat Sulaiman. He preferred not to occupy an official role in government, but became the Chief of the General Staff. His co-plotter, Abd al-Latif Nuri, commander of the First Division, had also taken the Sha'biyya oath and become a member. He occupied the Portfolio of Defence in the new cabinet. Abul-Timman, though a believer in al-Sha'byyia, was not enamoured of its socialist-based doctrines, and was keen on making it known that the government was reformist rather than socialist in nature. Timman became Minister of Finance. In fact, both he and Hikmat were reluctant to participate in the coup government following Ja'far 'Askari's assassination. Hikmat gave a curt acceptance speech on the day the government took office, leaving it to Timman to outline the government's programme in a speech more noted for its opening apologia than as a celebratory statement.[2] Kamel Chadirchi was perhaps the only al-Ahali cabinet member who truly believed in al-Sha'biyya principles. Although all the other ministers were al-'Ahali supporters, if not indeed members, they were reformist in their views rather than being strict adherents of al-Sha'biyya. It should be noted that although none of the younger generation or founding members of al-'Ahali occupied any ministerial posts, some months later Hikmat did offer Mohammed Hadid the Ministry of Finance, with the aim of moving Abul-Timman to Interior. But the decision was delayed and never implemented. However, in early 1937, Hadid became a member of the newly elected parliament, as did many of al-'Ahali's members and their supporters.

The reformist nature of the government became obvious almost immediately. Indeed, Sidqi named the force that marched on Baghdad 'The National Reform Force', placing it under his own command. Al-Ahali Group and their sympathizers in the cabinet (composed of Chadirchi, Timman, Naji al-'Asil and Yusuf Izzedine Ibrahim) in an attempt to give al-Sha'biyya a more formal political structure that proclaimed its liberal progressive credo, formed a group that they called 'The Popular Reform Society' (*Jam'iyyat al-Islah al-Sha'bi*).[3] Thus the whole Army/al-'Ahali/Sha'biyya nexus took on the features of a reformist movement, and became known to the country as such.

The people, unaware of the machinations behind the scenes that had brought about this much-desired transfer of power, supported the new government with something akin to fervour. On 3 November 1936, a massive demonstration walked across the capital proclaiming loyalty to the king, to the Armed Forces and to the 'People's Cabinet'. Citizens from all walks of life participated and the inter-mix of Iraq's diverse ethno-religious-sectarian groups, singing their respective folk songs and wearing their traditional clothes, moved the noted historian Majid Khadduri to say that this particular demonstration took on a dramatic and impressive face.[4]

Ja'far Abul-Timman's speech on 5 November 1936 (referred to earlier), announcing the government's programme, embodied the reformist agenda:

The Prime Minister has deputed me to make a short statement on the recent development in the country and on the policy of the new Government formed in accordance with the people's wishes. It will endeavour to preserve peace, security, and tranquillity, as well as to administer justice to all.

1. The exceptional circumstances which compelled your sincere brothers to co-operate with the gallant army officers arose from the despotic policy of the former Government whose conduct in violating the law and the constitution has exceeded the limits of the most despotic rulers, in such matters as causing bloodshed, suppressing liberties, and closing down liberal papers, in some cases even before publication, and persecuting liberals everywhere. The country has indeed passed through a period [of despotism] which she has never witnessed before, a period of martial law in which the prisons were crowded with your brothers and sons on the slightest suspicion. The despotic acts of the former Government and its arbitrary measures were not committed for the sake of public reforms, but merely for partial, nepotic, and personal ends. Such conduct has caused general dissatisfaction throughout the country and hastened the coming of the day of reckoning when the leaders of the National Reform Force asked his Majesty the King to entrust His Excellency Sayyid Hikmat Sulaiman with the formation of a new Government to realize the desires and aspirations of the people. The leaders of the National Reform Force have been prompted to do so, because they were aware of the difficulties and sacrifices, persecution and humiliation, which Hikmat and his colleagues have endured for the sake of the country's interests. The former cabinet, not satisfied with arbitrary and despotic rule, destructive and punitive measures, declaring martial law, exiling and sending to prison liberals, did not leave office before making heavy inroads into the Treasury—most instalments were not paid on the due date which endangered the carrying out of public schemes.

2. Every citizen of this country should know that the Government, having put an end to the period of persecution, transgression, and the suppression of liberties, is anxious to take all possible steps to respect life, property, liberty, religious rites and places of worship, religion or creed.

3. The Government will also aim at promoting the friendly relations of Iraq with other countries in general, and neighbouring countries in particular; the bonds of friendship with Arab countries will be strengthened, and co-operation with them in all matters promoted.

4. It is also one of the Government's decisions to draw up a general and sound plan for the reform of the system of education, and the encouragement of the spirit of culture which will ensure the unity of Iraq, but will not be inconsistent with the realization of Arab unity, in order to put an end to internal schisms and antagonisms.

5. The Government has decided to provide money for the improvement of land in general; it proposes to distribute uncultivated Government land, which is not privately held or leased, among the citizens of this country on the basis of public interest, taking into consideration in particular the custom and usage of the country; it intends to open new roads, improve the system of irrigation, encourage agriculture, commerce, and industry,

improve public health, and promote other vital schemes which are necessary for the happiness and welfare of all people.

To sum up, we do not intend to indulge in talking, since actions speak louder than words. If the Government is to carry out reforms properly, it will do so only with the unshaken confidence and support of the people. However great the responsibilities of the Government towards the country may be, the obligations of the people are still greater.

The speech, which aroused great interest in the press and in Baghdadi circles, was soon followed up by the government declaring a national amnesty for political prisoners (a demand often made by al-'Ahali and the populace prior to the coup). Masses of political prisoners crowding Iraq's jails, especially in the notorious Nograt Salman, were soon freed to the relief of their families and the general public. Tribal unrest which had been forcibly suppressed by the previous government was eased by assurances given to the tribes (thanks to both Hikmat and Timman's close relations with them). Restrictions on freedom of speech were lifted and the notorious Clause 3A of the Baghdad Penal Code, by which a political opinion could be punishable by law, was rescinded. Importantly, several newspapers whose licenses had been revoked were reinstated amidst a general lifting of the ban on freedom of the press—including *al-'Ahali*, which reappeared on the stands on 2 November 1936, and officially became the mouthpiece of 'The Popular Reform Society' (PRS). In a further move to assure freedom of speech and of the press, Hussain Jamil, a prominent *al-'Ahali* founder, was appointed head of the Publications Department at the Ministry of Interior.

Ja'far Abul-Timman's speech set the political scene around which the various camps gathered. It became the grounds for a confrontation between various parties. The speech received a joyous response from the liberal segment of Iraq's society, representing as it did their most ardent hopes. As promised, the government officially published its programme prior to the general elections that were about to take place.[5] But it was nevertheless no picnic for the government, as the 'nationalist' elements in Iraq's society responded with attacks on the government. They accused it of having come up short in embracing the Arab nationalist cause that its predecessor had adopted. Indeed, Hashemi, its former leader, was a well-known nationalist figure, not just in Iraq but throughout the Arab world. Thus, this criticism of the present government had the effect of rallying Hashemi's supporters, as well as other nationalist elements, to its cause. The opposition paper *al-Istiqlal* embraced the 'nationalist' banner and kept up an attack on the government. Many in the *ancien régime* hitched their wagons to the 'nationalist' cause, when all they were after was the restoration of the privileges they had enjoyed with the former government. Feudalist tribal leaders who were afraid of a land reform act that might reduce their land holdings also now jumped on the nationalist bandwagon.

The government tried by all means to steer a course by which it could satisfy both the PRS and the 'nationalist' elements. It made lavish promises to the nationalists to assure them that it intended to embrace the Arab cause fully. It issued many reminders that it had a different agenda to that of the PRS and that it had no intention of implementing the full PRS programme. It calmed those tribal sheikhs and landowners fearful of a land reform act, by stating that there was enough government land to distribute to the peasants without resorting to confiscation.[6] Hikmat was so effusive in his courtship of the nationalists that it might even be said that he actually went over to their side, more convinced by nationalist demands than by the PRS's programme of socio-economic reform.

The fissure between Sidqi and the PRS began soon after the coup. Far from keeping his pledge that the army would return to its barracks (the condition that al-'Ahali had set to enter government), Sidqi began to poke his nose into all matters, great and small. When the PRS held a meeting of its leadership (which included Prime Minister Hikmat), to elevate the society to the status of a fully-fledged political party, it decided to appoint a committee composed of five members to go into the details of implementation. Sidqi, using Hikmat as a conduit, managed to impose two of his supporters on that committee. Although this was distasteful to the reformists, they decided to go along with Sidqi's demand in order to secure a license for the proposed party, now named 'The Popular Reform Party'.

Within three months, Sidqi initiated an overt campaign to dominate the decision-making apparatus of the government. His estrangement from the reformists began to encourage members of the former government, as well as others who had experienced a loss of privilege, to further fan the flames between Sidqi and the reformists. The tribal sheikhs and the feudal class also spread unfounded rumours that sparked the fear that the PRS programme was a precursor to the introduction of communism in Iraq. Matters were not helped when PRS members such as 'Abd al-Qader Isma'il, known for his extreme leftist views, and certain members of the Communist Party too, began to beam their ideology at the army, in the hope of recruiting some of its members to their ranks. This irked Sidqi, who mounted a vicious attack on the leftists, with the result that the nationalist army officers began to think of themselves as the saviours of the country from a socialist—or worse still—a communist take-over. They suggested that the civilian leaders had made a mess of running the country, and that the military should therefore stay in government, despite their earlier promises to hand control to the civilians.

Matters began to go from bad to worse for the reformists. They had campaigned for free and honest elections, and for a new election law to replace the one inherited from the Ottomans and the British, which was fraught with fundamental flaws—anathema to a would-be democratic country. Sidqi, on the other hand, had decided that he would not allow a single PRS member to enter parliament. However, under pressure from Hikmat and Abul-Timman, Sidqi relented and allowed twelve PRS members (including those that were already ministers) to win seats. Considering that the total number of deputies was 108, the PRS, which was the actual government, ended up with only twelve seats, representing a serious fall from grace.

The writing was now on the wall. With alarming speed, the deteriorating situation began to affect the running of government as Hikmat leaned more towards Sidqi's position in his dealings with the reformists. Chadirchi was unrelenting in his advocacy of sticking to the reformist agenda, while Abul-Timman, although in agreement with Chadirchi, advised caution and patience. The fault lines dividing both sides were now patently visible. It was then that Chadirchi suggested to Hikmat that Abul-Timman be moved to Interior, and Mohammed Hadid be appointed to Finance, in an attempt to give the reformist agenda more muscle. Hikmat, as stated earlier, did offer the post to Hadid but, possibly because of the rapidly-deteriorating situation between Sidqi and the reformists, the decision was not implemented.

The reformists pushed ahead with their agenda despite strong opposition by some of the non-Sha'biyya ministers. Kamel Chadirchi (who was minister of economics) and Mohammed Hadid prepared a memorandum for the cabinet that outlined the one-sided aspect of the Oil Concession Agreement between Iraq and Britain. They proposed an extensive report to close the gaping holes in the agreement that put

Iraq at such a disadvantage. This memorandum sat ignored on the prime minister's desk, without even the courtesy of a reply.

Despite their differences with the government, the reformists did manage, together with the nationalists, to pass an amazing number of bills (forty-five) in parliament in its one session between 27 February 1936 and 20 June 1937. Parliament was never to sit again in Sidqi's time. Those bills promulgated new laws or were amendments of old laws and decrees, all concerned with improving the civil liberties of the people and their economic lot. However, the reformists found themselves in retreat against the nationalists in parliamentary debates, as it was only too easy for the latter to absurdly label every reformist idea as being a communist one. In his maiden speech, Mohammed Hadid stated the reformist position best by declaring that Iraq would never achieve the leap from a backward society to a modern progressive one without breaking the hold that feudalism had over agricultural life. Iraq was still basically an agricultural society, and therefore the most urgent reforms were those dealing with its agrarian problems.[7] This provoked a heated argument between Hadid and Salman Sheikh Daoud—one of Sidqi's candidates for the PRS executive committee— that again had the effect of dividing the PRS and nationalist camps, since it attempted to label the land policy advocated by the PRS as a communist measure. It is ironic that the PRS members in parliament were led by Hadid who, with Abul-Timman and Chadirchi, were descended from the wealthiest landowning families in the country. Yet all three were prepared to sacrifice personal wealth for the greater good of the country, and they certainly were not communist. Against them were arrayed the feudal landlords, fearful of the loss of their land holdings, who viewed the whole reformist agenda as a threat to their privileged socio-economic position. The landlords teamed up with nationalist deputies and further aroused their already anti-reformist feelings, attacking the PRS for not only its so-called 'communist' mantra, but also for its supposedly aloof attitude towards other Arab countries and for its allegedly irreligious ideology. Hikmat did his best to allay fears that the PRS was communist, but it was to no avail, as the axis of landowners, conservatives and nationalists now forced Hikmat to choose between them and the reformists. For the reformists, it became a situation of sink or swim. Hikmat, originally sympathetic to them, was now wavering. Sidqi, who had promised that the army had no ambition for the exercise of power, and would return to its barracks, thereby satisfying the condition that al-'Ahali/Sha'biyya Group had put down, was now meddling openly in all affairs of state. Worse still for the PRS, he was leaning towards the nationalists and taking Hikmat with him. The army officers, who were predominantly Pan-Arab leaning, had favoured the nationalists and the ideas promoted by the 'Muthana Club' which were anti-reformist.[8] They were now eyeing the government as their private domain, in the style of Turkey and Iran, and were not against the idea of declaring Iraq a republic.[9] The *ancien régime* still had its tentacles in the nationalist movement and in the army. These were busily stoking the fires against the PRS. Sidqi himself was moving inexorably towards the nationalist camp, where he found his comfort zone, considering it more aligned to his way of thinking than that of the reformists, with their progressive approach which he found beyond his regimented, if not simplistic, military mindset.

Sidqi was possessed of a ruthless personality. He now turned his venom on his erstwhile al-'Ahali/reformist supporters, with whom he was still supposedly associated. Matters were not helped when *al-'Ahali* newspaper wrote an editorial criticizing the government for its handling of the Diwaniyya Tribal Uprising. It was Sidqi himself who had decided on the use of overwhelming force to suppress that uprising. It was believed that Sidqi had dispatched the force to Diwaniyya even before the cabinet had approved his decision. Chadirchi, who had wanted to submit his resignation on two previous occasions, and had tried to persuade Abul-Timman to do likewise because of the increasing belligerence of Sidqi towards the reformists, now succeeded in tendering his resignation with three other ministers. They were aghast at rumours that Sidqi was not against eliminating his political opponents by assassination, a method that was complete anathema to al-'Ahali.[10]

The four resignations had the effect of a thunderbolt on Hikmat, who viewed them both as a personal affront and an attempt to scupper his government. He precipitously turned to the nationalists to fill the outgoing ministers' posts. This began an era of cooperation with this group and with supporters of the *ancien régime*.[11] Hikmat, probably prodded by Sidqi, now turned on his former PRS colleagues for their alleged left-wing, if not communist-leaning, beliefs. As an example, 'Abd al-Qader Isma'il, a founder member of al-'Ahali, a former editor of its newspaper and now a deputy in parliament, and his brother Yusuf Isma'il were stripped of their nationalities and deported. *Al-'Ahali* newspaper was shut down by orders of the government.

Mohammed Saleh al-Qazzaz, a labour leader, was exiled to North Iraq. Many other drastic measures—all calculated to diminish the power of the reformists—were also taken. But public opinion soon turned on Hikmat. He was seen as a turncoat, who had come to power on the promise of implementing the reformist agenda, only to do a U-turn and collaborate with the nationalists, who were the reformists' sworn enemies. To cap it all, Kamel Chadirchi began receiving threats to his person and decided to leave the country, which he soon did. It appears that Sidqi had a long 'hit list' of opponents both military and civilian. Rumours circulated in Baghdad about this list, and it must have reached Chadirchi's ears that he had become a target himself, which hastened his departure.

What then was the upshot of this roller-coaster sequence of events that started with the founding of al-'Ahali Group, their meteoric rise to power, and their downfall brought about by their own supposed members, Sidqi and Hikmat? Al-'Ahali Group had conceived the Sha'biyya idea, but was perhaps not as homogeneous as its members wished to believe. This divergence may not have been apparent at the outset, because of the youthful and dynamic nature of its leaders, bent on quickly propagating their liberal ideas, knowing well that the country was being run by a clique of elderly men, oblivious to the vital reforms a modern state needed. These young men even ignored the differences in their own educational, social and cultural backgrounds. Some came from a higher social class than others; some had been educated in Western universities and had the experience of the larger world, while others had studied locally in Baghdad. Such differences did not count when the group was formed, but began to do so later as members began to drift away. However, the original founders and leaders of al-'Ahali remained as the core group. These were Mohammed Hadid, Hussain Jamil, 'Abd al-Fattah 'Ibrahim and Abd al-Qader Isma'il. But even they developed ideological differences and began to split among themselves. Ibrahim, who had a serious clash with Chadirchi who had joined as an outsider, began to drift away from the group and left just prior to the Sidqi coup. Indeed, Mohammed Hadid and Kamel Chadirchi were the only two members who enjoyed unison of political thought and a common vision about the direction that al-'Ahali should take. Hussain Jamil was later to re-join them after the Sidqi coup, having been posted to a job outside Baghdad in the two years prior to the coup.

The differences that Chadirchi and Ibrahim experienced may have been an early warning of the split that was to occur in al-'Ahali later on. Ibrahim has not left a memoir and his version of the difference with Chadirchi can only be gleaned from the memoirs of others. Chadirchi's own memoir has several references to the episode, but the narrative is careful to portray it as a difference of opinion rather than a schism that represented something more serious.

'Abd al-Fattah Ibrahim was undoubtedly the leading light in the Beirut Group which went on to become al-'Ahali. He was the author of the al-Sha'biyya philosophy and it was he who developed its conceptual form when the Beirut and Baghdad Groups united under al-'Ahali. He most likely assumed a proprietary attitude towards it, and felt that other members should give him more credit. He was to receive a rude awakening when Abul-Timman decided to exclude him from a leadership role from the planned political party that was to be created based on al-Sha'biyya principles, since Ibrahim was too young and probably not from the 'right' social *milieu*. Controversially, however, Timman did not object to Mohammed Hadid, who was almost the same age as Ibrahim, but who came from a wealthier and perhaps grander background.

The more serious clash occurred between Ibrahim and Chadirchi. Chadirchi assumed a leadership role in the al-'Ahali Group as he was on average ten years older than the other members and far more experienced—but without being elected to do so. Ibrahim began to feel that the direction of al-'Ahali was being exercised by an outsider, and no longer by the founding members of the group. He began to cut back his connection to al-'Ahali, eventually severing it altogether. Ibrahim's unfortunate clash with the other al-'Ahali members was no doubt a microcosm of what was about to befall the group, exposing the differences in education, age, social background and ideology. The last of these was the most fundamental. Ideologically speaking, Ibrahim had moved more to the left of the other members, to a point approaching Marxism, a fact that created a noticeable schism between them. While still active in al-'Ahali, he insisted on writing and publishing '*Mutala'at fi al-Sha'biyya*' (Readings in al-Sha'biyya). This was a gratuitous act that labelled the whole group as socialists and, worse, as communists—a far cry from their actually much 'softer' ideology based on 'Fabianism' and the principles of the British Labour Party. The '*Mutala't*' ended up being attacked by both the right and the extreme left-wing Marxists. No persuasion on the part of Chadirchi and Hadid succeeded in averting Ibrahim from his task, and it could be said that the publication of *'al-Mutala'at'* did irreparable damage to the fortunes of the group as Hikmat, Timman and Chadirchi struggled in the coup government to dispel the accusations of communism that were constantly being levelled at al-'Ahali Group and the PRS.

The reformists and the military were finally estranged because what started with blood ended with blood. The reformists, who had been dead-set against a non-elected government, had been promised that the coup would be a 'white' one and that the army would return to its barracks once its task was over. The assassination of Ja'far 'Askari at the very outset was a harbinger of things to come. Sidqi joined the Sha'biyya through Hikmat but he never interacted in any meaningful way with the other members. Hence, he remained an unknown quantity to them. Nevertheless, the new government, for a while at least, enjoyed unparalleled popularity because of its civil liberties programme, its economic and social policies and its promise of free elections and a new parliament truly representative of Iraq's citizenry.

But the PRS misjudged the hidden intentions of the army officers, who proved to be more nationalist-leaning than was expected; in fact, much more fiercely so. That, coupled with the nationalist/reactionary/ *ancien régime* alliance against the government, finally persuaded both Sidqi and Hikmat to turn against the PRS, in order to ensure their own survival by aligning themselves with the nationalists. Furthermore, it became increasingly obvious that the army officers seem to have been more interested in establishing a military dictatorship than a parliamentary constitutional democratic monarchy. Both Sidqi and Hikmat might have been sincere at the outset in wanting to implement the PRS's liberal policies, but the army's ambitions became too over-powering to ignore. Both men finally found it easier to go along with the army who, after all, represented the backbone of the Sidqi/ Hikmat alliance.

The reformists did have massive popular backing, but were themselves guilty of allowing some of their members to flout extreme left-wing ideas that the country was simply not ready for—a refrain often repeated by Sidqi and Hikmat. When it finally dawned on them that the latter two had turned on them and with venom, they decided to disband and even leave the country, as Chadirchi had done already.

The 1936 coup was to prove a foray into the unknown for al-'Ahali Group, exacting a heavy political price from them. They were a fledgling group of liberal democrats, thrust into the fray of Iraqi politics, where the army, the nationalists, and the landlord-tribal sheikh cabal proved far too conservative to even begin to adopt their reforms.

5

THE ANGLO-IRAQI WAR OF 1941

The period 1937–42 saw al-'Ahali Group go into hibernation. Although much was happening in the country, they were no longer players at the time. Their meetings became restricted to social gatherings at Abul-Timman's or Chadirchi's houses, where the events of the day were discussed. Kamel Chadirchi had left the country for Cyprus, fearing for his life because of Sidqi's hit list of political opponents. He did not return to Iraq till after Sidqi's assassination. Abul-Timman abandoned politics altogether to manage his family's estates. Hadid, Jamil and Ibrahim all returned to private life, as did Hikmat Sulaiman. Yassin Hashemi died soon after the Sidqi coup and was buried in Damascus, a respected Arab nationalist. The epitaph on his grave reads: 'Here lies Iraq and the Arab World's leader'—an acknowledgement of his role in the nationalist movement both in and outside of Iraq.

   The period was a hotbed of intrigue as the palace and the British proved most active while the country was reeling from one coup d'état to another.[1] After the demise of Sidqi by a counter-coup, army officers swore allegiance to the new government, pledged to return to their barracks, and promised a return to civilian rule. Jamil al-Madfa'i was named as premier, and quickly proclaimed a period of healing and reconciliation known as *Isdal al-Sitar* (letting the curtain fall on the past) to allow the country to get back to some semblance of law and order. Madfa'i enjoyed a good reputation as an honest and straightforward leader. He must certainly have been a favourite of the British embassy, judging by the positive reports that the ambassador, Sir Maurice Peterson, regularly sent to London.[2]

Madfa'i wisely urged that the previous power struggle—that had pitched the Hashemi-Rashid'Ali axis against that of Hikmat-Sidqi, with the latter duo having to resort to a coup d'état to avert the usurpation of power by the former—be regarded as a thing of the past. Accordingly, all the exiles that had been deported by the previous government or had left of their own will now returned to Iraq, though with some restrictions remaining on their political freedoms. Ja'far al-'Askari was given a posthumous burial five years after his assassination with full military honours befitting the popular soldier/politician he had been.

Among the exiles who came back was Nuri al-Sa'id. He did not lose any time conspiring with anti-Sidqi army officers in clandestine meetings to force Madfa'i out, even by coup d'état if need be. He secretly contacted the British ambassador, Sir Maurice Peterson, to check out British government reactions to such a coup. Peterson rejected the idea flat out. He wrote in his memoir: 'I was in bed when a cryptic message reached me from Nuri indicating that that restless brain was planning a disturbance. I sent back a message entreating Nuri not to reintroduce the element of violence into Iraqi politics. I received no reply'.[3] The army officers that had led the anti-Sidqi coup were now gelling together into a bloc. They saw themselves as the rightful rulers of Iraq in the tradition of other countries such as Turkey and Iran. Officers such as Salah al-Din Sabbagh, Mahmoud Salman, Kamel Shabib, Fahmi Said and 'Aziz Yamulki (later joined by Hussain Fawzi and 'Amin al-'Umari) formed the 'Group of Seven'.[4] When news reached the 'Seven' that Madfa'i had got wind of their clandestine plans and was about to retire them from the army, they decided to strike first.

The game was up for Madfa'i. He was confronted with a *fait accompli*, since the army had lost confidence in his government and was prepared to remove him by force if necessary. Madfa'i was in no mood for a power struggle with the army and certainly in no mood to spill more blood. He asked the king to relieve him from the premiership, which the latter duly did. The king, ever familiar with army machinations, and probably mentored by the British ambassador, tried to dissuade the bloc from appointing Nuri, but the officers prevailed. Nuri was thus appointed prime minister on 25 December 1938. He had not headed a government since 1932, and this was now his moment to settle scores.

The period that started with Nuri's premiership and ended with the Anglo-Iraqi War of 1941 is shrouded in mystery. The country had witnessed three coups d'états in two years. It had seen the back of three governments (Hashemi/Rashid 'Ali, Sidqi/Hikmat and Madfa'i), but there was more to come. The leading players were now the military, Nuri al-Sa'id, the palace and the British.

Nuri, who wished to assume the mantle of a senior and benign statesman, chose the Muthanna Club (the bastion of the nationalist movement in Iraq) to deliver his programme of reform on 4 January 1939. Nuri's speech, which sounded candid and sincere enough, announced that the government would pursue a democratic agenda. It would work to restore constitutional rights to citizens, and promised it would accept parliamentary opposition, freedom of the press, and, through electoral reform, a parliament truly representative of the people.

But Nuri never got to implement his programme. He was sidetracked by the burning issue of Palestine, and the recriminations of members of parliament about the past. On 22 February, he dissolved parliament and many politicians returned to the old ways of protecting what political capital they had. Nuri kept his eyes wide open and watched his back for both the army and his opponents, lest they push him out of office as they had done his predecessors.

Nuri had promised to let bygone be bygones, and forgive those that were implicated in the assassination of his brother-in-law, Ja'far al-'Askari. He had even written to Hikmat Sulaiman assuring him that he harboured no ill-feeling towards him. But the mask he put on was soon to slip. In a fantastic plot he concocted, Nuri enlisted the support of Prince 'Abdulillah, a cousin of the king, to play a leading role. The plot, which was to be uncovered by Iraqi Military Intelligence, was to overthrow the present regime by inviting the king and 250 of the top civilian and military leaders to a banquet at 'Abdulillah's house, and there set upon them and massacre forty or fifty selected victims—including the king and Nuri himself! 'Abdulillah was then to be enthroned as king, and the plotters were to be named as Hikmat Sulaiman and other Sidqi supporters who would then form a new government.

'Abdulillah, first playing along with the plotters, would soon turn as witness against them. He informed the government of the details of their plan. Captain Hilmi 'Abd al-Karim, who allegedly was assigned to brief 'Abdulillah regarding the matter, confessed in court to his involvement which, with 'Abdulillah's evidence, was enough to put the plotters on trial.[5] Hikmat and his associates were duly arrested and tried by Military Court Martial. Hikmat and four of his associates received the death sentence, while others received sentences of varying years of hard labour. The verdicts drew many protests, causing most of the death sentences to be commuted to prison terms. The British took a dim view of these shenanigans, and their ambassador advocated a more lenient approach by Nuri. In his memoir, the ambassador stated 'Nuri plotted to have... Hikmat Sulaiman tried under the flimsiest evidence and sentenced to death by hanging. I intervened with Nuri to ensure that the sentence was not carried out'.[6] In any case, the British were not overly worried, as their interests were in no danger of being threatened—Nuri having made it a bedrock of his foreign policy to adhere to the terms of the Anglo-Iraqi Treaty.

To add to the confusion, King Ghazi was killed in a car accident merely a month or so after Nuri announced the existence of the plot. Ghazi's death, in what can only be described as improbable circumstances, sent a seismic shock throughout the kingdom. Nobody believed the version of the accident put out by the government and, lesser still, the sudden candidacy of 'Abdulillah as regent.[7] Sinderson Pasha, British doctor to the Iraqi royal family, arriving at the scene of the accident, refused—to his credit—to confirm when asked by Queen 'Alia to do so, that Ghazi had named 'Abdulillah as regent as he lay dying. Furthermore, he refused to certify that death had been caused by an accident. A local Iraqi doctor was quickly hustled in to sign just such a compromised death certificate.[8] 'Abdulillah, a much-reviled person, evev by the late King Ghazi, who always treated him with disdain, was named regent on the sole evidence of Ghazi's widow, Queen 'Alia ('Abdulillah's sister), and Ghazi's own sister, Princess Rajiha. This was that Ghazi's last words, before dying, were to name 'Abdulillah as regent. 'Alia, who had good reason to settle scores with her dead husband, who had preferred to spend his time drinking with his army buddies while she was left alone, did not want the rightful candidate, Prince Zeid bin Hussain (Faisal I's younger brother), to become regent, as this would have cast her into oblivion as a widowed ex-queen.[9] It is reported that Rajiha was at first hesitant at having to lie deliberately that Ghazi had indeed named 'Abdulillah, but the latter dropped to his knees sobbing and grabbed her by hers, begging her to go along with 'Alia's version of Ghazi's wish. True to form, once 'Abdulillah had become regent he quickly distanced himself from Rajiha, and cruelly would not even allow her to see her nephew, the now-fatherless infant, King Faisal II.[10]

The combined effect of Ghazi's death in hard-to-believe circumstances, together with the dubious naming of 'Abdulillah as regent, caused an eruption of angry national sentiment. Demonstrators marched through the streets of Baghdad as rumours flew about the city that Ghazi had been murdered in a plot put together by Nuri and the British. 'Thou shalt answer for the blood of Ghazi, O Nuri', chanted the crowds.[11]

Ghazi had endeared himself to the people of Iraq by taking an anti-British stand on Kuwait, Palestine and the Assyrian issue. He had set up a ham broadcasting station in al-Zuhour Palace. This ham radio station had been gifted to Ghazi by Fritz Gröbba, the German ambassador, who thought that Ghazi might have German sympathies. The station put out relentless attacks against Britain, courtesy of the broadcaster, Younis Bahri, and others, who were close to the four army officers who came to be known as 'The Golden Square'. Ghazi, despite his popularity, was a weak individual who was always searching for approval and acceptance. He wrote to the leader of the 'Square', Colonel Salah al-Din Sabbagh, on 1 March 1939: 'I realized, before it was too late, that your group is loyal and that you champion the Arab Cause... as such, I wish to be one of you and I join hands with you'. This letter was broadcast by Bahri to an adoring public on the al-Zuhour Palace station.

The British, who were watching the activities of Ghazi and his entourage with some trepidation, swung into action to tow Ghazi back into line. On 5 March 1939, Bahri was visited by the British consul-general, Mr. Monck-Mason, who threatened dire consequences if the king did not desist from his attacks on Britain and his close liaison with the army. The British ambassador, Sir Maurice Patterson, also entered the fray, with reports to the Foreign Office that Ghazi had to be reined in or gotten rid of altogether. In his memoir, Patterson wrote that 'it was plain that Ghazi had either to be controlled or removed', and he hinted as much to Ghazi himself in his farewell meeting with him.[12]

Younis Bahri, in his book *Harakat al-Thani Mais*, ('The Second of May Movement'), writes that he had communicated Monck-Mason's warnings both to Sabbagh and to Younis Sab'awi (another 'Golden Square' member). They saw the hidden hand of the British at play and, in turn, communicated their fears to Ghazi via Rashid 'Ali. They also put the army units around Baghdad on high alert, in case of any moves by the British.

Matters came to a head with Ghazi's 'meddling' in the Kuwait issue. From his clandestine radio station, Ghazi incited the Kuwaitis to rise against their ruler, throw away the shackles of imperialism that had them mired in obscurity, and join Iraq in its quest for modernity. Ghazi was fast becoming the subject of serious misgivings both by the British and their Iraqi political allies. The Foreign Office records of the time are fraught with insinuation and innuendo about Ghazi's fate.

Whatever the real story behind Ghazi's death, he ended up dying inside the palace grounds, despite the army's efforts to protect him outside it by placing all its units on high alert. The crowds in Mosul attacked the British Consulate—probably incited by Bahri—killed Monck-Mason and burned the building down. The German embassy, through its formidable minister plenipotentiary, Fritz Gröbba, with whom Bahri had been in constant touch, put the latter on a plane and got him out of Iraq to Berlin.[13] There, he lost no time broadcasting anti-British material starting on 6 April 1939—the day after his arrival there. In Iraq, he was sentenced to death *in absentia* for the murder of Monck-Mason.

'Abdulillah's appointment as regent was farcical. It was met with first stunned disbelief and then fury by the public. In addition to her testimony concerning Ghazi's dying wishes, Queen 'Aliya also swore that Ghazi had actually signed a document naming 'Abdulillah as regent in the case of his death so long as their infant son Faisal was still a minor. But no such document was ever produced. Dr. Sinderson, the family doctor, was once again asked to lie and corroborate her claim, but refused to do so. It was thus that 'Abdulillah—still in his twenties, and a useless lay-about, earning eighteen dinars a month at the ministry of foreign affairs and notorious for never showing up to work— became the effective ruler of Iraq, aided and abetted by Nuri al-Sa'id.[14] Nuri was now solidly manipulating the reins of government from behind the scenes. 'Abdulillah, who did not even possess an Iraqi passport, having preferred to keep his Hijazi identity, made parliament endure the absurd task of bestowing Iraqi nationality on him. He was effectively hardly more than a pariah living in a foreign land, having been kicked out of his own, when his father, King 'Ali, lost the Hijaz to Ibn Sa'ud. 'Abdulillah, who had failed to get so much as a high school diploma (despite having attended the famed Victoria College in

Alexandria, where the headmaster dubbed him 'lazy 'Abdulillah', which became a refrain that rang around the school), was selected to be regent over his uncle Zeid, a Cambridge University graduate and a seasoned and highly-respected statesman.[15]

Unfortunately for the country, this one foolish act effectively condemned the monarchy and the future of Iraq. 'Abdulillah would remain a figure of hate up and until the demise of the royal family in 1958.

One clever thing that 'Abdulillah did do was to recognize the power of the 'Golden Square' and cosy up to them. In his memoir, *Fursan al-'Uruba* (Knights of Arabism), Sabbagh wrote that the army went along with 'Abdulillah's appointment as they preferred him to his uncle, Prince Zeid, the choice of many senior politicians, including Jamil Madfa'I, that they had deposed.[16] Indeed, the 'Golden Square' officers may well have tipped the scales in 'Abdulillah's favour, as they had become by then the effective kingmakers of Iraq.

The death of Ghazi is key to understanding the national tragedy that befell Iraq, and the critical change of fortune that it experienced. In *Iraq*, 'Adeed Dawisha writes that 'little did Ghazi know that he had helped sow the seeds for the later destruction of the monarchy and the murder of his own son'.[17] Dawisha meant that Ghazi had crossed a line by becoming too involved with the army which became convinced, as a result, that it should rule the country instead of the civilian politicians. The fact that Ghazi and the officers he had befriended were anti-British may also have played into the drama that unfolded. There is certainly a wealth of academic, archival and memoir material to support this view. The officers adored Ghazi, and far from conspiring against the monarchy, they and the entire populace rejoiced in having a nationalist king. Ghazi had accomplished the national adulation that his father had always dreamed of. If Ghazi had not been killed, Iraq might well have had a more secure, flourishing and peaceful future, quite likely under a monarchy, as in Jordan still today.

The period from Ghazi's death which saw the rise and rise of the 'Golden Square' officers, who came to dominate Iraqi politics with Nuri directing the ship of state, to the declaration of the Anglo-Iraqi War of 1941, is noted for the deterioration of Iraq's relations with Britain. The declaration of war by Great Britain on Germany on 3 September 1939, had serious implications for Iraq because of its treaty of alliance with Britain. Nuri outlined Iraq's position thus: 'This country is bound to Great Britain by the Anglo-Iraqi Treaty of 1930, Article 4, which states that should either party become engaged in war, the other party should come to its aid. In this case, Iraq will furnish Great Britain with transportation and communications facilities that will include the use of its railways, rivers, ports, aerodromes, and means of communication'.

On 5 September 1939, Iraq severed relations with Germany, and deported all German subjects residing in Iraq, including the German minister, Dr. Fritz Gröbba. The regent, 'Abdulillah, sent a message to King George VI affirming Iraq's solidarity with Britain in her war against Germany. It should be remembered, however, that when Iraq went to war with Israel in 1948, Britain had no intention of fulfilling her obligations under the same treaty. The fact, though, was that there was considerable opposition to Nuri's excessive offer of facilities to Britain. Added pressure was applied by the officers themselves, who failed to convince Nuri to obligate Britain to support Palestinian rights (probably persuaded in this by the Mufti of Jerusalem, who had taken refuge in Baghdad) and to arm the Iraqi army. The officers severed their relations with Nuri because of his intransigence on the matter. However, Nuri insisted that Iraq's best interests lay with Britain, and that the officers' requests had to wait for a more opportune moment. With the murder of Rustum Haidar, a close supporter of his in the cabinet, Nuri decided to resign from the premiership, handing it over to Rashid 'Ali, but retaining the important portfolio of Foreign Affairs.

On 31 March 1940, Rashid 'Ali formed his government, resulting in the centre of gravity shifting squarely back to the officers, with the Mufti of Jerusalem lurking in the background.[18] The Mufti (known as 'The Red Fox' because of his red beard and piercing blue eyes) had set up a cabinet within a cabinet; so much so, that official ministers when leaving cabinet meetings would go straight to his house, to report on the government's deliberations.[19]

Despite the fact that Rashid 'Ali did not commit Iraq to either of the warring sides, he did state that his government would abide by the commitments of its predecessor, although he himself was not overtly friendly towards Britain. Since Britain had refused to make any pro-Arab pledges towards Palestine, and had been consistently anti-nationalist, her cause was not helped with the Iraqis who were now falling deeper and deeper under the spell of the nationalist/officer/Mufti constellation. The fall of France in June 1940 further convinced the nationalists of Iraq that Britain would be next to fall, and that their country had hitched its horse to the wrong wagon.

The ensuing months in Iraq dissolved into a phantasmagoric blur of further intrigue, as governments came and went through yet more coup d'états. Germany became an active player in the already complex Iraqi equation, as contacts with her through the Italian legation in Baghdad, mostly engineered by the Mufti, offered a new option to Iraqi leaders to ally themselves with Germany.

What marked this period of Iraq's history was Britain's flexing of her imperial muscle by declaring to the world at large, and to Iraq in particular, that her own interests were to be protected first and foremost. In the 1930 Anglo-Iraqi Treaty, Britain had ensured a dominant military presence for herself in the country with two air bases, one at Shu'aiba (near Basra), and the other at Habbaniyya (on the Euphrates, west of Baghdad). Both these facilities stood on the all-important air-route to India and the Far East. Defence of these facilities was provided by Assyrian levies.[20] The treaty provided an important right of transit for British military forces through Iraq in times of war and peace. During wartime, even if Iraq was not involved, the country was supposed to provide all possible facilities—including the use of railways, rivers, ports and airfields—for the benefit and movement of British armed forces. Furthermore, the air route between the United Kingdom and India took on an even more important role. With Italy in peacetime threatening East Africa, it was reasonable to assume that enemy attacks on British military assets might come from the Red Sea area. Hence, for London, Haifa, Baghdad, Basra and the Persian Gulf had to be developed as alternative routes.

Doubtless, and more important than the geographic imperatives, Iraq's rich oil deposits—situated in the area around Mosul and Kirkuk—figured high in British economic and geopolitical strategy. The fact was that Shatt al-Arab, into which the Tigris and Euphrates merged to flow into the Persian Gulf, was the natural channel for the export of oil. The oil from northern Iraq was transported by pipeline to Haditha on the Euphrates, where the line forked south to Transjordan and Palestine, and north through Syria to Tripoli.

Oil from that area represented one of the single most important strategic assets for the British war effort. If the Axis powers could lay their hands on either Persian or Iraqi oil, the results would have been dire indeed for Britain. The proximity of Habbaniyya and Shu'aiba to the two vital oil regions and their total protection became of paramount importance. Obviously, keeping a friendly and compliant Iraqi government in Baghdad guaranteed the smooth running of British imperial policies. However, Germany's resounding military successes, coupled with the innate hatred that Iraqis felt for the occupying British, had a profound impact. After all, no propaganda ever provided a better elixir in times of war than victory.

Had 1940 been a year of Allied triumphs, it is debatable whether German propaganda would have had the same effect. Axis radio stations, broadcasting in Arabic, saturated the airwaves with the achievements of German forces. The Japanese, still technically neutral, were nevertheless aiding and abetting to undermine the British position. The Mufti of Jerusalem, who had taken sanctuary in Iraq, further inflamed national feeling with pointed descriptions of Britain's treacherous attitude towards the Palestinians, and their infamous Balfour Declaration.

In February 1941, Sir Kinahan Cornwallis, a trusted friend of Faisal I and by then an old Iraq hand, was appointed ambassador in Baghdad.[21] London was unhappy with Rashid 'Ali's anti-British stance, but for the moment they were not going to interfere, provided Iraq stuck to her obligations under the treaty. Cornwallis's mandate was made clear to him by Churchill: Basra was to be turned into a great troop assembly base. He had to do whatever it took for Iraq to deliver on its treaty obligations—even more if necessary, to ensure that objective. Cornwallis should take no heed to demands made by the Iraqi government to limit the number of British troops to that agreed on in the treaty, or decide on their movements. There was to be no bargaining about acceding to British demands, in return for British pledges on Palestine. Cornwallis should not engage in explaining anything about the British position.

The first British troops disembarked in Basra on 17 April 1941. The Iraqi government assembled a military force to oppose their disembarkation. Cornwallis informed Rashid 'Ali that the British government would recognize his regime (which it had not done yet) if he was to turn a blind eye to the terms in the treaty regarding troop limitation, and allow the arrival of British troops regardless of numbers. Rashid 'Ali appeared seemingly happy with the arrangement; indeed, for the next two days, troops poured into Basra by sea and by air, without opposition from the Iraqis. Rashid 'Ali may have overplayed his hand, because by 19 April, a note was sent to the British ambassador by Iraq, laying down the country's conditions as called for in the treaty on troop landing limitations. Direct pressure was now being applied by the 'Golden Square' officers on 'Ali. He was accused of blatantly degrading the authority of the government, in the face of Britain's flagrant flouting of the treaty's already British-favoured provisions.

Both sides were now squaring for a fight. The Iraqis began making preparations for war and the British began mobilizing their forces to oust Rashid 'Ali and the colonels. British subjects were evacuated, and relations between Rashid 'Ali and Cornwallis, never friendly, now hit rock bottom. When the British landed further troops on 29 April in defiance of Iraq's protests that this was in stark contravention of the treaty, both sides knew that they were heading for a showdown.

Ironically enough, it was the British—though in clear contravention of their own treaty—who started the war. Admittedly, the Iraqi army had surrounded the British base at Habbaniyya, but at 5am on 2 May, Air-Vice Marshall Smart gave the order for British planes to attack the Iraqi army without giving it any ultimatum. Cornwallis informed the Foreign Office that he regarded any Iraqi threat to Habbaniyya as an act of war.

War erupted between the two sides, and became known in Iraqi history as *Harakat al-Thani Mais* (The Second of May Movement). The Iraqis acquitted themselves well, fighting a courageous but expectedly unequal battle against a massive invading British army. As in 1920, the overwhelming difference that the British enjoyed in technical superiority, especially in the air, proved yet again to be the decisive factor in the outcome of the war. Christopher Buckley, in his book *The Five Ventures*, argues that the invasion of Iraq by British forces in 1941 was a strategic necessity for them, in view of German advances into Greece and Yugoslavia and the rapidly developing aim of Hitler to invade Russia. Yet Buckley describes the advance on Baghdad as having encountered a skilful and courageous counter-attack by the Iraqis.

Buckley relates in the book that Iraqi morale must have suffered a blow when their gunners fired by mistake on a plane bringing Major Axel von Blomberg to Baghdad to help direct Luftwaffe operations there. He was pronounced dead on arrival. In total, military operations lasted one month, with one hundred dead on the British side and 497 on the Iraqi side. Ten thousand Iraqi soldiers were taken prisoner and the Iraqi air force was totally destroyed. Buckley describes Rashid 'Ali's relations with the Germans as having been perfunctory before the war, but adds that Hitler and the German general-command did not fully exploit the opportunity open to them at that critical moment (in their favour) to establish a foothold in Iraq, and actualize the long-held German dream of a warm-water port in the Gulf. This was what the Baghdad-Bahn project—a German engineering scheme of major scale to connect Berlin to Baghdad by rail—had initially been designed for.

On 30 May 1941, Rashid 'Ali—accompanied by the new regent, Sharif Sharaf, and together with the Iraqi chief of staff and the four colonels—fled Iraq to Iran. An Armistice was declared on 31 May 1941, and signed that day by the remaining top brass of the defeated Iraqi army.[22]

Hanna Batatu, in his seminal work *Old Social Classes and Revolutionary Movements in Iraq*, writes: '1941 was seen by the outside world as a movement with a pro-German/Nazi colouring. It was nothing more than a continuation, in another form and by other social forces, of the 1920 Uprising. In 1920 it was the tribal sheikhs and Sayyids who were the motivating force. In 1941 it was now the Pan-Arab middle-class army officers. The principle immediate aim was the same: the elimination of British influence from Iraq'.[23]

The return to power of the unpopular 'Abdulillah precipitated an unfortunate incident involving the Jews of Iraq that became known as the *farhood*.[24] It throws light on how the British tended to spin news, in this case by engineering 'Abdulillah's return so as it was not seen as having been orchestrated by them, as indeed was the case. On 1 June 1941, which happened to fall on a Jewish religious holiday, a large group of Iraqi Jews went to the airport to watch the festivities which were meant to celebrate the return of the ex-regent on board a British aircraft (he, in fact, ended up returning by another route). At the same time, another group of Christians and Muslims had gone to the airport for the same reason, and an altercation occurred between the two disparate groups, which resulted in the injury of seventeen Jews, and the consequent death of two of them. Although normality returned to the city that night, the Jews continued to display great delight at the return of both 'Abdulillah and the British. On 2 June 1941, as the Iraqi army marched back into the capital defeated and humiliated, it was subjected to taunts from young Jewish members of the community. This led to another altercation, which sadly deteriorated into a bloody battle. As the capital was bereft of any central government control and any semblance of order, massive incidents of looting of Jewish homes occurred, with great consequent damage to property, and the instilling of fear amongst the Jewish community. It must be remembered that British forces had already surrounded Baghdad and could easily have marched into the capital with no resistance from an already collapsed Iraqi army. The British could have certainly prevented the *farhood* from happening, but they made no move for two days, supposedly to allow the regent ('Abdulillah) to arrive and enter Baghdad on his own, without being tainted as having returned on British wings.

Finally, the highest ranking officer in the army contacted the regent, and a force was belatedly put together, which then entered the capital accompanied by armoured cars. These opened fire on the crowd, resulting in 110 dead and many more injured. Curfew was declared and punishment by execution was threatened for anyone who attacked others' property.

The now-defeated government leaders fled to Iran where they were accepted as political refugees, with the exception of Salahudin al-Sabbagh, who managed to go on to Turkey, as did the Mufti, who then made his way to Italy with the help of the German embassy there. Gailani also took refuge in Turkey. As for the rest, they were arrested by Iranian security forces, and handed over to the British authorities, whose forces had occupied Iran on 24 August 1941. They were placed on a British ship, and taken to Salisbury in Rhodesia, to await sentencing by Military Court in Baghdad. On 15 March 1942, the British government agreed to hand over 'the criminals of April-May 1941' to the Iraqi government. On arrival, they were placed in the concentration camp of Abu Ghraib (still notorious to this day), and languished there in chains. There they were visited by the regent—their erstwhile friend—who proceeded to spit into each of their faces as they lay helpless in their chains. The Baghdad newspapers followed the regent's lead and poured scorn and insult on them. They were full of praise for Iraq's present rulers, who had been returned to power by the British. On 14 May 1942, executions were carried out on those found guilty and all the others received long prison sentences.

The Second of May 1941 movement was yet another *cri de coeur* by Iraqi politicians and army leaders for freedom and independence. These leaders attempted to apply this not just to Iraq, but to other Arab countries that were subject to foreign imperialism, especially Palestine. It served to revive the national fervour that Arabs everywhere felt for the achievement of their independence, and for Palestine, which was now falling under Jewish control. As far as Iraq was concerned, its army had fought an honourable battle with great courage, given the disparity in arms and expertise between the two adversaries. The morale of the army and the people remained high and the movement enjoyed genuine popular support. No period of anarchy or mob rule followed the collapse of the Iraqi army. Quite the contrary, it was rumoured that even criminals ceased their activities in the void created by the collapse of the government.[25] The fight went out of the leaders when they saw that they were no match for British military power, especially in the air. Leaders such as Younis Sab'aoui, possibly with the support of his brother-in-law, Siddiq Shanshal, wanted to carry on fighting with guerrilla forces. Both were apprehended by the British and accused of treason. If fortunes had been reversed and the Iraqi side had won, it would have been 'Abdulillah and Nuri who would have awaited the hangman's noose. Whatever the other merits of the 1941 movement, it was certainly fuelled by nationalist ideals of freedom and independence, essential for nation building. The movement was a cat-alyst for spreading nationalist fervour in other Arab lands, especially Palestine and Lebanon. It was credited with planting the roots of the Egyptian Revolution of 1952 and the Iraq Revolution of 1958. It was no coincidence, therefore, that after the 1958 revolution, 'Abdulillah was left hanging in the very same spot Salahuddin Sabbagh had been strung up from outside the ministry of defence. In the ensuing period, the British wished to name Dr Sami Shawkat as prime minister, pro-vided he undertook to carry out the executions of the movement's lead-ers. He agreed to take the post only if the sentences were not carried out as he, like other Iraqis, believed that the leaders had been moti-vated by nationalist causes and should be exiled from Iraq instead as ambassadors, as was then the Arab custom. Nuri was named prime minister, and did obtain death sentences for the leaders. The British occupied Iraq, and did not depart until 26 October 1947, two years after the end of World War II.

6

AL-'AHALI BECOMES THE NDP

In the post-1941 coup era, Iraq—now under actual British military occupation—had returned to business as usual. The palace was entirely under the influence of the regent, 'Abdulillah, deputing for the infant king, with pro-British Iraqi politicians in government and the British firmly in control. Al-'Ahali Group, dormant since their foray into government with Sidqi, began once again to agitate politically. The group had splintered since the Sidqi coup, with its meetings becoming mere social gatherings. It no longer had the force of a political movement. However, after 1941, Kamel Chadirchi, Mohammed Hadid, and 'Abd al-Fattah'Ibrahim began to function again in unison, as in the old Sha'biyya days first associated with al-'Ahali.

This revival happened to coincide with the active campaign that the Allies now waged against fascism, seeking to promote the concept of freedom, coupled with social and economic reform. Western embassies were tasked with contacting the liberal leaders in the countries they were posted in, with the objective of developing a dialogue with them. In the case of Iraq, the ruling regimes in both the pre- and post-1941 eras resisted such activities by the Allies but, under heavy pressure from the British, the post-1941 regime was forced to relent, not so much out of conviction, but as a way of neutralizing the counter-campaign waged by the Axis countries. The resulting relaxation by the government of its draconian clampdown on civil liberties resulted in a limited re-emergence of political life. In the case of al-'Ahali, it meant the return of more progressive elements to its fold, with the intention of restarting political activities and re-publishing its newspaper, al-'Ahali.

In 1942, it was rumoured that Sir Stafford Cripps, prominent member of the British Labour Party and a future cabinet minister in the Labour government during the war, was sent on a mission by his government to India and had planned a stop in Baghdad en route to his destination. Since Iraq was under British occupation at the time and since the British government had let it be known that it was interested to know how the country was faring, Hadid, Chadirchi and Ibrahim decided to present Cripps with a memorandum describing the conditions prevailing at the time. This stressed the necessity of the Iraqi government's introducing immediate reforms, and relaxing its suppression of civil liberties.

The memorandum was prepared but, at the last moment, Cripps changed his schedule and by-passed Baghdad altogether. Nevertheless, this document is worth summarizing here, as it depicts both the problems then facing Iraq and al-'Ahali's views on addressing them.

The Stafford Cripps memorandum (1942)[1]

This memorandum was put together by Kamel Chadirchi, Mohammed Hadid and 'Abd al-Fattah'Ibrahim, together with other progressive individuals then in Iraqi politics. Its aim was to lift the cover on conditions in the country, especially those that affected democratic public opinion, which was unable to express itself through party life.

The memorandum at the very outset attributed the foundation in 1921 of the Iraqi state to the Iraqi Revolution of 1920, which itself was the offshoot of the Arab Revolution. Iraq was caught between its population's interest in Woodrow Wilson's famous Fourteen Points, and the desire of the imperialist powers to continue to have designs on its land. A unique 'compromise' solution was reached: the mandate system was invented—under the auspices of the League of Nations—supposedly to help those under-developed countries that the Allies had occupied attain self-rule. It was an unwritten condition, however, that the tutor nation that held the mandate was to receive special strategic and economic considerations from the mandated state. The system failed because of the inordinate greed shown by the mandate nations to extract the last drop of commercial advantage for themselves, and because the men entrusted with the running of it were of the old imperialist school, and had absolutely no intention of furthering national-ist aspirations. The resulting fissures began to manifest themselves in all aspects of the political, social and economic life of the country; by 1932—when Iraq was deemed ready to join the League of Nations—conditions there had failed to change for the better since its creation by the British, except that there was now a clear demarcation line in those areas that the mandate power wished to suck dry economically. Iraqi society, which long had hoped for reform and political change, was in 1932 still facing the same wolf—now in wolf's clothing!

The basis of the new Iraq was supposed to have been constitutional and parliamentary, and its form of government democratic. Essen-tially that meant in the context of the time the application of Wood-row Wilson's Fourteen Principles. Unfortunately, all the literature generated in the writing at the constitution, of parliamentary practices and other democratic principles, proved to be mere ink on paper, for Britain never had any intention of actually implementing what was written down.

At the outset a semblance of democratic life manifested itself in the formation of political parties, though in rudimentary form, with the establishment of a token opposition in parliament. But these embry-onic entities never took shape. They attained mere formulaic status, and were deliberately and continually weakened, so that by the time the World War II broke out, Iraqi's system of government was far more like a dictatorship, despite the show presence of a constitution and parliament.

In order to be able to push through pro-British legislation and com-mercial agreements, the government constantly manipulated the com-position of parliament, so that it always was weighted in representation in favour of the countryside. The majority of the rural population was composed of smallholding landlords and farmers, who were politically ignorant and often illiterate. The regime relied on municipal leaders to recommend such names for parliament seats, and they were then appointed to them by the central government in Baghdad. In this way, the government guaranteed itself a parliamentary majority always ready to vote in its favour. Unfortunately for Iraq, this continued unal-tered as successive governments discovered the comforting succour that a pliable majority gave to government. From the liberal democ-racy and freedom of speech point of view, this of course was an unqualified catastrophe. Personal rights were denied, parties disbanded, freedom of the press suppressed, and the judiciary system made a tool in government hands, with which to apply pressure where it was needed. Governments began to be composed from networks of nepotism and favouritism. Anything that was even vaguely progressive, by way of political, social or economic programmes, was deliberately stalled, and even stopped.

Given such conditions, it was not surprising that there emerged in the populace a ferocious anti-government feeling. In the absence of any political parties or political platforms to express dissent, violence became the only conduit left with which to effect change. The first manifestations of violence came from the Euphrates tribes, who had in the past often conspired with some of the power blocks in government to gain a way of manipulating the political system. Quite often, the central government had resorted to the army to quell such uprisings, and sometimes it had succeeded in doing so.[2] (End of Cripps memorandum summary.)

The worsening economic and social conditions, mostly caused by the war, practically bankrupted the government. It nevertheless had to continue its import of goods imposed upon it by Britain as a contribution to the war effort. Those still existing al-'Ahali members felt that they had to find their group's voice again, in order to be able to vent the frustrations of an angry public and regain the progressive high ground that it had been known for.[3] It became obvious very quickly that their newspaper, *al-'Ahali*, needed to reappear on news-stands. It was decided that this time round, the mission of the publication should be better defined so as to avoid the disputes between members and editorial staff that had occurred in the past. They invited 'Aziz Sharif (one of their original members who was known for his progressive views) to join a new al-'Ahali nucleus. Sharif recommended his nephew 'Abd al-Rahim Sharif, to become editor (but not director of the paper's policy) and this was accepted by the other members. The paper was often forced to change its name slightly in order to evade consecutive closing-down orders.

On 23 September 1942, *Sawt al-'Ahali* was licensed to appear on the stands, which it did under the ownership and management of Kamel Chadirchi.[4] The policy of the paper remained the same, in that the editorials and main articles were first discussed by the members before a final text was published. The paper, as before, called for:

• Free elections.

- Freedom to organize political parties and trade unions without outside interference.
- Freedom of the press and freedom of association.
- Implementation of state law in dealing with political disturbances.
- Resolving problems in the education and public health sectors.
- Raising the standard of living across the board, especially among the poorer segments of society.
- Resolving agrarian and labour problems.
- Combating Fascism.
- Working for the Arab cause, with special emphasis on the Palestinian situation.

But, within months, the disputes of the past returned to haunt al-'Ahali Group. This time, the differences were between Hadid and Chadirchi on the one hand, and 'Abd al-Fattah'Ibrahim and 'Aziz Sharif on the other. A further problem loomed when Sharif's nephew, and editor of the paper, began to exceed his authority by including radical views that did not reflect al-'Ahali's outlook. With other infractions in his work, he was fired from his job, which led to his uncle 'Aziz Sharif leaving the group as well. 'Abd al-Fattah'Ibrahim stayed on for a time, but his differences with Hadid and Chadirchi continued to grow, and he finally quit the group altogether. The work of writing the editorials was now placed squarely on Hadid and Chadirchi's shoulders, though they would occasionally enlist the help of outsiders when they offered articles for publication.

The momentum built up by the call for meaningful freedom by *al-'Ahali* newspaper, crystallized for al-'Ahali Group the idea that they should at last become a fully-fledged political party.

The British (via their embassy in Baghdad) played an active role in seeking to sway the government to introduce much-needed reforms. Their occupation of the country at the time had given the Iraqi government a pretext to eliminate most political 'enemies', and crush all freedoms. However, the British were alarmed at the popular anger this was causing, which they feared would blow up in their face. The ambassador, Sir Kinahan Cornwallis, made his displeasure known with Nuri's mishandling of government affairs. In a memo of November 1943, he wrote:

I attacked His Excellency for the endless failure of his government to tackle the economic problems honestly and boldly, for the manner in which they have tolerated dishonesty and inefficiency in the public services, for the resultant weakness and corruption in the police, the unreliability of the army, the mis-handling of the Kurds, the shameless land-grabbing carried on by prominent personalities, the general lack of courageous leadership and the wide gulf between the Government and the people. I complained, too, of the harmful effects of widespread nepotism and about the low moral tone of public life.[5]

Sir Kinahan observed rightly that Iraq had changed and a new edu-cated young class was emerging, which was demanding far more free-dom of expression than the government was prepared to allow. The old-style parliament—where 50 per cent of the members were tribal sheikhs always supportive of the government—was not the formula to build a new, post-war Iraq on. The growth of the press and a far more knowledgeable and politicized public made this impossible. In another note about Nuri to the Foreign Office, Cornwallis warned (presciently as it turned out): 'I remind the Prime Minister that there had been a radical change in the attitude of the people during the last twenty years. They were no longer as long-suffering as of yore. In the towns especially, education had brought about a new outlook, and I warned His Excellency that, unless account were taken of these facts, the old order might be very rudely disturbed at no very distant date'.[6]

Even the unpopular regent, Prince 'Abdulillah, joined the gathering momentum when, in a speech in December 1943, he referred to the possibility of re-introducing political parties to Iraqi life. Indeed, 'Abdulillah submitted a memorandum on political and other reforms to the British embassy in early 1944 that Sir Kinahan found somewhat 'jejune'.[7] It took another two years for the regent to actually act on the speech he gave, and announced this in a follow-up speech on 27 December 1945. The prime minister of the day, Hamdi al-Pachachi, resigned a month later and was replaced by Tawfiq al-Swaidi, who then proceeded to carry out several of the long-promised reforms.

In his memoir, Kamel Chadirchi reaffirms the drive for civil liberties, and the re-emergence of progressive elements in Iraq's political life combined now to operate more systematically as political parties. The first group to do so applied to be licensed as the Sha'b Party (the Peo-ple's Party), but their application was turned down by the government. The reason for the rejection may well have been that among the extreme left-wing members of the party, there may have been some who were communist. A sharp exchange between this group and al-'Ahali took place, directed mostly at Kamel Chadirchi, who was leader.

Al-Sha'b taunted al-'Ahali for not forming themselves into a political party. This was a signal for al-'Ahali to distance themselves from the communists and the more extreme leftists, with Chadirchi plainly telling 'Abd al-Fattah'Ibrahim that he could no longer work with him in the same party, because of the latter's strident political views.

Al-'Ahali wished to bide their time. They did not want to rush into forming a party, though they maintained an ongoing dialogue about the specific principles for such a party, as well as the criteria for the election of its future members. In this same period, *al-'Ahali* newspaper kept up a constant barrage of articles, reminding readers of the necessity for clean party-politics and real parliamentary life.

The process of recruiting members from the educated young generation that had congregated around al-'Ahali, but were not necessarily members, now began to pick up actively. Names such as 'Abd al-Karim al-'Uzri (a graduate of the London School of Economics and an up-and-coming civil servant); 'Abd al-Wahhab Murjan, graduate of the Baghdad Law College, and an emerging lawyer from the Middle Euphrates area; and 'Abud al-Shalchi, another graduate of the Baghdad Law College, a prominent lawyer and scion of a well-known Baghdad family, all underwent interviews with a committee composed of Kamel Chadirchi, Mohammed Hadid, and Hussain Jamil (who had rejoined al-'Ahali after resigning his judgeship), to ascertain the commonality of their political views. The consensus of these leaders was that all three candidates fitted in well with al-'Ahali's worldview of liberal democracy and social justice.

Hadid, Chadirchi and Jamil now put forward a *pro forma* proposal for a political party manifesto. They opted for the 'National Democratic Party' as a name for this new group. On 5 March 1946, this group submitted an application for a license as a political party. The signatories were Kamel Chadirchi, Mohammed Hadid, 'Abd al-Karim al-'Uzri, Yousuf al-Hajj Ilyas, Hussain Jamil, 'Abd al-Wahhab Murjan, 'Abud Shalchi, and Sadiq Kammuna. On 2 April 1946, the party was licensed and the National Democratic Party came into actual being. *Al-'Ahali* newspaper became the official mouthpiece of the party, publishing in detail the exact procedure that the party had undergone, from application to license. Leading articles now openly carried the names of their writers, which included Hadid, Chadirchi, Jamil and 'Uzri.

It is of note that on the same day (2 April 1946) four other parties were also licensed. These were:

The Independence Party (IP) (*Hizb al-'Istiqlal*): It adopted a nationalist position calling for conservative political and social reforms. The founders were, *inter alia*, Mohammed Mahdi Kubba, Dawud al-Sa'da'i, 'Isma'il al-Ghanim, Fayiq al-Samurra'i, Siddiq Shanshal, 'Abd al-Razzaq al-Dhahir, Razzuq Shammas, and Fadhil M'ala.

The Liberal Party (*Hizb al-'Ahrar*): It called for political and social reforms within the prevailing constitutional framework and regime. The leadership consisted, *inter alia*, of Tawfiq al-Swaidi (the then prime minister), Dakhil al-Sha'lan, Sa'd Saleh (the then minister of interior), Mumtaz 'Ali al-Daftari (the then minister of finance), and 'Abd al-Wahhab Mahmud (the then minister of justice). The party's make-up derived mostly from old-style politicians and former members of parliament.

The National Unity Party (*Hizb al-'Ittihad al-Watani*). This party's command structure consisted of 'Abd al-Fattah'Ibrahim, Mohammed Mahdi al-Jawahiri, (the well-known communist poet), Jamil Kubba, Moussa al-Shaikh Radi, Edward Qulayan, Musa Sabbar and 'Ata al-Bakri. The party espoused a socialist/neo-Marxist programme.

The Peoples' Party (*Hizb al-Sha'b*): This party had a distinct Marxist position and many of its founding members were well-known lawyers and Marxists. These members were, *inter alia*, 'Aziz Sharif, Tawfiq Munir, 'Abd al-Amir Abu Tarrab, 'Abd al-Rahim Sharif, Ibrahim al-Darkazli, Na'im Shahrabani and Gerges Fathallah.

Another group of individuals applied to found The National Liberation Party (*Hizb al-Taharrur al-Watani*), but the government decided that the founding members were communists, and their application was turned down on that basis.[8]

The National Democratic Party's (NDP) manifesto was published and called for widespread reforms in Iraq's political, economic, social and cultural life. Those reforms were planned with the objective of raising the standards of the country from those of a backward nation to a modern democratic state.

The foreign policy of the party was to seek to bring about the full independence of the country from the British by replacing the 1930 Anglo-Iraqi Treaty with a pact based on mutual interests, thereby setting the two countries on an equal footing in accordance with the United Nations' Charter. The manifesto advocated a federal system in which Arab countries might unify under one command structure, which would nevertheless allow each country to deal with its own important local issues on a local level. The Arab League would be relied upon to streamline such a structure. Iraq would assist other Arab countries that had not yet attained statehood to achieve their independence. It was to resist with all its power the establishment of a national home for the Jews in Palestine, insuring instead the formation of an independent Arab state there.

The political agenda of the party was to achieve a democratically-elected parliament to which the government would be accountable. Constitutional rights, freedom of speech, of the press, of association and of political beliefs; all were to be defended by the party through its paper al-'Ahali at any time that the party felt they were under threat. The party also called for the modernization of the army, so that it would be ready and able to defend the country; for the independence of the judiciary system; for the guarantee of all rights and liberties, and with effective legislature that would ensure these objectives.

Regarding Iraq's different factions, the manifesto stated categorically: 'The Party does not differentiate between Iraqis. It considers them all as one, irrespective of sect, religion and ethnicity, believing that they should all participate in the building of their country and should benefit equally from any progress resulting there from. The Iraq homeland is open to every citizen to freely cooperate for the public good, be they Arab, Kurd or pertaining to any other background in Iraqi society, on the basis of tolerance and in an atmosphere of freedom, equality and justice'.[9]

On the economic front, the party considered that the basic malaise from which the country suffered was its low production levels and the inefficient distribution of products to markets. Furthermore, the party called for widespread reforms to combat illiteracy; to rescue the dysfunctional health care system; and to alleviate the crushing poverty in Iraq by carefully-planned economic and social programmes, that would ensure an efficient distribution of wealth and the raising of the overall standards of living. The economic section of the manifesto spelt out in detail the methods that the party would employ in order to implement its programme.[10]

The manifesto also dealt with the social and cultural challenges facing the country. On the social front, it dealt with health care, local elections, municipal reform, low-income housing, the modernization of farming, prison reform, and social welfare, the happiness of the family unit and women's rights—insisting on the importance of Iraqi women taking their place fully in the social, political and economic life of the country.

On the cultural front, the party called for compulsory and free education for all children up to primary school level, as well as the initiation of a campaign to combat widespread illiteracy. It recommended a wider catchment area of secondary schools at the state's expense. It called for the establishment of vocational schools, of higher education, and the founding of an Iraqi university. It recommended the establishment of public libraries throughout the country; the encouragement of the translation of foreign works, as well as the promotion of fine arts and Iraqi artists.

Following its license as a political party, the NDP invited applications from the public to join, and hundreds of applicants immediately came forward. The party held its first conference on 26 April 1946, to elect an executive committee. The number of members attending was 736 and the following members were then elected: Kamel Chadirchi, Mohammed Hadid, Hussain Jamil, 'Abd al-Karim al-'Uzri, Sadiq Kammuna, 'Abud Shalchi and Zaki 'Abd al-Wahhab. 'Abd al-Wahhab Murjan, though a prominent member, failed to garner enough votes and resigned from the party soon afterwards.[11]

The newly-elected executive committee soon met to elect Kamel Chadirchi as leader, 'Abd al-Karim al-'Uzri as deputy leader, and Hussain Jamil as secretary general. Rumours abounded, though, that the real command structure of the party consisted of Chadirchi, Hadid and Jamil, and that there was an internal 'Office of the Party Leadership' which actually decided the direction that the party took. This, however, was denied by Mohammed Hadid in his memoir, as was the rumour that these three men had been appointed to any such office. Hadid did allow that it was a known fact that it was these three leaders who had shepherded the original 'Jama'at al-'Ahali' of the thirties to its present structure as a political party, and that they had presided over its intellectual and political evolution during that same period.[12]

Perhaps it was inevitable that the NDP should experience some teething problems upon its setting-up as a party. It happened that the system put in place for vetting applicants before they could become members was inadequate. In consequence and within a few weeks, widely-varying currents of political beliefs began to manifest themselves among members. These went from extreme left to extreme right. The first evidence of such divergences appeared when the party held its first meeting on 11 May 1946, in order to discuss the Palestine issue. At the meeting, 'Ali Jalil al-Wardi delivered a fiery speech, which even included a vicious attack on the NDP itself. This received the noisy approval of a group of attendees belonging to the Iraqi Communist League (*Rabitat al-Shuyu'iyyin al-'Iraqiyyin*), whose leader was Dawud al-Sayigh.[13] The party was compelled to conduct an investigation after this episode, to question the motives of the members that had sided with al-Wardi and had so publicly taken an anti-NDP position. As a result, it felt obliged to dismiss these individuals and withdraw their membership.

When the Tawfiq al-Swaidi government licensed the parties mentioned above as well as their newspapers, political life and debate increased considerably in the country. Almost all the newspapers initiated a robust campaign to criticize the government for its lax approach to pushing forward democratic progress. Obviously, such criticism was not looked upon favourably by those in power. Rather, it occasioned the belief in conservative politicians that the Swaidi government had gone too far in its political freedom programme. Under pressure, Swaidi and his government resigned and was replaced by 'Arshad al-'Umari as prime minister.

This new government, which was formed on 1 June 1946, was immediately viewed by the political parties with alarm, no doubt, due to 'Umari's well-known impulsive character. Mohammed Hadid, in a leading article published on 26 February 1946, in *al-'Ahali* newspaper, warned of a possible clash between the government and the political parties, due to the still very divergent manner in which each side viewed the process of democratic reform. Generally speaking, though, the parties did not adopt an anti-government attitude, preferring to give 'Umari's government every possible opportunity to carry out its promised reforms.

But an editorial by Kamel Chadirchi on 16 April 1946 spelled the end of the honeymoon between the NDP and the government. Swaidi, in an interview with the Egyptian magazine, *Rose al-Yusuf*, defended the current-style of government by his generation of politicians and the old traditional elites that Chadirchi had attacked. He further added that he hoped that by allowing political freedom to come into being, he would be exposing the empty promises that the emerging democratic forces and new political parties were making to the public.

Sawt al-'Ahali newspaper was now in full flow against the new 'Umari government. Mohammed Hadid, in a leading article published on 2 June 1946, decried the pointlessness of such changes of government, and the adverse effect this had on the vital transition to democratic life. The paper followed with another article commenting on the rumour that 'Umari was intending to cancel all licenses for political parties, hardly two months after their formation. The paper firmly stated that political freedoms were written into the constitution, and could not be deleted according to the whims of incoming governments. Chadirchi followed with a leader on 23 June 1946, reiterating forcefully that freedom of the press was an indivisible part of political life; that the government's closure of three political newspapers, a literary magazine, and its warning of a closure of two other newspapers, was an intolerable interference in Iraq's democratic process.

Matters came to a head on 28 June 1946, a Friday. A demonstration of students and young people was met by a police force which tried to disperse them. The police eventually opened fire, killing five people—including a child of ten—and wounding scores of others. The country was outraged and the NDP immediately demanded an official inquiry into the affair. In several follow-up articles, it denounced what was a total absence of political freedoms, and a regime which would not even tolerate a peaceful demonstration. The 'Umari government was sternly reminded that it was nothing but a transitional one on the road towards the establishment of democracy. By its actions and its inactions too, it was told, it had set back the process by many years.

The five opposition parties met to discuss the catastrophic consequences of opening fire on unarmed demonstrators. They decided to send a unified memorandum of protest to the government, in addition to requesting a meeting with the vice regent, Prince Zeid. The memorandum they did send was wide-ranging in its coverage of the political freedoms due to the people of Iraq. It included a programme of implementation to accelerate the process of democratic reform. This document has an important place in Iraqi history, as it signalled a second coordinated stand by the five parties (the first being over the Palestine issue). The battle remained ongoing with the 'Umari government, despite the fact that the leaders of the five parties had had meetings with both the prime minister and the vice regent to discuss their demands.

There followed concerted efforts by the NDP and *Sawt al-'Ahali* to remind the government of its duty to implement the programme for democratic reform, without which it was not eligible to embark on its recently-announced ten-year reconstruction plan. Mohammed Hadid, in an article in the party's paper on 8 July 1946, estimated that the government had abandoned its transitional, caretaker role altogether. It had become instead one that was opposed to the very institution of democratic practices. This rendered it quite unfit to assume responsibility for such an important programme.

While the government was under attack from the opposition parties, another incident occurred which further inflamed public sentiments. This was the 'Kawerbaghi Strike' of Kirkuk, which saw the workforce at the oil company there go on strike on 3 July 1946, demanding an increase in wages; the provision of housing; provision of transport to and from the workplace; and the same wartime bonus as was paid to workers in those oil companies operating out of Haifa and Abadan. The strike continued daily until 12 July 1946, when police opened fire on the strikers, killing five of them and injuring fourteen.

As can be imagined only too readily, the incident had an inflammatory effect on the Iraqi populace as well as on the media. *Sawt al-'Ahali* mounted a blistering attack on the government, culminating in a leading article by Mohammed Hadid, who demanded the resignation of 'Umari's cabinet and its immediate replacement by a democratically elected one. The government's foolish reaction to these attacks was to resort to prosecuting the newspapers and their owners. This resulted in the permanent suspension of *Sawt al-'Ahali* by the government, with the last issue of the paper coming out on 13 August 1946. On that same date, Kamel Chadirchi was sentenced to six months in jail.

On 27 August 1946, the Court of Appeal overturned the court's order, Chadirchi was released, and *Sawt al-'Ahali* returned to the newsstands. On 21 August 1946, the NDP had issued a communiqué, signed by Mohammed Hadid, decrying the confiscation of a booklet containing the minutes of Chadirchi's trial. It lamented the government's bullying tactics in seeking to restrict political freedoms and party life.

Since most of the opposition parties had faced similar harassment from the government and the NDP, together with the National Unity Party (NUP) and the Peoples' Party, decided to hold a meeting at the Central Office of the NUP on 30 August 1946. The meeting was attended by over 3,000 people. The opening speech was given by 'Abd al-Fattah 'Ibrahim, leader of the NUP. This was followed by a keynote speech by Mohammed Hadid, who delivered a stinging attack on the

'Umari government because of its relentless persecution of party members and its violation of the most basic principles of freedom. Party members, he said, were now being arrested for the simple act of registering as members of a given party. Both Ibrahim and Hadid's speeches were published by *Sawt al-'Ahali* on 1 December 1946. The paper also published the trials of members, including those of Nadhim al-Zahawi, Sharif al-Shaikh, 'Abdallah Mas'ud, and Musa Shaikh Radi. On 16 September 1946, Chadirchi published an article in which he attacked the government for its suppressive measures, and was arrested once again as a result! An appeal for his release was refused. However, following a furious article by Hadid on 20 September 1946, which further attacked the government, the Court of Appeal once again ordered Chadirchi's release. The newspaper continued its confrontation with the government and was suspended once more on 3 October 1946. It did not reappear again until 27 November 1946, after the fall of 'Umari's government.

The 'Umari government became the focus of such utter revulsion amongst the populace, including within Iraq's most important social and political circles, that coupled with a ceaseless campaign by the opposition parties and their papers to expose its failings, the powers-that-be decided to bring its run to an end, and appoint a more acceptable government that might manage to regain some popular favour. Prior to its enforced resignation, Kamel Chadirchi was contacted by his brother-in-law, Mahmud Subhi Daftari (a former cabinet minister and mayor of Baghdad) who invited him to dine at his house together with Nuri al-Sa'id. Chadirchi accepted the invitation and at dinner, Nuri informed Chadirchi that the 'Umari government was about to fall, and that he, Nuri, had been charged with forming a transitional coalition government to oversee a general election, which would herald in a new parliament. Nuri suggested the inclusion of the NDP as well as the Liberal Party, together with some independent political personalities that had gravitated around Salih Jabr. Chadirchi told Nuri that he had no objection to such a proposal, on condition he could prove that it would be a real transitional government, whose mandate was to oversee fair and honest elections, the freeing up of personal freedoms as spelled out in the constitution, as well as the return to normal party life. Chadirchi made these comments a condition for presenting Nuri's proposal to the central executive committee of the NDP for approval.

Soon afterwards, the executive committee of the NDP met to discuss Nuri's proposal and Chadirchi's conditions for cooperation. They decided to accept that an NDP leader should represent the party in the proposed cabinet. Chadirchi suggested Mohammed Hadid, and this was approved by the committee. In his memoir, Hadid writes that Mahmoud Subhi Daftari later told him that his name had been discussed as the NDP candidate for a post in the cabinet prior to the dinner that Chadirchi had had with Nuri. However, Chadirchi put forward Hadid's candidature to the NDP executive committee as though it were a personal initiative from him.[14]

On 21 November 1946, Nuri formed his coalition government, with Mohammed Hadid representing the NDP and 'Ali Mumtaz Daftari representing the Liberals. The two parties had developed no joint strategy prior to entering government, nor had either party developed one with the independent members of the cabinet, who included Saleh Jabr and Sadiq al-Bassam. This, regardless of the fact that these groups had had many consultative meetings together, and had even become known, informally, as *al-Kutla* (the 'Bloc').

Shortly after, the NDP held its first Party Conference on 28 November 1946, in the Farabi Building in Baghdad. The conference was well attended by delegates from all over the country, but it was not long before differences of opinion began to surface, related to the actual wisdom of allowing the party's leaders to participate in the Nuri government. Chadirchi, in his opening speech, reviewed the formidable opposition that the party had come to represent in the country, supported by its newspaper, as it had sought to stop, again and again, a host of suppressive measures taken by the 'Umari government. Chadirchi also stated that the question of whether or not to participate in Nuri's government would be put to a vote. This was followed by Mohammed Hadid, vice president of the party, who in his speech assured his audience that he had never yet in the past, nor would ever in the future, agree to participate in a government on an individual basis, but would do so only if he were representing the wishes of the NDP.

Thus the issue of participation in Nuri's government was put to the vote. It resulted in 132 votes for participation, and twelve votes against. Despite such an overwhelmingly affirmative vote, there was nevertheless discernable fear—coupled with extreme caution—about the inherent dangers of playing into Nuri's hand, especially where foreign policy was concerned. The differences in opinion that emerged within the party at this juncture were useful, as they served to define the party's objectives more clearly. They also led some members to resign, but those were more than compensated for by new members joining. The latter included two members that were soon elected to the central executive committee—Tal'at Shibani and Raji al-Safar. The two members of the committee who resigned were 'Abd al-Karim al-'Uzri and 'Abud Shalchi.

The pragmatic participation of the NDP in the Nuri government did not stop the party or its newspaper from continuing its ideological campaign for the consolidation of democratic life and the holding of fair and honest elections. *Sawt al-'Ahali*, for example, carried a leader on 3 December 1946, entitled 'The Duty of the Present Government to ensure Freedom of the Press and of Civil Liberties'. It called in particular for the lifting of the ban imposed by the 'Umari government on newspapers. On 4 December, it ran another leader entitled 'The Necessity of Speeding up the Licensing of Party Branches outside the Capital'. Other leading articles followed, dealing with the freedom of trade unions, as well as stressing the necessity of an honest electoral process. In one article, Chadirchi referred to his dialogue with the prime minister. Despite the latter's good intentions, Chadirchi wrote, Nuri was still under pressure from any one of possible outside sources—a party, a sectarian group or a political bloc—not to relax his grip on power-sharing.

As it turned out, the pressure on Nuri came from the bloc of Saleh Jabr, the minister of finance, who had seen fit to make a blunt statement opposing electoral freedom and all talk of democratic practice. Complaints now began filtering through of interference in elections in the more far-flung cities of Iraq, though Baghdad and the big cities were still relatively free of it. There, however, the regent himself was sabotaging the electoral process, by pushing for the election of his own candidates. Rumours even suggested that the regent was using Saleh Jabr's bloc to ensure the 'election' of their joint candidates.

When Nuri showed no inclination to stop these flagrant interferences in the elections, nor any sign that he would implement conditions which the NDP had insisted upon in return for its joining the government, the matter was referred to the central executive committee of the party. Mohammed Hadid, who had continuously harried the prime minister on the promises he had made to the NDP, submitted his resignation from the government on 26 December 1946—a mere five weeks after joining it.

During this period, and especially on 26 December 1946, the party was rocked by yet another important resignation of a member of its central executive committee. This was Sadiq Kammuna. In his letter of resignation to the party's leader, Kammuna objected that there was a conflict of interest as a result of individuals occupying decision-making positions both in the party and on its newspaper. Kammuna was referring pointedly to Chadirchi himself, who was then both leader of the party and editor in chief of *Sawt al-'Ahali*. It was a case, Kammuna stated categorically, of the tail wagging the dog. The paper had taken to dictating the direction that the party should adopt over certain given issues, whether party members actually agreed with the paper on such issues or not.

In his reply, which ran to ten pages of print, Chadirchi defended the roles that both the party and the newspaper were playing in implementing the party's objectives, and robustly denied any conflict of interest arising from their relationship.[15]

The NDP suffered further problems when another difference emerged between members over the forthcoming elections that Nuri's government were supposed to launch. Some members thought the party's decision somewhat controversial, in that it had recommended Mohammed Hadid's resignation, but had gone ahead with preparations to enter the elections nevertheless. The party faced criticism from other political fronts which pursued a clear policy of boycotting the elections. Within the NDP itself a group of members, calling themselves 'The Rescue Appeal Group' (*Nida'al-Inqadh*), published a memorandum in the press attacking the party for deciding to join in the elections that Nuri was planning.[16] Their memorandum went on to say that the NDP had diverged from the common path agreed upon with other parties to boycott the elections. This action, the memo continued, had alienated it from the people that made up the nationalist movement in Iraq.

These 'tear-away' members were investigated by the central executive committee for possible infractions of party regulations. The result of the investigation was that their memberships were suspended. Chadirchi actually was relieved that the leader of the group, Kamel Qazanchi, had been suspended thus, since he had always suspected him of leading an extremist group within the party, with worrying ties to parties of the extreme left. This, in Chadirchi's view, could only constitute a deliberate wrecking exercise which the NDP now was well rid of.[17]

In the meantime, the Nuri government was pressing ahead with preparations to hold elections, and on 10 March 1947, these were indeed held. The NDP had submitted a list of members to stand in the provinces of Baghdad, Mosul, Basra and Kut. But it was soon to realize that the government had already surreptitiously sabotaged the electoral process by flagrant interferences with the party's chosen candidates. Mohammed Hadid, who was standing for a seat in his hometown of Mosul, discovered to his shock that the government had informed the electoral officials there that Hadid should not win, and that that it was their own candidate who must! The person heading the electoral committee happened to be Hadid's cousin. He was too embarrassed to execute the government's dictatorial order, so he simply absented himself from the proceedings, so as not to take part in this fraudulent act.[18]

Hadid, Chadirchi and Jamil reacted strongly in articles in *Sawt al-'Ahali*. They exposed the election fraud being perpetrated, and submitted a note of protest to the prime minister. The paper also published detailed accounts of other electoral frauds that had occurred in Kut, Mosul and several other election centres.

In the end, only four NDP members succeeded as candidates. These were Hussan Jamil for Baghdad, and Ja'far al-Badr, 'Abd al-Jabbar al-Malak, and 'Abd al-Hadi al-Bjari for Basra. However, as a result of the electoral fraud that had taken place, the party decided to boycott the parliamentary sessions and withdraw its members in protest. This it did on 17 March 1947, in a communiqué that spelt out the reasons for this decision. Hussain Jamil withdrew immediately, but the other three members preferred to leave the party rather than lose their seats. One of them, Ja'far al-Badr, who was to return to the party at a later date, continued to maintain his opposition to the government as a member of parliament.[19]

The withdrawal of the NDP and the Liberals played right into Nuri's hand. Coupled with his manipulation of the election results, this left the field clear for Saleh Jabr to form a new government, exactly as Nuri had planned. Such a government was to pave the way for a new Anglo-Iraqi Treaty. The NDP lost no time in exposing the hidden agenda of the government that Jabr formed on 29 March 1947. On 30 March, Hussain Jamil wrote the leader in *Sawt al-'Ahali* in which he accused the government of being unrepresentative of the Iraqi people. It was there, he continued, merely to execute the imperialist plans that Britain had drawn for the country. On 31 March, a communiqué was issued by five political parties. Signed by each party's respective leader, it described the decline of political conditions in the country, first under the 'Umari government, then under Nuri al-Sa'id. The latter had come to power on the promise of free elections. But the elections that had been held were anything but free. As a result of such electoral fraud, two important signatory parties—the NDP and the Liberals—had had to withdraw from the electoral process. This important communiqué considered the new parliament to be outright illegal, and insisted that it had no right whatsoever to condemn Iraq to agree to yet more onerous and exploitative foreign treaties.

Whilst the NDP and other opposition parties were conducting their campaign against the government, the latter was secretly planning the next Anglo-Iraqi Treaty. In Chadirchi's words, this was to 'further shackle Iraq to the wheels of British imperialism'.[20] The government was also planning a campaign of silencing all opposition so that the treaty would not be subject to any criticism by the parties or their newspapers. Within a month, the parties' anxious premonition proved only too real, as the government suspended the opposition press and launched a campaign of persecution of the parties and their leaders—some of whom were even put on trial. Kamel Chadirchi and Zaki 'Abd al-Wahhab—editor in chief of *Sawt al-'Ahali*—were accused of sedition because of NDP articles that Chadirchi had penned. These had fiercely attacked the proposed Iraqi-Turkish Treaty for which the newspaper had been banned.[21] Sharp exchanges followed between Chadirchi and the government. Chadirchi was put on trial on 1 July 1947. Hussain Jamil acted as his defence counsel. After much to-ing and fro-ing between the Primary Court and the Court of Appeal, Chadirchi was acquitted with a symbolic fine. The party's newspaper was suspended for two months. With all this legal wrangling, the paper was not to return to the stands for several months, since the final legal verdict was not pronounced until 2 December 1947.

The second NDP Party Conference was scheduled for 27 November 1947. The party was still reeling from the aftershocks of the first conference, when a few of its members upset party policy, with divisive calls against entering into a government led by Nuri and not participating in the planned general election. This was followed by yet more divisive action, initiated by Kamil Qazanchi and his 'Rescue Appeal Group'.

The effect of these actions led to the resignation or the expulsion of many members. These either belonged to the dissenting groups or had been scared off by government threats of punitive action. Matters took a turn for the worse when two prominent members of the central executive committee resigned just prior to the conference, because of differences to do with the documenting of the philosophy and objectives of the party. This was followed by a mass withdrawal of members of the committee, who decided not to put their names up for election.

The idea of documenting (i.e., putting into a distinct written form) the philosophy and objectives of the party had been initiated by Chadirchi in the summer of 1947. The principles of socialism were, in Chadirchi's opinion, not sufficiently well defined when al-'Ahali Group had adopted al-Sha'biyya as its political programme. Al-Sha'biyya, in his opinion, was trying to widen its appeal and be all things to all men (and women) by adopting some elements from each of socialism, capitalism, and democracy. As a result, it had become difficult to spell out its specific credo. Chadirchi wished to give the NDP a distinct political philosophy, in order to distinguish it from parties to its left or to its right. The party's newspaper, which saw several reincarnations under varying names—but with the word *al-'Ahali* always featuring in its title—had developed a more consistent political identity, according to Chadirchi. This identity was on the whole democratic, but it relied on socialist principles in order to provide solutions to the pressing economic and social problems that abounded in the country. Mohammed Hadid, commenting on this matter in his memoir, wrote:

Chadirchi had specific socialist and democratic ideas that reflected themselves in his writing. He differed in his thinking from other NDP leaders, in that there were members more right-wing than he would have wished, while others were more left-wing, almost approaching communism, than he would have liked. Intellectually, he was closest to my own and Hussain Jamil's outlooks in the first degree, and to Zaki 'Abd al-Wahhab and Tal'at Shaibani in the second degree.[22]

Chadirchi also thought that the lack of a clearly-defined ideology in the party was placing it in a grey area in relation to how it was perceived by the government, the people, and by other political parties. To alter this, Chadirchi wrote a thirty-page memorandum. In it, he traced the history of the NDP from its al-'Ahali origins in the thirties; the impact of other left-wing movements in the country on al-'Ahali; and the way it evolved into the NDP.[23]

The memorandum was officially presented by Chadirchi to the members of the executive central committee on 15 August 1947. It was marked 'Confidential'. In it, Chadirchi categorically stated that the party was not associated with communist beliefs, but that it was a democratic socialist party modelled along the lines of the British Labour Party. He granted that the NDP was associated with larger progressive movements in the world which, by definition, did include communists, democratic socialists, radicals, liberals, and national democrats in what was an international reform movement. Chadirchi believed—with acute political premonition, as it turned out—that the party should uphold the principle that change of government should come about not by revolutionary means, but by the gradual application of democratic values, as espoused by the party and propagated by its newspaper. On the economic front, it should seek to advocate a gradual nationalization of the country's basic industries within a fixed-time plan, while allowing free enterprise to operate widely and freely. It should strive to raise the country's standard of living at all levels of society; achieve social justice; both assure and extend civil liberties; and ensure a thriving party political life while enforcing parliamentary sovereignty. If socialism could be achieved by democratic means, then there would be no need for revolution. But if all doors were shut in the face of such attempts to achieve democracy, then there would come a moment when there would be no choice but to use force to effect the massive changes that were needed.

The executive central committee discussed Chadirchi's memorandum over ten long meetings, the first of which took place on 7 October 1947.[24] Hussain Jamil led the dissenting view, stating that he saw no need for the party to lock itself into the aim of achieving socialism, when its manifesto did not call for it to do so. Zaki 'Abd al-Wahhab also rejected Chadirchi's memorandum on the 'socialism' issue, by saying that the Iraqi people remained too under-developed to fully understand socialist values. Mohammed Hadid suggested that the word 'socialism' could be substituted for other values that the Iraqi people could indeed relate to, such as the notion of civil liberty, or working within a constitutionally-elected parliament, and resisting all forms of dictatorship, including that of the landed classes. But many members were against adopting socialism as a philosophy for the party. On the tenth and final meeting, on 5 November 1947, and after the concluding discussion of his memorandum, Chadirchi announced that his proposals had been rejected by the committee.

On 6 November Chadirchi resigned from the executive central committee and from the party too. Some thought that this was a somewhat petulant position to take. The effect of Chadirchi's resignation caused quite a stir among the rank and file of the party. It had become evident that the majority of the members of the executive central committee were not buying into Chadirchi's proposal for an officially-declared philosophy for the party. As the vice president of the party, Mohammed Hadid concluded that the only way of persuading Chadirchi to withdraw his resignation, thus averting a major existential crisis for the party, was to change the make-up of the committee itself. Thus, Hadid took a personal initiative by asking whether Tal'at Shaibani—who had been the most vociferous voice in his rejection of Chadirchi's proposal—was prepared to resign if that would allow Chadirchi to return. Shaibani told Hadid that he had already written his letter of resignation prior to Hadid's request, and that he certainly would have submitted it if Chadirchi returned. He stressed to Hadid that he was resigning not because of his political argument with Chadirchi, but because he felt that Chadirchi's memorandum had relegated the far more crucial issue of British imperialism in the country to a secondary place, to be addressed after the party had adopted Democratic Socialism as its credo. To Shaibani at least, this seemed an intellectually unacceptable—even dangerous—position to hold.

The NDP committee, which met on 12 November, rejected Chadirchi's resignation and appealed to him—in a letter signed by Mohammed Hadid—to reverse his resignation decision, arguing that the damage to the party otherwise would be incalculable. On 14 November, Chadirchi replied to Hadid with a letter of acceptance. Hadid had stated already that he himself would refuse to accept the leadership position if Chadirchi demurred.

On 16 November, Tal'at Shaibani submitted his resignation, which was followed on the same day by the resignation of Zaki 'Abd al-Wahhab, another prominent member of the executive central committee. This was a double blow to the party. It came at a critical juncture in Iraq's struggle for democracy, and no doubt weakened the party's important confrontational role *vis-à-vis* British imperialist plans and a compliant Iraqi government. Both resignations were rejected by the committee, and an appeal was made to both resigning members to delay their decision—till after the party's second National Annual Conference at least. But both men refused to withdraw their resignations and did not even attend the conference. At the conclusion of its Annual Conference, therefore, both resignations were accepted by the party.

In his memoir, Mohammed Hadid recounts that in a private conversation with Hussain Jamil, the latter was critical of the stand Chadirchi had taken in his memorandum. As Jamil saw it, Chadirchi's concern was superfluous, considering that other matters of greater urgency had still to be resolved by the party. Indeed, Jamil was critical enough of Chadirchi to suggest that he was no longer fit to lead the party. Perhaps out of respect for Chadirchi, Hadid never shared this conversation with anyone, till he included it in his memoir some fifty years later. However, Chadirchi himself did reveal to Hadid that Jamil had communicated similar feelings to committee members Qasim Hassan and Nadhim Hamid—who had seen fit to tell Chadirchi what Jamil thought of him.[25]

Hadid, too, thought the timing of Chadirchi's memorandum inappropriate. After all, the party did have a well-defined agenda that mapped out a strategy of how it intended to deal with Iraq's political, economic and social problems. In Hadid's opinion, this was well-attuned to the country's needs, and there was no pressing reason to tie the party down to any particular ideology. Furthermore, the party had always attracted a diverse membership from both right and far left, though each group had its own outlook on how best to achieve the party's aims. The extreme leftists were against the memorandum because it fell short of their Marxist beliefs, while the rightists thought that Chadirchi's democratic socialism went far beyond what they were prepared to commit to. Thus the memorandum that Chadirchi hoped would provide a united ideology for the party had the opposite effect exactly. It caused further fissures in a party already weakened by the resignations of prominent members in its critical formative period. The party's main aim had been to create a welfare state in Iraq—very much along the lines of the internationally much-admired British model. In Hadid's own opinion, this was aim enough, and therefore there was no need to declaim any further ideology. Though Hadid was against Chadirchi's proposal, he decided not to make a political issue of it by resigning, as this would have torn up the party even further. He continued to believe that Chadirchi had never intended for his memorandum to become such a major bone of contention, but had simply wanted a party 'motto', that could eventually come to hang proudly on the wall of the party's office.[26]

But it was Chadirchi himself who gave the best rationale for his insistence on such a memorandum. In his memoir, he includes the full textual exchanges between himself and the party's dissenting members, as well as the memorandum's full text, to allow his readers to reach their own conclusions. However, he writes that his main reason had been to give the NDP a specific ideology that would serve to set it apart from other Iraqi political parties. The NDP, after all, had attracted a very wide range of progressive elements to its ranks at its formation. This had led to the resignation of many members, who claimed to have discovered that they had joined the wrong party. Chadirchi reasoned, therefore, and sensibly, that giving the NDP a fixed ideology would deter both Nuri's manipulative accusations of communism, and clarify once and for all what the party actually stood for, in his opinion at least. The memorandum was killed, however, and Chadirchi suffered a loss of confidence in both the left and the right.

7

THE PORTSMOUTH TREATY AND *AL-WATHBA*

27 January 1948 may not be a date that many in Iraq today can remember, lesser still those in the Arab world or elsewhere. It is, nevertheless, the date that has gone down in Iraqi lore as *Yawm al-Wathba* (the Day of the Uprising). It is when the Iraqi people rose against their government, and succeeded in forcing it to cancel a planned treaty with Great Britain, designed to replace the much-hated 1930 Anglo-Iraqi Treaty. Such an act of defiance would have been unthinkable at the time of the signature of that first 1930 Treaty, and represented a great leap forward—or '*wathba*' in Arabic—for the Iraqi people. The new treaty came to be known as the Portsmouth Treaty, since it was signed in that British port.

The route that led the Iraqi delegation to go to Portsmouth in 1948 to sign the new Anglo-Iraqi Treaty began in Turkey in September 1945. The regent and Nuri, who had been on a visit to the United States and Britain, received an invitation from the Turkish prime minister, İsmet İnönü, to visit Turkey. In the aftermath of the demise of the Saadabad Pact, Turkey was looking for a new regional agreement commensurate with the imperatives of the post-World War II world order.[1] The Turks needed to balance out the loss of their former possessions in the Balkans to the Soviet Union, and now turned eastwards to seek a Middle Eastern pact. This fitted in well with the Anglo-American plan for a strategic containment of Soviet expansion into the Middle East, a region very rich in oil and warm-water ports. The Turks therefore initiated the idea of a Turkish-Iraqi treaty, to fit in with this overall Anglo-American scheme.

Nuri, who had stayed behind in Turkey after the departure of the regent, began preliminary negotiations for the treaty without even bothering to consult the Iraqi prime minister, Hamdi al-Pachachi, or his government. In March 1946, under a new government with Tawfic Swaidi serving as prime minister, Nuri signed a treaty of *Bon Voisinage* (good neighbourliness) with Turkey which only just fell short of being a full treaty. Confronted with a *fait accompli* in the text of the treaty, Swaidi was startled to find that it even specified certain regional security implications. He felt that these would be at cross-purposes with Iraq's commitments to other Arab countries. Swaidi—not wishing to incur the displeasure of the Turks—suggested including a proviso to the treaty warning that it should never clash with Iraq's commitments to the Arab League. Turkey rejected this proviso outright. However, and sadly for Iraq, the incoming cabinet under Saleh Jabr approved it with no qualification or qualm.

Nuri, in addition to the regional security aspect of the treaty, had sought other clandestine aims from it. He, along with others in the ruling establishment, wished to tighten the noose on the Kurdish movement and put a halt to its frequent mutinies inside Iraq. For this he needed Turkish help. Furthermore, he sought to suppress the communist movement in Iraq by expatriating all persons against whom any judgment for sedition had been passed. Nuri also wanted the trading of intelligence information between the two countries on all their known dissidents.

The treaty was heavily attacked by the opposition parties for its weakening impact on the Arab League and for embroiling Iraq in needless foreign adventures. But despite the national resentment to it, the treaty was nevertheless made to pass in parliament by a 101 to thirteen vote—a clearly absurd count, considering the fierce opposition to it in both Houses. Kamel Chadirchi, in a series of four articles in *al-'Ahali*, attacked it as being anti-Arab League, anti-Kurdish, against the country's best interests and involving it in unnecessary alliances. It needed to be rejected by all Iraqis, he insisted. These were followed by a communiqué from the NDP as well as communiqués from other opposition parties reviling the treaty.[2]

In an almost simultaneous move, Iraq and Jordan concluded a Treaty of Brotherhood and Alliance (*Mu'ahadat Ikhwa wa Tahaluf*) on 15

April 1947. This purported to prepare the terrain for a union between the two countries. The initial idea for this scheme had originated in 1941, when the Arab Legion under Glubb Pasha had moved on Iraq from Jordan to support the regent against the Rashid 'Ali coup of 'May the Second'. This had left a sour aftertaste, with Iraqis witnessing the spectacle of a foreign army—in name an Arab one but led by a British general—invading its territory to crush a nationalist movement that had just waged a war against the British. The Iraqis had lost that war and found their country occupied for a second time by the British. Thus the idea of a union with a British-controlled Jordan was anathema to the Iraqis, yet one further scheme that aimed to shackle their country to Britain. Furthermore, the scheme was met with great hostility by the Arab League, as well as by Syria and Lebanon. These were all suspicious of being dragged into the larger scheme of the 'Fertile Crescent'.[3] The treaty was fiercely criticized from all quarters, which obliged the government to water it down to a mere treaty of friendship.

The role played by the National Democratic Party and its paper in opposing both the Turkish and Jordanian schemes led to its paper being shut down on 8 June 1947. Both Kamel Chadirchi and Zaki 'Abd al-Wahhab (the paper's editor) were put on trial.

No research yet has provided firm evidence that this heavy traffic of treaties between Iraq-Turkey and Iraq-Jordan was a preamble to a grander scheme linking the area via Iraq to yet another new treaty, and one which aimed to secure for Britain its economic, political and security interests in the area. It was to become patently obvious, however, that the Portsmouth Treaty was intended exactly for that purpose. The pressure had been mounting from nationalist quarters for the dissolution of the 1930 Anglo-Iraqi Treaty, and the substituting of it with one that reflected the aspirations of the Iraqi and British people on a basis of fairness and equality. The former treaty was a minefield of onerous conditions that the Iraqi people came to detest. By inference, they came to view both Britain and its Iraqi allies with the greatest suspicion. The stream of newspaper print, party political speeches and communiqués had been ceaseless in demanding the renegotiation of this treaty. In the period dating 1944–5, all opposition opinion was unanimous—even in its use of language—that Iraq must be rid of the 1930 Treaty.

It is not certain whether the regent actually initiated the idea of negotiating a new treaty because of the pressure building up to help him garner popularity after the 1941 Anglo-Iraqi debacle; or whether, having prior knowledge of Britain's desire for a new order in the area, he decided to try and negotiate a better deal for the Iraqis. Phebe Marr, in her book *The Modern History of Iraq*, believes that this was the second part of the regent's reform plan—the first having been to allow political parties to be active in 1946. But Marr believed the regent to have been misguided, and that his timing left much to be desired: 'The Regent hoped to modify the treaty in Iraq's favour, believing that such a change would go far toward meeting the objections of the opposition and recouping some of his lost prestige'.[4]

The regent further compounded his difficulties by appointing Saleh Jabr to head the cabinet that was to renegotiate the treaty. Jabr came from a Shi'a family of modest means from the south. After graduating from Baghdad Law College, Jabr had risen through the ranks as a judge and a provincial administrator. He was disliked by the opposition nationalist parties for his support of the regent during the 1941 coup, and by others for his sectarian politics. He also suffered from a social stigma, looked down upon by the more patrician men in politics. Regardless, Jabr was proof of the way that the ruling establishment was now absorbing capable men, who might once have been considered less acceptable from a social or sectarian standpoint. For that reason alone, perhaps, Jabr remained always eager to please the 'Establishment', which included both the British and their men in Iraq—often made up of older-generation politicians. For all this, and for the fact that he was the first Shi'a ever to become prime minister, it was Jabr who was selected to renegotiate the 1930 Treaty.[5]

Marr writes that, in actual fact, there had been no need to renegotiate the 1930 Treaty, since it still had ten years to run. On the pragmatic basis that 'if it ain't broke, don't fix it', Britain and her Iraqi allies would have been better advised to leave well alone.[6] But Marr was mistaken in this argument. The 1930 Treaty was odious to the Iraqi people and their nationalist leaders who had always been dead-set against it. The demand for its renegotiation had been a national priority from the very day of its signature. Between 1944 and 1945, this demand became the nationalist cry, especially following the Egyptian leader Nahhas Pasha's demand for a renegotiating of the equally-hated Anglo-Egyptian Treaty.[7]

Al-Nida's newspaper of 4 July 1945 best summarized the need to renegotiate the Anglo-Iraqi Treaty:

1. Iraq's Defence needs should not be provided by the British, but by the articles of the League of Nations, of which Iraq was a member.

2. The presence of British armed forces in Iraq, protected by special concessionary tax and other financial privileges, was depriving Iraq and other nationals from free competition in Iraq's own market. This not only represented a loss of revenue to the Iraqi Treasury, but had an adverse effect on Iraq's international business reputation.

3. The employment of Iraqi Assyrians (the Levy) on British bases in Iraq as mercenaries was unacceptable.

4. The realignment of the Iraq Army with the British Army was possible only in consultation with other Arab countries.

5. British shipping entering Shatt al-Arab needed to receive Iraq government clearance. Merely informing the Iraq government would not suffice.

6. Iraq's diplomatic representative in Britain (and in the U.S.) needed to be elevated to ambassadorial level in order to become equal to that of Britain's representative in Iraq.[8]

7. The administration of Iraq's railways, as well as its maritime port of Basra, needed to cease to be British-controlled and must be turned over to the Iraqis to administer.

The Swaidi government's licensing of political parties in 1946 saw those parties spring into action, raising the clamour for Iraq to be rid once and for all of the 1930 Treaty. The NDP took the position that Iraq and Britain were now on a collision course if the 1930 Treaty was not renegotiated. After all, Iraq was a sovereign state, a member of both the League of Nations and the Arab League, with duties and responsibilities to both. To be shackled by the 1930 Treaty with its unjust pro-British conditions—such as the retention of British military bases; the freedom of transit by British troops through Iraqi territory in both peace and wartime; the forced adoption by Iraq of Britain's foreign policy; and its enforced ties to British-designed Western pacts—were all seen to be unacceptable. Worse still, the economic stranglehold enjoyed by Britain over Iraq's oil wealth, its endless economic privileges in Iraq's markets, and its political manoeuvring of government machinery—either directly or through compliant Iraqi allies—had by then reached intolerable levels.

When it became clear that Nuri, (obviously aware of the terrible shortcomings of the 1930 Treaty), had 'cooked the books' in the election in order to ensure a majority vote that would guarantee a safe passage for the new treaty being devised, the country was enraged. His appointment of an only too eager Saleh Jabr to head the new cabinet was evidence enough that a new pro-British treaty was in the offing. The pieces of the puzzle were now falling into place. The British and their Iraqi allies were busy configuring this new treaty to satisfy British foreign-policy planners, in their determined quest for bi-lateral treaties with client Arab countries. These would provide the infrastructure for an entire Middle East defence strategy. For Iraq's rulers, this would also provide a dignified exit from the hated 1930 Treaty, and silence the stiff opposition to it. Thus, when the regent visited Britain on 15 June 1947, he initiated preliminary contacts with the foreign secretary, Ernest Bevin, in a meeting on 18 June. On the same day, the regent wrote to his prime minister, Saleh Jabr, that Bevin had said: 'We are prepared to have an honourable long-term agreement'.[9] The regent's letter also indicated that negotiations could start at the end of September of that same year.

The regent, who had extended his stay in London for this purpose, did not actually succeed in commencing full negotiations as had been scheduled in September with an Iraqi delegation. Instead, he continued the talks himself, sending Jabr a series of telegrams advising him of the progress—or lack of it—in the discussions. The British preferred to delve deeper into the issues to be covered by the new treaty, especially concerning the air bases of Habbaniyya and Shu'aiba. They wanted to have them discussed at their full cabinet meeting. Bevin therefore informed the regent that the British side would only be ready for talks in November. On 19 October, the regent finally returned to Baghdad, but was soon informing Jabr that the British would not yield on the critical point of handing the two air bases over to the Iraqis. Jabr threatened to resign, stating that this inflexible position represented a U-turn by the British. He stressed that the Iraqi side had, during the secret negotiations for a new treaty that had been held since May of that year, always inferred that the two bases would be returned to Iraq.

Jabr stood his ground. This forced the British to send a delegation to Baghdad, which met with the Iraqis on 22 November, in order to refine the treaty more to the Iraqis' satisfaction. Although these negotiations supposedly yielded control of the bases to the Iraqis, the British continued to occupy them as before. Details were left to be worked out in face-to-face meetings between Jabr and Bevin in London, which would conclude with the treaty's signature.

The advantages accruing from a new treaty to replace that of 1930 were not lost on either Nuri or the regent. If the treaty was accepted by the Iraqi people and by the opposition parties, it would be a win-win situation for all concerned. The regent—scenting a possible revival of his sinking popularity—acceded to Nuri's idea of diffusing the basic outline of the new treaty to the Iraqi people. Hoping to score a big public relations coup thereby, he convened a meeting on 29 December composed of Iraqi statesmen, former prime ministers, members of both Houses of Parliament, and former cabinet ministers. At his al-Rihab Palace he conducted an open forum discussion of the new treaty in order for it to be carried by the press.[10]

The decision by the regent and Nuri not to invite the leaders of the opposition parties to this sensitive palace meeting backfired. An inference was drawn that this was yet another 'plot' by Nuri to fall in with British imperialist designs on Iraq. It was a major political mistake to try and cut out the opposition parties from a decision-making process concerning such a highly influential treaty with Britain, which was likely to run for decades and determine a host of vital economic and security issues.[11]

It is curious to ponder why the regent and Nuri made such a colossal error of judgment. The 'elder' politicians—though concurring that Iraq still needed Britain, given the new world order—insisted nevertheless that the treaty should indeed be worded on the basis of equality and the protection of mutual interests. Most of them even insisted that the evacuation of British troops must be made a condition, but accepted that the use of the air bases should be granted to Britain.

The opposition parties all protested against their deliberate exclusion from such a critically-important meeting, which was effectively deciding the very future of Iraq. They lamented the fact that such a decision had been left in the hands of a government that bore little association with national Iraqi aspirations. They now demanded transparent and free elections that would put in place a government truly representative of the Iraqi people that would be able to negotiate a new treaty with the British on a fair and equal basis.

On 3 January, the regent convened another meeting at Rihab Palace to which he invited the prime minister, Saleh Jabr, Nuri al-Sa'id, Tawfiq al-Swaidi and 'Ahmad Mukhtar Babban, the minister of court. A draft copy of the treaty in English was circulated, with the participants suggesting changes related to the two air bases and, particularly, to their use in peace time; the discontinuation of the out-dated practice that all foreign experts had to be British; the cancellation of the Railway and Ports Agreement and the return of these to Iraqi management; as well as the modernization and re-equipment of the Iraqi army.

The regent suggested that Nuri and Tawfiq al-Swaidi accompany Saleh Jabr and the Iraqi delegation to London. Both demurred at first, only to acquiesce finally to the regent's insistent supplication. According to his British biographer, Lord Birdwood, Nuri did not see the need for a new treaty, and had suggested to the regent that the whole issue be postponed. Furthermore, according to Birdwood, Nuri believed Saleh Jabr to be too unpopular to carry forth the treaty in the face of opposition from political parties that he would not be able to win over. Though Nuri tried hard to persuade the regent of the futility of a new treaty, the latter would not countenance any of it, and insisted that Nuri himself join the delegation, which the latter did unwillingly.[12]

Prior to the delegation's departure for London, Fadhil al-Jamali, the Iraqi foreign minister who had preceded it there, made an outrageous, if not blundering, statement to the British press, suggesting that the opposition to the 1930 Treaty was limited to a few dissident parties, and was not shared by the Iraqi public as a whole, who actually understood the value of the treaty and its intrinsic use to their country. He added that the Iraqis should show gratitude to Britain for agreeing to renegotiate a treaty that still had ten years to run.

Iraqis certainly did not share Jamali's somewhat ersatz opinions. On 6 January, a demonstration by the students of the Baghdad Law College marched in the streets of Baghdad, only to be ruthlessly put down by the police. The government promptly suspended classes in the college. Both the NDP and the Istiqlal Party protested vehemently to the minister of interior against the use of such unwarranted force to suppress the lawful right of citizens to express dissent on a matter of such grave import to their country's future.

On 11 January, the government issued a communiqué stating that the 1930 Treaty was now cancelled, and that the prime minister had initialled his agreement to a new treaty. On 15 January, the treaty was signed in a meeting with Bevin in Portsmouth dock on board the British battleship 'Victory'—thereby becoming known as the Portsmouth Treaty.[13] Saleh Jabr called it a 'Treaty between Equals' (nadd lil nadd). Bevin cabled the regent, saying that the treaty would become 'the foundation stone that will define future relations in the Middle East'. While the two sides were exchanging self-congratulatory speeches in Portsmouth, and while cables were flying between King George and the regent praising the treaty, Iraq was about to erupt in a massive uprising—*al-Wathba*—that only ended when the ill-fated Portsmouth Treaty was cancelled and relegated to the dustbin of history.

Many observers of the period agree that the treaty was nothing but the 1930 Treaty warmed up again, albeit with adjustments. Phebe Marr writes:

The Portsmouth Treaty was undoubtedly an improvement over the 1930 Treaty. It provided for the removal of British troops from Iraqi soil and gave Iraq sovereignty over the bases, but it was hardly a treaty of equals as the regime claimed. A joint defence board composed equally of Iraqis and British gave Britain a say in Iraq's military planning—and given the relative military strength of each partner—one might say a predominant say. Iraq was still tied to Britain in terms of supplies and military training, and the agreement to surrender the bases to Britain in time of war negated any possibility of future neutrality. Lastly, the new treaty extended to 1973 whereas the old one was due to expire in 1957. However, the actual provisions of the treaty were not at stake; what was at stake was the continuation of the need of a treaty at all and the whole issue of the British tie.[14]

Majid Khadduri, in his book *Independent Iraq*, offers the view that: 'This Treaty was certainly an improvement on the Treaty of 1930. It sought to establish the alliance on the basis of respect for Iraqi independence and mutuality of interest... As Bevin pointed out, everything in the old treaty was removed from the new treaty, since its purpose was to put "friendship into words". And yet the treaty was repudiated by a popular coup d'état as soon as the news of its signature reached Baghdad'.[15]

This was because the new treaty was not different from the old treaty. There may have been a few sweeteners thrown in to camouflage certain imperialist interests that had to be protected at all costs; and those were cunningly hidden into the annexes of the document. The new treaty basically retained all the imperialist advantages that had accrued to Britain in the old treaty, while adding new ones.

For example:

• The new treaty stipulated that it would always prevail, irrespective of what occurred in other countries that Iraq had relations with.
• The two parties committed to come to the aid of each other in the event of a war with a third party, clearly a nonsensical article, since Britain certainly did not come to Iraq's aid in its war with Israel that

same year. That Iraq should have to enter a war on Britain's side was yet an additional burden placed on it that had not existed in the 1930 Treaty.

- The treaty allowed Britain to keep her troops in the air bases that were supposedly now reverting to Iraqi control, another condition not available to Britain under the old treaty. The British, by supposedly passing 'control' to the Iraqis, craftily passed the financial burden of running the bases to Iraq while they continued to enjoy their use, only now for free.
- The Joint Defence Committee set up under the new treaty obliged the Iraqi army to be equipped with the same weapons used by the British army. It thus obliged Iraq to buy its weapons from Britain alone.

The *Manchester Guardian* confirmed that the new treaty hid its pro-British articles in the annexes. It stated in its edition of 16 January that the crux of the treaty still lay in retaining Iraqi air bases to secure Britain's geopolitical imperatives. However, the rest of the British press was effusive in its praise for the treaty, with *The Times* of 16 January stating that the Portsmouth Treaty was a fine successor to the Saadabad Treaty, since it satisfied the security needs for the Near, Mid and Far East regions. It called for similar bilateral treaties to be drawn up with all other Middle East countries.

The reaction that met the announcement of the treaty in Iraq on 16 January took the force of a tsunami. The three main opposition parties—the NDP, the Liberals and the Independence Party—issued fierce criticisms of it. The NDP stated on 18 January that the basis for such treaties was no longer valid. Iraq might perhaps be a small country that both the British and their Iraqi allies had pretended was in need of an alliance with a powerful country like Britain to provide its security needs. But Iraq was now a sovereign state; a member of the United Nations and, like scores of other small countries around the world, membership in such an international organization should be sufficient to provide for its security needs. The Portsmouth Treaty was therefore seen as nothing but simply an extension of the 1930 Treaty. Under the prevailing international environment and the Wilsonian new world order, it was yet another imperialist example of a wolf in wolf's clothing.

Thus, the conclusions of the opposition parties were to appeal to the Iraqi people to reject the treaty at whatever cost. This appeal by these parties certainly lit the fuse that triggered the massive uprising known as *al-Wathba*. The students of Iraq's universities walked out *en masse*. What started as a peaceful, three day demonstration beginning on 17 January, only a day after the announcement of the signing of the treaty by the government, turned violent on 19 January, though until then it had remained without incident.

The students, bolstered by the opposition parties' furious, anti-treaty declarations, held a massive demonstration on 20 January. They were met by police who opened fire on them as they tried to cross a bridge linking one side of Baghdad to another. Four students were killed while both sides suffered grave injuries. The bridge has been named 'Bridge of the Martyrs' ever since. By this time, thousands of citizens had joined the students in their demonstration, and on 21 January, an even more massive and angry demonstration was determined to carry the bodies of those students that had fallen the day before to their graves. The students headed for the Royal Hospital, in an attempt to take the bodies of their fallen classmates, but they were met again by police who pursued them even inside the hospital, opening fire and killing two, while injuring seventeen others. The students then carried the body of one of their dead friends into the office of the Dean of the Pharmaceutical College, who was so outraged by this spectacle that he immediately tendered his resignation.[16] This was followed by mass resignations by the members of the faculty, across the full spectrum of teaching institutions. It was coupled with the resignations of 110 doctors and department heads. The Medical Society issued a strongly worded statement, addressed to the government, decrying in the strongest language possible, the state-terrorism tactics of the police, and their horrific use of machine-guns fired point blank at unarmed students. It is worthy of note that the students had tried to persuade the police at the very beginning of the day that their demonstration would be a peaceful one. They even suggested that the police should accompany them as they carried the bodies of their fallen to the graveyard. But the police ignored the students' pleas, attacking them mercilessly, first by beating them with batons and then by opening fire. By now, the demonstrations had spread across the country, with the local citizenry joining the students on their marches. This prompted the deputy prime minister, Jamal Babban, to cable the prime minister, Saleh Jabr in London, to report the gravity of the deteriorating situation, asking for his immediate return to Baghdad. Jabr did not heed his deputy's plea and did not return to Baghdad until 26 January. It was reported that his wife persuaded him to delay his trip back home, in order to spend a few days shopping in London.[17]

On the same evening of 21 January, the regent convened an emergency meeting at the Royal Diwan, to which he invited several former prime ministers, the leader of parliament, several members of both Houses and the leaders of the three opposition parties—Kamel Chadirchi, 'Ali Mumtaz al-Daftari and Mohammed Mehdi Kubba. The meeting lasted five hours, in which the deputy prime minister gave the government's point of view that the police action was in self-defence; that the demonstrations were a threat to public order and safety; and that 'destructive' elements (meaning the hapless communists), which the government was intent on crushing were behind them. Chadirchi's reply was that the government should wake up to reality, and see the demonstrations for what they really were: a massive popular uprising against the attempt to drag Iraq into unnecessary and onerous treaties, which the people of Iraq wanted nothing to do with. He criticized the government's actions to silence popular dissent by suppressing political party life and closing down party offices and newspapers. Like all the other opposition leaders who spoke at the meeting, Chadirchi called for the immediate resignation of the government.

The regent asked Jamal Babban to contact Jabr at once and ask for his immediate return to Baghdad. Babban, in an interview with the Iraqi chronicler, 'Abd al-Razzaq al-Hassani, reported that he did speak by telephone to Jabr in the presence of the regent. To his amazement, Jabr sarcastically dismissed the demonstrations as something that he would easily crush upon his return. He was equally dismissive of the meeting that the regent had convened with the opposition leaders, and of the fact that he had not consulted him about it beforehand.[18]

The regent, perhaps correctly judging the gravity of the situation (and possibly taking fright, since the events of 1941 were still fresh in his memory), partially yielded to the opposition parties, by announcing in a royal communiqué that the consensus opinion of the participants at the Royal Diwan meeting was that the treaty did not fulfil national aspirations, nor provide a solid basis for consolidating British-Iraqi relations. As the cabinet had not yet ratified the treaty, the regent promised that no decision would be taken that did not guarantee Iraqi rights and national aspirations.

In London, the regent's proclamation was viewed as a *volte-face*, and as a slap in the face for the British foreign secretary. The British press were quick to criticize it. In Iraq, however, the proclamation was met with approval by the opposition parties and their members in parliament, as well as by the populace in general. On the next day, a massive peaceful demonstration of over 10,000 people came out in celebration of the regent's decision, led by Hussain Jamil of the NDP, among other opposition leaders.

In London and in a radio interview, Saleh Jabr, ignoring the regent's proclamation, denounced the demonstrations as the work of the disruptive opposition parties, which he vowed to deal with upon his return. He also said that once the Iraqi public and parliament fully understood that the treaty did satisfy national aspirations, the overwhelming majority would support it. Meanwhile, Ernest Bevin stated in parliament that he decried the position regarding the treaty taken by the regent and the opposition parties and declared that 'there must have been some misunderstanding in Baghdad. Neither I nor the Iraqi prime minister would have set our signatures to any document which ignored the aspirations of the people of Iraq… I hope that the Treaty which has been worked out with such care, will serve as a model, when it has been carefully studied, for other Middle East defence arrangements'.[19] Jabr, still smarting from this reversal, sent a cable to his deputy to ascertain the veracity of the regent's declaration, which the former duly confirmed.

Nationally, the situation took a turn for the worse. On the morning of 23 January, a demonstration by left-leaning workers led by Kamel Qazanchi and organized by the far-left National Cooperation Committee, took to the streets. The communists infiltrated the demonstration and pressed their advantage with banners glorifying communism. The IP (*al-Istiqlal*) pleaded with these demonstrators to quit this show of strength, in view of the encouraging position taken by the regent regarding the treaty. The NDP, however, insisted that the pressure be kept up until the capitulation and resignation of the government, in order to ensure that no political plotting could reverse the advantages gained by the people due to their unified stand.

Saleh Jabr finally arrived in Baghdad on 26 January. He proceeded immediately to the Rihab Palace for a meeting with the regent and with his deputy, who had preceded him there. He tore viciously into the deputy prime minister—in the presence of the regent—that the demonstrations were all his fault, since he had erred in releasing student activists that he, Jabr, had arrested on 5 January—the very day of his departure to London. The deputy, Jabr continued, had also erroneously reversed his order to close down the Baghdad Law College after his departure, and had not used sufficient force to put down demonstrations. Nuri and Swaidi now joined the meeting; while the latter advised the conciliatory manner that the regent had taken, the former supported Jabr's hard-line position. Jabr stated that he was prepared to submit his resignation, but nevertheless requested that he be given twenty-four hours to deal with the situation.

On the evening of 26 January, Jabr addressed the nation and listed the advantages of the new treaty, requesting that the public be made aware of all its provisions before deciding on its qualities. Rather than resign, he ordered the police to use any means at their disposal to stop all demonstrations that might take place. This incited people into an even more violent eruption. This marked the following day, Tuesday 27 January 1948, as a seminal date in Iraqi history—'The Day of the *Wathba*'.

'Abd al-Razzaq al-Hassani described this day thus:

Demonstrations erupted everywhere in the country. The capital became a war zone as the police planted themselves at all the main arteries to the city, with machine guns at the top of buildings and armoured cars patrolling the streets. Students of both sexes assembled at 9 am and began their march, only to be mowed down by police gun fire, killing four of their numbers. Baghdad was practically set on fire as students set police vehicles and motor-cycles alight. They began converging on the centre from both sides of the river; a hail of machine gun fire mowed them down as they tried crossing but, in a battle that lasted half an hour, they succeeded in overwhelming the police and crossing to the Rasafa side of Baghdad, despite their great casualties.[20]

To add to the gravity of the situation and paralyzing the country even further, the railway workers went on strike on 27 January, thus joining the demonstrators and bringing to a head a highly-critical moment in Iraq's struggle for democracy, in which the Iraqi people would decide the sort of government they actually wanted. The end came when the leader of parliament, together with thirty members, the deputy prime minister and two other ministers, tendered their resignations. The regent—sensing that the situation had now turned into an existential battle for the survival of the monarchy if Jabr were to remain as prime minister—immediately demanded his resignation. He even went on Baghdad Radio to announce it and to express his regret at the events that had taken place, adding a plea to the Iraqi people to return to calm and order.

The most defining feature of *al-Wathba* was that by the time the regent demanded Jabr's resignation, the uprising had engulfed not just the students who had initiated it, nor just the opposition parties and their adherents, nor just the trade unions and their members; indeed, it was no longer limited to the capital Baghdad, but constituted the entire population of ordinary people in Iraq, who were collectively demanding their democratic rights that they felt were usurped by a succession of overly-compliant pro-British governments. Majid Khadduri's view of the uprising can be summarized thus:

> ... the Portsmouth Treaty was not the real cause of the Uprising of 1948; it was rather the culmination of a series of episodes which demonstrated public lack of confidence in the ruling oligarchy... The new Treaty would have never been regarded as evidence of friendship and cooperation between Iraq and Britain, due to Britain's pro-Zionist role in Palestine. Moreover, it was signed by a prime minister who had already been denounced as an enemy of the political parties, having interned many of their leaders, and had also roughly handled the press. His treaty was condemned even before it was scrutinized.[21]

Many of the books and memoirs dealing with *al-Wathba* have omitted the role of the army in this very significant event in Iraq's history, possibly because the army did not then play an active part. But what is worth mentioning is that the regent and the government did indeed consider deploying army units to quell the uprising, but decided on balance that, by doing so, it might invite even more problems, such as a coup d'état by the army itself. This was something of a premonition for what was to come in 1958.[22]

On 28 January, a new government with Sayyid Mohammed al-Sadr as prime minister (it was argued that since Jabr had been a Shi'ite, he should be replaced by another Shi'ite, so as not to inflame sectarian feelings). The new government promptly repudiated the treaty on 2 February, and parliament was dissolved on 22 February.

The bringing down of the Jabr government and the unpopular treaty was a seminal achievement for the nationalist/democratic forces in Iraq. The opposition parties had empowered the people to find their voice and, justifiably, thought that a giant leap had been taken towards constitutional representative government. It must be remembered that what happened in the uprising was the result of a series of suppressive measures conducted by a series of governments from 'Arshad 'Umari's to Saleh Jabr's. These had entailed the continuous arrests of citizens and their leaders; the falsifying of election results; the restricting of civil liberties; and, by the time of the uprising, a worsening economic situation too. Of equal importance was the question of Palestine, which had deeply affected Iraqi national sentiment. Some British officials were persuaded that anti-British feelings ran high in Iraq not so much because of the treaty but because of Britain's behaviour over Palestine. In the final analysis, however, all this hardly made a difference to the British who, although annoyed by Iraq's repudiation of the new treaty (especially after all the congratulatory statements that had been exchanged by both sides), now fell back on the old 1930 Treaty, which still had ten years to run and which was, for all intents and purposes, the very same treaty as the new one would have been. More importantly, they no longer felt they could count on the regent. In the long term, they now viewed Nuri al-Sa'id as Britain's sole fervent ally and the only strong pillar of the regime.[23]

On 28 January, the new Sadr government allowed a demonstration in which the populace could express its feelings for the fifteen students killed in the uprising. It was reported that over 100,000 people marched in the demonstration, led by the prime minister himself, together with most of his cabinet. The leaders of the opposition parties and a large contingent of the country's leading politicians were there too. The regent was elevated to hero status, as the crowds hailed him for his wise handling of the crisis, while banners written in blood attacked Jabr and Nuri, demanding that they be put on trial.

The after effects of *al-Wathba* on Iraq were far-reaching. Nuri al-Sa'id blamed the regent for doing a *volte-face*. Nuri could not see the need for a new treaty, and felt that he had been pushed into supporting such a document by the regent, who had urged him to accompany Jabr and his delegation to London, much against his will. When the new treaty failed to gain acceptance in Iraq—with the delegation still in London—the regent quickly backed down and acceded to the opposition parties' demands, leaving Nuri out in the cold. As a result, relations between Nuri and the regent cooled. This was to the detriment of the regime, and to the gain of the opposition members, who were now pushing for real reforms. This was to be a critical factor, as the opposition now kept up a barrage of demands for change that the regime found hard to accept, without offering any programme for reform. The regime faced the dilemma that, failing to satisfy the ever-strengthening opposition, its demands would soon escalate to a call for the replacement of the entire regime.

For the NDP, the uprising was positive proof that the population of Iraq was now ready for the next phase of democratic evolution. The party then was bereft of its mouthpiece *al-'Ahali*, to put into words what was transpiring on the streets and to criticize the treaty itself.[24] However, the NDP leadership, particularly Chadirchi, Hadid and Jamil, met every day to discuss the rapidly evolving situation and to plan the party's support for the uprising in the form of memoranda and communiqués that were issued daily. Hussain Jamil took a direct role (recalling his younger days as a student activist) by going to colleges and leading the students out on demonstrations. Even the party's executive central committee met daily to define the position the party should take *vis-à-vis* events as they were occurring. The four opposition parties—the NDP, the Independence Party, the Liberals and the National Front—also met frequently to coordinate their stand towards bringing down the government and repudiating the treaty. Towards the end of the uprising, those parties met daily, usually in the evening, to plan the next day's actions and to communicate them to student leaders, the trade unions and the other worker and professional organizations, such as the Chamber of Commerce.

Viewed from a historical perspective, the opposition parties held the key for a meaningful leap (*wathba*) to guide Iraq towards democracy. Unfortunately, as things turned out, they seem to have been united only in their determination to bring Jabr down and tear up the treaty. They had devised no post Jabr-treaty joint plan. When Sadr was planning his cabinet following Jabr's ouster, the only opposition figure who would accept a post in it was Mohammed Mehdi Kubba, leader of the Independence Party. The Liberals refused to participate and the NDP were not invited.[25] Mohammed Hadid, in his memoir, recounts the extreme surprise of the NDP and the Liberals when learning of Kubba's decision to join the Sadr government. His decision went against the spirit of cooperation that had prevailed amongst the opposition parties. This surprised attitude turned to dumbfoundedness when the Independence Party then took a hostile, unilateral stand against all other political groups that had participated in the demonstrations. These were the ones that had followed the uprising, including that of 28 January—a massive demonstration (later known as the March of the Martyrs) which had walked out to lament the death of students killed by the police. Kubba in his memoir states that such measures were only taken against 'communist' elements in the crowds, who were bent on disrupting and destabilizing the status quo.[26] But according to Khadduri, the communists had played an equal role in the uprising as any other opposition party. Their demands for repudiating the treaty, and for the reforms that should follow, as stated in their manifesto put out on the eve of the formation of the new government, were identical to those of the other parties.[27]

The months of March, April and May 1948, were marked by a wave of political dissent that spread through the whole country.[28] It was as if a volcano had erupted with the uprising, and the months following were the after-shocks. Every corner of Iraq was now demanding reform and the retreat of the reactionary forces in power. Demonstrations covered the country, distinguished by their well-planned organization and intent on achieving their goals. The trade unions became the centre of gravity of the forces of dissent, and the very heart of the national movement. This collective pressure put on the government succeeded in forcing it to allow greater measures of constitutional and civil liberties. In that sense, the period immediately following *al-Wathba* may be considered a major victory for the democratic and reformist forces in Iraq.

8

THE YEARS 1948–1952

Apart from repudiating the Portsmouth Treaty, the next major outcome of *al-Wathba* was the dissolution of parliament and the announcement of new elections. All parties—public or clandestine—declared that they were entering the elections. However, the 'Portsmouth Group'—in other words, Nuri al-Sa'id and Saleh Jabr—began to prepare a joint bloc to fight these elections. As the opposition parties—the NDP, the Independence and the Liberals—and the Nuri-Jabr Bloc squared up to fight each other, it promised to be (and indeed became) the most dramatic battle in Iraq's short-lived electoral history.

Despite the parties' clamour for the strict application of the constitution to allow for a free election, it soon became apparent that candidates were being terrorized and that considerable interference in the electoral process was being practised by the authorities. The 'Portsmouth Group' called a tribal conference which was attended by most tribal leaders. These took some melodramatic decisions on how to deal with the elections. One was that tribal leaders should enter towns fully-armed to terrorize the electors in a style reminiscent of Hollywood Westerns. This took place in several towns, including Kut and Sulaimaniyya. On 28 April 1948, Sheikh Hamed al-'Ajeel, the NDP electoral representative and head of the party's branch in al-Swaira, was killed by his own pro-government uncle, Sheikh Mizher al-Samarmard, who was vying for the same electoral seat. On 12 May, an Independence Party representative, Selim al-Durra, was also killed in

Baghdad. This murderous rampage reached its peak in a battle between Independence Party followers and armed tribesmen loyal to the Portsmouth Group—and, in particular, to Shakir al-Wadi, minister of defence in the Jabr government. The result of this encounter was five dead and forty-seven were wounded.

The situation now went from bad to worse as the government failed to curb the excesses of the Portsmouth Group. The opposition papers were relentless in exposing the atrocities committed, accusing the 'ancien régime gang' of receiving foreign aid to promote the chances of its candidates, and ridiculing the BBC for broadcasting propaganda that the Portsmouth Gang (as they became known) represented the majority of Iraqis.[1]

As the violence mounted in the face of inertia by the government, the latter now declared a State of Emergency and Martial Law on 15 May. This action became a cover for more government interference in the electoral process under the handy pretext that the army—then engaged in the war in Palestine—had to be protected. Both state and unchecked individual terrorism against nationalist candidates now became the norm in Iraq. If the government's intention was to curb the success achieved by the opposition parties with these methods, it temporarily gained that objective. For example the NDP, whose candidates had been threatened with assassination or even killed; whose branch offices were attacked; and whose leaders arrested (e.g. Mohammed al-Sa'dun), presented a memorandum to the prime minister which stated: 'Martial Law is being used by local government authorities as a pretext to threaten parliamentary candidates to withdraw their candidature or risk being tried under it. Several candidates who refused to withdraw were in fact brought before the Martial Law Tribunals'.[2] The NDP newspaper, Sawt al-'Ahali, followed with a leader saying that the government of the day was exercising the same oppressive measures to interfere in the electoral process as the outgoing government had done, and which had incited the events that eventually led to that government's downfall.

Kamel Chadirchi himself felt obliged to withdraw his candidature for his electoral district (the Third District), when many of his supporters were prevented from reaching the ballot boxes by supporters of his rival for the seat, 'Ali Mumtaz al-Daftari of the Liberals. Chadirchi accused Daftari (who incidentally happened to be a relative of his) of having positioned armed men from his nearby farm to stop NDP supporters from voting. This incident provoked a war of words between two leaders who were supposedly representing the allied parties of the NDP and the Liberals.[3] Chadirchi's withdrawal was soon followed by that of the leader of the Independence Party, Mohammed Mehdi Kubba, who resigned from his post as cabinet minister. Another distinguished politician and cabinet minister, Daoud al-Haidari, had also resigned from the government in protest prior to Kubba. Both wrote letters of resignation which described the sorry state of political affairs, saying that the government had reneged on its promise of free and honest elections, acquiescing instead to the most flagrant interferences in the electoral process by both state operatives and other unauthorized individuals.

On 15 June 1948, the election finally took place. The results were a rude shock for the opposition parties, as only a handful of their candidates were successful. This was an absurd result, considering the massive outpouring of support that the public had shown for these parties during the tense months leading up to the election. The total seats won by the opposition were a paltry seven. Two for the NDP (Mohammed Hadid and Hussain Jamil), four for the Independence Party (Mohammed Mehdi Kubba, Fa'iq Samira'i, Sa'ad Saleh and Isma'il Ghanem) and one for the Liberals ('Ali Mumtaz al-Daftari). As for candidates from the extreme left and other independent groups, including the communists, not one candidate was successful. Daftari's response to Chadirchi's accusations of election fraud was, surprisingly, that the elections were the first in Iraq's history that had been conducted in total freedom.[4] He went on to accept a cabinet post in the new government headed by Muzahim al-Pachachi.

On 21 June, the regent inaugurated the new parliament with a speech from the throne. In it, he announced the resignation of the Sadr government, stating that it had accomplished its mission of shepherding in a new parliament. This was clearly a fallacy, as the entire nation knew that the Sadr government had come to power only due to *al-Wathba* (the uprising), which had forced Saleh Jabr's departure and had repudiated the Portsmouth Treaty.[5] The public was expecting that the incumbent government would commit to those reforms that the uprising had called for and paid for in blood, and that it would remain in power until these were carried out.

On 26 June, Muzahim al-Pachachi was asked to form a new government. His choice by the regent reflected the latter's idea that the country needed a strong man to hold it together after the grave deterioration of the government apparatus under Sadr. The NDP and the other opposition parties viewed this choice with caution, since Pachachi had seen no compunction in using ruthless tactics against dissidents when he was minister of interior in Nuri's government. When Mohammed Hadid commented on Pachachi's appointment, he reflected this caution in his speech to parliament, which the NDP's newspaper carried in full. The party's position was that Pachachi—despite his extensive experience in foreign affairs as Iraq's representative abroad—was not a member of parliament, and that even in Iraq, which still had no more than a semblance of democracy, the prime minister certainly should have been drawn from the ranks of elected representatives.

To understand this period in Iraq's history, the question of Palestine must be introduced, and its profound importance to the Iraqi people explained. Palestine had been a major political issue since the 1930s, when Iraq became the first Arab country to join the League of Nations and have its voice heard in international forums. It had also become the crux of the Arab nationalist movement, on which all Arab countries had pinned their political hopes. The make-up of the old-style Iraqi politicians was strongly nationalist. The Second of May Movement, which had resulted in the Anglo-Iraqi War, had a strong Palestine overtone, which was heightened by the presence of the Mufti, 'Haj Amin al-Hussaini, in Baghdad. When nationalist leaders were put in jail or sent into exile following the end of the Anglo-Iraqi War, the democrats and the communists continued to raise the Palestine Question in articles in their newspapers and publications.

In April 1946, when the Swaidi government licensed the five opposition parties—the NDP, Independence, Liberal, the People's Party, and the National Union—the only common theme they shared in their political programme was the question of Palestine. When in April 1946 the Anglo-American Joint Committee was set up to study the subject of Jewish immigration to Arab Palestine—after President Harry Truman had asked for 100,000 Jews to be allowed to settle there—issued its recommendations to allow the 100,000 in, the Arabs realized that another major betrayal was about to be perpetrated on them. Iraqi political parties gave vent to the general bitterness in the area with an avalanche of articles, decrying this Anglo-American action.

When on 29 November 1947, the general assembly of the United Nations voted in favour of the division of Palestine, the deception of the Arabs was complete. It was another day that lives on in infamy for them. The Assembly had voted thirty-three to thirteen in favour of division, with ten abstentions. It recommended a two-state solution—one Arab and one Jewish—with Jerusalem remaining as an international city. Sensing trouble, Britain quickly decided to terminate its mandate and pull its troops out of Palestine on 14 May 1948. The Arabs then saw another deliberate act of deception being perpetrated by the U.S., after Roosevelt and Truman in turn had promised the Arabs that no solution to the Palestine question would be considered without both Arabs and Jews giving their seal of approval to it. It was absolutely clear where the Arabs stood on this burning issue. They had made every effort on the international scene to tell the world, and specifically the U.S. and Britain, that they were dead-set against the division of Arab Palestine.

The simultaneous occurrence of both the Portsmouth Treaty and the Palestine debacle had massive repercussions in Iraq. Arab armies entered Palestine to wage war on 15 May 1948. On that same day, the state of Israel was declared, and was met with immediate recognition by the U.S., followed shortly by the Soviet Union. The rapid recognition of Israel by Truman was considered a slap in the face by the Arabs and a reneging on the promise that he had made to them. He was lambasted by the Iraqi and Arab press. All political parties in Iraq were incensed; the NDP issued stinging attacks on both the U.S. and the Soviet Union, calling on Arabs to unify their political and economic strengths against nations that supported Israel, using an Iraqi oil embargo. Indeed, the NDP went further. It called for the shutting down of the pipeline that pumped Iraqi oil to Haifa, and the stopping of all Arab oil shipments out of Libya.

The Arab states, unaware of the strength of the British-trained and -backed Israeli fighting force, which had been so well-armed by Britain, imagined that the war in Palestine would be a 'cakewalk', to use that notorious term, and that Jewish claims on this crucial part of their territory would be dealt with militarily in a mere matter of days. Fadhil al-Jamali, a former Iraqi foreign minister, later wrote in his memoir: 'the Arab States belittled the strength of the Zionist force and thought that the saving of Palestine would be no more than a military picnic. They soon discovered otherwise by the resistance and the fight to the death put up by the Zionists'.[6] By the time the second Armistice was accepted by the Arab states—with the exception of Iraq and Syria—on

18 July 1948, their armies were practically destroyed and their defeat complete and humiliating. It is not in the remit of this book to analyse the reasons for this Arab defeat, as considerable literature now exists about it. Suffice it to say that far too many questions remain unanswered about exactly how the war was conducted from both the Arabs' political and military standpoints.

In Iraq, Muzahim al-Pachachi formed his government on 29 June 1948. This was in the aftermath of the downfall of Saleh Jabr; the repudiation of the Portsmouth Treaty, and the catastrophic defeat in the war for Palestine. Pachachi continued with Martial Law conditions that had prevailed under the previous government, arguing that this was for reasons of state security, since the country and the army were still at war. As though this was not bad enough, within three months of the formation of Pachachi's government, the latter thought fit to bring into his government Shakir al-Wadi as minister of defence. Wadi had been a prominent member of what became known as the 'Portsmouth Group', i.e., those members of Jabr's cabinet who had negotiated the much-despised Portsmouth Treaty. Wadi's appointment was widely resented by the public, especially since his appointment also coincided with the return to Baghdad of both Nuri al-Sa'id and Saleh Jabr, who had both been lying low waiting for the 'Portsmouth storm' that they had created to subside.

The opposition parties' pressing fear of a return to the use of draconian measures by the government to suppress civil liberties and freedom of the press were realized only too soon. Using Martial Law, the new cabinet (with Nuri's man, Omar Nadhmi, as interior minister) cracked down on the parties and their newspapers. The opposition members in parliament mounted a sustained campaign against these government policies, but this was met with abusive threats by the majority pro-government members. It ended in violent verbal exchanges between the two sides. The situation became such that the NDP and the Liberals decided jointly to suspend their parties' activities. Both parties came to feel that the pressure being applied by the government in its use of Martial Law against opposition parties, its censorship of their newspapers and its sustained persecution of their members left them no alternative but to cease their activities for a time. Both parties decided to announce this decision after their respective Party Conferences. The NDP's third Party Conference was held on 29 November 1948. It was sparsely attended due to the crackdown by the government on all party branches around the country. Kamel Chadirchi announced the party's decision to cease its activities. This caused great consternation among members present, who agitated to delay the decision in order to vote on the issue the following day. On the morrow, the majority did indeed agree that it would be best to cease party activity. On 3 December 1948, *Sawt al-'Ahali* carried the news of the decision on its front page. In doing so, the paper removed the heading from the top of the page—which usually announced that it was the voice of the NDP (*Lissan al-Hizb al-Watani al-Democrati*)—in order to reflect this new development.

Apart from the Independence Party and those few opposition members still in parliament, the voice of the opposition had been—for all intents and purposes—silenced. The military censor also tightened the noose on *Sawt al-'Ahali* and its successor, *Sada al-'Ahali*.

This ruthless persecution of opposition parties and the heavy-handed silencing of their voices hardly guaranteed the survival of Pachachi's government. It had by then fallen totally under the influence of the 'Portsmouth Group', and was criticized bitterly for this in parliament. It eventually buckled under and resigned due to the combined weight of constant criticism in parliament and the catastrophic Palestine debacle which caused a massive public outcry. When Pachachi finally resigned, he was replaced by Nuri al-Sa'id on 6 January 1949.

Nuri lost no time in escalating the reign of terror on the opposition. Although censorship had been lifted as of 20 May, Nuri pursued his avowed aim of suppressing all opposition to his rule with added vigour. He started by crushing the Communist Party with an iron fist, and sent many of its leaders and lesser members to jail, where the worst forms of torture were meted out to them, not to mention the appalling conditions in which they were incarcerated. He then turned on the NDP, deliberately targeting their newspaper, *Sawt al-'Ahali*, after it had published an article by Chadirchi which praised those opposition members in parliament who had been freely elected, and who had therefore spoken with more liberty than those planted by the government. Nuri took offence at this and ordered the pro-government members to call for the disciplining of the newspaper. Chadirchi was put on trial and received a four month suspended prison sentence. The courts did not order the newspaper to be shut down, but Nuri took it upon himself to suspend the paper indefinitely by resorting to the Martial Law regulations still in force. At the same time, and for good measure, Nuri suspended 237 other newspapers and magazines around the country.

The NDP presented a memorandum on 14 August 1949, to the deputy regent, Prince Zeid ('Abdulillah being on holiday out of the country), protesting against Nuri's draconian measures. The party requested the abolishment of Martial Law, and the reinstatement of civil liberties. This was followed by a request to re-license *Sawt al-'Ahali*, which was accepted. The paper reappeared on 18 September, with a leader entitled 'The Suppression of a Free Press and its Serious Consequences on Public Policy'.

Nuri, now aware of having gone too far in repressing freedoms and causing two main opposition parties to cease their activities (a matter that had not only produced a great public outcry in Iraq, but in other Arab countries as well), launched a scheme which called for a 'National Pact'. This was his attempt to bring together as one party all the national political groupings in the country, with the intention of creating a one-party system. Nuri was at this stage being vilified by a public that blamed him for ordering the Iraqi army to withdraw from the positions it had held in Palestine, and hand them over to the Israelis. His orders had incensed Iraqi and Arab nationalists.

In practice, however, Nuri ended up asking only the Independence Party to join his 'Constitutionalist Pact', calculating that a mutual hatred of the communists would make them natural bedfellows. The Independence Party did not reject Nuri's proposal off hand. It proposed, instead, its own version of such an arrangement, which it renamed the 'General Pact'. This put a priority on persecuting the communists, as Nuri had shrewdly predicted. But he ended up rejecting the Independent Party's Pact after all, since the two sides could not reach an agreement. Nuri went it alone and set up his 'Constitutional Union Party' (CUP) (*Hizb al-'Ittihad al-Dusturi*) on 21 November 1949, which was duly licensed three days later. Simultaneously, Dr. Sami Shawkat—a staunch Nuri supporter—set up his own party. This he called the Reform Party (*Hizb al-'Islah*), with a newspaper carrying the same name. This party lost no time in joining up with Nuri's CUP.[7] Chadirchi, in his memoir, states that Nuri and the feudal reactionary forces in the country were now running scared of the opposition parties. They certainly feared the sway that these had on the public. They thus countered with a balancing act, by forming their own political bloc.[8] 'Abdel-Razzaq Hassani, in his seminal *Tarikh al-Wizarat al-'Iraqiyya*, describes the composition of the new party's founding committee as being a mix of Nuri's and the regent's men. The party was met with derision by the public, who saw it as a tool in the hands of the British, with which to implement their colonial plans. The membership, Hassani wrote, was made up of feudalists as well as opportunists, seeking as their prize a lucrative cabinet post or membership in parliament.[9] On 10 December, Nuri resigned. He claimed that he had accomplished what he had come into government to do. 'Ali Jawdat al-'Ayyubi was then asked to form a new government, which he did on the very same day of Nuri's resignation.

Almost in tandem, the opposition parties—possibly inspired by those independent members in parliament who had simultaneously taken to voting as a bloc—decided to develop further the idea of a 'National Front'. A meeting took place in Mohammed Hadid's house, attended by many prominent opposition leaders as well as by the independents, to discuss the formal formation of such a bloc. Chadirchi pointed out that Nuri was floating the idea of a coalition government, and added that the NDP, the other opposition parties, and the independent politicians should all be ready to act together should they be asked to participate in such a government. Several further meetings took place but the group failed to take the proposal to a higher level, despite having reached agreement on a pact that would embody the demands of this proposed bloc as a condition to joining any Nuri coalition government. This failure was indicative of the weakened state of the Iraqi opposition at the time. The Liberals had lost Tawfiq Swaidi (who had withdrawn from the party) and Sa'ad Saleh, who had died. Saleh had been a leading Liberal personality (in fact, the Liberals disappeared as a party soon after his death). The NDP had been inactive for several months and this, together with the lack of any committed enthusiasm by the Independents, may have led to the failure of the scheme.

The opposition's weakness did not go unnoticed by the British embassy. It sent several missives from the ambassador, Sir Henry Mack, and from his oriental counsellor, Douglas Busk, to the Foreign Office. These suggested that the opposition had no real grass roots support in Iraq and that Nuri was still Britain's best bet there. In what was a case of wishful thinking, the embassy may have under-calculated the membership numbers of the opposition parties. The NDP, considered the party with the largest membership (more than 7000 members in April 1947), was estimated by Britain's representatives in Iraq to possess only 1000 members.[10]

Whether or not it was as a result of Nuri's idea of a 'Constitutional Pact' bringing all political groups together under one umbrella to serve the country's needs, the idea of a new government in which the opposition could participate began to take shape. Kamel Chadirchi no doubt had had a premonition that this might happen when he urged his fellow opposition groups to ready themselves by adopting their agreed pact as the condition for entering any such coalition government. Chadirchi was worried that even his own NDP members might be tempted to join a government of this kind without reference to their party (especially since the party virtually had ceased its activities) and without consulting him as NDP leader before accepting a government post. Chadirchi feared that entering government without party support could only weaken further still what was already an ailing party that had shut itself down—albeit, temporarily.[11]

On the evening of 15 November 1949, Mohammed Hadid received a call from the former prime minister, Muzahim Al-Pachachi, asking whether Hadid could meet with him at his home. Hadid informed Chadirchi of this, and they decided that they would meet right after Hadid's visit to Pachachi. When Hadid arrived at Pachachi's house, he found his friend, former classmate from the AUB and ex-'Ahali member, 'Ali Haidar Sulaiman, waiting there as well. Without much ado, Pachachi came to the point of the meeting. He said that the regent had asked 'Ali Jawdat al-Ayyubi to form a government to succeed that of Nuri's. Al-Ayyubi had been given *carte blanche* to select ministers to execute a programme befitting the country's needs. Ayyubi had decided not to include members of the Portsmouth Group—i.e. Nuri or Shakir al-Wadi—in order to start with a clean slate *vis-à-vis* the opposition. He wanted to include Mohammed Hadid and Hussain Jamil from the NDP; Pachachi himself and 'Ali Haidar Sulaiman as independents; and Mehdi Kubba from the Independence Party.

Hadid, along with Hussain Jamil and Chadirchi, met right after the meeting. They discussed the possible entry of Hadid and Jamil into government (they were to be appointed finance and justice ministers respectively, according to Pachachi), and the ramifications this might have on the party. Whether these two NDP members should join the government as individuals or as party members was discussed carefully. Indeed, in their separate memoirs, Hadid and Chadirchi devote considerable space and detail to this episode, reflecting its gravity for the party at the time.[12]

The main issue centred on Hussain Jamil's wish to join the new government in an individual capacity. Mohammed Hadid, on the other hand, turned down the offer to join the cabinet from the moment it was made, in spite of strenuous attempts by Pachachi and by Sulaiman pressing him to accept. Hadid made his position clear. He would only join if the NDP's central executive committee approved such a decision—despite the fact that the party was at the time inactive. Hadid also made it clear that he would never join a cabinet in which Nuri al-Sa'id and Shaker al-Wadi were members. Hadid feared that 'going-it-alone', in his case or in the case of Jamil, would not only weaken the party further, but might even lead to its demise. This, he feared, would be the fulfilment of Nuri's long-held desire.

This left Jamil to decide whether or not to join unilaterally, leaving the question of his status—in other words, his joining as an NDP member or in his own individual capacity—in suspense. In his memoir, Chadirchi writes that he had suspected, as had others, for over a year that Jamil might be tempted to accept a cabinet post and in any government if one was offered him.[13] Chadirchi's biggest fear—as was Hadid's—was not only that Jamil might behave in a maverick manner and enter a coalition government of his own volition, but that in doing so, he might bring down the whole of the NDP with him. This was because Jamil was a founding member of the party, and such action would have struck the NDP's rank and file as a worrying sign of weakness and conflict at the top. Chadirchi had never forgotten the many defections that the party had suffered since its inception (especially those of 'Uzri, Marjan, Kammuna, and Shalchi) and was only too aware that yet another defection, and by the general secretary himself, might suddenly relegate the party to political oblivion. To make matters worse, Jamil had intimated first to Hadid (who had honoured the confidence) and then to others (who had not) that Chadirchi was no longer fit to lead the party, and that he saw no future for it under his leadership. He also thought that a generational shift to himself and Hadid to lead the party (possibly with him as leader) would eliminate Chadirchi from being a constant thorn in Nuri's side and allow a new style of politics to emerge. In Jamil's view, it was time that the NDP realigned itself with other like-minded parties in order to form a new grouping able to take on Nuri's newly-founded party. He felt that this was most unlikely to happen under Kamel Chadirchi. Furthermore, Jamil no longer believed that the party could be brought back to life any time soon. He therefore felt himself free to enter government without consulting the party, for the simple reason, he argued, that there was effectively no party to consult!

Chadirchi was made aware of Jamil's hostile feelings towards him by those that Jamil had confided in (though not by Hadid). He must have been sufficiently affected by Jamil's lack of confidence in his leadership to discuss it with him in private, though Jamil insisted that it was nothing personal. In spite of this, Chadirchi must have suffered a loss of esteem both for himself and for the party. So much so, that he asked Mohammed Hadid (who had been approached to join the new government even before Jamil had been—and who had debated the wisdom of joining on any individual basis) obviously somewhat dejectedly that if Hadid were to finally decide to join as an NDP member, he should ask the coalition government to consult with him (Chadirchi) as leader of the party about Hadid's joining. This was Chadirchi's way of saving face and of restoring both his own authority as well as that of the party. Mohammed Hadid, who since the very outset had made his entry into government conditional on NDP approval, now did so officially. This was refused by Jawdat (the proposed prime minister) on the basis that if it were allowed, then Nuri's party, which enjoyed an already dubious majority in parliament, would ride rough-shod over any government programme of reform, and especially those the NDP put forward. Hadid therefore refused to join and withdrew. Jamil, on the other hand, did not even discuss his participation in the new government with Chadirchi, and only notified him after he had accepted to join. This was a slap in the face for the older leader.

As was feared, the ramifications of Jamil's entry into government were grave for the NDP. The Independence Party, too, refused to join the government, giving the same reasons as Hadid had done, which only highlighted Jamil's going-rogue behaviour. Rumours were rife that Jamil was about to quit the party altogether, or that Nuri had once again lured away yet another NDP member, to weaken the party and destroy Chadirchi—who was his *bête noir*. There had been earlier warnings as far as the Nuri-Jamil political courtship was concerned. Nuri had asked Jamil to join him on a 'Palestine Oversight Committee', which had drawn much criticism of Jamil cosying up to Nuri. Nuri then did what he did best, which was cunningly to entice his new 'catch' into his web, promising the prospect of power and privilege. This he undertook with determined skill, to such an extent that Nuri and Jamil were soon spending hours in private meetings at the prime minister's office. In a breach of the usual etiquette, it was said, VIP guests were made to wait as Nuri and Jamil huddled in private session together. This struck many people as a bizarre shift from the Jamil they knew, who only a year or so before had marched alongside students in the *Wathba*—or 'the Portsmouth Uprising'—dodging police bullets with the best of them.

The gravity of the Jamil crisis that now engulfed the NDP was of sufficient importance for Chadirchi later to devote more than 150 pages of his memoir to it. For Chadirchi and Hadid, this crisis—coming along at a time when the party had shut itself down—signified either the end of the party or its forced merger with other like-minded political groups, which was what Jamil had been advocating all along.[14] Hadid was then of the opinion that the NDP crisis was still an internal storm that had not been exteriorized. The outside world still believed that the NDP enjoyed huge political capital, both inside Iraq and in the greater Arab world. Its leadership was still held in high regard for its consistent political stance and its integrity. Though Chadirchi concurred with Hadid's view, he had witnessed, over a long political career, the fragility of Iraq's political parties and their unfortunate tendency to fragment. He feared that this same fate might still befall the NDP. The al-'Ahali Group, which had morphed into the NDP, had had a fifteen-year track record. Chadirchi, its leader for all of that period, was not prepared to let the party die without a struggle, and nor indeed was Hadid. While talk of Jamil's somewhat opportunistic wish to become minister at any price was rampant in Baghdad's social and political circles, rumours were also circulating that heralded the demise of the NDP. From an NDP tactical point of view at least, the worst were those that had it that Jamil was leaving the party because the leadership was dead-set against his joining the government. If this was allowed to gel into political fact, then it would have meant the death-knell for the NDP.

In a meeting with Jamil, Chadirchi warned him that he was putting both his own political credibility and the party's at risk by accepting a government post. He cited Hadid's refusal to do so unless he joined as an NDP member. Jamil's response was that he had seen no need to consult with the NDP as the party was then a moribund entity. Furthermore, he believed Hadid's refusal to join was an error of judgment on the latter's part, given the importance of the two ministries that they

149

were offered (Justice and Finance respectively). This, Jamil argued, would represent an opportunity for them to implement NDP programmes, such as the revocation of Martial Law and the complete review of those sentenced to prison by Martial Courts which, in fairness to Jamil, he fought hard to achieve in government (as detailed below).

The British position *vis-à-vis* the opposition parties seems to have been confused during the formation of the Jawdat government. Whilst the opposition thought the British had finally seen sense and were now advocating the inclusion of more moderate elements in the new government, the British in actual fact still imagined that their long-term interests were best served by the tried (if not true) formula of a Palace-Nuri nexus. The British knew that they were hugely unpopular, because of their role in the 1948 Uprising in Iraq and in their siding with the Zionists in Palestine. However, their interests remained well protected under the 1930 Treaty, and they saw no point taking any position as Iraq grappled with governments that would hardly see the year out. All Iraqi politicians—with the exception of Nuri—took to British-bashing as a standard practice, but the British simply turned a deaf ear to it all.[15]

On 10 December 1949, the new government was formed under the premiership of 'Ali Jawdat al-Ayyubi. Jamil was named minister of justice. On 17 December 1949, he issued an order revoking Martial Law. He also suggested that all cases of political prisoners held under Martial Law be reviewed, but the cabinet resigned before it could authorize any such review. Chadirchi nevertheless wrote a leading article in *Sada' al-'Ahali* on 18 December in which he questioned the new government's ability to deal with a mountain of problems inherited from previous governments, despite the obvious relief that the public had shown at its appointment. The article embarrassed Jamil sufficiently for him to call Mohammed Hadid and ask him to intercede with Chadirchi in the hope that he might show more restraint in his writings. Hadid did communicate Jamil's concerns to Chadirchi, but the latter defiantly stated that he was merely doing his job and would continue to do it regardless.[16]

The dilemma facing the NDP because of the Chadirchi-Hadid position versus the Jamil position regarding participation in the 'Ayyubi government may have prodded the party to look inwards and reassess its very *raison d'être*. Chadirchi initiated this process of reassessment by floating the idea of totally re-establishing the party. He wished to coordinate such an action with the Liberal Party (which had also suspended its activities) in order to gain maximum impact, to stage a joint re-entry into Iraq's political life. On 19 December 1949, the NDP central executive committee members met (without Hussain Jamil, who sent regrets due to cabinet duties) to discuss the new start-up of their party.[17] This was in light of the revocation of Martial Law and the lifting of the particular difficulties that the opposition parties had had to endure under it. It raised the possibility of joining with like-minded political entities to form a bloc.

The NDP committee met again on 25 March 1950. It adopted a resolution to re-start the party by an overwhelming majority. The committee also called on its members to become more active in recruiting new elements into their party. It carried out an in-house review of its operating methods. It also called for the formation of a new national front of like-minded parties and individuals, who were ready to work on a united plan of action. Interestingly, Hussain Jamil, who by then was no longer a cabinet minister due to the government's resignation, opposed the committee's resolution, and stated that in his view the party was not ready to re-enter politics. He said that back-channel negotiations with other political entities and individuals should be carried out before the party could re-establish itself. He also said that he would respect nevertheless the opinion of the majority, and would implement any task assigned to him by the committee, but would not serve as general secretary if the party went ahead with its restart.

On 5 February 1950, Tawfiq al-Swaidi was asked to form his third government in which Saleh Jabr was named minister of interior. This was Jabr's first re-entry into government since the 1948 Uprising against the infamous Portsmouth Treaty. Swaidi's government was met with a barrage of hostile articles in the opposition press, and by hostility too in the opposition bloc in parliament. *Sada' al-'Ahali* led the outcry with a series of articles critical of the government. It also published the speeches of Mohammed Hadid and Hussain Jamil in parliament, speeches that had caused violent verbal exchanges to take place with pro-government members, leading to the resignation of thirty-seven members of parliament who would not support the government.

On 6 March 1950, the resignation of the thirty-seven members *en masse* was presented to the leader of the house. He, in turn, presented it to the House, which sat in session on 12 March 1950. Despite their agreed intention to resign as a unified bloc, some of the parties to which these members belonged—such as the Independence Party— gave reasons for their members' resignation that differed from those given by the other parties. The government deliberately speeded up the resignation process, and accepted all thirty-seven resignations at once, in order to rid itself of awkward opposition members in parliament.

In his memoir, Mohammed Hadid writes that although he resigned willingly as part of a resigning bloc of members, his view remained that these resignations were a strategic error of judgment. The opposition in parliament had been incrementally gaining strength. It was held in high regard by the public, and would almost certainly have increased in number at the next election. It had become a major barrier to the government's unpopular programmes, even succeeding time and time again in defeating them. Furthermore, opposition members had played an important watchdog role in guarding against many government schemes that failed to conform to democratic and constitutional practices. Thus the sudden disappearance of most of the opposition from parliament made it easy for subsequent governments to foist unpopular programmes on the public. The starkest example happened in 1954, when Nuri withdrew the licenses of all political parties, along with that of their newspapers. He then appointed a parliament without as much as bothering to hold an election in order to get through his hugely-unpopular 'Baghdad Pact'. Such reckless political high-handedness may well have been the beginning of the end for Nuri al-Sa'id and the monarchy. It was a direct contributing factor to the 14 July 1958 Revolution.

Although the question of what fate befell Iraqi Jews in this critical period of Iraq's history is not part of the main story of this book, it certainly merits a pause here, and not only because of the inferred Jewish ties to Iraqi communists and the Iraq Communist Party (ICP). Iraqi Jews were one of the oldest communities living in Iraq. They had enjoyed a peaceful co-existence with their countrymen for thousands of years. When the new state of Iraq was founded in 1921, one third of the population of Baghdad was Jewish. The first minister of finance in the first Iraqi government (Sasson Heskiel) was Jewish.

The rise of Zionism, the Palestine war and the subsequent defeat of the Arab armies at the hands of British-trained and armed Zionists— including those of Iraq—placed the Iraqi Jewish community in a vulnerable and precarious position. By the end of 1949, many of its members attempted to leave the country for the new state of Israel—

often by illegal means—in order to escape dangers to their ancient community.[18] Those dangers were heightened by two separate incidents: the arrest of the chief rabbi, Sasson Kh'dhouri and the execution of Shafiq 'Adas, a socially prominent and wealthy Jew. The latter was convicted of several alleged sales of scrap metal to Israel, even though his Muslim partners were acquitted.[19]

The link between the Iraq Communist Party (ICP) and Iraqi Jews is germane to this narrative, specifically because of its trickledown effect on the fortunes of the NDP. The ruling regime in Iraq—and especially Nuri al-Sa'id himself—feigned ignorance about what the NDP actually stood for, which was mild socialism. The regime and Nuri always deliberately tried to associate the NDP with communism and with communist dogma. During the period of Martial Law, the ruling regime used it to persecute communists, Jews and, for good measure, the opposition parties too, especially the NDP.[20] Regardless of this, there was a link between the ICP and Iraqi Jews. Many of them were leading members of the ICP, and had suffered greatly during the Pachachi government's purge of communists—later continued by the Nuri government that followed it. In fact, four leading communists were executed, resulting in angry protests in the world's communist press. One of these was Yahuda Siddiq, an Iraqi Jewish member.[21] Iraqi Jews, like Jews everywhere in the first part of the twentieth century, were drawn particularly to communism and socialism. This may well have been because there were large educated elites in their communities, which counted among their members an agitating intelligentsia preaching social justice (justice being one of the key tenets of Judaism). World-wide Jewry became divided to a considerable extent between those who espoused communism, and those who became ardent Zionists.

When the general assembly of the United Nations voted on 29 November 1947 for the partition of Palestine, the Iraqi Communist Party favoured the UN decision, calling for the establishment of an Arab Nation in the partitioned Arab part. This was not so much because of Jewish influence, as Arab histories conventionally have it, but rather because of Soviet influence. Communist parties world-wide tended to vote on issues exactly as Moscow did. This would not change till much later on in the century. The ICP was hoping also that such a resulting nation would be socialist, and would come under the sphere of Soviet influence. This decision by the ICP was immediately attacked by the NDP. Their newspaper, *Sawt al-'Ahali*, accused the communists of outright treachery—and even of espionage. Populist opinion attributed this worrying ICP stance to the presence of Jewish members in the party's hierarchy. These, it was decided, had found in the ICP a perfect vehicle to approve a national home for world Jewry in Palestine. Many Iraqi Jews began flocking to the ICP and propagating its doctrine, and may have offered perhaps financial aid to help create as much local disruption as possible, to deflect public opinion from the far worse treachery about to be perpetrated on the Arab people of Palestine. Such moves did not go unnoticed by the other opposition parties, who assumed from then on an adversarial position *vis-à-vis* the ICP and its Jewish members in the highly-disturbed period of 1948–9.[22]

Whatever evidence there was to prove a link between the ICP and Iraq's Jews, there was also an attempt by the ruling regime to insinuate a link between the NDP and the communists and by inference with the ICP position *vis-à-vis* partition. Incongruous as such linkage was, it did succeed, and the NDP from then on was always obliged to adopt a self-defensive position in order to allay any tinge of communist association. The communists had incurred the Iraqi public's wrath due to their position on Palestine. At the fourth Party Conference in November 1950, one of the three principal topics on the agenda was Chadirchi's revived suggestion that the party name Democratic Socialism as its philosophy. The conference did in fact end up adopting his idea, despite the fact that the majority of members were against it, including party leaders such as Mohammed Hadid, simply due to Chadirchi's stubborn insistence.

On 2 March 1950, the minister of interior, Saleh Jabr, introduced a bitter law permitting Iraqi Jews to leave the country provided they relinquished their Iraqi nationalities and left all their assets to the state. The government calculated that only some 10,000 Jews would leave, as their patriotism (and their anti-Zionism) were not in doubt (bar a few exceptions), and it was thought unlikely that they would think it worthwhile to forfeit all their assets. But much to the government's shock, the number wishing to leave reached 113,000. Those that chose to remain behind were the wealthier members of the community, who decided to stay on as Iraqi subjects for reasons of pragmatism. The loss of Iraq to the Jews was highly traumatic. So was the loss to Iraq's society of its Jewish community, with all its manifold skills and varied talents, which left a discernible void in the economy and in many of the professions, including medicine and the law.

By September 1950, Swaidi's government (which had barely been in existence a few months) had already outlived its usefulness to the regent. 'Abdulillah now developed a system of appointing certain governments and men to carry out specific tasks. When a task was accomplished—or even more usually when a task failed—the government would unceremoniously be dismissed. In this case the regent dropped Swaidi and asked Nuri to form a new cabinet. Nuri, in any case, already enjoyed a majority in parliament and could therefore manipulate members at will and bring a government down if he so wished. Between 'Abdulillah and Nuri al-Sa'id, the Iraqi people were, in matters of state, disdainfully ignored.

Having disposed of the irksome Palestine issue, which in his own heterodox view went totally against Iraq's interests as far as its ties to Britain were concerned, Nuri's arrival in government at this stage was for the purpose of renegotiating the oil concessions with Britain.[23] Nuri had already given a hint of what he planned to do in a press conference on 10 August 1950, in which he discussed the history of the oil concessions and the pressing need for their renegotiation. This was immediately taken up by *Sada al-'Ahali*, which published two successive leading articles by Mohammed Hadid on 13 and 14 August, entitled 'The New Oil Agreement'. Hadid pointed out that Nuri could always be relied upon by the British to 'negotiate' their oil agreements with Iraq, as he had done in 1931. Hadid went on to list the onerous features of that 1931 concession and expressed Iraqi fears that the new concession would prove to be equally damaging to the country's interests. Nuri formed his new government on 16 September 1950, and went on to sign the new oil concessions on 3 February 1952. A year before, the Iranian prime minister, Mohammed Mossadeg, had nationalized the Iranian oil industry. Nuri seemed strangely unmoved by this historic act of independence and patriotism, on the contrary, he set the tone for what direction his government would take in a lecture that he gave on 14 November 1950. He stated clearly that his government was dead-set against the idea of political neutrality, and as far as he was concerned, Iraq's interests lay firmly with the West. This lecture, not surprisingly, caused an angry stir. The Directorate of Public Propaganda was forced immediately to begin to spin the news so as to lessen its damaging impact both inside and outside of Iraq. *Sada al-'Ahali* in its issue of 21 November commented negatively on Nuri's lecture, as did Chadirchi in a speech he gave to the NDP's conference on 29 November 1950.

With regards to the question of neutrality (or as it would become later known, non-alignment), the NDP and its mouthpiece, *Sada al-'Ahali*, decided to join other developing countries in adopting neutrality as a vital political principle. They did not wish to be in league to either the Western or Eastern bloc. The party swung into action with a series of articles published in its newspaper which argued against political and military pacts in general, and the Iraqi case in particular. These pleaded that Iraq needed to detach itself from the Western camp if it were to have any hope of real independence. These were received with such enthusiasm by the public that other opposition parties and independent individuals decided to join the NDP in issuing a communiqué announcing a common adoption of political neutrality as their principles. A stellar list of opposition and independent names appended their signatures to the communiqué. These included Muzahim al-Pachachi, Mohammed Hadid, Kamel Chadirchi, Taha al-Hashemi, Hussain Jamil, Abdul-Hadi Dhahir, Ja'far Hamandi, 'Arif Qaftan, Saleh Shakara, Hussain Fawzi, Abdul-Razzaq Dhahir, Burhan al-Din Bash 'A'yyan, Abdal-Jabbar Joumard, 'Abd al-Rahman al-Jalili, Na'el Simhairi, Mahmoud Durra, and Qassem Hassan.

This communiqué was very well received in the Arab world. Egypt's National Party sent a telegram to the NDP, signed by its general secretary, Fathi Radhwan, supporting the stand taken by the Iraqi opposition. The idea of neutrality then spread like wildfire around the world and was adopted by important developing countries such as India under Nehru, Indonesia under Sukarno, and Egypt under Nasser. This movement, which famously became known as that of 'Non-Alignment', resulted in the important Bandung Conference. This was held in a cool hill station in Java, and attended by Nehru, Sukarno, Tito, Nasser, and Chou En-lai. Nuri's Iraq, gallingly going against the grain of the rousing spirit of the time, sent Fadhil al-Jamali to represent it at the conference. He gave the Iraqi government's adversarial, if not flaccid, position to the concept of non-alignment.

The momentum created by the coming together of the opposition parties in Iraq resulted in this grouping assuming an official political structure. It was named *al-Jabha al-Sha'biyya*, or 'The United Popular Front' (UPF). A manifesto was prepared for the new grouping, which was signed by most of the same leaders who previously had signed the neutrality communiqué. An application was made to license the grouping as a party, but the government refused the application on the basis that the grouping already contained a political party—in other words, the NDP. The grouping therefore went ahead to reapply without the NDP, and obtained a license that way. They then signed an agreement with the NDP to act jointly in all future decisions and to hold joint executive committee meetings. The Independence Party also joined the grouping and although this was not given an official stamp, as was the case with the NDP, the opposition in Iraq from that moment onwards began to function as a united national front.

In 1950, Nuri's government enacted a law (conceived during Swaidi's tenure as prime minister) that set up a Development Board to which all oil revenue was diverted. In 1952, this was amended to 70 per cent of the total oil revenue. Revenues in 1949 stood at just under four million dinars, equivalent to twenty million dollars in present value money (2011). This figure was expected to quadruple in the near future. Indeed, in 1951, Iraq embarked on a new economic age as the creation of the Development Board expanded its activities. The Board, however, soon became unpopular with the public as it quickly mushroomed into a state-within-a-state entity. An argument in its favour by Iraqis with vested interests and sizeable foreign elements benefiting from it was that the Board 'offered continuity, efficiency, and freedom from political considerations which had scarcely existed before'.[24] Nuri bragged that the Board had been his creation and that he had managed single-handedly to re-negotiate an increase in oil revenue without the need for such a matter to be debated by the government. But this optimism with which the Board's early beginnings had been met by some in Iraq, soon evaporated amidst accusations of favouritism and corruption—not to mention the huge foreign influence and pressure that was applied to its decision-making process. The Board's projects proved to be far too slow and future-oriented, like the Tharthar Dam Project, for example, for average Iraqis to feel any obvious benefits. But they did eventually bear fruit. And by that time, in order to play down criticism, the Board had been downsized and its employees downgraded in both status and salary. Many resigned as a result. Those who remained suffered from dejection and low morale. In 1959, the Board was abolished entirely and replaced by the Ministry of Planning.

The opposition had been clamouring for a revision of the oil concessions that were granted to foreign oil companies for some time. Mohammed Hadid in particular was writing pointed articles about this issue in the NDP's newspaper. The oil concessions consisted of three agreements: the first was signed on 24 March 1925, with the Iraq Petroleum Company (IPC); the second with the Mosul Oil Company on 25 May 1932; and the third with the Basra Oil Company on 13 November 1938.

Nuri opened negotiations with the oil companies in June 1950. Although these negotiations yielded an increase in revenue and in production, the two sides could not agree on the pricing of the product, which was tied to the price of gold, as had been agreed by both sides in the 1925 concession. The Iraqis wanted to price their product based on the market value of gold. The companies, however, insisted on a punitive fixed price in pound sterling. The market value of gold had risen appreciably against sterling and would have represented a marked rise in Iraq's revenue from oil, had this been accepted. The Iraqi government decided to sue for their rights, although they did continue to negotiate with regard to matters relating to the Mosul and Basra concessions. Nuri failed to persuade the British oil companies to compromise, despite his warnings that the threat of nationalization was now hanging in the air. In addition, he informed them, they were letting him down—their most devoted Iraqi friend.

In 1951, that nightmare scenario for Western oil companies finally did happen. Iran, under the premiership of Dr. Mohammed Mossadeg, nationalized its oil industry. The Iraqi public, as well as all the opposition parties, warmly welcomed Iran's move, and immediately saw the need of replicating it in Iraq. Siddiq Shanshal, general secretary of the Independence Party, asked Nuri al-Sa'id point blank in parliament why Iraq could not take similar action to nationalize its own oil industry. Nuri hemmed and hawed in his reply. This resulted in Independence Party members, together with some others—totalling eighteen members of parliament—submitting a request on 25 March 1951 for the nationalization of Iraq's oil. The request set out in detail the abject economic conditions prevailing in Iraq, and the country's dire need to benefit from this vital natural resource. Since Iraq owned this abundant source of wealth, it was patently absurd that it should be forced to hand it over to any foreign entity at such a punishingly low ratio. As if to strengthen Iraq's case further, Saudi Arabia had just signed an oil agreement with ARAMCO (the Arabian-American Oil Co.) that stipulated a fifty–fifty sharing of profits. Unfair as this was, it highlighted even more starkly the paltry share that Iraq was being given.

Both the NDP and the Independence parties now went into overdrive to push the government into nationalizing the oil industry. For the NDP, Mohammed Hadid wrote a series of leading articles that appeared in *Sada al-'Ahali*. In the paper's 15 May 1951 issue, Hadid's article 'An Equal Share in Oil Itself and not just in its Profits is the Minimum Demand by Iraq until its Oil is Nationalized', was read and quoted widely both inside and outside Iraq. On 19 May, he followed up with another leader that argued that after Iran's nationalization of its own oil, a revision of Iraq's oil concessions had become the harsh reality for the oil companies that they could no longer afford to ignore. Kamel Chadirchi made a straight out call for nationalization in an interview with the Iranian newspaper, *'Itila'at*.[25] The pace of public demand for nationalization picked up alarmingly as far as the pro-Western government was concerned. It therefore launched a campaign of persecution, arresting scores of citizens on the charge that the call for nationalization was communist-inspired, and meant as a way of overthrowing the regime!

The oil companies must have taken fright—heightened by Nuri's warnings to them that public anger might well spill over into a full demand for nationalization as happened in Iran—and agreed to hold negotiations with the government. These went on for several months, but ended only with an equal profit-sharing agreement, initialled by both sides on 13 August 1951. Nuri signed off on this agreement on 3 February, and parliament passed it on 13 February 1952.

The NDP and the UPF issued a joint communiqué, in which Nuri's re-negotiated oil agreement was exposed as a sham containing yet another hidden agenda to deprive Iraq of its lawful share of its oil wealth. The importance of Iraq's oil deposits to the foreign oil companies became even more obvious after Iran's loss to them, especially as world demand for Iraqi oil expanded as a result. Thus the NDP, through several articles by Mohammed Hadid, repeatedly called for either an equal share in the quantity being produced if not in the profits or, far better still, complete nationalization of oil—the latter being the only way for Iraq to finally benefit fully from its major natural resource. Hadid's articles went on to illustrate how the agreement was phrased in such a way that Iraq would never actually receive its 50 per cent share of the profits, as by the use of artful accounting, the oil companies had made it so that the country would receive only 35 per cent of the profits. The UPF, through its mouthpiece, *Jaridat al-Jabha al-Muttahida*, was equally critical of the government for its over-accommodating attitude towards the oil companies, which had resulted in the blatant abuse of Iraq's oil rights. The other parties were equally vociferous and anti-government in their criticisms. These included the Ba'th Party, as well as the Peoples' Socialist Party (Hizb al-'umma al-'ishtiraki) which was Saleh Jabr's party (the supposed ally of Nuri's). The PSP published a detailed study contained in a booklet, in which it set out the many deficiencies of the oil agreements signed by the Iraqi government. Although Jabr's party did stand for an equal sharing of the profits of oil, it stopped short of calling for outright nationalization.

The public outcry reached such a pitch that the political parties called for a general strike to protest the signing of the oil agreement. The strike, which took place on 19 February 1952, had widespread and huge participation. Parties, labour movements, students, and all political and populist groups took part. The strike was not without incident, however; strikers clashed with police, who opened fire, and wounded hundreds. This was followed by a wave of arrests as well as the dismissal of scores of students from universities and colleges. This action, in turn, brought out the whole student body for more demonstrations and protests.

Despite the fact that in many of its aspects, the new oil agreement was a marked improvement over previous ones (for example, equal profit-sharing exactly as Saudi Arabia had negotiated; a 12 per cent share of crude production; the employment of Iraqis in technical and administrative jobs—as opposed to manual jobs only as before—and the setting up of a scholarship programme to send fifty Iraqi students annually to Britain for further studies), it failed to convince the Iraqi public that Britain did not have imperialist designs on their country and on its abundant natural resources. In addition, the oil agreement had been foisted on the public without as much as a debate in parliament. The presence of air bases in Iraq that were still occupied by British forces rankled too, as did the fact that Iraqi oil did not 'belong' to the nation. The idea of a fifty–fifty split had become totally unacceptable to Iraqis once they could see what Mossadeg had achieved in neighbouring Iran. Even tiny Kuwait—which Iraq had always claimed as a part of its territory—was now pulling in the equivalent of fifty million Iraqi dinars per annum—a sum far in excess of what the whole of Iraq was earning from its oil!

One positive development that Kamel Chadirchi could see emerging from this period was the coalescence of the opposition parties, who were now beginning to act as one power bloc. The NDP, UPF and the

Independence parties were all working hand in hand to confront the government over issues of major public concern. They were also joined by student and labour organizations, including far-left groups such as the Peace Partisans ('*Ansar al-Salaam*).[26] Chadirchi, however, did not see a positive development emerging to unite the opposition parties after their attempt (failed as it was) to stop the signature of—or at the very least, extract any real benefits from—the new oil agreement.[27] Indeed, by the end of 1952, the immense efforts that had gone into tying all these groups into one united front failed to reap political benefits. The UPF refused to join a coalition for fear that it would gradually become controlled by the Peace Partisans. Chadirchi did his best to persuade the UPF leader Taha al-Hashemi to agree to join such an important united front, but his efforts proved in vain.

It was agreed, however, that each party would prepare a separate memorandum to be presented simultaneously to the regent on 28 October 1952. Generally, the memoranda contained a list of public grievances that included:

- A call for the abrogation of the Anglo-Iraqi Treaty of 1930.
- The relaxation of all restrictions on civil liberties.
- The end of police state tactics by the government.
- The revision of the electoral law to allow for direct elections.
- The protection of local and national industries.
- Agrarian reform and the distribution of crown land to farmers.
- The nationalization of oil.
- Freedom for workers to form or join trade unions.

The UPF memorandum went further still. It reminded the regent and the government of events in both Egypt and Lebanon, where two coup d'états had brought about a total change of government. It predicted that a similar fate awaited Iraq if the regent and government failed to grant Iraqis their rights to a parliamentary and democratic life as was guaranteed them in their constitution.

On 3 November, the regent invited all party leaders, together with all former prime ministers, to attend a conference in the palace to discuss the memoranda. What happened in that meeting is described best by Kamel Chadirchi in his memoir.[28] Chadirchi writes that just prior to it, he, Taha al-Hashemi (the UPF leader), and Mehdi Kubba (the Independence Party leader) met in order to align their positions so as to present a unified response to the matters contained in their memoranda and to restrict discussions to matters contained in these memoranda. They agreed to attend as listeners rather than as speakers in order to hear what 'Abdulillah had to propose.

The meeting started well enough. Nuri al-Sa'id opened with his statement, followed by Tawfiq al-Swaidi, Kamel Chadirchi, Taha al-Hashemi, Jamil al-Madfa'i, 'Ali Jawdat Saleh Jabr, Hikmat Sulaiman and Mohammed al-Sadr. Of those, Taha al-Hashemi was the bluntest in addressing the regent. He plainly told him that the time was fast approaching when he would have to hand over the reins of the monarchy to the new king, Faisal II, who was to attain majority and the kingship on 2 May 1953. It therefore behoved him to leave a clean slate behind for the young king's benefit. Hashemi also warned that the situation in Iraq was of such gravity—and the coup d'état in Egypt (of July 1952) so fresh in Iraqi minds—that a similar fate might well befall Iraq's monarchy if it did not acquiesce to popular demands.

The regent, visibly irritated, left the meeting abruptly several times while these leaders were speaking. When the last leader had finished, the regent, now in an agitated state, responded by saying that from the time he had arrived in Iraq as a refugee from the kingdom of his deposed father in the Hijaz, he had heard Iraqis talking about the very same topics being raised at the meeting at hand: fraudulent elections and parliaments; tribal uprisings; governments coming and going rapidly through coup d'état or other such upheavals; politicians plotting to assassinate one another, and scores of other matters that the royal family had absolutely nothing to do with, and could not possibly be blamed for. He accused all those present of being liars because they would not admit that the present state of the country was one of their own making. He then suddenly turned on Hashemi, and abused him personally and viciously by screaming repeatedly: 'Liar! Liar!' Hashemi got up and said simply 'I am an honourable man!' and walked out of the room.[29] Chadirchi immediately followed Hashemi out, with the regent's offensive parting words 'You can get out too! GET OUT!' ringing in his ears.

The regent's insult to Hashemi became a major topic of discussion, with some important repercussions. The UPF, the NDP and the Independence Party leaderships were so incensed by the incident that they agreed a protest note that was to be signed by all three leaders and published the next day in their respective newspapers. Strangely enough, it was Hashemi who demurred. He refused to sign the protest note himself, despite having been the person who had been insulted. The regent, in the meantime, perhaps feeling some remorse because of his outburst, visited the houses of all those who had been present at the meeting—with the exception of those of Hashemi and Chadirchi—to leave a note of apology.

The importance of this heated palace meeting cannot be stressed enough, as it led to the rapid evolution of the political situation. One aspect of this evolving political situation and the Hashemi incident was the doubling of efforts by the political parties—now joined by the Peace Partisans—to organize themselves into one united national front.[30] The parties agreed to form a liaison committee to study a possible structure for a national front which, though not given a formal status, became a tool that was to prove most useful when the Intifada erupted later that month. This structure helped orchestrate the actions of the parties (although the UPF still refused the inclusion of the Peace Partisans on the basis that they would attempt to dominate the committee). The committee that emerged finally represented only the NDP, the UPF and the Independence parties. Possibly because of this new-found political unity on the part of the opposition, the government, yielding to one of its demands, authorized the principle of direct elections. Thus, on 6 November, the cabinet agreed to accept the principle of direct elections and to present it to parliament for approval. On 17 November, the prime minister, Mustapha al-'Umari, asked all parties to nominate a representative to sit on a government committee of leading jurists and civil servants in order to draw up a new electoral law. However, all the parties refused to join this committee with the exception of Nuri's Constitutional Union Party (CUP). The others said that this would prove a futile effort by the government, unless the proposed amendment included full guarantees of freedom of choice for electors and a clear undertaking that future governments would desist from fixing election results.

The gathering momentum generated by a resurgent coalition of opposition forces was to lead inexorably to a collision with the government. This happened in what would become a landmark in Iraqi history, known as the 1952 Intifada.

9

THE 1952 INTIFADA AND THE YEARS 1952–1954

By the end of 1952, Iraq was ready to erupt. A series of consecutive governments had failed to bring about either social or political change to a country that was growing fast in political consciousness. Political parties had finally managed to overcome their chronic divisiveness, and had begun to act in unison. The country had grown weary of the older-generation politicians, of their cronyism, and their penchant for fixing election results as well as important parliamentary decisions to suit their vested interests. Nuri al-Sa'id's perennial grip on power had begun to seem without end, discouraging even those who supported him from ever reaching leadership positions themselves.

In March 1950, when thirty-seven members of parliament resigned *en masse*, the beginnings of a new opposition grouping—which included the NDP and the UPF—appeared on the Iraqi political scene. Both these parties were composed of younger-generation politicians. They wanted to make their country more democratic and more socially just. They were tired of the machinations of the older politicians. They now wanted to attain power in order to implement the many reforms they knew were needed. This was well demonstrated when Saleh Jabr—ostensibly an ally of Nuri's—established his own party, the Peoples' Socialist Party (PSP) (*Hizb al-'Umma al-'Ishtiraki*), which was later to break ranks with Nuri al-Sa'id and join the opposition.

Outside factors also contributed to Iraq's internal turmoil. Mossadeg's election in Iran, and his dramatic nationalization in 1951 of

Iranian oil, lit the Iraqi fuse for Iraq to nationalize its own oil, or at least to revise its oil concessions. On 23 July 1952, a coup d'état in Egypt removed the monarchy and installed a group of young army officers in its place, with the charismatic Gamal 'Abd al-Nasser as their leader. The significance of the Egyptian coup on a foreign and fragile monarchy such as Iraq's, with its infant king and hugely unpopular regent, was not entirely lost on the regime. After all, the role of 'Abdulillah in Iraq was not unequal to that of the British and/or successive pro-British governments in stifling civil liberties. The regent, who possessed neither culture nor a proper education, appeared on the Iraqi scene by pure coincidence—some say even by skulduggery—when King Ghazi had died suddenly in a car accident. 'Abdulillah was ill-equipped for such a role, and soon developed his own particular system of 'government-by-intrigue' that would prove disastrous for Iraq. The events of 1941 no doubt affected him greatly, when he only just managed to escape the country during the Rashid 'Ali coup. He would remain forever grateful to the British who had brought him back after their victory and their occupation of Iraq following the Anglo-Iraqi War of 1941.[1] 'Abdulillah developed a sinister sense of vendetta against all those who had participated in the 1941 coup, imprisoning and executing many of them. Indeed, he was known to bear a grudge forever against any survivor of his punishment. He retained a visceral fear of a '1941' happening again. In 1948, when the Portsmouth Treaty Uprising (al-Wathba) called for the removal of the monarchy and the establishment of a republic, he immediately took fright and cancelled the treaty, despite the fact that his prime minister was still in London, celebrating its signature with his British counterparts. Although this cancellation caused a momentary spike in the regent's popularity in the period 1948–50, 'Abdulillah failed to gain the high ground by effecting a rapprochement with the opposition parties during a problematic period for them. Though continuing to press for political reform, those parties themselves were losing ground due to their internecine wrangling, which eventually led to the disappearance of some of them from the political scene altogether. It was the 1952 Intifada that was to become the event that would change the political landscape in Iraq, and to shake the country to its core in the same way that al-Wathba had done four years earlier.

The timing of the Intifada was spontaneous and unplanned. It came at the end of a whole series of events—Iraq's political neutrality or non-alignment; the revision of its oil concessions; Mossadeg's astounding nationalization of Iran's oil; the coalition between the NDP, UPF and the Independence Party—which itself was unexpected and came about as a result of a relatively minor incident.

In mid-November, 1952, the Dean of the College of Pharmacy and Chemistry in Baghdad amended an internal college regulation. This made it so that a failed student would have, from then on, to re-sit all his or her subjects, and not just those they failed. The students felt that this action by the Dean was not fair and went on strike on 16 November. Other colleges—those of Medicine, Law, and Commerce—went on strike in support and sympathy. This soon necessitated the intervention of the government, which cancelled this contentious amendment by the Dean. The students terminated their strike peacefully, and went back to their colleges on 19 November. However, four unknown thugs came into the college on that same day, and began to indiscriminately beat up the students, causing severe injuries to some. The police arrived on the scene and did manage to arrest three of these offenders. This, however, did not satisfy the students as they continued to accuse the Dean of complicity in this sordid affair. He, on the other hand, aggravated the situation even more by letting it be known that he had taken slight at the government's rescinding his regulation. The students went on strike again on 20 November, threatening to remain on strike until the government carried out an investigation into the affair that recommended the removal of the Dean.

The government did remove the Dean from his post and ordered a further inquiry, but this did not pacify the students. By this time, the affair had assumed quite a different dimension—that of a political rebellion, which was being directed by leftist elements such as the Peace Partisans. By then, the strike included the entire student body and the political opposition parties, and had spread to other Iraqi cities. The police sought to suppress the demonstrators, with many casualties falling on both sides. The demonstrators accused the pro-government police force of treason and called for Iraqi national aspirations to be realized, and not through the use of force. By 21 November, the student demonstrations had swelled to include large numbers of the public. The next day, the authorities were no longer in control, even though the police had fired on demonstrators, causing many casualties and fatalities. There was no choice left for Prime Minister Mustapha 'Umari except to resign along with his government.

The demonstrations continued unabated on 23 November, and in the absence of any government. The regent first asked Nuri, then Jamil al-Madfa'i, and then Hikmat Sulaiman to form a government, but they all declined in turn. The failure of the police to restore public order obliged the regent to call in the army, with specific orders not to fire on the crowds. He was told, however, by the chief of the general staff, General Nur-al-Din Mahmoud, that the army would not be able restore order if it were not allowed to use live ammunition. In order to circumvent the legal technicality of who would give the order for the army to fire on citizens, the regent appointed General Mahmoud as prime minister, so that he, as PM, could issue the order.[2] By this time, the demonstrations had reached fever pitch, and constituted an avenging mob. They attacked the United States Information Service offices and set fire to its books and papers, and burned down the offices of the English-language *Iraqi Times*, as well as the offices of the British airline, B.O.A.C. Two police stations were attacked and set on fire, killing the four policemen who were inside them. Their bodies were dragged out to the street before they, too, were set on fire. The army was called to try and rescue the situation that a now helpless government could not handle.

At 6pm on the evening of 23 November, General Mahmoud announced on Baghdad Radio that he was heading a military government that had just come into being. At 10pm, Martial Law was declared, and General 'Abd al-Muttalib 'Amin was named as military governor of Baghdad. On 24 November, a sweeping wave of arrests took place, when over 1,000 homes were raided. The raids that were carried out against the homes of party leaders were deliberately carried out at night to make sure the police got their men. These arrests eventually reached 3,000 in number, and included 220 members of the opposition.[3] The military government then ordered the five political parties dissolved; seventeen newspapers suspended; all educational establishments closed, and a Martial Court set up to try those arrested. Among the leaders arrested were Kamel Chadirchi, Hussain Jamil, and others from the NDP; Fa'iq al-Samerra'i, Siddiq Shanshal and others from the Independence Party, and 'Abd al-Wahhab Mahmud, president of the Lawyers' Association and leader of the Peace Partisans. Members of the UPF and several leaders of other political organizations were also arrested. Mohammed Hadid was absent from the country at the time attending to a sick relative in London, and would certainly have been arrested had he been in Baghdad. In London, he carried out a campaign in the British press and on the BBC, which was highly critical of the government's violent actions.[4] Hadid personally met with several leading newsmen such as Kingsley Martin, and with politicians such as Aneurin Bevan and Willie Greaves (both MPs and leading members of the Labour Party) to champion the cause of the Iraqi opposition, and describe the depths of despair that the country had descended into.[5] Hadid's BBC radio broadcasts (aired on the BBC's Arabic Service), as well as the articles that he wrote that managed to reach Baghdad, had a wide and appreciative impact on the public in Baghdad.

Despite the draconian measures adopted by the government and their implementation of Martial Law, the crowds still defiantly went out on the streets of Baghdad on 24 November, calling for the resignation of General Mahmoud and the appointment of a national government headed by Kamel Chadirchi as prime minister. The army stood in wait for the demonstrators, and opened fire just above their heads, but could not deter them. They continued to occupy the streets till late that evening. Similar demonstrations took place in other Iraqi towns, such as Basra, Najaf, Kerbala, Hilla, Diwaniyya, Kut and 'Amara. In all cases, the army was unable to restrain the demonstrators, except by the use of excessive force.[6]

Ironically enough, Sir John Troutbeck, the British ambassador who enjoyed privileged access to Selwyn Lloyd, the foreign secretary, sent reports of the Intifada back to London, which did not match up to reports of the events on the ground and as later unearthed by academic research. Sir John reported that the number of people demonstrating was small and that Nuri al-Sa'id had intimated to him that 'the whole agitation that led up to those events was a monstrous bluff that could easily have been called by a determined government'.[7] As further proof of the Intifada's weakness, Troutbeck continued, factory workers had not joined the demonstrators. He also reported that Nuri had told the regent that he (Nuri) could form a government that could bring the situation under control.

As regards the actual numbers demonstrating, the size and severity of the demonstrations must have been large enough to overwhelm the police as they were unable to exercise adequate crowd control. This forced the government to resign, obliging the regent to call in the army that had to resort to orders to shoot to kill. A military government had to be formed, which immediately declared Martial Law. Highly serious measures, one might conclude, to deal with such an insignificant event as described by Nuri, and gullibly believed and reported back by Troutbeck. As for Troutbeck's claim that factory workers had not participated in the demonstration, that was wrong too, as they had actually participated in great numbers, including workers from the Qadhimain factories in Baghdad.[8] As for Nuri al-Sa'id offering his services to the regent, Troutbeck must have gotten that one wrong as well. Nuri, in addition to Jamil Madfa'i and Hikmat Sulaiman, was offered the premiership by the regent, but declined it because of the severity of the crisis.[9] It is indeed bizarre, if not somewhat remiss, that neither Troutbeck nor his oriental secretary ever took the initiative to speak to the leaders of the opposition in order to get their views and comments on the situation. Most of the British ambassador's information seems to have been gleaned either from the palace or from persons close to palace circles. Therefore, Troutbeck's assessments of the events of 1952 reflected an uninformed personal view that had not been tested on the outside world.[10]

On 16 December 1952, the military government issued a Royal 'Irada (Order) making direct elections an integral part of Iraq's Electoral Law. The government had withdrawn the army from the capital on 13 December. In spite of this, Martial Law was retained for another year, and political party leaders remained in detention until after elections were held on 17 January 1953. They were released without even having been tried, all having refused bail, defying the government to try them instead. The latter must have seen the dangerous potential consequences of such trials, and so began releasing them gradually, with Kamel Chadirchi being the last allowed out of the Detention Camp. Indeed, the camp was shut down with his departure.

Given the restrictions imposed by the government, political life came to a standstill, with the banning of political parties, the closure of their newspapers and the arrest of their leaders and many of their members. General Mahmud submitted his resignation and that of his government on 22 January 1953. He claimed that his mission of pacifying the country had been accomplished. However, it was believed widely that Mahmud had resigned only reluctantly, having acquired a taste for power himself. This reluctance was perhaps a harbinger of the 1958 Revolution, when military men did take over. Mahmud may have eyed an appointment to the Senate, but the regent offered him an ambassadorship instead, which apparently had rankled with him and his army officers, who thought this an inadequate recompense for 'services' rendered.[11]

Muzahim Al-Pachachi, the former prime minister, wrote in his memoir that the events of 1952 actually spelt the beginning of the end for the monarchy in Iraq. Empowering the army had brought younger army officers into line with popular sentiment and demands. Seeing the relative ease with which the army in Egypt had disposed of its monarchy—that had ruled for 150 years—gave such men ample reason to think that they could pull off the same coup in Iraq, which indeed they did in 1958. In Pachachi's view, 'Abdulillah's decision to bring the army into politics was a suicidal act. It condemned him and the royal family to death, and an ugly one at that.[12]

All the opposition leaders now lobbied the prime minister with memoranda decrying the actions of the previous military government. They demanded the termination of Martial Law, the return to party political life, and freedom of the press. The cumulative effect of this avalanche of criticism did prove effective, as the government soon passed a law sanctioning direct elections (a priority of the opposition) and even called a date for them to take place.[13] Khalil Kanna, an avowed supporter of Nuri's (and related to him by marriage), was clear-sighted enough to declare that the ruling regime was setting a grave precedent in involving the army in the political affairs of the country. This, he warned, would one day have serious repercussions, and the regime would have to pay a very high price indeed—words that proved prophetic.[14] Chadirchi declared that the Intifada had been a cathartic release for the public to voice its dissatisfaction. It had been a wake-up call, too, for the opposition parties to unite in action. It was the first time in Iraq's young history that crowds had called for the abolition of the monarchy and the army had been used to crush its own citizens and halt a popular national movement.[15]

The NDP and the IP refused to participate in the general election held by the Mahmud government, but the UPF and the PSP agreed to do so. However, Saleh Jabr, the PSP leader, later declared that he had evidence of massive interference in the electoral process from the government side, and that his party was withdrawing from the elections as a result. It was extraordinarily foolish that the government should commit election fraud against a pro-government party such as the PSP. It was soon rumoured that this had happened on the direct orders of the now overwrought regent.[16] The NDP and the IP decisions to boycott the elections were applauded by the public. These two parties were proven right about the dishonesty of the electoral process. The pressure that they continued to apply on the government was eventually rewarded, when the latter cancelled most emergency laws, with the grave exception of Martial Law, which was not abolished until 15 September 1953. It also allowed political parties to function once more without government restrictions.

On 2 May 1953, King Faisal II reached the age of maturity and was crowned king of Iraq. This made Prince 'Abdulillah redundant as regent, though he was named crown prince. The latter seemed undeterred by the dramatic change in his status and treated the whole matter as back to business as usual, with his same coterie of palace advisors and older generation politicians. Majid Khadduri writes that the king 'was too young to exercise his royal prerogatives independently, and his uncle and heir apparent, the former regent, was too close to him to let him learn from experience'.[17] The public had hung great hopes on the young king, and they were keen to see the regent's disappearance from the political scene.[18] Iraqis had grown weary after fifteen years of his unconstitutional meddling in state affairs, and of his constant trashing of those democratic values that the constitution was supposed to guarantee. Sadly, however, all the public got after the young king's accession was an even bigger dose of 'Abdulillah, who quickly relegated Faisal to a ceremonial role, as he continued to exercise an iron grip on the conduct of state affairs. 'Abdulillah decided which politicians the king could meet with and showed documents to Faisal merely for rubber-stamping. Some senior Iraqi politicians were only too aware of the manner in which 'Abdulillah was jeopardizing the king's reign from its very beginning. They suggested that he accept an ambassadorship to London or to the United States, which he disdainfully refused.[19] Mohammed Hadid, in his memoir, attributes 'Abdulillah's negative influence on Faisal and his arrogating power to himself as if he were the ultimate authority in the land, as important factors that brought about the Iraq Revolution of 1958.[20]

Kamel Chadirchi lost no time in appealing to the young king to involve himself in national causes. In a memorandum that he submitted to Faisal on 18 May 1953—a mere sixteen days after his accession—Chadirchi summarized the abject social and political conditions in the country that had led to the Intifada. The memorandum also listed the warnings that the opposition already had given to the regent in the ill-fated Palace Conference; and the disdain with which the regent had treated such warnings. Chadirchi spelled out the dangers of governing by Martial Law with all the consequential loss of civil liberties. He also spelled out the danger of handing government over to the military. He wrote how the NDP had submitted several memoranda to the prime minister, decrying the restrictions imposed on the parties and the closure of their newspapers, which had been to no avail. He concluded that the NDP held high hopes that the king would initiate a reign that would respect the constitutional freedoms that the Iraqi public was now clamouring for.

Phebe Marr writes that at the outset of his reign, the king was handed but missed a great opportunity to gain support among the young generation in general, in politics in particular. She says that 'his enthronement should have initiated a new era. He was young, Western-educated, and had democratic ideas. As a member of the younger generation he might well have been able to identify more readily with the newly-emerging, Western-educated class in the cities, the group that was giving the regime so much trouble. Many Iraqis liked him. However no such transition took place'.[21] She attributes Faisal's supine personality to his shyness and inexperience, suggesting that he lacked the leadership qualities of his second cousin, King Hussain of Jordan. He was raised by his aunts, having lost his father as a child and his mother when he was only fifteen. His education at Harrow—an elitist school in England—and by British tutors in Baghdad, not only kept him out of touch with Iraqi youth of his own age, but also put him out of touch with Iraqi popular opinion as a whole. What further worsened matters was that he was only allowed to socialize with boys drawn from Iraq's wealthy sycophantic and pro-monarchist families.

In spite of this, Faisal had no real excuse to plead ignorance of what was transpiring in the country, since Chadirchi's memorandum and those of many other party leaders did alert him to what actually was going on. Chadirchi received a polite but vague reply to his memorandum—and only from the prime minister, Jamil Madfa'i—and not the king himself, in which the former promised that a return to proper political life and a termination of Martial Law was on his government's agenda. The indefatigable Chadirchi replied to the prime minister's letter saying that it was constitutionally illegal (quoting Article 120 from the Basic Law) to maintain Martial Law when the reasons for it no longer prevailed, which was certainly the case then in Iraq. He further pointed out that even Madfa'i's deferred promises to return freedom of the press and of political life were illegal under the constitution and the Basic Law, as neither document allowed for these freedoms to have been suspended in the first place, nor allowed for any government to promise to reinstate them at an unspecified future date.

The NDP kept up a barrage of memoranda that were submitted to Madfa'i, all requesting the return of civil liberties to the people, to which Madfa'i did not even bother to respond. When he resigned and was replaced by Fadhil al-Jamali as prime minister, the NDP submitted another memorandum to Jamali, in which it reiterated the need for a return to free political life, urging him to take immediate action. It pointed out that the situation in the country was worsening and that officials of the government—especially the police and the prison administration—were exceeding their authority and perpetrating the worst kinds of atrocities. These could not now be reported on by a free press. The banning of political parties meant that there were no bodies left to monitor the actions of the government.[22]

Thus Fadhil al-Jamali became prime minister on 17 September 1953, to replace Madfa'i, who had completely failed to restore public confidence in government by perpetuating the cruel measures of his predecessor. Although Jamali's government arrived on the scene in the same unelected manner that its predecessors had—and contained amongst its members the usual coterie of pro-establishment figures—it did nevertheless include members from the UPF (Hassan 'Abd al-Rahman and 'Abd al-Rahman al-Jalili) and the IP (Roufael Batti). In the meantime, the NDP and the UPF had set up a liaison committee to realign the positions of both parties and to present a united front. This arrangement broke down unfortunately in this instance, as no consultation took place between the two parties regarding UPF members joining the new government. This was the third failure of the two parties to present a united front (the other two being the failure to form a National Front, and the disagreements resulting from the Palace Conference), This was to spell the end of the collaboration between these two opposition parties.

Batti had also joined the government in his personal capacity, and not as an IP member. The cabinet also included technocrats and younger-generation politicians such as 'Abd al-Karim 'Uzri, 'Abd al-'Amir 'Allawi and 'Abd al-Ghani al-Dalli, in addition to prominent lawyers such as Sadiq Kammouna and Mohammed Shafiq al-'Ani. The cabinet included seven Shi'a members—the highest number ever yet in any Iraqi cabinet, signalling the growing empowerment of the Shi'a and the palace's acknowledgement and support for it.

Bowing to a cumulative pressure, the opposition parties were applying to the government, Jamali cancelled Martial Law on 5 October 1953. He also sanctioned the return of political parties and their newspapers. The NDP reopened its doors and *Sawt al-'Ahali* returned to the stands on 6 October. It decided, however, to assume a cautious observational approach to the new government, and to comment only on specific actions taken by certain ministries that it did not agree with.

The British obtusely took the view that the activities of the NDP and the IP in pressing for the return of civil liberties were ones that did not reflect national demands, but were 'another reason to use such restored freedoms as an opportunity for further irresponsible behaviour'.[23] The unfortunate Sir John Troutbeck reported: 'It is generally expected that the lifting of martial law will be followed by attempts by the communists, probably in co-operation with the leaders of the Istiqlal (IP) and NDP to provoke disorders... The motives of Kamel Chadirchi and Muhammed Mahdi Kubba (IP) in wishing to create disorders will be the simple ones of trying to bring down the government so that they will be given portfolios in the next'.[24]

It was not long before Jamali's government ran into difficulties, when a series of industrial strikes rocked the country. A strike in a cigarette factory in Baghdad was followed by another strike in the oil fields of Basra in December 1953. Clashes between police and strikers occurred and were reported by the press. The government declared Martial Law in Basra and closed nine non-party newspapers. *Sawt al-'Ahali*, which was very active in reporting the strikes, was the first casualty. Its managing editor, Hassan Jum'a, was brought before a Martial Court for questioning. The paper immediately protested this action with a blistering attack on the government. It wrote that it was absurd that the paper's managing editor should be questioned in Basra when the so-called offending article had appeared in Baghdad. Nevertheless Jum'a received a heavy fine, whilst the paper's Basra managing director, Mohammad Rashid, received an eight month prison sentence. The Basra paper, *Nida' al-'Ahali*, was closed down for a year.

The campaign that *Sawt al-'Ahali* conducted focused attention on the Basra strike to such an extent that the two UPF ministers in the cabinet were moved to submit their resignations. This caused the collapse of the Jamali government, which resigned, only for the palace to ask Jamali to form a new government. The NDP which had taken a neutral stand *vis-à-vis* the first Jamali government decided, in view of recent events, to take an adversarial stand against his second government. This was reflected in the opinion pages of its newspaper.

At the NDP sixth Party Conference, which had been postponed due to the Intifada, but was eventually held on 27 November 1953 (i.e. a full year later), Chadirchi reviewed the events that had occurred in the previous two years since the party's fifth conference in 1951, and their huge effect on the country as well as their effect on the party itself. Chadirchi attacked Jamali's government as being far too subservient to Anglo-American designs, which were in the early stages of preparing the area for military pacts to serve their strategic interests. Mohammed Hadid, in his memoir, writes that the Jamali government was complicit in paving the way for the notorious Baghdad Pact with earlier bilateral pacts—such as those between Turkey and Pakistan, and between Turkey and Iraq—signed as part of the greater scheme in development in the planning departments of Washington and London.[25]

By 19 April 1954, the palace—cognizant of the suppressive measures of the Jamali government, including the use of Martial Law under the pretext of halting the spread of industrial strikes, and their repercussions on an increasingly dissatisfied population—dismissed Jamali and appointed 'Arshad al-'Umari as prime minister. This was in the hope of pacifying the public before disclosing the plan to enter into the ill-fated Baghdad Pact.

To put its plan into action, the palace began consultations with political party leaders in order to calm public sentiment. Chadirchi was invited for a one-to-one meeting with the king, as were the leaders of the UPF and the IP. Chadirchi recounts in his memoir that he was asked by the king to offer his view on Jamali's resignation, as well as his view on electing a new parliament and appointing a government that enjoyed a majority in parliament. Chadirchi told the king plainly that the crisis that had led to Jamali's resignation was not new. Its cause was the chronic accumulation of demands by the public and by the opposition parties for the return of civil liberties, as called for in the Iraqi constitution. He also pointed out that the NDP and the other parties had sent a stream of memoranda to the palace, as well as to sitting prime ministers, warning of the explosive situation that might well arise from the continued deprivation of democratic rights. Chadirchi told the king that the present parliament was not legally elected, warning that the public would no longer stand for another Nuri government based on a 'majority' resulting from a sham parliament.

Sawt al-'Ahali published a summary of Chadirchi's meeting with the king, as well as a summary of the two other meetings the king had had with the leaders of the UPF and IP, which had voiced the same views expressed by Chadirchi.

'Umari's appointment as prime minister was met with trepidation by the opposition parties, as he had a reputation for using violence in politics, as evidenced by his government of 1946. *Sawt al-'Ahali* published a leading article on 30 April 1954—the day following 'Umari's appointment—in which it chronicled 'Umari's past violent acts and those of his previous government. In the paper's view, these disqualified him from presiding over the proposed elections. The paper added that 'Umari had no background whatsoever as a reformist, and that he was ill-suited to assume such a role if the new government was to accomplish its plans. The paper warned that 'Umari might well be nothing but a cover for Iraq's entry into military pacts engineered by Western imperialism, and demanded his speedy resignation.

On 3 May, the NDP presented another memorandum to the king, setting out a summary of its misgivings about 'Umari and his government. The paper published the full contents of the memorandum the next day, as did the IP in its newspaper, *Liwa' al-'Istiqlal*.

The government announced that elections would be held on 9 June 1954. All political parties decided to participate. The NDP, through its newspaper, announced that it would join in the elections, remaining nevertheless vigilant in case the government resorted to electoral fraud as had been its wont in past elections. The paper set out in detail what it perceived as the demands of the public for civil liberties and political reform, which became the basis for the formation of the National Front Pact that came into existence a few days later.

On 12 May 1954, the National Front was formed. Its charter contained *inter alia*:

- The freedom of civil liberties, including the freedom of speech, freedom of the press, and of association; the freedom to demonstrate and strike; the freedom to form political organizations and trade unions.
- The maintenance of the integrity of elections.
- The abrogation of the 1930 Treaty; the evacuation of all foreign troops from Iraq, and the closure of all foreign military bases.

177

- The refusal to join foreign imperialist military pacts and the refusal to accept any aid from the United States if tied to entry into military pacts.
- The cancellation of all foreign oil concessions.
- Closer cooperation with the Arab world in order to rid it of foreign interference and occupation and the closing of Arab ranks in order to liberate Palestine.
- The termination of feudalism, and the encouragement and protection of local industry.

The pact was signed by representatives of the NDP and the IP; and by those of workers, students, farmers, doctors and lawyers.

The result of the election was contested by the National Front, which had entered the election as a bloc. The NDP in particular accused the government of election fraud. It gave examples of its occurrence in named locations, where the secret police had cruised voting stations to frighten voters. The Front won ten seats out of a total of thirty-seven candidates entered. This gave the government an overwhelming majority. Nevertheless, the Front did have a voice in the new parliament through its ten members. This gave it historical value as the last parliament ever to have a nationalist group of members. However, even this was not to last, as Nuri—who now headed the majority in parliament—attempted to dissolve it in order to be rid of the opposition, despite their small numbers. He wanted above all else to be rid of Kamel Chadirchi, who had won a parliamentary seat.[26]

Forty days passed without the new parliament sitting in session. It finally met for the first and last time on 26 June when the king gave a speech from the throne, and a president ('Abd al-Wahhab Murjan) was elected. The king's speech was received in stony silence, even by Nuri's majority CUP Party. The prime minister visited the palace the next day to protest at Nuri's behaviour. He offered to resign if the palace would not instruct Nuri's CUP to back his government.[27] On the very following day, parliament was suspended until November 1954. Nuri had been secretly planning to conclude the Baghdad Pact, and could neither tolerate nor afford to have a cohesive opposition like the National Front in parliament attacking his plan. He figured that even if he could silence the opposition and their newspapers by the usual strong-arm tactics of closure and suspension, he could not stop the opposition members in parliament from speaking their minds. The possibility of their speeches leaking out to the general public or being reported on by other newspapers was too big a risk for him to take.

Nuri, now in a fit of pique, left the country and refused to come back, thereby signalling his anger at the result the election had produced, and at the presence of what, to him, was the pesky opposition. His intransigence forced the hand of 'Abdulillah to travel personally to Paris, where Nuri had taken refuge, in order to seek to woo him back to Iraq. Nuri was promised that if he did come back, he would be allowed to form a new government. Parliament would be dissolved too if he so wished. 'Abdulillah had already foreseen such an eventuality, and had extracted a letter of resignation from 'Umari dated 17 June 1954. 'Abdulillah now accepted this, so as formally to ask Nuri to form his twelfth government. Such manoeuvrings did not go unnoticed by the opposition, who were alarmed at the dangerous palace-Nuri-British agenda that was about to unfold.

Nuri set about implementing his plan. His first political act was to dissolve the new parliament that had hardly started its tenure, and had met only once. He also set about stifling civil liberties once again, and suppressing the opposition parties. Under the pretext of cleaning government from 'destructive' and 'corrupt' elements, Nuri began a wanton reign of terror, carrying out the arrests of citizens under the flimsiest of charges—usually for being communists—without ever bothering to prove the charge in any court of law. He justified his dissolution of parliament under the pretext of renegotiating the 1930 Treaty. Nuri claimed disingenuously that a new parliament would be very much like holding a referendum, which would give him the mandate required to proceed with a new treaty. He issued laws that were not sanctioned by parliament (since he had suspended it) and were clearly illegal. These laws dealt with curbing the individual Iraqi's activities, as well as those of non-governmental organizations and groups (which included the Peace Partisans). The laws sanctioned the government to take the extraordinary measure of stripping citizens of their nationality, and holding them in detention until they could be expelled from Iraq. The laws could also shut down trade unions; close down clubs and societies; cancel newspaper licenses; prohibit freedom of association; ban demonstrations or give the authorities the right to disperse them with violence.

Nuri dissolved his own Constitutional Union Party as a precursor to dissolving all other parties. In so doing he paved the way for an unopposed march towards the signature of the Baghdad Pact. Salih Jabr's party, the PSP, followed suit, although this was due as much to divisions within its own ranks. Jabr himself, perhaps aghast at such measures, took a decidedly anti-Nuri stand, but remained unable to persuade others in his party to do the same. Nuri also dissolved the IP Party. With that measure, he practically put paid to any pluralism in Iraq's political life. The NDP issued a communiqué decrying Nuri's draconian new laws, especially the one relating to stripping citizens of their nationality for any alleged misdemeanour. It issued another declaring that it was boycotting the forthcoming elections. In punishment, Nuri withdrew the license of the party and of its newspaper for a whole year. The NDP contested the closure, but the authorities rejected the contention, as well as the party's application to obtain a new license, claiming that the reasons for closure would apply as much to the new party as they had done to the old.

The NDP did indeed boycott the elections but some IP leaders decided to participate in their personal capacity since their party had been suspended. When the blatant fraud that had been perpetrated in order to obtain pro-government results became clear—with 121 candidates standing unopposed out of a total of 135 candidates—Mohammed Mehdi Kubba, the former IP leader who had been elected on an individual basis, resigned his seat in protest at the shameless nature of the whole affair.

Phebe Marr describes this period in Iraq's history as one where the laws that Nuri forced through, and the fake elections that he engineered, effectively stifled political life for the next four years and turned the country into a police state. She writes that: 'There is little doubt that this suppression produced sufficient stability to shepherd the Baghdad Pact through parliament and later ride out the Suez Crisis. But it ultimately had fateful consequences. It put almost complete power in the hands of a man increasingly unable to come to terms with the new forces about to shake the Arab World'.[28] She might well have added that the opposition failed—yet again—to form into a unified bloc to stand up to Nuri. It was a chronic failure that continues to be a persistent flaw in Iraqi politics even to this day.

10

THE BAGHDAD PACT AND THE YEARS 1954–1958

On 3 August 1954, Nuri al-Saʻid replaced Arshad al-ʻUmari as prime minister. He immediately embarked on preparing the ground for launching political programmes he had planned by issuing laws that empowered the authorities to silence all opposition, prohibit demonstrations and suppress any expression of opinion, be it in newspapers or by individuals. The opposition's failure to unify and block Nuri's plans for the country allowed him to proceed unhindered towards shackling Iraq to a new Anglo-American scheme for the region.

Nuri knew that the 1930 Anglo-Iraqi Treaty—which was heavily weighted in Britain's favour—was about to expire, and another arrangement would have to be agreed to take its place. Nuri also knew that any such new pact would be strongly opposed by the public and by the political parties of the opposition. This was bound to be doomed in the same way that the 1948 Portsmouth Treaty had been. The geopolitical imperatives of the United States and its NATO allies (including Britain) were such that a collection of compliant countries whose cooperation could be counted on had to be found in order to form a tier (which later would come to be referred to as the 'Northern Tier') that could separate the two Cold War adversaries. This was the Eastern Bloc—composed of the Soviet Union and the Warsaw Pact—and the Western Bloc—made up of America and its NATO allies. The British needed Iraq to be counted as a member state of that latter tier, and for Nuri al-Saʻid to facilitate its entry.

181

Nuri was far too cunning to spring such a scheme in its entirety on an already seething Iraqi public, preferring to divulge its components in small doses and in progressive steps. The first step was a Mutual Cooperation Pact between Iraq and Turkey that he signed on 24 February 1955. His handpicked Iraqi parliament rubber-stamped this for him with hardly a ripple of discussion. The second step was completed on 4 April 1955, when Iraq and Britain signed an agreement that governed their overall relations, conceived to replace the 1930 Treaty. On 5 April, Britain joined the Iraq-Turkish Pact. This event was not reported by Nuri to parliament, who claimed that Iraq was not entering into commitments that required any further parliamentary approval.[1] With the addition of Britain as a new 'member' of the Iraq-Turkish Pact, and since this pact was signed in Baghdad, it became known from then on as the 'Baghdad Pact'.[2] The third step was for Pakistan to join, as it too had signed the Anglo-Turkish Pact on 23 September 1955. The fourth step was for Iran to join, and this it did on 23 September 1955. It was thus that the Baghdad Pact came to form the 'Northern Tier' of countries: in other words, Britain, Iraq, Turkey, Pakistan and Iran all now standing as a Western shield against the Soviet Union. The inaugural meeting of the pact took place in Baghdad on 21 November 1955.

The prevailing political environment at the time must have seemed opportune enough for Nuri to embark on a scheme as ambitious as the Baghdad Pact. He enjoyed a close relationship with the Conservative Party in Britain, who happened to be in government at the time with Winston Churchill as prime minister. He shared their view that such a pact would cement the ties between Baghdad and London. At this time, too, in the area, there was a pro-Western government in Lebanon while in Syria, the military government of 'Adib al-Shishakli had fallen by coup d'état and had been replaced by a more pliable pro-Western military regime. Pro-American Saudi Arabia was neither involved with nor interested then in Iraq's schemes. So, when the British and the Americans successfully engineered the downfall of Mossadeg's government in Tehran, the last nationalist obstacle in the way of Iran's joining in the British scheme of things was removed and it was made to return to the Western fold. For Nuri al-Sa'id, all this provided a perfect regional setting in which to enter into a new relationship with Britain, to replace the 1930 Treaty—disguised with the useful smokescreen that the pact also involved four other countries.

The United States—which had been expected to join the pact—decided against joining as an official member, preferring instead to join specific committees of the pact as an observer. One reason why America did not officially join was because the US Congress demanded that the Baghdad Pact guarantee Israel's borders as a condition of entry. This was a condition that the American administration of the time—not yet trapped in Israel's sway as later administrations have become—knew would be unacceptable to Arab and Islamic public opinion. The American government therefore pretended to opt for a 'minor' role as an observer although, in practice, it actually operated as a full member.

The British and the Americans made great efforts to have Jordan join the pact. Despite several seductive offers of aid, Jordan was forced to decline, as massive demonstrations rocked Jordan's cities, clearly proving that there was stiff popular resistance to such a scheme. The request to join was also put to Egypt; or at the very least, Egypt was asked to take a neutral position *vis-à-vis* the scheme. That effort failed as well when an increasingly nationalistic Egypt declined on both counts.

Why Iraq joined the Baghdad Pact has remained something of a historical mystery. Apart from the attempts by the British and by Nuri al-Sa'id to cloak naked British interests in a new guise that would supplant the much-hated 1930 Treaty, later writing on the topic has provided no truly convincing explanation. Nuri's determination to alienate the Iraqi public, stifle political life and drive the opposition parties underground in order to secure the freehand he needed to join such a pact is ample proof of his reckless single-mindedness in its favour. His highly unpopular actions eventually succeeded in galvanizing the opposition parties to reluctantly cooperate with the army to mount the successful 1958 Revolution which toppled his pro-British regime. Not surprisingly, one of the first major measures undertaken by the revolutionary government was to cancel Iraq's membership in the widely detested Baghdad Pact.

Books favourable to Nuri's decision to join the pact often cite his rabid anti-communism as his compelling reason, or even his active dislike of the opposition parties in Iraq.[3] In his memoir, for example, Waldemar Gallman, the U.S. ambassador to Iraq at the time, wrote that Nuri's decision to join the Baghdad Pact enjoyed great popular support and was overwhelmingly voted for in parliament by 112 votes to four, a majority of 108 votes. He refers to this vote as an impressive parliamentary endorsement of Nuri's plans.[4] He quotes Nuri's response to one of the 'lone' dissenters in parliament, Mohammed Ridha Shabibi (the only member of the opposition who did manage to enter into and remain in parliament), who advocated the opposition view that Iraq should remain neutral, as not being representative of the Iraqi people—'99.75 per cent' of whom were in favour of the pact.[5] Gallman's breezy glossing over the fact that an election fraud had been perpetrated in order to secure a 'rubber-stamp' parliament appears to be quite disingenuous.

Though Nuri was oblivious to the Iraqi public's genuine opposition to the pact, he seemed eager for Egypt to join in nevertheless, even though the Egyptians had made it more than clear to him that they were totally opposed to all such schemes. He must also have been oblivious to the failure of similar foreign-led schemes, including the non-aggression 'Sa'dabad Pact' involving Afghanistan, Iran, Iraq and Turkey (signed on 8 July 1937, at Sa'dabad Palace, the Shah's summer residence); or MEDO (Middle East Defence Organization), brain-child of John Foster Dulles (the then U.S. secretary of state) which received a cool reception even by those Arab states which were supposed to be its potential members; and Alpha, the Anglo-American scheme which purported to deal with the Arab-Israeli conflict in such a way as to make it run in tandem with the 'Northern Tier' concept.

Current research has revealed that the Baghdad Pact was a weak political and military concept that stood little chance of succeeding, especially in Iraq. The pact could never have withstood the many pitfalls inherent in the strained Arab-Western relationship. When the Suez Crisis took place, with the actively tripartite military attack on Egypt by Israel, Britain and France, Nasser was pushed into the Soviet camp, thus vitiating the entire concept of a 'Northern Tier'. The Soviet Union managed to leapfrog into the very heart of the Arab world, not so much through its own power, but through European partiality and political short-sightedness—strikingly—represented by Anthony Eden's personal and obsessive hatred of Nasser.

Ironically enough, as it turned out, the pact was not very high on the American list of alliances. Indeed, this may have been an early example of the United States supplanting an increasingly weakened Britain in the region. Few historians who have written on the topic chose to consider the pact as an exemplar of Anglo-American relations or as a significant example of alliance formation.[6] Rather, some have argued that the U.S. did not actually join as a full member simply because it suspected Britain of being far more interested in creating another Anglo-Iraqi arrangement than a genuine multilateral security pact.

Additionally, the mix of countries in the pact proved to be too disparate, and so like the Sa'dabad Pact before it, it too was destined to fail. The pact did give Turkey increased political status but this was resented by the Arab states (many of which had not forgotten yet their Turkish overlords of the near past). The Soviet Union, which had become alarmed at Iran's new pro-Western stand, certainly did not wish to see Iraq go down the same route, and was especially hostile to the pact as a result. In addition, Iraq's relations with her sister Arab countries were impaired. It came in for heavy criticism for causing divisions within the Arab League by its 'going-it-alone'—and needless—pro-Western security policy.

One bizarre feature of the pact was that neither Iraq nor Pakistan shared borders with the Soviet Union. In addition, their relationship to each other was tenuous, as they shared neither language nor common national characteristics, apart from their official state religion of Islam—hardly a common bond in a period that long predated the rise of Islamic internationalism.

The Baghdad Pact is now considered to have been quite useless as far as defending the area or keeping the Soviets out was concerned. If anything, Soviet interest in certain Arab states increased after its signing and the pact is viewed as having failed to achieve a single one of its set objectives.[7]

Egypt was not content to just say 'NO' to Nuri al-Sa'id when he asked it to join the pact. It unleashed a vicious, anti-pact campaign through its popular radio station '*Sawt al-Arab*' (the Voice of the Arabs), which was widely listened to across the Arab world.[8] The Egyptians, in general, and Nasser in particular, came to represent a real personal nightmare for Nuri, who was reduced to having to utter nervously and repeatedly, 'I have done no wrong'.[9] In private conversations, in statements to parliament, and in interviews with the press, he was from then on always on the defensive—feeling suddenly obliged to justify his policy. He was deeply worried by charges that he had deserted the Arab camp; and by the aspersions cast on his loyalty to Arab nationalism, when he had been one of its early protagonists, possibly even before Nasser was born. Cairo radio was relentless in its attacks, however, using the anniversary of the Portsmouth Treaty to vilify Nuri further, and to incite the Iraqi public to rise up against what it considered a far worse replacement treaty. The broadcasts even warned the palace of the ire of the Iraqi people, reminding it of the adverse consequences of Nuri's past ill-judged actions. It even called up the anti-Arab racism of the Young Turks for good measure, asking Allah to rescue the Arabs from 'the calamity of the Nuri-Menderes alliance'.[10] To highlight the political pitfalls inherent in such a pact, Nasser called for an emergency meeting of Arab prime ministers and foreign ministers, but Nuri feigned illness and did not attend. In private, however, he confessed that he was certainly not about to go to Cairo in order to be pilloried!

The NDP—as was the case with all other Iraqi political parties—had remained inactive in the period under review. Party leaders were forced to restrict their meetings to private gatherings in each other's houses, though in their individual capacities, they continued to pursue their personal political agendas. The idea of a new joint party, to be called the National Congress Party (NCP) *Hizb al-Mu'tamar al-Watani*, along the lines of the one formed in India, was already taking shape. Several preparatory meetings about it were held in the closing months of 1955, just as the furore over the Baghdad Pact was building up. On 29 December 1955, a note signed by Kamel Chadirchi, Mohammed Hadid and Hussain Jamil (NDP), and by Mohammed Mahdi Kubba, Siddiq Shanshal and Fa'iq Samara'i (IP) was presented to the king. In it, the two parties pointed out that Iraq—which had been at the forefront of the Arab independence movement—now found itself isolated from the new direction that the Arab countries were taking towards freedom and independence from foreign rule and interference. The note demanded Nuri's resignation, along with a return to democratic party life and the guarantee of civil liberties. This was the only route open to Iraq, the note continued, that could avert the dangers spawned by its joining of the Baghdad Pact. This would see Iraq return to the Arab fold by realigning its policy with that of its sister Arab countries.

The two parties submitted a request, signed by the full leadership of both the NDP and the IP on 16 June 1956, for the new party (NCP) to be licensed by the government. The request was turned down. Almost a full year later, the two opposition parties still wished to function legally and politically together. When, on 20 June 1957, Nuri resigned and 'Ali Jawdat replaced him as prime minister, Mohammed Hadid and Mohammed Mahdi Kubba (Chadirchi was in jail at the time) met with Jawdat to request that he reverse the earlier negative decision and allow the new party to be licensed, but he, too, declined, claiming that he did not wish to countermand a decision that had been already taken. This was a decision, however, that the regime came to regret bitterly. As a result of it, the opposition began to operate underground, only re-emerging after the 1958 Revolution in the unexpected form of the new government.

On 26 July 1956, Gamal Abd al-Nasser announced that the Suez Canal Company was to be nationalized. This historic announcement was met with great intensity and delight by the Arab public, and Iraq certainly was no exception. Popular reaction was on a scale similar to that which greeted Dr. Mossadeg's cathartic announcement of the nationalization of Iranian oil.

Unbeknownst to the Iraqi regime at the time, Suez was soon to prove to be the downfall of both Nuri al-Sa'id and the monarchy. As luck would have it, when Nasser announced the nationalization of the Canal, Nuri, Faisal and 'Abdulillah were in London on a state visit, and were dining with the British prime minister, Anthony Eden, in Downing Street. Eden's secretary approached him and handed him a note. Eden read it, turned pale, and said to his guests that Nasser had just announced the nationalization of the Suez Canal Company. Eden, who viewed Nasser as his nemesis, blurted out to his dinner guests that this time Nasser had overstepped the mark. He must be hit, hit now and hit hard. Nuri apparently encouraged Eden to carry out such an action against Nasser, as confirmed by Hikmat Sulaiman (who had gone to visit Nuri soon after his return to Baghdad from this state visit) to Mohammed Hadid. Nuri, Sulaiman told Hadid, had said that Nasser was going to be hit by the British and that he was finished.[11] Further evidence of Nuri's encouraging Eden to carry out his anti-Nasser plan is provided by Tariq al-'Askari, the then Iraqi minister at the London embassy, and Nuri al-Sa'id's nephew (son of his sister who had been married to Ja'afar Pasha al-'Askari—the former Iraqi prime minister). Tariq al-'Askari, who was known for his Arab nationalist views, had visited Muzahim al-Pachachi in Geneva (which the latter was visiting) and told him that a member of the British House of Commons had quoted Eden to him as having said that Nuri al-Sa'id had encouraged him (Eden) to 'hit' Nasser, even assuring him that Iraq would be willing to assist in such an operation.[12]

Nuri's increasingly bellicose attitude seems to have hardened during 1956 to such a point that he began contemplating military action against both Syria and Jordan. When the situation in Jordan worsened for the British after the dismissal of Glubb Pasha, Nuri consulted with some of Iraq's former prime ministers to secure endorsement for his Arab policy. He met with Jamil Madfaʻi, ʻAli Jawdat and Mustapha al-ʻUmari. The meeting went badly for Nuri, as the consensus opinion of the group was that Nuri's attitude was creating unnecessary tensions for Iraq with Egypt and other Arab countries, and that another prime minister, not associated with Nuri's views, should be appointed to defuse the situation. Matters were not helped when Salih Jabr told the British ambassador that Nasser was 'a megalomaniac whose ambition was to supplant Britain throughout the Middle East', and that Britain and Iraq should intervene in Jordan and Syria if need be to bring them into line. A week later, and perhaps as a result of this intelligence from the ambassador, the deputy director of Britain's Secret Intelligence Service, George Kennedy Young, was reported as having discussed taking exactly such an action with his CIA counter-parts.[13]

Nuri, according to the British ambassador, was also contemplating restructuring Iraq's political life along British (and/or Turkish) lines by having a two-party system. This he wished to be composed of a government party (ostensibly his own CUP) and one other party made up of independent members of the IP and other opposition groups who shared a pro-Western outlook. As 'proof', the ambassador recounts that when the opposition parties got wind of Nuri's scheme, they rushed to apply for a new party to be named the National Congress Party. Nuri had discussed their application in cabinet, and had decided to make them wait for a month for his reply—so as to give the impression that the government was seriously considering their request—only to turn it down when the time came. Nuri claimed that refusal then did not mean that permission might not be granted later when his own single government party was announced that autumn. These best-laid plans, however, were thwarted by the Suez Crisis.[14]

Despite this linkage with events surrounding Nuri's viewpoint, the evolution of the idea of the National Congress Party (NCP), has been carefully chronicled by the leading Iraqi politicians from both the NDP and the IP in their memoirs. All give accounts that are at complete variance with Nuri's version of events. The very idea that the NDP and IP leaders who submitted an application for the new party on 16 June

1956, were somehow 'inspired' to join a pro-Western, two-party system led by their nemesis, Nuri al-Sa'id, is simply a case of wishful thinking and quite absurd to anyone who is familiar with Iraq's modern history. This would have been obvious from the first demand listed by the new party's manifesto which was the immediate removal of Nuri from office. Furthermore, and despite the government's refusal to grant a license for a new party, Kamel Chadirchi and Mohammed Mehdi Kubba—the leaders of the NDP and IP respectively, who were probably the very last two people in Iraq who might contemplate collaboration with Nuri—began signing all memoranda and communiqués jointly in the name of this new virtual party.

The period following the exhilarating nationalization of the Suez Canal was one of frantic activity in Iraq. All the opposition parties, including the ICP (Iraq Communist Party), were holding meetings to discuss ways and means of unifying their efforts. Mohammed Hadid describes in his memoir a secret meeting with Salam 'Adil (aka Hussain Ahmad al-Radi), the general secretary of the ICP, who wished to sound out whether his party and the Ba'th Party could unite their efforts with the NCP under a single national grouping. Hadid informed 'Adil that the NDP saw no objection to this, provided that the new group would work towards certain specific and clearly-defined goals, which were:

• To support Egypt in its nationalization of the Suez Canal.
• To mobilize the public and the army in the event of an attack on Egypt.
• To lend Iraq's support to the Palestinians.
• To release all political prisoners.
• To return to the era of civil liberties.
• To call for free elections.
• To call for freedom of the press and freedom of association.
• To call for Nuri al-Sa'id's removal from government.

'Adil promised to relay those demands to the Ba'th Party. Both he and Hadid decided to leave the Kurdish issue open for future discussions, since it might have caused friction with the IP—which had strongly-held nationalist aims—that might well have clashed with the aspirations of the Kurds of Iraq, who were seeking then (as now) to win autonomy.

The idea of a new grouping was adopted and became known as The National Union Front (NUF). This grouping now included the NDP,

IP, ICP and the Ba'th Party. Its members were Mohammed Hadid (NDP), Mohammed Mahdi Kubba (IP), 'Aziz al-Shaikh (ICP) and Fu'ad al-Rikabi (Ba'th). Kamel Chadirchi could not participate as he had been arrested (alongside other leading members of the NDP and IP) after his return from Damascus where he had attended the Popular Congress organized to show solidarity with Egypt over the Suez Crisis. It is revealing to note that the British ambassador, reporting to the FO, stated that Nuri had come down hard on the opposition. Nuri, the ambassador wrote, had made an example of Chadirchi for having spoken 'traitorously' in Damascus not only about the Iraqi regime itself, but also about the destruction of the Syrian pipeline by Syrian army units (which was viewed as an anti-British act) which Chadirchi had commended.[15]

Egypt was attacked on 29 October 1956, when Israel invaded its territory. Israeli troops crossed the frontier into the Sinai, allegedly to destroy the bases of Egyptian commandos. The first sign of collusion between Israel, Britain and France came on the same day, when the Anglo-French ultimatum was handed to Egypt and Israel, before Israel had even reached the canal. British bombing destroyed the Egyptian air force, and British and French paratroopers were dropped over Port Said and Port Fu'ad. The Egyptians put up fierce resistance to this massive attack on their territory. Ships were sunk in the canal to prevent transit. In the battle for Port Said, some 2,700 Egyptian soldiers and civilians were wounded or killed.

In the Arab world, this was yet another event that would live on in infamy. Arab anger was unfathomable, and the event came to be seen as the one that would change the political map of the region. For Iraq, tied in its alliance with Britain by the Baghdad Pact, the situation became untenable. Sir Michael Wright reported that Nuri al-Sa'id had naively expected that Britain would consult with all its partners in the Baghdad Pact before launching into such an attack. He describes Nuri being stupefied with a bitter sense of personal betrayal when it dawned on him that Britain 'intended not to take action against the invader but only against the invaded (as much as he desired to see Nasser brought down)'.[16] Yet again, Sir Michael's missives to the Foreign Office belie historical accuracy. If Nuri's excitable words of support to Anthony Eden, when the latter intimated that Nasser was going to be hit and hit hard back in the previous July were true, that would mean that Nuri was now only play-acting by pretending to be betrayed—or that

Wright was wrong himself or was wrongly briefed by his own subordinates at the Baghdad embassy about Nuri. Nuri, well-aware of the dangers awaiting the regime from an outraged Iraqi public, quickly reinstated Martial Law and broke diplomatic relations with France, but tellingly not with Britain. He brutally put down a massive demonstration on 21 November 1956, when several students were killed and more than fifty policemen were wounded. He closed down all schools and colleges. Nevertheless, strikes spread throughout Iraq's cities, where there were occasional clashes between police and civilians. As stated earlier, Syria had blown up the Iraq Petroleum Company pipeline in November, thereby putting a dent in Anglo-Iraqi finances—another cause of annoyance for Nuri.

The country was in uproar. Students and other civilians—especially the intelligentsia in Baghdad—were now prepared to risk arrest in order to demonstrate their political anger and bitterness. Research has since revealed that the same bitterness had penetrated the army, which began to form secret cells which eventually became known as the 'The Free Officers' Movement'. The opposition parties, which had been driven underground, were hard at work too. On the foreign policy front, Iraq was now surrounded by hostile Arab states—save for pro-British Jordan—all baying for Nuri's resignation or even his head. To be fair to Nuri, he did attempt to submit his resignation to the palace on several occasions, probably as a result of panic at the escalating situation, but his resignations were not accepted.

Curiously enough, the British embassy continued to report that Nuri was in control. In one such report, the British military attaché, Major Lawson, went on a tour of the countryside to assess the situation there. He reported bizarrely that most of the mayors (*mutasarrifs*) remained solidly behind Nuri and went on to say that many of them thought that the attacks on Egypt were merely coincidental, and that they were far more offended by Cairo's 'vicious attacks' on Iraq than they were by the Anglo-French-Israeli attacks on Egypt.[17] Another bizarre report was sent by the ambassador himself in April 1958, only three months before the July Revolution. The ambassador agreed with Major Lawson's analysis, seeing no danger of a revolution coming from the countryside and believing that there was little chance of a change of regime in Iraq. Sir Michael stated in his report that he too believed the regime to be sufficiently well-organized to prevent either an urban revolution taking place or a military coup d'état.[18] In yet another muddled report to the Foreign Office, Wright reported on an interview that Salih Jabr had given some American journalists, in which Jabr described the Iraqi parliament as 'having been packed' (i.e. fixed) and that there were 'thousands' of political prisoners. Sir Michael described Jabr's statements as 'demonstrably inaccurate as well as being patently irresponsible', as the figure for those under detention for political offences was only around 200. This was a clearly serious under-estimate by the British, considering that thousands of political prisoners were released only weeks later, shortly after the July Revolution.[19]

Nuri al-Sa'id limped along for a few months more until 18 June 1957, when a new government was formed under 'Ali Jawdat. The British embassy thought that Nuri 'had steered Iraq successfully through the months since Suez, when a weaker hand or a less-cool head might have involved the country and the régime in catastrophe'.[20] Nuri had hoped that the benefits of his development programme would have a trickle-down effect which would mollify public anger, since his Tharthar Barrage project had just saved Baghdad from flooding. But all this was to no avail, as the palace, in consultation with 'the elder statesmen' and quite likely with the British embassy too, decided to give Nuri a 'rest' and appoint Jawdat in his place.

In Jawdat's first statement as prime minister, the Baghdad Pact was deliberately left out, much to the anxiety of the British ambassador. Jawdat spoke of the need to clear the air between Iraq and its sister Arab countries, which was at variance with the palace's desperate assurances that the Iraqi regime's support for the Baghdad Pact would remain unaltered. It was still widely assumed that Jawdat would adopt a more liberal attitude towards dissent than his predecessor had. He was quick to demonstrate this by lifting the order to jam radio broadcasts from Cairo, Damascus and Moscow. Jawdat wisely recommended a 'soft' power approach, by upgrading the quality of Iraq's overall media operations—including radio and television—and a reorganization of the whole information apparatus in the country. However, restrictions on the press continued, though the government announced it was prepared to consider new applications for licences. Jawdat continued his conciliatory approach by releasing a few political prisoners, especially those that had recanted their communist beliefs—presumably under duress or torture.

Jawdat eventually fell foul of 'Abdulillah over Syria. The latter had never given up hope of meddling there in order to secure a Syrian crown for himself, now that Faisal II had become king of Iraq. Jawdat thought 'Abdulillah far too trigger-happy in wanting to embroil Iraq's army in a military venture to topple the Syrian regime. In this he was perhaps in cahoots with the United States, unhappy with the recent Soviet penetration into that country. Jawdat also believed that 'Abdulillah was totally out of touch with public opinion. In this he was backed by several palace courtiers, including the chief of the Diwan. On 14 December, Jawdat tendered his resignation in protest at 'Abdulillah's intransigent attitude to government recommendations to hold new elections. Jawdat left government having accomplished little except to prevent 'Abdulillah from a military misadventure in Syria.

Jawdat was replaced as prime minister by 'Abdul Wahhab Murjan on 14 December 1957. Murjan's cabinet was described by Sir Michael Wright as 'a Cabinet of Nuri's supporters without Nuri', and Murjan as 'somewhat lacking in personality'. His first controversial act was to brandish his support for the Baghdad Pact. The composition of his cabinet indicated that Nuri was still in office, but by proxy. It was not long before the new cabinet faced its first foreign policy crisis when on 1 February 1958, Egypt and Syria announced the formation of the United Arab Republic (UAR). For the British and their Iraqi regime, this represented a grave challenge that was sure to provoke further unrest amongst an already-restless Iraqi public. The latter could now see a glimmer of hope of Arab unity afforded by this union, which might yet present an existential threat to their hated political masters. The ramifications of this union of Syria with Nasser—which made him capable of exercising direct control over Iraq's pipeline which crossed Syria—posed threats to many British interests in Iraq, including the possibility of political blackmail and extortion. A further nightmare for the Iraqi regime was the threat presented by the Soviet Union, which was now well-established in Syria through its material support of many economic projects, most importantly the development of a dam on the upper waters of the Euphrates.

Feeling the noose tightening, the Iraqi regime, together with its Jordanian counterpart, embarked on a Union project of its own. Britain was asked to press Kuwait into joining this new Union, but Britain prevaricated. It claimed that it would have to grant Kuwait its independence before such a move could be made possible. 'Abdulillah, King Faisal and King Hussain became the ill-starred figures behind the Union, with 'Abd al-Wahhab Murjan acting as facilitator. They managed to cobble together an agreement within two weeks of the proclamation of the UAR. The actual Union, however, had to wait for the approval of both countries' parliaments.[21]

On 2 March 1958, Murjan resigned to make way once more for Nuri, who engineered a new election with his old method of preordaining results by making certain that all members of the chamber committed to his government. On 12 May 1958, parliament ratified the constitution for the Arab Hashemite Union and on 19 May, the last government under the monarchy was formed with Ahmad Mukhtar Baban, a Kurd, as prime minister. Nuri held the somewhat vainglorious title of 'Prime Minister of the Union'.

Nuri al-Sa'id and the palace continued their efforts to press the British to bring Kuwait into the Union. Nuri intimated to Sir Michael Wright that this was the only way for the Union to succeed. He warned that, otherwise, Kuwait, Jordan and Iraq would all be lost. When Wright continued to procrastinate, Nuri threatened to annex Kuwait himself. He, like all Iraqis—including Saddam Hussain—considered Kuwait to be no more than an amputated part of Iraq, detached from it by a wily Britain when Iraq was still a helpless part of the Ottoman Empire.

In July 1958, a crisis in Lebanon alarmed Nuri sufficiently for him to consider military intervention, in case the crisis came to affect Jordan too. When his appeals to Britain and the United States to intervene on behalf of the Lebanese president, Camille Chamoun, failed to exact any response, Nuri decided to send a division of the Iraqi army to the Jordanian border, where it would await further instructions as matters developed.

Ironically, as it turned out, this army division, instead of going into Jordan as Nuri had planned, marched on Baghdad. It staged the revolution of 14 July 1958, bringing to an end thirty-seven years of British-appointed monarchy rule in Iraq.

11

IRAQ ON THE EVE OF REVOLUTION

The 1958 Revolution in Iraq was an event waiting to happen. The excesses of the ruling establishment had reached eruption point. On 14 July 1958, the country exploded. Although most of the factors that contributed to the downfall of the monarchy and its support systems have been written about in detail, it might be useful to summarize them here from eyewitness accounts, scholarly works, and other sources that have become available in recent years.

Many have attributed the regime's downfall to Nasser's ascendancy in Middle East politics, especially after the Suez Crisis with its accompanying vitriolic but highly effective campaign that Cairo's radio station, *Sawt al-Arab*, unleashed against Nuri al-Sa'id. In actual fact, however, anyone familiar with Iraqi politics can retrace the hardening of Iraqi public opinion in both actions and reactions to well before 1952 and the arrival of Nasser. Bakr Sidqi's 1936 coup; Rashid 'Ali's Second of May Movement; the 1948 Uprising against the Portsmouth Treaty and the 1952 Intifada, all provided proof of the Iraqi people's mounting dissatisfaction with the palace and with Nuri's handling of state affairs—aided and abetted as he was by a towering British presence in the country.

The root of Iraq's continuous state of open revolt against successive governments stemmed from the fact that Iraqis had never taken to the idea of monarchy—let alone an imported one. The very concept of monarchy was an alien one to them. One must bear in mind that modern Iraq was a British creation, and that before the nation's birth in 1921, it had consisted of three city-states—Baghdad, Mosul and Basra—that were disconnected from each other. The people inhabiting these cities were of different religious and ethnic backgrounds. In the case of the Sunnis and the Shi'a, they were religiously divided; and in the case of the Kurds, they were self-referentially insular.[1] To hrow all such sectarian and ethnic contradictions into one melting pot under a foreign monarchy and expect a result other than chaos, was wishful thinking on the part of the British. Furthermore, to even begin to expect such a complicated mix to evolve quickly into a viable nation-state along the modern Western model required nothing short of a socio-political miracle.

When the mandate system was imposed upon the Arabs, and Arab lands divided up between England and France, the French established republics headed by indigenous leaders, while the British imposed monarchies and kings. In this way each mandatory power perhaps was seeking to recreate its own political and cultural systems. Unfortunately, the monarchs chosen by Britain—although Arab—were 'strangers' with no visceral ties to the countries they were brought in to rule. Consequently they could not belong and suffered initially from being isolated and unable to inspire a local following. In the case of the newly-created Iraq, Faisal I had a first-class royal pedigree, but most Iraqis thought his choice as king was a political sham plainly organized by the British. This negative view of Faisal was shared by local candidates such as Talib al-Naqib—who was unceremoniously shuffled off in a British tank to be exiled in Ceylon, and 'Abd al-Rahman al-Naqib (no relation) who swore to Gertrude Bell that he preferred the return of the Ottomans a thousand times over than forcibly accepting the Sharif Hussain or any of his offspring to rule Iraq.[2] Given the huge popularity and standing of these two Naqib men in their respective communities of Basra and Baghdad, it is hard to believe that Faisal, an outsider and unknown to Iraqis, actually could have garnered 97 per cent of the vote, as the British pretended he had.[3]

Faisal may not have been aware of British machinations in preparing for his coronation as king. Most likely he believed them, as well as the Iraqi ex-Ottoman army officers among his advisors who had been with him in the Arab army, who assured him that the local people wanted him to be their king. He had, after all, been king of Syria, albeit for a few weeks only, before the French unceremoniously ejected him from that position. Faisal had by then become a burden even to the British themselves as he shuffled back and forth, seeking some convincing role to play. The British began to treat him with benign neglect. Their ingratitude must have grated, especially after all that Faisal had done for them in their war against the Ottomans.[4]

Faisal was caught in a vice from which he could no longer escape. He was expected by the British to remain forever grateful to them (even against his better judgement) for having put him on the throne of this new country called Iraq. Another reason for this required gratitude was that when the Hashemites were driven out of their ancestral home in the Hijaz by 'Abd al-'Aziz bin Sa'ud, the British allowed them to take refuge in Iraq and Jordan—two countries then under British tutelage. One grave consequence was that 'Abdulillah, son of the exiled Hijazi King 'Ali, was to become the single most important contributor to the Iraqi monarchy's downfall, due to his overbearing character and deep unpopularity with the Iraqi public.[5]

The die was cast with Faisal's coronation. It was an entirely British-controlled and concocted deal, whereby a new country is 'invented'; a new king beholden to the British is crowned; and a supporting cast of parvenu Iraqis (mostly ex-Ottoman army men, that came to be known as the Sharifian officers) became cabinet ministers, together with whatever opportunistic local gentry willing to collaborate with such a hurriedly put-together regime. Simply put, the British ran the show. The newly-minted Iraqi Court became a parody of British royal life, replete with an outlandish palace etiquette, and with a Western-sounding national anthem, more often than not played out of tune! There were Rolls-Royces, a royal hunt, and even a second-hand horse-drawn carriage sold to the Iraqis by Buckingham Palace. There was the usual coterie of *arrivistes*, who normally congregate around monarchies for personal gain and social advantage. The whole scene was straight out of Kipling, and completely out of place in a Baghdad where most of the population was living in abject poverty and squalor, and viewed this British-style 'Court' spectacle with a mixture of disdain and ribald amusement.

To Iraqis, the monarchy appeared alien, not just because of its foreign origins, but because of its silly mimicking of British court manners, too. Faisal I hardly knew the country when he arrived, and spoke a different and hardly understandable dialect of Arabic. He himself understood the Iraqi accent even less. In later years, 'Abdulillah, Faisal's nephew who came to live in Iraq after being evicted from the Hijaz when his father lost his kingdom to Ibn Sa'ud, did not even bother to take up Iraqi citizenship until after he was named regent, preferring to cling to his Hijazi nationality instead.[6] This royal scene did not change except in two instances: one was when Ghazi became king, and espoused national causes and an anti-British stance; and two, when his son, Faisal II, was crowned, and gave the population new hope for a future without 'Abdulillah's sinister meddling in the country's affairs. Towards the end, however, the unpopularity of the monarchy was manifest. When a royal would pass on the streets of Baghdad, there was never more than a smattering of lukewarm applause. And when Faisal II became engaged to the Egyptian-Ottoman princess, Fazilet, the Nizam of Hyderabad, her relative by marriage and a contemporary of Faisal's at Harrow, on a visit to the king in Baghdad shortly before the revolution, had decided to go to see a film at a local cinema. When he returned to Turkey, he advised Fazilet's family to break off her engagement to Faisal. He told them that at the cinema in Baghdad he had attended, Faisal and 'Abdulillah's pictures when flashed on the screen during the playing of the national anthem had been met by raucous booing.[7] Another ominous reflection was made by 'Abd al-Razzaq al-Hasani, the noted and prolific Iraqi chronicler, who wrote that as crown prince, 'Abdulillah had had his own eye on the Iraqi throne and was not about to hand it over to the boy Faisal. According to Hassani, 'Abdulillah was not keen on Faisal marrying at all, as that might risk producing a male heir to the throne, which would have relegated him at once to a secondary role. 'Abdulillah hoped that if he could continue to delay such a marriage and, consequently, delay the possible birth of an heir, Faisal, who suffered from severe asthma, might even succumb to an attack of it and die, leaving the scene for 'Abdulillah, as crown prince, to become king instead. According to Hassani, this was a well-established rumour among knowledgeable people in Iraq and indeed was often repeated in private by Prince Zeid bin Hussain, Faisal I's brother, and uncle to 'Abdulillah, to his intimates.[8] When 'Abdulillah got wind of these fast-spreading rumours about his reasons for delaying Faisal's marriage, he quickly initiated contact with the Moroccan royal family for a possible union between Mohammed V's daughter, Princess Lalla Aicha, and Faisal. The Moroccan princess, however, threw cold water over the whole idea.[9] This episode is quoted in full in the memoirs of 'Ahmad Mukhtar Baban, a former prime minister and one of the closest people to the Iraqi throne.[10] The Moroccan side of the story was confirmed to the author by Princess Lalla Aicha herself, in a private meeting in July 2010, in Rabat. The princess said that although she had gone through the motions of meeting with Faisal's family, who had come to ask for her hand in Paris, she never had any intention of trading a liberated existence in Morocco for a life in purdah in Baghdad.

The Iraqi constitution that was drawn up was farcical. It was only a pretence at democracy; it gave the monarch dictatorial powers, which the British then could manipulate from behind the scenes to serve their own interests. Faisal I was a nationalist, but his attempt at kingship was that of an unsuccessful juggler, hopelessly trying to reconcile nationalist aims with the realpolitik of a British colonial presence. He was also the product of an old-fashioned Ottoman style of leadership, which was top-down and authoritarian. This was not a style of government that would have endeared him to democrats. His style of governance (both in Syria and Iraq) was flawed, and eventually failed even by his own admission, judging by his account in the secret memorandum he distributed to those closest to him.[11]

This style of government, consisting of prime ministers and ministers (all of whom had to be both pro-palace and pro-British in order to keep their membership in this select club) saw its first danger signal with the 1936 coup of Bakr Sidqi. It should have been clear from the population's massive support for both the coup and King Ghazi that the whole governing system needed to be overhauled to allow for the emergence of the type of democracy that had been advocated by *al-'Ahali*. But this was not to be. In fairness, the Iraqi people themselves were partly responsible for the coup's failure because of their penchant for divisiveness and their inability to unite under one banner. Five years later, the Rashid 'Ali coup of 1941 and the bitter Anglo-Iraqi War took place. Regardless of what foreign accounts or pro-palace writers have said about this coup, the case was that the whole Iraqi nation stood behind its army during its short-lived war with Britain. The regime fled the country (but pointedly not the infant King Faisal II who remained in-country with his coterie) and was only returned to it with British assistance. It was from then on viewed by the Iraqi public as having betrayed the nation in its hour of need in the most ignoble fashion.

The 1941 coup was the event that set the scene for 'Abdulillah to resume his role as regent, but this time with vengeance and vindictiveness. This was to make him the most detested figure in the Iraqi royal family.[12] He stripped Rashid 'Ali of his personal and financial assets, and insisted on the execution of the four 'Golden Square' colonels. 'Abdulillah simply could not understand what every citizen of Iraq understood so clearly: that all of Iraq's army was at war with Britain, and not just a small pocket of revolutionaries seeking to oust the monarchy. Both Nuri and 'Abdulillah were seriously marked by the event. It can be said that from that point on in Iraqi history, the two men formed an unholy alliance which manifested itself in the catastrophic decisions they took regarding Iraq and its people. Such decisions were to push Iraq inexorably towards revolution.

On the eve of the revolution, Iraq had been reduced to nothing more than a police state. Corruption was widespread: ministers, their sons and relatives amassed wealth that was way out of proportion to their government salaries. Compliant businessmen were allowed a virtual monopoly on big contracts, with a kick-back system involving cabinet ministers and members of parliament, together with innumerable parasites all the way down the food-chain. It was public knowledge who the corrupt ministers were; also public knowledge was the behaviour of their sons in Baghdad night-clubs, who took it upon themselves to break the law shamelessly in Baghdad's streets, with no fear of reprisal. This was a tradition that was later revived by Saddam's sons, who set new and obscene levels of abuse of authority.

Worse still, Iraq was at the nadir of its political fortunes, if, indeed, it had any left at all. The regime was being savaged from all sides. From the opposition parties that now had to operate underground; from Nasser and the vitriolic attacks by *Sawt al-Arab*; and from most other Arab countries, which despised Iraq's singular involvement in the Baghdad Pact. Nuri, although at the apex of his power, had become hopelessly out of touch with the facts on the ground. He apparently thought that he was only opposed by a negligible minority—most of whom he thought communist, his overriding and peculiar obsession—and that he was still firmly in control. A favourite saying of his was '*dar al-sayyid ma'muna*' (the master's house is safe). He viewed anyone with an even mildly liberal opinion as a communist. This endeared him to the Americans, who tended to embrace anyone as neurotic about communism as they were. It also served as cover-up for the country's corrosive corruption, in that any criticism of this state of affairs could be dismissed as being communist-inspired. Caractacus writes that: 'From his (Nuri's) point of view, his critics were interfering in the specialized business of government. It was not for ordinary citizens to have opinions about what was done by their rulers, or about what went on in their country. They must be punished. Probably he was not vindictive like 'Abdulillah. Cruelty for Nuri served a purpose... Nuri al-Sa'id seemed to be a tyrant of the most classic and traditional kind'.[13]

Nuri now unleashed a campaign of terror in the country, where the police and the army were entitled to intrude into anyone's privacy or home with utter impunity. Nuri's repetitive orders to round up the 'usual suspects' (as in the film *Casablanca*) became a disagreeable feature of many an Iraqi's life. Those imprisoned suffered the worst form of human rights abuse. In prisons such as the now notorious Abu Ghraib, men were locked up in tiny cells with no windows and were allowed no exercise. The only outing a prisoner could make was to a water closet. Those in solitary confinement literally rotted in their cells, exactly as prisoners later did under Saddam Hussein. As a result, by 1958, most men with any political or fighting spirit had been cowed and broken in Iraq.

Khalil Kanna—Nuri's supposed heir apparent, and a relative by marriage—gave a perceptive evaluation of Nuri in his memoir. In successive chapters on the revolution, the first of which he aptly titled 'The Beginning of the End', Kanna states that Nuri thought of Iraq as a father might think of a child. He (Nuri) felt responsible for its upbringing, and for its disciplining if necessary. Nuri's shortcoming, according to Kanna, was his love of power at any price, which eventually spelled his downfall. Kanna believed Nuri's worst trait was that of over-confidence. He surrounded himself with sycophants and profiteers, although he (himself), in the author's view, was honest to a fault.[14]

It is not within the scope of this book to detail the actual planning and execution of the revolution. However, it had a huge impact on prospects for a democratic future in Iraq and certain relevant aspects need to be recounted nevertheless. Perhaps a convenient starting point would be a description of the formation of a group of Iraqi army officers, who styled themselves upon and even took the name of their Egyptian counterparts, the 'Free Officers'. It is a sad reflection on Iraqi political life and its characteristic of divided loyalties that the two officers that soon emerged as leaders of the coup—'Abd al-Karim Qassem and 'Abd al-Salam 'Arif—had both been protégés till the bitter end of leading men in the monarchy. Qassem was a protégé of Nuri's (who took to calling him by the intimate nickname of 'Karrumi'), and 'Arif was a protégé of General Rafiq 'Arif (no relation), chief of the general staff. Furthermore, one of the plotters, Lieutenant-Colonel Wasfi Tahir, had been Nuri's personal Aide-de-Camp. The plotters must themselves have experienced the feeling of such divided loyalties as all army officers then had to take an oath of loyalty to king and country. The Free Officers, however, must have harboured such intense ill-feelings towards the monarchy and its supporters that they abrogated this moral promise to serve the king, by considering that they were serving their country and their people instead. Another factor, suggested by the historian Caractacus, is that few men would jeopardize their entire careers, if not their lives, to publicly denounce what they disapproved of in such an outright manner. In the case of the Free Officers, it took some mental toughness on their part to be able to maintain seemingly-conformist behaviour in public, whilst secretly plotting the overthrow of a regime that they—like most other segments of Iraqi society—had come to hate.[15]

The Free Officers, unfortunately, have left no record of their deliberations in the period in which they planned the revolution (minutes etc.) for the obvious reasons of security. A researcher therefore cannot determine with any precision how specific the aims of the revolution were at that nascent stage, and/or what direction the officers would have liked them to take. What has survived are the personal recollections of some of the Free Officers (though many were not senior enough to be writing first-hand and not through hearsay), and the testimony of those Free Officers who appeared before the infamous Mahdawi 'Peoples' Court'. The officers had apparently agreed (some, it is said, tacitly) to abide by a 'Pact' (*Mithaq*) that supposedly embodied the aims of the revolution. Other officers deny that such a pact existed in written form, but agree that it was only agreed verbally. The aims, written down or not, were the following:

- Iraq should be declared a republic.
- The government should be a parliamentary democracy.
- Nuri al-Sa'id and 'Abdulillah should be eliminated (either by trial or by outright execution), but the young King Faisal II should be spared.
- A civilian prime minister should be appointed (the names of Kamil Chadirchi, Hikmat Sulaiman and Rashid 'Ali were considered).
- Iraq should subscribe to the UN Declaration on Human Rights.

- The country should declare its neutrality in world affairs.
- Agrarian Reform should be introduced to end the state of feudalism in the country.
- Reform of the educational, health and cultural systems in the country should take place, with the state assuming responsibility for its success.
- The Kurdish demand for autonomy should be addressed, and satisfied by more decentralization but not by the granting of full autonomy.

Opinions are mostly unanimous that the officers' outlook—apart from their wish to topple the monarchy—was politically simplistic and strategically ill-conceived. Many of them adhered to widely-differing political affiliations. It soon became apparent that this lack of political cohesion in their outlooks was to spell trouble for the revolution. Qassem leaned towards the NDP; 'Arif and Rif'at Haj Sirri held Pan-Arab ideas and advocated immediate union with the UAR. Others, like Wasfi Tahir and Isma'il 'Ali, leaned towards the communists, while Mahdi 'Ammash was a Ba'th Party supporter.

Although the officers may have been political lightweights in seeking to formulate a proper working ideology to guide their revolution, they did, nevertheless, initiate secret contacts with all the opposition parties. In that sense, they probably wished to hand over the political compass and to delegate the future direction of the government to a civilian leadership—if indeed they did wish to keep their promise of steering clear of politics. It is only after the revolution that a number of politicians told of their individual contacts with the Free Officers' group. In his memoir, for example, Mohammed Hadid writes that in 1956, he was contacted by Rashid Mutlaq—a business associate of Hadid's and a democrat—to inform him that something was afoot in the army, and that a movement to topple the regime was by then a work-in-progress. Mutlaq enquired whether Hadid was prepared to meet Qassem who wished to ask of Hadid—perhaps relying on his financial and economic expertise—the specific time-frame that the country could hope to survive if all external sources of finance dried up after a coup. Although Hadid never met Qassem until after the revolution, he did send word to him (via Mutlaq) that, in his estimate, and with strict cutbacks on spending and an overall tightening of the economy, the country could still survive for six months.[16]

In early September 1956, Hussein Jamil met with Hadid and Chadirchi to inform them that a senior army officer (through a mutual friend that he did not name) had contacted him. Nuri al-Sa'id was prime minister at the time, and the army officer intimated to Hussain that an army movement was afoot to remove Nuri from office. He wished to know whether the NDP would be willing to support this movement. The three NDP leaders thought it wise not to commit themselves or their party yet, but would review their position if the movement did indeed manage to progress. The subject never came up again, except that very much later (in the 1980s), Jamil confided in an interview he gave to the Iraqi press that the army officer referred to was Qassem himself, who had despatched Rashid Mutlaq (who came from Jamil's neighbourhood) to seek his advice. Qassem asked if Jamil would accept the premiership of the new government. He also requested that Jamil travel to Egypt to meet Gamal Abdel-Nasser to seek his support for the planned coup. In the interview, Jamil stated that he did go to Egypt and did meet with Nasser, who offered total support for the movement.[17]

Hadid, on the other hand, was asked by Qassem—yet again via the conduit of Mutlaq—to meet with Nasser to ask him specifically for Egypt's support and for that of the Soviet Union. Nasser was to be asked personally to seek the support of the USSR and, more crucially, to determine on behalf of Qassem the extent to which it would commit to countering any Anglo-American move to thwart the revolution. Hadid informed Chadirchi (who was in jail at the time) of this request and both decided that Hadid should proceed with it. Hadid met with Nasser in Cairo and briefed him fully on the internal political situation. He said that the political opposition—left and right—including the NDP, IP, Ba'th and ICP, had grouped secretly under the banner of a National Union Front; and that he (Hadid) had been asked by a senior army officer, Abdal-Karim Qassem—one of the leaders of the Free Officers' movement—to inform Nasser that a movement to topple the regime was in preparation. Qassem wished Nasser to know that he considered the unqualified support of Egypt, political and material, as absolutely critical to the success of this Iraqi movement. He therefore needed to know the potential extent of such support. Hadid also conveyed to the Egyptian president Qassem's request for Nasser to personally seek an undertaking from the Soviet Union to intervene to foil any attempt, military or otherwise, by outside forces to crush the revolution. Nasser told Hadid that Egypt would stand fully behind the movement, as it would behind any movement against foreign alliances such as the Baghdad Pact. Nasser also undertook to seek the required assurances from the Soviet Union.

Hadid intimated to Nasser's aide who was escorting him back to his hotel, and who was aware of the content of Hadid's meeting with Nasser, that as the National Union Front in Iraq was working underground, they were lacking in liquid funds to finance their activities, as they could not risk open banking operations because of the government's scrutiny and wide net of spies. Hadid then travelled to Beirut to join his family on a private visit. Three days later, Hamid Franjiyya, a former cabinet minister and a leading Lebanese nationalist leader, contacted Hadid at his hotel (though Hadid had no idea how Franjiyya knew where he was actually staying) and asked to meet with him. Franjiyya came to Hadid's hotel and handed him a packet of Iraqi dinars. He said that this was from Mohammed Fu'ad Jalal, Nasser's aide—the same aide who had escorted Hadid back to his hotel in Cairo. Hadid duly delivered the funds to those individuals responsible for finances in the National Union Front.

Hadid and Jamil were not the only Iraqi opposition leaders that the officers made contact with. Siddiq Shanshall of the IP was in contact with the officers, as was 'Adil Salam of the ICP. Furthermore, judging from the memoirs of the few Free Officers who wrote years after the events, it seems that every faction among the officers had asked a favourite Iraqi politician to go visit Nasser on a 'personal' basis, to extract from him a message of support for the revolution.

By the spring of 1958, Mutlaq contacted Hadid again, telling him that Qassem was now pressing to receive a reply from the NDP—and from Hadid personally—as to whether the party was committed to the revolutionary movement or not. If not, Qassem told Hadid via Mutlaq, then he (Qassem) would not give the order to mount the coup. Qassem said that such a coup would simply fail if it did not have the unqualified support of the opposition parties, as only they could guarantee the support of the public. Qassem thought that such support might not be forthcoming if the military were to embark on its mission alone. By this same reasoning, Qassem said that it was essential that the government of the revolution be a civilian one that would enjoy the support of the public.

Hadid consulted with the other major opposition party, the IP. He and Siddiq Shanshall, the IP general secretary, then went to see Chadirchi in prison, to decide whether to join the new government or not.[18]

Chadirchi was supportive of the coup but hesitant about involving the NDP at the initial stage of the revolution. He was still in a state of denial about the Bakr Sidqi coup of 1936, and did not wish to repeat the same mistakes. Thus he preferred that the army should govern the country for a period, before transferring government to civilian leaders. Hadid and Shanshall told Chadirchi that the military were adamant that the politicians, and specifically the National Union Front (NUF), should go into this operation hand in hand with them or else the coup leaders would simply abort the whole operation. Hadid and Shanshall had concluded, and told Chadirchi so, that if the military aborts this particular coup, that would not mean that another military group might not mount its own splinter movement, with political goals and objectives that were unknown to the NUF and might even turn out to be anathema to it. At least with Qassem, the NUF was being asked to lead the revolution, and implement their political aims and objectives. After much deliberation, a decision was taken to back the revolutionaries, and for Hadid and Shanshal to join the new government.[19] This decision was relayed at once to Qassem via Mutlaq.

Despite their insistence that the NUF should enter the scene as the new government of the revolution, the military chose not to deal with the NUF as a whole, but rather deal with each NUF leader separately. No NUF meeting by all its component groups seems to have occurred for the purpose of comparing notes, although all knew of the on-going individual contacts. The sole exception was when Mohammed Mahdi Kubba, the IP leader, stated in an NUF meeting in early 1957 that certain army units coming back from Jordan were crossing Baghdad upon their return, and might well be attempting a coup while in the city. Nothing ever came of that, and this possible first attempt was never mentioned in the few memoirs that the Free Officers have left.

The authorities seemed to have been totally unaware that the entire military-political body in the country now agitated for revolution. Several warning lights had come up and though some action was taken, Nuri al-Sa'id continued to stubbornly believe in his mantra that 'there was no one yet born who could kill Nuri'. Several incidents did occur that should have alerted the authorities. Most visible of all was the case of Qassem himself, whose conduct had been reported to Nuri as suspicious. Qassem was summoned to Nuri's office to explain his behaviour, but he managed to sweet-talk himself out of the situation, relying on the fact that he continued to enjoy protégé status with Nuri.

Further reports about Qassem were again passed to Nuri, but the latter had such a close relationship with Qassem that he simply ignored them. Similarly, General Rafiq 'Arif, chief of the general staff, was warned about his protégé, Colonel 'Abd al-Salam 'Arif's, own suspicious activities, but he too was beyond reproach as far as the general was concerned. Col. Rifa't Haj Sirri, one of the first Free Officers, was hauled before Nuri and accused of suspicious activities. Sirri pleaded his innocence and Nuri, probably due to loyalty to Sirri's uncle who was the former prime minister, Jamil Madfa'i, simply decided it best to retire Sirri from the army, warning him that 'in case you ever succeed in your coup, remember that all you and your cohorts will achieve, is to build hanging blocks for each other'.[20] Nuri's words were to prove sadly prophetic, as later events would show.

A meeting the Free Officers held at Qadhimain (a suburb of Baghdad) in a garden which belonged to the brother of a Free Officer (Ismail'Arif) was leaked to the authorities. This obliged the chief of staff to re-locate many of the officers to desk jobs rather than risk taking harsher measures that might have ignited powerful sentiments amongst an already highly charged corps of younger men. This move to re-locate the officers certainly had its effect. It paralyzed the movement, reducing it to splinter groups that had to make separate plans for a revolution that never seemed to see the light of day, until the movement managed to regroup in 1957–8. In an incident, whether deliberate or accidental, but which was soon attributed to one of the so-called splinter groups, a bomb was fired at a tent where Faisal, 'Abdulillah and Nuri were observing army manoeuvres in Western Ramadi. It was later said that the bomb was fired by the officers to remind Qassem that he now should proceed with his movement, although the investigation that followed revealed that it was an accidental firing by a soldier.

The British were not standing still either. Their intelligence both in-house and in-country from their Iraqi agents was informing them all the while that something was afoot. In one telling incident, Mohammed Hadid was invited for tea at 'Aziz Yamulki's house. Yamulki, a Kurd, had been a high-ranking officer during the 1936 Sidqi coup. When he arrived there, Hadid was taken aback to find Sam Falle, the oriental secretary at the British embassy, who had well-known links to British intelligence, there too. The conversation turned to the worsening situation in Iraq and the increasing stranglehold the regime was applying on civil liberties. In all likelihood, Yamulki (an ex-revolutionary himself and still in touch with fellow-officers) may have gotten an inkling of a possible coup to be mounted by the Free Officers. It was quite obvious to Hadid that Yamulki and Falle had become more than acquaintances, and Yamulki may well have hinted to Falle of his suspicions of a coup-in-the-making. Yamulki had invited Hadid to tea without telling him that Falle (whom Hadid had met socially at embassy functions) would be there, in order to see whether Hadid, a leading figure in the NDP, would deny knowledge of any such coup. Falle quickly warmed to his subject. He put it to Hadid that since the country was up in arms against the regime, was it not logical to assume that dissatisfaction had reached the military too, and that there was now a movement afoot to launch a coup, since there were precedents in Iraq of the military intervening in politics as a last resort. Hadid simply replied 'Who knows?' and soon afterwards left the two to their tea-party. Shortly after the revolution of 1958 had taken place, Falle visited Hadid at his home to enquire about the aims and objectives of the revolution. During the course of the conversation, Hadid turned to Falle and said: 'Do you see now? The answer to the question you asked at Yamulki's house was that there *was* a military movement at the time to do away with the monarchy'.[21]

In fact Falle had sensed enough that day from Hadid's reply to prepare a detailed report for the ambassador, Sir Michael Wright, in which he warned of a possible revolutionary trend emerging. There was certainly a pressing need for this eventuality to be addressed by the governing authority, as well as by the British themselves. He suggested that the palace mount its own 'white' revolution by appointing a new cabinet with an able army officer acceptable to both the palace and the opposition parties as prime minister. The new government should include a wide selection of opposition leaders and other officers popular in the army in order to ensure the army's loyalty. Nuri should be retired from politics, as he was now too old and too out of touch, and Crown Prince 'Abdulillah, who was uniformly disliked, Falle warned, should be sent away to the United States as ambassador, so as to allow the young king to become his own man. The young king and a new government might just about be able to save the country from escalating public discontent. Falle suggested that the British ambassador should adopt a hands-on approach to dealing with Nuri and 'Abdulillah in the manner proposed. The proposal was communicated to the latter but, according to Majid Khadduri, 'Falle's advice seemed to have fallen on deaf ears'![22]

Sir Michael Wright and Sam Falle visited 'Abdallah Bakr, chief of the royal palace, a month before the revolution, seeking to impress upon him the need for radical change. Majid Khadduri, who interviewed him many years after the revolution (in 1966 and again in 1968), says that Bakr told him that 'Sir Michael almost prophetically gave warning that if reforms were not carried out, there would no longer be a monarchy'.[23] On a separate visit to Bakr, Sam Falle warned that reform in the political and social spheres had become a necessity if the regime was to survive at all and that the days of illiterate tribal sheikhs sitting in parliament as a sphinx-like support team to rubber-stamp whatever the government of the day put before them were long over.[24]

The story of Iraq on the eve of revolution would not be complete without mentioning certain tangential but *a propos* issues. The first of these is the still unanswered question of whether the Anglo-American intelligence services operating in the area had any inkling of what was about to take place. Rumour has it that the regent, while attending a dinner at the Rihab Palace on the eve of the revolution, was passed a note which seems to have distressed him enough for him to rush to a telephone and attempt to advance the plans for the royal party's departure from the country to the very next day. Faisal, 'Abdulillah and Nuri were all, in any case, scheduled to leave for Istanbul to attend a Baghdad Pact meeting, as well as to finalize arrangements for the king's wedding to the Egyptian-Ottoman princess, Fazilet. 'Abdulillah apparently spoke to the pilot who was to fly the party there, but the latter claimed that the flight could not be advanced, as the plane required certain technical checks. Iraqi memoirs in which this episode is recounted, however, discount this account, as they claim that had 'Abdulillah known about, or even suspected, imminent action by the army, he would have initiated immediate checks and counter-checks to determine the authenticity of such reports. Furthermore, it would seem that both foreign and local intelligence services were taken by complete surprise when the revolution occurred, despite their suspicions that something was brewing.

King Hussain in his memoir, *Uneasy Lies the Head*,[25] claims that he was the purveyor of a warning passed on 'personally' to King Faisal, regarding a plot that intended to overthrow both his own and his cousin's regimes. The Iraqi chief of staff, General Rafiq 'Arif, was despatched by the palace (in Baghdad) to Amman, where he was briefed on King Hussain's intelligence report. 'Arif, somewhat rashly as it transpired, dismissed the report as unlikely, insisting that the loyalty of the Iraqi army was beyond reproach.

Many have posited that British intelligence did know of the plot, if indeed they were not an actual party to it. This theory concerned the union between Iraq and Jordan that Nuri al-Sa'id wanted Kuwait to join. Kuwait had become a vital factor in Nuri's mind that could contribute to the success of such a union, and thus balance out that between Egypt and Syria. It would increase considerably the economic power that Iraq and Kuwait could jointly deploy. Kuwait, however, turned Nuri down. This only served to heighten his ire towards the Kuwaitis.[26] In fact, Nuri then began making threatening noises concerning Kuwait. This raised serious alarm bells with the British, who were not about to allow Kuwait to be lost to some last-ditch, ill-fated, notion that Nuri had concocted for a Hashemite union meant to combat Nasser. According to the theorists of this scenario, the British on balance decided to lose Nuri rather than risk losing Kuwait. According to this version of events, the British were either participants in the 1958 coup, or at the very least, did nothing to stop it. But Mohammed Hadid in his memoir discounts such a scenario as being implausible, seeing that the British had vast interests in Iraq to protect, and needed to maintain the monarchy and the status quo—including a prize asset such as Nuri himself—to continue guaranteeing those interests.[27] Indeed, documents released after the expiry of the Official Secrets Act reveal that both British and American Intelligence were taken totally by surprise by the revolution on the day that it happened. The event even became a case study for future agents to be more alert in situations such as those that prevailed in Iraq at the time, in order to avoid such nasty surprises and intelligence failures in the future. In the case of the British, not acting more forcibly on the intelligence on the ground provided by their embassy in Baghdad must have grated back in Whitehall, seeing that Iraq could have averted revolution as a result. Had the National Union Front been empowered under the plan suggested by the ambassador and Sam Falle, the opposition would have had no need to cooperate with the coup leaders, of which they knew little and were weary of after the 1936 experience.

As for simultaneous coups hatched by various army officers that have since come forward with memoirs of their endeavours, many might certainly be based on fact, but few of them ever had any chance of succeeding. The only really serious attempt—and the only one that might possibly have succeeded—was the one that came about as a result of the interaction between the Free Officers led by Qassem and 'Arif, and the National Union Front of Iraqi opposition leaders. However, two other endeavours that were reported after the revolution are worth recounting. The first was revealed by General Ghazi al-Daghestani, one of Iraq's most brilliant soldiers and Qassem's immediate superior. Daghestani, who was a loyal supporter of the monarchy, claimed that he had planned for a 'Palace Revolution' in which a new government would be named that would be supportive of the king, but which would brush aside Nuri and 'Abdulillah and strip them of all power.[28] Furthermore, it is claimed that Daghestani was approached by Lieutenant Colonel Rajab 'Abd al-Majid to lead the Free Officers' movement. Daghestani declined, remaining loyal to the monarchy to the end. He nevertheless respected the confidentiality of the offer by not revealing it to the authorities at the time.[29]

The second endeavour was an indirect, if not somewhat risky, attempt by the Free Officers to recruit the chief of the general staff, General Rafiq 'Arif, to head their movement. This endeavour is still shrouded in mystery but it might well have been likely, given that 'Arif was aware of the officers' movement, since he was the one ordered by the king to investigate rumours that had reached the palace of an impending coup, together with the actual names of the officers involved. 'Arif was irritated that outside intelligence sources were bypassing him to go directly to the palace, since he had total faith in his own army intelligence. He therefore went on to defend the suspected officers in no uncertain terms. It is claimed that 'Arif preferred to remain silent regarding the suspicious activities of the Free Officers because he knew that dissent in the army had reached an unstoppable point by then. It was known that he had harboured hopes of being made prime minister under the monarchy, but had never been elevated to that position, despite the promises that may have been made to him. Whether it was for selfish reasons or otherwise, the consensus opinion has been that 'Arif had finally lost all faith in the regime. He no doubt saw that it was a hopeless undertaking—from an army point of view, at least— to seek to defend it any further.

12

THE 1958 REVOLUTION

THE BALANCE SHEET

The Iraqi Revolution of 1958 ranks as the most important event in Iraq's modern history with the exception of the American invasion of 2003, which must count as an external event. For reasons of limited space, this book cannot include details of the planning and execution of the coup itself. However, for the reader, there is a plethora of books and memoirs about the topic—the most important primary sources being, naturally enough, written in Arabic. The purpose of this chapter is to evaluate the achievements and failures of the revolution in the light of the involvement of the country's democratic forces with the military to guide the revolution to its declared aims.

On 14 July 1958, Baghdad woke up to see the army strategically placed and already in control of all the major government establishments, as well as all the arteries leading in and out of the capital. By 6am the royal palace was surrounded, as was Nuri al-Sa'id's house, though the latter managed to escape, disguised in a woman's *abayya*.[1] 'Abd al-Salam 'Arif had led the army into the capital, while Qassem stayed behind as an auxiliary force at his divisional headquarters in Miqdadiyya, ready to march on the capital if 'Arif encountered resistance. At 6.30am Baghdad Radio went on air to announce communiqué number one, which had been prepared beforehand by Qassem and 'Arif, and possibly by others too. It was read out by 'Arif. He announced the downfall of the monarchy, and declared Iraq a republic, now headed by a three-man Sovereignty Council, composed by a member of each of Iraq's three main groups: the Shi'a, the Sunnis and the Kurds, in order to represent the unity of the country.[2] The selection of the cabinet was also announced by 'Arif. This, too, was something the officers had dealt with during the planning stage of the revolution. The cabinet was remarkable for its inclusiveness, in that almost all the opposition parties were represented. Two cabinet posts went to the NDP (Mohammed Hadid at Finance and Hudaib Hajj Hmud at Agriculture); one cabinet post each to the IP (Siddiq Shanshal at Guidance) and the Ba'th Party (Fu'ad Rikabi at Development); a post to a Marxist (Ibrahim Kubba at Economy); a post to a Kurd (Baba 'Ali at Communications); a post to an independent ('Abd al Jabbar Jumard at Foreign Affairs), and one post only to a Free Officer (Naji Talib at Social Affairs)—and possibly only in order to kick Talib upstairs.

Phebe Marr describes the composition of the cabinet as a 'master stroke' for its inclusivity and its real connection to Iraq's political, religious, ethnic and sectarian spectrum. She writes that the cabinet propitiated the entire opposition movement. Because of the high regard that most of the opposition leaders commanded, the regime was lent instant legitimacy and respect that would have been difficult to achieve as a mere army movement.[3] It would be fair to say that whatever befell the Qassem regime in its later stages, Iraq could not have gotten off to a better start, given the tectonic upheaval brought about by the 1958 Revolution.

Communiqué number one set out the aims of the revolution. These were based on the National Pact but, surprisingly enough, did not emphasize the Arab nationalist view of entering into immediate union with Nasser's United Arab Republic (UAR). Rather, the communiqué stressed Iraqi unity. 'One homeland and one people', the communiqué stated clearly at the outset. A republic was declared, and this was to be run by a government elected by the people and for the people. In another plea for Iraqi political homogeneity, the republic was to 'uphold the complete unity of the country'. Whether this was a deliberate hint to Egypt and to the Pan-Arab movement that Iraq would take its time over any 'union' with the UAR is not specifically known. What is known, though, is that the communiqué certainly stressed— and repeatedly—Iraq's 'separate existence', with mere lip service paid to its association with other Arab or Islamic countries. There was a reference to Iraq's adherence to United Nations principles, as well as to Iraq's neutrality *vis-à-vis* the two super powers along the lines of the Bandung Conference resolutions.

The news of the revolution was met first with incredulity which instantly turned into spontaneous jubilation. The streets of Baghdad were flooded by people from all walks of society all united in their opposition to the *ancien régime*. Indeed, it was noteworthy that the power structures which had supported the monarchy simply failed to react to protect it, as the police—who certainly could have resisted a small army force such as the one led by 'Arif, and who were more than used to putting down large popular uprisings—preferred to remain inert. The army units loyal to the monarchy showed no resistance either, and Baghdad was taken virtually without opposition.

Not even a brief account of the revolution such as this one can be made without a reference to the ugly fate that befell the royal family and Nuri al-Sa'id. To this day, opinions are divided on whether the massacre of the members of the monarchy was committed on the orders of the revolutionaries or not. Many an Iraqi army officer has written memoirs claiming to have been an eyewitness to such a decision being taken. The more senior officers' memoirs, however, cast doubt on those of the junior officers as being unreliable and self-serving. There was no question that the arrest of 'Abdulillah and Nuri—if not their immediate liquidation—was high on the officers' agenda. The officers had not forgotten previous coups (those of 1936 and 1941), when both these men had been returned to power by the British; and in the case of 1941, by an occupying British army. The fate that befell the king remains to this day controversial. It is still not known whether his assassination had been premeditated or not.[4]

Mohammed Hadid, in his memoir, writes that outside the tight circle of Qassem and 'Arif themselves, nobody knew what the plan to deal with the royal family actually was. Was it a planned assassination or simply a vengeful event that occurred on the spur of the turbulent moment? Hadid adds that neither Qassem nor 'Arif left memoirs that shed any light on this particular topic. In Hadid's view, the liquidation of 'Abdulillah and Nuri had most probably been planned, but certainly not in the ghastly manner in which the assassinations were ultimately carried out. Nor were the revolutionaries necessarily to blame for the ensuing mob hysteria and the later snatching of their bodies, which were dragged through the streets of Baghdad till their very features rubbed off—a grotesque act known as '*sahl*' in Arabic.[5] And though the body of King Faisal was taken immediately for burial in the royal mausoleum (a significant act of sympathy for Faisal and his late father Ghazi), the mutilated one of 'Abdulillah was left hanging from the very same lamp post that the regent had once ordered the corpse of Colonel Sabbagh, leader of the 'Golden Square' movement of 1941, to be hung from. Whether this was a spontaneous act by the mob, or actually ordered by the army as vindication for its humiliation by 'Abdulillah in 1941 may never be known, though later opinions have tended to credit the latter version.

Although many have contextualized that such barbaric acts are typical of revolutions everywhere; and that the French Revolution, for example, had witnessed far worse acts of barbarity and over a far more protracted period, Iraq was to remain tainted by the palace massacres. To this day, those acts continue to associate Iraqis with wanton violence. It is true that a street mob took over as the day of revolution progressed. Fuelled by 'Arif's inflammatory broadcasts, it went on a rampage to destroy all vestiges of British colonial power and of its acolytes—including the statue of General Maude (who had led the British army to occupy Baghdad in 1917). It set fire to the Chancery of the British embassy, and tore down the statue of King Faisal I. The mob then attacked and plundered the royal palace. It disinterred the body of the king, as it did the next day the body of Nuri al-Sa'id. The corpse of 'Abdulillah was handed over to a baying crowd. By noon, the situation was rapidly approaching mayhem. This forced Qassem, now the new commander-in-chief of the army, to declare an emergency and impose a curfew.

If one were able to set the miserable and macabre massacre of the royal family aside, the revolutionaries did restore calm and a return to ordinary life relatively quickly and with minimum loss of life. Uriel Dann, in *Iraq Under Qassem*, writes: 'If we take the background, the casualty list is very short; great credit must be given to 'Abdi (Brigadier Ahmad Saleh 'Abdi, the military governor-general) for restoring a deteriorating situation with the minimum of brute force'. Dann quotes and agrees with Qassem's statement that only nineteen people—including the royals—were killed in the revolution.[6] Given that a country's political anger had boiled over after thirty-eight years of political frustration and communal hurt, a few hours of savage mayhem were sadly only to be expected.[7]

216

It is the contention of this book that, despite the pitfalls inherent in imposing change through the military, the best democratic opportunity for Iraq presented itself with the 1958 Revolution.[8] For the first time in its short history, the country had a government that represented all its major ethnic, sectarian or religious groups; its opposition parties that had stood up to the *ancien régime*, as well as its army—which had always been a shadowy partner in the running of Iraq's affairs from the very first day of its 'invention' as a country.[9] Khadduri writes that: 'the masterly fashion in which the July Revolution was carried out, and the relative ease with which the Old Régime was disestablished, raised high hopes that the new régime would wipe out past injustices and open a new era which would provide freedom, prosperity, and progress'.[10] Qassem himself was the product of a Sunni father and a Shi'a-Kurdish mother (or a Fayliyya), a fact that he announced proudly on innumerable occasions.[11]

The most pressing problem facing the new government was the question of international recognition. The first country to recognize the Iraqi republic was the UAR. It immediately sent a new ambassador there, backed up by a strong staff that included 'Abd al-Majid Farid as military attaché. The latter had the lead role in the embassy, but his intrigues and scheming in the early period of post-revolution Iraq had a highly damaging effect on the stability of the government.[12] The Soviet Union was next in recognizing the republic, sending as ambassador the high-flying Grigory Zietsev. This was followed by most of the socialist regimes in Eastern Europe as well as by India and Indonesia—both these non-aligned countries sent dynamic ambassadors to Baghdad who were to leave their mark.

The big issue for the government was to see if and when recognition would be forthcoming from Britain and the United States. 'Abd al-Karim Qassem, possibly advised by Mohammed Hadid, was well aware of 'Abd al-Salam 'Arif's constant fiery rants in public about the revolution and the urgent need to enter union with the UAR, and was therefore careful not to rock the boat further with actions that would seem to threaten Western interests. Although the Baghdad Pact was perceived as dead in the water, there was no actual official withdrawal from it by the new Iraq. Oil agreements as well as all other international commitments were declared to be binding. The government was confident that Britain eventually would come through by recognizing the Iraqi republic. The U.S., however, remained uncomfortable about extending recognition to a regime it knew so little about.[13]

On 31 July 1958, Britain did indeed recognize Iraq. The recognition came after a private meeting between Sam Falle and Mohammed Hadid at the latter's home. Hadid assured Falle of the government's commitment to democratic reform, and of its desire to remain neutral as far as its foreign policy was concerned. Hadid's presence in the government as a leading member of the NDP was no doubt a factor that helped persuade Falle of the stability of the regime. It led him to write in his report to London that the new government was serious about honouring its international relations, that it was reformist in outlook, and that British interests would be best served by recognizing Iraq.[14]

Be that as it may, the revolution began showing signs of fissure almost from its inception. The personal rivalry between Qassem and 'Arif that soon became apparent was only a reflection of the divisions that existed in the broader Free Officers' movement. Although the central committee had unanimously agreed Qassem's selection as leader, it seems that his colleagues had not envisaged him in such a role prior to this selection. This hesitancy derived from the Free Officers' own failure to adhere to any united form of post-revolutionary programme. The political affiliations of these officers were not developed enough to enter national politics or even to remain as part of the political decision-making process. The impulsive behaviour of 'Arif and his half-baked ideas provoked President Nasser, in the days just after the revolution when he met him in Damascus, to exclaim: '*Meen il 'ayyel dah?*' (Who is this rash kid?).[15] Indeed, only weeks after this major and important encounter the rift between Qassem and 'Arif became apparent.

Many of the Free Officers—including Brigadier Nadhim Tabaqchali and Colonel Abd al-Wahhab Shawwaf—only gave Qassem tacit approval as leader, preferring to adopt a wait-and-see policy. They, like Brigadier Naji Talib, saw themselves as alternative (if not better) candidates to Qassem to lead the revolution.[16] Such divided loyalties came to the fore in the revolt mounted by Shawwaf in Mosul. This pitted Shawwaf and Tabaqchali's Pan-Arab group, representing as it did the vested interests of the rich, against Qassem's 'wattani' group, which was supported by the poor, the disenfranchised and by Iraq's minorities.[17] On a more blatantly ideological scale, the Mosul revolt was precipitated in part by a vast invasion of the city by the Peace Partisans, a quasi-communist organization which inflamed Mosul's conservative society, and brought to the fore the split between the Qawmiyyin and the Wattaniyyin. This split may have been an early harbinger for both 'Arif's dismissal and Qassem's eventual execution.

There is a general consensus among Iraqis (understandably excluding most that belonged to the *ancien régime*) that the 1958 Revolution was no mere coup d'état, but an event that had a tectonic impact on the future of Iraq as a nation.[18] For the first time in their short history, Iraqis of all classes and backgrounds felt that there was hope for a bright democratic future and a decent life. They were agreed that a much-hated regime was now got rid of, and with it the heavy burden of Western imperialist designs on Iraq. A feeling of liberation and pride in the country filled the air and pervaded the whole nation. There was a return of control over the country's natural resources, most importantly its oil. It was the first time in centuries that Iraq had been governed by Iraqis for Iraqis.

The American ambassador, Waldermar J. Gallman, chose to view the cataclysmic events of 14 July as a simple seizure of power by a small but determined group, which in no way should be considered a revolution. He saw the demonstrations that accompanied the event as devoid of all spontaneous character, and the 'hordes of utterly jubilant people who took part in them' as a bunch of 'hoodlums' recruited for the event.[19] Hanna Batatu dismisses Gallman's assessment by saying that surely the participation of 100,000 people in the pro-revolutionary demonstrations constituted something more than what Gallman suggests. Batatu goes on to say that revolution, as a happening, is never a peaceful walk in the park, but rather, an 'indelicate, rough and violent affair'. Although Batatu agrees that the 14 July events were organized in secret by a small group of determined individuals, in the wider view, these events were no doubt the 'climax of the struggle of a whole generation of the middle class, lower-middle and working classes. It was the culmination of an underlying, deeply-embedded insurrectionary tendency of which the 1936 coup, the military movement of 1941, the *Wathba* of 1948, the Intifada of 1952 and the risings of 1956 were similar manifestations'.[20] Batatu concludes that the 14 July events were a major milestone in Iraqi history—'indeed a glance at the consequences is enough to make us realize we are in the presence of a genuine revolution'.

One can safely make the assumption, therefore, that the Iraqi Revolution was a genuine, massive cry, by a people that inhabited a land cobbled together into a country by a foreign power. Iraqis now were reaching out for nation-statehood under a genuine leadership that would represent their political wishes and aspirations. On paper, this was the most unique opportunity to have presented itself in centuries, when a power take-over was made by them, rather than by a foreign entity that merely wanted to exploit their country's geopolitical location and rich natural resources. Furthermore, the revolution now genuinely offered a 'melting-pot' scenario for the emergence of a new Iraqi identity. This was an opportunity to create a new society, throwing off one that had always been divided by sectarian, religious, racial, class or cultural differences. It now had the chance to become a free, independent country which, while respecting the rights of its various communities, could also be active in the defence of Arab-Islamic issues; would establish gender equality, equalize employment opportunities; fight illiteracy, encourage education, and be in control of its own natural resources. Government would come about by freely-elected officials, who would be accountable to a constitutionally-elected parliament.

All the above and more were on offer in the declared aims of the revolution. And they were certainly not empty promises. Far from it, they were aims taken straight out of the pages of the political programmes of the opposition parties and the banners of their decades-long struggle to establish freedom and democracy in Iraq. It must not be forgotten that the opposition parties had re-aligned themselves into a bloc, which was named 'The National Union Front' (NUF) *al-Jabha al-Wataniyya al-Muttahida.*[21] This bloc—now empowered as the new revolutionary government—held the possibility of delivering on an immense political, social and economic agenda that was well within its grasp.

On paper, a better scenario could not have been written for a revolution to succeed. The military, that had only a superficial grasp of how to go forward, were totally reliant on the civilian opposition leaders for guidance. It was only logical that the military—which had risked so much to mount the coup—should hold portfolios that dealt with internal and external security, plus some minor portfolios handed out to senior officers as sinecures. Otherwise, all cabinet posts were occupied by NUF members. Of critical importance was the fact that Qassem himself was a NDP fellow-traveller. He relied on Mohammed Hadid for advice in the early stages of the revolution and later in the crucial promulgation of the landmark Law 80 which nationalized Iraq's oil industry, and of which Hadid, though already out of office by then, was the architect and author.[22] Hadid was committed to the NUF, as were Independence Party members in government, which included Mehdi Kubba (a member of the Sovereignty Council), and Siddiq Shanshal (the party's general secretary, and minister of guidance). Others, not necessarily party members—such as the Independents' 'Abd al-Jabbar Joumard, minister of foreign affairs, as well as the Marxist Ibrahim Kubba, minister of the economy—were equally committed to the aims of the revolution.

Qassem himself was a perfect fit for the new Iraq. As stated earlier, he was half Sunni Arab and half Kurdish Shi'a. He related emotionally to the under-privileged and poor, because he was one of them. All important books and memoirs have praised his simplicity and his fairness. Adnan al-Pachachi, scion of a distinguished political family, had this to say about Qassem:

Qassem was possessed of great simplicity which much endeared him to people who surrounded him. I toured Baghdad at night with him and like most Baghdadis who loved living at night, we finished up at dawn with a simple breakfast of grilled kebabs brought to us from a simple popular restaurant near Qassem's office... Qassem was loyal to Iraq's cause and appreciated those that were loyal to Iraq like himself. In fact, he dedicated his picture to me with the words: "To Adnan al-Pachachi in appreciation for his loyalty to his country"... Qassem was dedicated to building Iraq into a modern state and to raising the standard of living of the poor to partake in the economic benefits of the country.[23]

Perhaps the last word on Qassem should go to Mohammed Hadid, his closest collaborator in the early years of the revolution:

When I met Qassem and 'Arif for the first time on 15 July 1958 (the day following the revolution), and during subsequent meetings, I was fully persuaded that Qassem was the person who should lead the revolution forward despite the emerging rivalry between him and 'Arif. He was a democrat who displayed poise and an inner calm when dealing with people or situations... Although my cooperation with Qassem barely lasted two years and our future contacts remained limited after that, they did include the oil negotiations that resulted in Law 80 which returned to Iraq its usurped rights. I disagreed with the authoritarian style with which he came to run the country, but I still found him to be a humane, modest and good-hearted person who bore no ill-will towards anyone and a nationalist who wanted to realize benefits for his country and prosperity for his people... In the end he came to run the country as he would his brigade before the revolution which inevitably led him to be overthrown. His demise put paid to the last opportunity Iraq had to put into place a democratic system that was both balanced and moderate. In any case, his regime was better than any other that followed.[24]

If Iraq ever had a democratic moment, this was it. In an atmosphere of unprecedented public optimism, the government got off to a flying start, bringing much promise of social and economic reform. In *Iraq Under Qassem*, Uriel Dann calls this period 'a harvest of socio-economic and socio-political measures that rendered it the golden age of the Qassem era'.[25] Within a fortnight, Mohammed Hadid had set the economic policy of the government as that of a welfare state.[26] A new tax law was introduced to equalize the tax burden, so that citizens would pay their fair share in more equitable taxes. The law was designed to lay the foundations for a stable economy and a stable society, with social justice as its guiding principle. Industry, then relatively small, would receive a fiscal impetus to invest in plant and machinery and would be protected by laws against imports. Several other cabinet ministers were busy upgrading their ministries from sluggish and often corrupt systems that were inherited from the former regime. Many introduced measures typical of a welfare state, such as a compulsory savings scheme where employers and government contributed the lion's share. A mortgage bank was set up to allow easier loan facilities to needy applicants. A rent control act followed, which allowed both landlord and tenant to have a fairer relationship, which included a restriction of the landlord's power to evict tenants unpredictably at will.

Qassem's earliest achievement was to deal immediately with the atrocious housing conditions in which the poor lived, which had been a mark of shame on the previous regime. Particularly shameful were the *sarifas*, or tin shacks, where displaced peasants who had come to seek work in the city lived in the most abject conditions imaginable. There were no sanitation facilities, no running water or utilities of any kind, and disease and pollution were rampant there. Qassem simply bull-dozed this whole area, and put up modern housing facilities in its place for its inhabitants. These stood as an early monument of one of the revolution's greater achievements. By that one social achievement alone, he won the gratitude of the poor forever.[27]

Price controls on foodstuffs were introduced and merchants were scrutinized for excess profits on their products. All low-level government salaries were adjusted upwards to allow a better standard of living for employees. The working day for industrial workers was reduced from nine to eight hours, and overtime was charged at a higher rate. The former method of workers labouring from dawn till dusk on the same pay scale was abolished. All industrial establishments now came under supervision to ensure proper health and safety measures. Labour exchanges were set up all over the country, where employers were under obligation to announce any job vacancies. Social welfare institutions were set up by the appropriate ministries to look after orphans, disabled children, juvenile delinquents and the destitute. All prison sentences were reduced by one fifth, and former methods of whipping and chaining prisoners were abolished. A law designed to bring prostitution under control was brought in, and heavy prison sentences were imposed on procurers, while rehabilitation centres for the prostitutes were set up.

In the time frame of the Qassem era (which lasted no more than four and a half years), and despite the mammoth internal and external problems that emerged within weeks of the revolution, an impressive list of aims were nevertheless achieved. These were:

1. Iraq's exit from the Baghdad Pact. This spelled freedom from Western security schemes that it had been made to join against the will of its people. Extricating Iraq from the Baghdad Pact was top priority for the NUF and, by inference, for the vast majority of Iraq's people. On 24 March 1959, the revolutionary government gave notice of its total withdrawal from the pact.

2. Iraq's exit from the Sterling Area, which had shackled Iraq's finances to the pound sterling.[28] This had helped prop up the British economy and, by leaving it, Iraq could finally liberate its currency and bring it under the control of its own Exchequer and Central Bank.

3. The promulgation of Law 80 which nationalized Iraq's oil, and brought 99.5 per cent of lands that were part of the oil concession under Iraq's sovereign control.[29]

4. The promulgation of the Association Law that regulated the formation and operation of political parties, and political societies, as well as the press and its freedom.[30]

5. The promulgation of the Agrarian Reform Act, which limited unfair landholding and distributed land to needy farmers.[31]

6. The abolition of Tribal Law.[32]

7. The legal acknowledgement of women's rights under the newly passed gender equality law. The law was the first of its kind in the Arab world, and it was further given confirmation by the appointment of Dr. Naziha al-Dulaimi as minister of health—this being the first appointment of a woman to a cabinet post in the Arab world.[33]

8. The active widening of the education process, to include all stages of education—at primary, secondary and university levels.

9. The active widening of health services in all of Iraq to include more hospitals and clinics.

10. The encouragement of workers to insist on their rights, to be bestowed by trade unions and by new vocational laws, as well as the encouragement of students to form their own student unions.

11. The encouragement of professionals such as doctors, lawyers, engineers, teachers, etc., to form their own unions, and to exercise their rights under the law. Free land was even offered by the government in order to build and house such organizations.

12. The improvement of the work conditions of both civil servants and military personnel by the passing of laws that guaranteed them benefits.

13. The creation of urban zones in which professionals could build new homes for themselves with generous financial aid packages from the government.

14. The establishment of a ministry of planning to replace the Development Council (Majlis al-'I'mar) which had acquired a reputation for being under foreign control.

15. The elimination of religious and ethno-sectarian divisions in Iraqi society by the offering of equal educational opportunities to all citizens, as well as equal job opportunities too.

16. The encouragement of national industries by the provision of protection when needed; by increasing investment in real estate development; by increasing the national level of commerce; as well as by offering the maximum number of import licenses to a wide list of merchants.[34]

In summary, the revolution removed every barrier that stood against the advancement of the people of Iraq, be it through class, ethno-sectarian bias, or educational and employment favouritism. It heralded a new era for Iraqis in which they could aspire to build their country on solid foundations.

However, in order to present a true and fair balance sheet of the 14 July Revolution, one must also list the negatives. These negatives became more obvious with time. In the case of the opposition political parties, for example, it was hard to envisage that the vital political cohesion that held them together would come unglued so quickly. The two principal parties—the NDP and the Istiqlal (IP)—failed to see the communists and the Ba'th as being the two elephants in the room. They made a strategic error not to combine and consolidate as one party, as they had planned to do in 1954. After all, they did share more or less the same values and political objectives. But sadly, they suffered from the perennial Iraqi flaw of falling out over who should be leader.[35] Since the Free Officers were unable to deal with complex political issues, they might well have been persuaded to hand over to a united, though transitional, civilian government with a solid programme of reform behind it, in order to transform Iraq into a parliamentary democracy.

Qassem sought to align himself with political moderates right from the outset and make them 'the backbone of his regime'.[36] The NDP especially should have therefore cosseted Qassem from the beginning and maneuvered to dominate the government, conceivably with his blessing. The reasons for the NDP's failure to do so will be returned to further on in this chapter.

The first negative in the balance sheet was certainly the atrocious massacre of the royal family. If ever a saying were true that what starts with blood must end with blood, it was definitely true of the 14 July Revolution. It is telling that every account given by individuals directly implicated in the decision to eliminate the royal family flinched from accepting responsibility for it. The Free Officers had been in touch with all the leading politicians in the opposition, and is it not odd that none of these had demanded what fate awaited the royal family? Surely this should have been a priority topic, as their treatment would reflect on the very character of the revolution. As far as the outside world is concerned, the killings proved to be a major public-relations disaster, quite apart from being a macabre human tragedy. The Free Officers did not seem to have agreed among themselves on a plan of how to dispose of the royal family. Qassem and 'Arif were later to blame each other for what happened. This proved to be an early and horrible harbinger of one of the main weaknesses of the revolutionaries: that they had no fully-developed plan, not just about what to do with the royals, but about what to do in general once their revolution had succeeded.

The second negative was soon to follow. This came in the form of 'Abd al-Salam 'Arif, a loose cannon if ever there was one. The Free Officers did not seem to want anything to do with him when their movement first started, precisely because of his dangerous impulsiveness. But they bowed to Qassem's insistence that he should be allowed to join the movement. Within five days of the revolution, 'Arif had gone rogue and met with Nasser in Damascus, to seek immediate union with the UAR without consulting with Qassem and the RCC. Nasser, ironically enough, had a lot to do with destabilizing the revolution, as he had had with supporting it before it took place.[37] The very fact that Nasser came to Damascus to meet with 'Arif showed ill-judgment on the part of this great leader, in not letting the Iraqi Revolution settle down before discussing critical issues concerning its future. Nasser also placed himself in an adversarial role *vis-à-vis* Qassem, who obviously heard of his encounter with 'Arif. Qassem reprimanded 'Arif for such a maverick move, warning him to remain silent on the question of union until it could be discussed calmly with the revolutionary government.[38]

The issue of whether Iraq should immediately leap into a union with Nasser's UAR opened up a Pandora's Box for the country. By September, 'Arif had outlived his usefulness to Qassem, and was dispatched to Bonn as ambassador. He had pulled a gun on Qassem during a heated argument about 'Arif's deviation from the path of the revolution.[39] The real damage brought about by the Qassem-'Arif conflict was that their conflict now pitted the communists against the Ba'thists. 'Arif's Pan-Arab enthusiasm had made him espouse Ba'thist beliefs, while Qassem—who believed in an Iraq-First policy—first turned to the NDP for support, but when he found it wanting, turned to the communists instead. These were only too happy to lend Qassem a hand. The NDP had not been willing to support Qassem unreservedly without the guarantee that he would take measures to convert his government to a democratically-elected and parliamentary one. However, the NDP may have exposed its own weakness by withholding such support. In so doing, it became increasingly clear that its core support was among the intelligentsia and professional middle classes, but not from the ordinary man on the street. This had always been the private reserve of the communists, a fact that became patently clear to Qassem, who found in the communists a perfect foil to the Ba'thists. They could move the masses; were ready to counter Ba'thist propaganda with a superior one of their own, and were already parading in the streets with pro-Qassem banners. For Qassem, this was an offer of political support that he simply could not refuse. Perhaps this support was to turn into the kiss of death for Qassem. Though he knew that he could eventually get rid of the communists—and eventually did get rid of them, as will be detailed later—he never again managed to regain support among the Pan-Arabists, a political failing that no doubt weakened him fatally.

The third negative was the Mahdawi Court. This was the infamous 'Mahkamat al-Sha'b' (or Peoples' Court), presided over by Colonel Fadhil 'Abbas Mahdawi, a cousin of Qassem's and an obese bully. Mahdawi was a boor of limited education, singularly unprepared for the major task he was about to assume from either a legal or any other standpoint.[40] He managed single-handedly to give the Iraq Revolution a black eye, the effects of which are visible even today.

Though no one has questioned the basic and—following a revolution—perhaps even necessary need to try members of the former regime for legitimate cause, but putting such a task in the charge of a person of such limited culture and education was the nearest thing to shooting oneself in the foot. Mahdawi faced persons whose culture and intelligence were patently superior to his own (even though they may well have been guilty of their alleged crimes). He certainly managed to make himself a laughing stock, though maybe not to the illiterate masses that avidly watched his show every night. His was a kangaroo court and whilst providing as it did amusement to its popular audience, it was nevertheless dealing with subjects that were no laughing matter. However, if the dead-serious purpose of the trials were to be disregarded for a moment, the proceedings themselves were often fraught with unintended hilarity.

Mahdawi became vaingloriously persuaded of the vital service he was rendering to the country and to its leader. He developed ridiculous majestic overtones, which he assumed when lording it over some cowering victim. Sam Falle, the British oriental counsellor who attended several trials at the Mahdawi Court, remarked that on days when Mahdawi did not insult the accused, this was taken to be a form of benign mercy.

No thanks to Mahdawi, the evidence provided by those accused to his 'court' does nevertheless provide a treasure trove of historical data. The trials of 'Arif, Rashid 'Ali, Ghazi Daghestani, Sa'id Qazzaz, Bahjat 'Attiyya and others, offer fascinating insights into the workings of the former regime. The trials—had they been conducted in a civil and fair manner—could have yielded not just vital historical data, but would have presented Iraq's plight and struggle for freedom in a manner befitting of the seriousness of that struggle. The flip side of the coin of these aspects of the Mahdawi Court was the total transparency with which the trials were actually held. The trials were broadcast live. No trials were ever held *in camera*. All transcripts were published the following day for the public to read. All accused could freely name their defence attorneys, have the court name an attorney for them, or decide to defend themselves in person. All spoke with total freedom, and many managed to gain the sympathy of the public. The trial proceedings are all documented and can be found in public libraries around the world. None of this would have been remotely imaginable under the former regime, let alone under later ones. Yet, the burlesque manner in which the trials were conducted erased the positive gains that might have accrued. The final joke, as ever in such matters, was on Mahdawi himself. By the end, he was trying 'enemies' of the post-revolution period, while the 'enemies' of the pre-revolution period were all laughing at him from afar—by then having safely and comfortably relocated to Beirut, London or elsewhere.

One of the biggest negatives was Iraq's unreadiness for political cohesiveness. The almost immediate split between the Pan-Arabists/Ba'thists (Qawmiyyeen), and the Qassem/communist axis can be said to have rung the death knell for the revolution, without the players even knowing that they were already marching in their own funeral. The scenario then unfolding came to spell the same death knell for the NDP too, as the failed revolution took this party down with it as well.

Gamal Abd al-Nasser's meddling in Iraq's affairs so soon after the revolution was also a major factor in destabilizing the regime. He was then at his gung-ho phase of launching ill-thought out misadventures abroad, before he retrenched into an Egypt-First (nationalist) policy following his massive defeat in 1967 at the hands of the Israelis. His over-reliance on his sinister intelligence services (the notorious *al-Mabahith* service) was to prove catastrophic in the cases of both Syria and Iraq. He was to learn his lesson in Syria, when the much-vaunted UAR broke up in shambles and to the relief of both parties after a ludicrously short time. In the case of Iraq, he committed a critical error of judgment by allowing himself to be goaded by the impulsive promises of 'Arif and by the spurring on of his own intelligence services. He made the mistake of making an outright enemy of Qassem, when the latter was not at all opposed to a future alliance with Egypt or with Syria. Amazingly, Nasser and Qassem never met. Talib Shabib (a future foreign minister in the post-Qassem government, and supposedly anti-Qassem) nevertheless wrote:

Nasser rashly precipitated a quarrel with Qassem. He discussed Qassem's fate with 'Arif a mere five days after the revolution. Qassem viewed this act as a blow below the belt and a plan for future intrigue. Nasser later [barely a year had passed since the revolution] sent arms and a powerful transmitter to Colonel Shawwaf [infiltrated through Syria to Mosul, where Shawwaf mounted his revolt] to aid in the latter's insurgency against Qassem. He [Nasser] even came to Damascus on a visit which he prolonged to await the results of that revolt… Despite Qassem's friendly overtures to Egypt, perhaps more so than any other regime in the Arab World at the time, Qassem was rightly weary of handing over Iraq to Nasser as the Syrians had done with their country, only to find that in actual fact they had handed it over to his *Mabahith*.[41]

The Iraq-Egypt war of words soon descended into farce. Egypt started a vitriolic campaign against Iraq and against Qassem's person in particular (or 'Qassem al-'Iraq', as *Sawt al-Arab* intoned). This soon had Colonel Mahdawi (who could certainly match *Sawt al-Arab's* vitriol with massive doses of his own) responding viciously. Mahdawi lacked the intellectual capacity to understand that, outside all the ranting from Cairo, Nasser's serious message to Iraq was that it was not headed for the promised democracy under Qassem. Though this was clearly an absurd accusation, since Nasser had dismissed notions of parliamentary democracy in his own union with Syria, had not instituted it in Egypt itself, and yet was demanding that Qassem implement it in Iraq in the short space of the few turbulent months immediately after the revolution.[42] Quite apart from Egypt and Syria, no country in the Arab world at the time had even the vaguest notion of the democracy that Nasser was demanding of Iraq. Shabib correctly states that had Nasser approached his plans by conciliatory and quiet diplomacy, a future for an important Arab union might well have been a lot more conceivable.

The last negative was the collapse of the NDP that for decades had represented Iraq's forlorn hope of democracy. In the run-up period to the revolution, contacts by the revolutionaries with the NDP (as indeed, with all other leaders of the NUF) were achieved through Mohammed Hadid and Hussain Jamil—Kamel Chadirchi being in prison at the time. Chadirchi was nevertheless kept fully apprised of all contacts made, but withheld his full support for the NDP to enter a future post-revolutionary government, preferring instead a wait-and-see policy. He was worried—and rightly so, as it transpired—about how matters would evolve with the military. Once in power, he was not convinced that they would return meekly to their barracks and hand over the reins of government to civilian politicians. Chadirchi was still deeply affected by his experience in 1936 when he personally, and together with al-

'Ahali as a group, supported the Bakr Sidqi coup to their eventual detriment. Mohammed Hadid visited Chadirchi in jail accompanied by Siddiq Shanshal, the general secretary of the IP, who had himself been briefed by the revolutionaries, and whose own party, much like the NDP, was a pillar of the National Union Front. Both men informed Chadirchi that the military was not going to make their move without full NUF support. The political situation in the country was extremely grave and there were rumours of other groups—including groups loyal to the monarchy—mounting their own operations. At least, Hadid and Shanshal argued, they were dealing with the Free Officers' movement, the best placed group to carry out such an action. The devil you know, they argued. After a frank discussion with Chadirchi and a full analysis of the situation, he was finally persuaded to back the movement and to participate fully in the new government, resulting in its success. His decision was passed on to the Free Officers.

The politicians in the NUF had absolutely no face-to-face contact with the military and all communications were handled through third parties. This was a regrettable way of communicating, as it was often less than accurate but, for the sake of secrecy, it was understandable. In the event, it brought together several groups with a common vision for the future. However, they lacked a cohesive and manageable plan of action, having not resolved in advance their different approaches to the problems facing the country. This was to cost many of them dearly, particularly the NDP.

When the revolution took place, and was met with unprecedented popular support, Chadirchi was, in the first months at least, a fully paid-up participant and supporter—delighted that it had brought such joy to Iraq's cities. So much so that he volunteered to go personally to Cairo to meet with President Nasser, to try and plead for calm in the crisis that soon erupted between the NUF and the Free Officers, over either an immediate union with the UAR, or a federal solution that put Qassem and 'Arif in opposing camps. Chadirchi did go to Cairo on 14 September 1958. He met with Nasser to inform him of the crisis and of the Iraqi public's preference for the federal solution. Nasser, Chadirchi reported back to Hadid on his return, had said that he welcomed any decision that the Iraqi public took on the issue.[43]

After the trip to Cairo, Chadirchi seems to have returned to his former recalcitrance *vis-à-vis* support for the revolution. He was worried that the Qassem-'Arif feud could develop into a contest for leadership

between the two, to the detriment of democratic plurality, not to mention the irresponsible throwing of Nasser's name into the mix by those
who would have him become sole leader. And Chadirchi had a second
reason to be wary. He had begun to notice the growing brittleness of
the NUF, and could see that it might well come apart as each group
gravitated to one or the other of the new Iraqi military leaders. The
NUF actually was conscious of its own failings, and the need to pump
new life and vigour into its creaking structure. The four parties making up the NUF (the NDP, IP, ICP and the Ba'th) met at Chadirchi's
house to discuss the situation and concluded by signing a pact reiterating their original intent. They even decided to hold a general conference to reassure their followers of that intent.

The combined conference did take place in Sahat al-Kashshafa, a
large stadium in Baghdad, which for some unknown reason Chadirchi
failed to attend. Chadirchi may have known something that those that
did attend did not. The division between the NDP/ICP and the Pan-
Arabists had begun to grow ugly. It coagulated around those that
backed Qassem's Iraq-First policy, and those that backed immediate
union with Nasser.

Resignations of ministers from the NUF suddenly came thick and
fast. The nationalist ministers (or Qawmiyyeen) resigned en masse.
This act was a significant set-back to Iraq's democratic prospects, as it
dealt a knock-out blow to the NUF which became, for all intents and
purposes, a moribund entity. Sadly enough, no other political formation with such lofty hopes for democracy was ever to succeed it in
modern Iraq.

On the heels of those nationalist resignations, Chadirchi asked his
two cabinet minister NDP colleagues (Mohammed Hadid and Hudaib
al-Haj Hmoud) to consider tendering their resignations too. Both
Hadid and Hmoud agreed to withdraw from the government, submitting their resignations both personally and then jointly at a meeting
with Qassem. The latter pleaded with both to reconsider, assuring
them that he had been reared on NDP philosophy, and was intent on
fulfilling the party's political agenda. Hadid and Hmoud agreed to
withdraw their resignations. Chadirchi—obviously displeased with
their decision—now called for a meeting of the entire NDP leadership,
together with all the leading independent democrats that were not affil-
iated with the party. The idea was to have an in-depth debate about the
wisdom of the NDP supporting the government. The result was an

overwhelming decision not only to support the government but to cooperate with it fully.

Not one to be rebuffed so publicly, Chadirchi packed his bags and pointedly left for Moscow for 'medical treatment'. In his absence, conflicts between the NDP and the Communist Party escalated, not just into open media warfare but into physical violence as well. The communist tide had reached its zenith, and communist members were near to burning their bridges with the general public, not to mention the middle and professional classes, that had grown weary of their methods. Hadid, now leader of the NDP, and possibly with Qassem's acquiescence, decided to freeze all NDP political activity. This was followed by a government order to freeze all political party activities, including that of the ICP.

This was a well-calculated stroke that not only dealt the communists a knock-out punch, but it put paid to their erstwhile domination of Qassem himself, of the Iraqi street, as well as some other political groups. The blow dealt to the communists has been a subject much debated in all books written about this period of the revolution. Qassem never left a memoir or a diary to give his version of how this plan was conceived. Hadid, however, the other party to the plan, is unequivocal about its origin. He writes in his memoir that 'the idea behind freezing the party's activities was strictly mine and was one that Qassem adopted. I reached that decision alone because of the general deterioration in relations between political parties in general, and between the NDP and the Communist Party in particular'.[44]

Hanna Batatu writes that Qassem began the process by calming the fears of industrialists and 'men of capital', in a speech that emphasized Iraqi freedom of action and neutrality—stressing that he himself was against parties and 'partyism' in the manner then being practised. Batatu continues that 'cunningly and with the help of Mohammed Hadid… Qassim defied the communists to choose between hanging on to his sleeve or striking out entirely on their own'.[45] Uriel Dann says that Hadid, now leader of the party during Chadirchi's absence, took a distinctly hostile attitude towards the communists and the ICP, which followed in the wake of government curbs on the communists' free-ranging domination of public life. When Chadirchi returned from Moscow, he made a bid to reassume the leadership of the party, asking the party to reverse the course it had adopted towards the communists.[46] This pitched Hadid and Chadirchi into direct confrontational mode over the most fundamental issue now facing the party—and possibly even the country—over the direction it was heading. Hadid had asked the question: did the NDP wish to support the government or not? Chadirchi and his followers' answer was a definite no; whereas Hadid and his supporters' reply was a resounding yes.

The Chadirchi-Hadid conflict regarding NDP support of Qassem and the revolutionary government—or the withdrawal of such support—has been the reason given by many writers for the eventual demise of the NDP. The true reason, however, may be attributed to the inability of the NDP to readjust to those new circumstances thrown up by the revolution and, especially, to the entry of two new players into the political arena. These were the communists and the Pan-Arabists/Ba'thists, who proved to be more wired into the popular psyche of the time than the NDP was. Several analysts have put the blame for this on Chadirchi himself, for being too old and too mired in thirties-type politics to be able to flexibly change direction.[47] But this is something of a fallacy. Chadirchi was only sixty years old in 1958, and was more than capable of taking a leading role in the government, had one been offered him. Others have spoken of the blow to his supposedly well-known vanity when he was sidelined by Qassem in favour of NDP members of Qassem's own age (Hadid, Jamil, Hmoud) who were all in their fifties. Many memoirs by *ancien régime* personalities (Khalil Kanna, Ahmad Mukhtar Baban), may have also exaggerated the frivolous aspect of Chadirchi's so-called vanity, but such observations had to be balanced with the accolades he richly received as Iraq's foremost national leader.[48]

The truth is that Chadirchi had every right to expect to be rewarded for his long years of struggle, mostly spent in Nuri's jails, by being named president of the new Iraq. After all, during the massive demonstrations during the 1948 Uprising (*al-Wathba*), the crowds had proclaimed his name as their choice for prime minister. Chadirchi was the quintessential national leader, the best kind that Iraq—with its tortured political history—could produce. The scion of a wealthy and prestigious upper-class family, he was totally dedicated to bringing democracy to his country, and found the right vehicle to actualize his dream in the NDP. The party's founding members had pioneered those democratic aims but none could dedicate themselves so totally to the task as he did, simply because unlike him, they had to earn their livelihoods.

Qassem's electrifying appeal to the masses, however, was a factor that neither Chadirchi nor any other patrician Iraqi politician could possibly match. Mohammed Hadid recounts that when he and Chadirchi attended the Arab Lawyers Association's annual general meeting, which was held in a vast auditorium in Baghdad (Qa'at al-Sha'b), the crowds went ballistic when cheering Qassem's entry into the hall. Hadid writes that he 'was pained to see the look on Chadirchi's face that probably reflected the latter's understandable dismay that a political non-entity like Qassem, who had played no role in the long national struggle, should now stand before such hero-worshipping crowds while he, the true national leader, sat there as a mere spectator'.[49] Qassem's approach to governing Iraq, naive as it may have been, went to the very root of the Iraq riddle, unsolved as it remains to this day. This riddle was: who and what was an Iraqi? Qassem tried to simplify the answer by making two assumptions. One, that there was indeed an 'Iraqi people'. Two, that the inhabitants of the land could be made loyal to an 'Iraqi state'. Qassem relentlessly plugged the theme that the revolution presented a unique opportunity for Iraqis to 'bury their feuds'; that doomsayers who said that Iraqis were a deeply-divided people were wrong, and that the revolution had made unity a graspable national hope. He exhorted Iraqis to forge a unique identity that would embrace all of Iraq's multi-racial, religious and ethnic groups that could learn to be tolerant of each others' needs. According to Qassem, thanks to the revolution, all classes of the Iraqi people had now merged.[50]

The heady, idealistic potion that Qassem was now serving up was near-nigh impossible for any politician to even begin to compete with, let alone Chadirchi or the other members of the NDP. Their appeal was in any event more slanted towards the intelligentsia and the professional classes. Chadirchi's character in particular has bedevilled many a writer. Uriel Dann returns to the theme of Chadirchi's vanity, as does Khadduri, both alluding to a personal factor that may have been at play, causing Chadirchi to feel that he was now 'the exasperated veteran superseded by his juniors (obviously referring to Hadid and Jamil)'.[51] Qassem made several attempts to befriend Chadirchi, but the latter spurned all his approaches. Isma'il 'Arif recounts that Qassem spent an entire night in 1961 trying to persuade Chadirchi to enter a coalition of all parties, but Chadirchi continued to demur saying that he would only consider such a proposal after a general election. Chadirchi apparently was even rude to Qassem at that meeting. When Qassem said that he considered Chadirchi his teacher in democracy,

Chadirchi churlishly refused to accept that Qassem shared the al-'Ahali vision as he claimed to. When Qassem said that General 'Abdi, the military governor, was looking into the question of political arrests, Chadirchi is reputed to have replied 'What? That 150 kilograms of meat [a reference to 'Abdi's obesity]? He is incapable of any kind of decision'. When Qassem took Chadirchi to tour the city with him in his car—which was immediately surrounded by rapturous well-wishers—Chadirchi told Qassem that the presence of those well-wishers had been arranged beforehand.[52] Isma'il 'Arif, in his memoir, writes that Qassem told him personally the next day that Chadirchi had thrown cold water on his plan to form a coalition government of all parties. Chadirchi also told Qassem that it was undemocratic of him to parade around town with the public's applause ringing in his ears (no doubt a bitter reference to the two men's drive around Baghdad).[53] Despite Isma'il 'Arif's exhortation to Qassem to go ahead with his plan, Qassem feared that the other parties would follow Chadirchi's stance, and therefore deferred implementing his idea.

Some writers have wrongly concluded that Chadirchi harboured pro-communist sympathies, and was incensed that Hadid and Qassem between them had struck down the ICP. Chadirchi has gone on record as saying that had he had any communist affiliations, he would not have shirked from declaring them publicly. Although he was no communist, Chadirchi nevertheless genuinely believed that the communists had a constructive role to play in the politics of Iraq; that they were both popular and patriotic and had paid their dues in the national struggle—perhaps more heavily than most considering Nuri's phobic animus against them. Like Chadirchi, they too were wary of military rule, and were proved right in the end.

Chadirchi and Hadid were now poles apart. Hadid took the firm view that the revolutionary republican regime had not disappointed the hopes that it had inspired at the time of the revolution, and that much had been accomplished already from the NDP agenda which would have been beyond the party's wildest dreams under the monarchy. Hadid was candid about the shortcomings of the regime and knew that much was remiss, but he thought that the best way to go forward was to assist the government in rectifying its mistakes. Hadid felt that the very last thing that the NDP should do at such a critical time was to go into opposition, as this would render the party meaningless, devoid of all influence and dangerously detached from political reality. In its present position, and with Qassem openly declaring his NDP sympathies, the NDP could position itself so as to carry out much of its agenda in the fullness of time. Isma'il 'Arif writes of this situation: 'Mohammed Hadid's short presence in the government [two years] provided ballast for the government and stopped Qassem from embarking on many extremist schemes that other political groups were trying to lead him into and that had instilled fear in Iraqi society'.[54]

Chadirchi let it be known that he was prepared to reassume the leadership of the party, if his condition of the party withdrawing its support from the government was met. Hadid, on the other hand, was sure of his position, and equally sure that a majority in the party took the same position. He was pained that the dispute of whether to support the government or not had become an existential issue. For this reason, he announced that for the sake of party unity, he would resign from the government. But he also added that he would resign from the party as well, as he could no longer be a member of a party that held a position so diametrically opposed to his own. It is not known whether Hadid could have been persuaded to change his mind, as Chadirchi himself had been made to do so many times in the past when he had resigned. Instead, Chadirchi immediately accepted Hadid's resignation. Shortly thereafter, Hussain Jamil also resigned, fearful of the party's quick slide into ill-conceived alliances with the Communist Party. So, too, did the editor of *al-'Ahali* newspaper. Chadirchi—long a beacon of the national struggle for democracy—now stood alone amongst the party's shattered remains, polemicizing against the regime and against what he called his 'renegade' friends.

On that day the NDP died, and with it, the hope of democracy in Iraq.

13

THE AFTERMATH

On 8 February 1963, a military coup succeeded in toppling the Qassem regime. Qassem was summarily tried and shot by firing squad, after a trial that can only be described as a travesty. In the light of what had been meted out to the royal family and to Nuri al-Sa'id, it was proof of the old axiom that what starts with blood, ends with blood. Qassem, like Nuri before him and Saddam after him, failed to realize that a similar fate awaited him.[1] Many writers—some of whom were pro-Qassem—have suggested that he would have been better off had he fought on till the end, or even taken his own life. The coup leaders, terrified by Qassem's huge popularity with the masses, took the gruesome decision to exhibit his corpse on public television, so that Iraqis would be convinced once and for all that he was in fact dead. In a macabre scene reminiscent of a horror film, Qassem (who had slumped dead in a chair in an office of the broadcasting station) was grabbed by a clump of his hair by a soldier, who lifted his head up and spat in his face in full view of the camera for all to see. This was the manner by which Iraq's new coup leaders announced their arrival. Talib Shabib, who became a minister in the new government and was witness to Qassem's end, nevertheless spoke kindly of him. He wrote many years later, and with hindsight, that Qassem had been the most clement of all of Iraq's leaders. He had not dipped his hands in the state coffers to enrich himself, like all those who came before him and all who came after him; he had worked selflessly for the good of his country, even if later it was in a dictatorial style. Qassem certainly did not deserve the shabby and tragic end he was made to endure. Shabib claims that 'it was best that he was executed, since if he had been tried, as he was demanding, his trial would have been a gross travesty, much in the style of Mahdawi, and would have subjected him to worse forms of humiliation. Immediate summary execution may have been a form of mercy'.[2]

Qassem's end was no unique event in Iraq's sanguinary modern history. Most movements against the state finished in blood. Ja'far al-'Askari was assassinated (1936); Bakr Sidqi was assassinated (1937); the 'Golden Square' colonels, led by Salah al-Din Sabbagh, were executed (1941); the royal family was executed (1958); Nuri al-Sa'id was either killed or committed suicide (1958);[3] Qassem was executed (1963); and Saddam Hussein was first dragged out of a hole in the ground and subsequently hanged, while being jeered at and insulted even as he hung from the gallows (2006). Such examples of sheer brutality might lead one to sadly assume that Iraqis came to establish a certain trend in how they deal with their soon-to-be ex-leaders.

Ironically, Mahdawi appears to have shown great courage by leaving the relative safety of his home in order to traverse Baghdad and join Qassem at the ministry of defence, where Qassem was hoping to mount a counter-attack to subdue the rebels. Mahdawi could easily have hid or left the country, but instead, he stayed with Qassem till the very end. He received a bloody beating when Qassem surrendered and died by firing squad, with blood already streaming from his face.

Qassem had fallen. The leaders of the NDP, the NPP and the IP had all retired from politics. With them went the NUP, with its once lofty goals for Iraqi democracy. This left the scene entirely open to the army officers, to the Ba'thists, the nationalists and the communists. Chadirchi died on 1 February 1968, a deeply disappointed man. He had watched as the democracy house of cards collapsed around him despite his and the NDP's long and valiant struggle to build a solid base for it. At his memorial service, Mohammed Hadid was asked by Chadirchi's family to deliver the eulogy. It must have been a poignant moment, as the two men (described by Sir Sam Falle as 'the Gandhi and the Nehru of Iraq') had fallen out after a lifetime's political comradeship and solidarity.[4] In his eulogy, Hadid said:

Kamil Chadirchi's passing represents not just a loss for Iraq but for the entire Arab nation. He fervently believed to the last breath of his life in democracy as Iraq's one and only way to solve its society's problems. Chadirchi was the quintessential example of a statesman, who blended wise reasoning with impeccable manners, and rejected the idea of the end ever justifying the means—this unfortunately being the method of practicing politics in Iraq. He was the symbol of the democratic ideas propagated by al-'Ahali since their formation in the thirties, and their later transformation into the National Democratic Party in the forties and beyond.[5]

Mohammed Hadid himself was arrested by the coup leaders on 8 March, and imprisoned together with others who had collaborated with Qassem. This was in spite of Hadid's departure from government years earlier, and his isolation from Qassem in the last years of the latter's rule, when Qassem had taken a distinctly hostile posture towards both the democrats and the communists. In one petty instance, for example, Hadid's application to renew his passport to travel abroad was deliberately delayed to signal Qassem's displeasure. Hadid, held without charge, was subjected to offensive behaviour by the new coup leaders (Saleh Mehdi 'Ammash and Taher Yehya, in particular) who would visit him in jail for no other reason than to use vindictive language, with the former ordering Hadid's incarceration in solitary confinement for forty days. 'Ammash grandly ordered the prison director, a certain Hazim Sabbagh (known as 'Hazim the Red' not because of his politics but his red hair) who hailed from Mosul like Mohammed Hadid himself—and whose father had been the Hadid family barber—to deprive Hadid from seeing 'the sun and the sky' to which 'Hazim the Red', perhaps enjoying the moment, replied 'your orders are my command, Sir'. Hadid's vindictive treatment by the Ba'thists was frowned upon by public opinion inside and outside Iraq—though not by members of the *ancien régime*, now basking in affluent freedom in Beirut. Hadid later wrote in his memoir that the most vociferous, not to say the most ungrateful, amongst them were those that he had intervened hardest with Qassem to save (and in some instances plead for their very lives to be spared).[6] The Qur'an puts it thus: '*Ittaqi sharra man ahsanta illaihu*' (Beware evil from he that you have been good to) and the Old Testament similarly: 'No good deed goes unpunished'.

Eventually the coup leaders, unable to find anything to accuse Hadid of, trumped up the absurd charge that he had authorized the striking of silver coins to celebrate an anniversary of the revolution, and demanded that he reimburse the state in full for this cost. When his accusers discovered that the price of silver had in fact risen since the striking of the coins, and that the government had made a neat profit, they backtracked somewhat, but not before trying to save face by asking the then governor of the central bank, Khair al-Din Hassib, to demand that Hadid pay 3,000 dinars as penalty.[7] Majid Khadduri, whose book *Republican Iraq* is considered an unassailable classic, mistakenly states that 'Qassem's ministers were rounded up for irregularities or corruption'—an error of fact, as most ministers who were arrested were released within a month and not one was charged with corruption.[8]

Mohammed Hadid's treatment was no different to that meted out to other Iraqi leaders who had to endure humiliation by a competing political power newly arrived on the scene. There was never any question of acknowledging the services rendered by such individuals to their nation. This included everyone in Iraq's short modern history, from Faisal I to Saddam Hussain. Yet whilst they were in power, they had their fawning supporters and were cheered by the masses. This may have been why Faisal I pronounced his haunting and blunt verdict on his newly-acquired Iraqi subjects that they were devoid of patriotic ideas, prone to anarchy and ready to rise against any government.[9] Nor was this treatment by any means the special preserve of Iraqis. All Arab nations with a history of similar upheavals have treated their former statesmen with appalling cruelty and ingratitude. In Britain, the mandate nation that was supposedly meant to teach Iraqis the mores of a modern state, such leaders would have ended up sitting in the House of Lords (or Majlis al'A'yan in the case of Iraq), so that the nation might continue to benefit from their political experience, despite the real or imagined wrong-doings of their time in office. For this reason, many Iraqi statesmen ended up frittering away their time and skills in Beirut cafés, leading the bitter and empty life of exiles, when they could have been, and would have much preferred to be, of continued use to their country. It was completely absurd that a great national leader like Kamel Chadirchi should have spent so much of his most productive years in Nuri al-Sa'id's jails, and on the flimsiest of charges. Nuri's infantile efforts to brand Chadirchi and the NDP as communist only showed Nuri's inability, real or feigned, to differentiate between the NDP and the ICP. The social irony in this role reversal was that Chadirchi, who hailed from an aristocratic and wealthy Baghdadi family, should have been the politician advocating right-wing attitudes, whilst Nuri, who came from impoverished and humble stock (as indeed, did most of the Sharifian officers that Faisal chose to appoint as the new governing class of Iraq when he was anointed king by the British) should have been the national democrat.

The Ba'thists pointedly ignored Hadid's invaluable contribution to his country; the fact that he was the architect of Law 80 that had nationalized Iraq's oil—widely accepted as the 1958 Revolution's major accomplishment—should have been enough to guarantee him an exalted place in Iraq's history, regardless of the petty changes in party politics. In fact, when the Ba'thists ordered their soldiers to ransack Hadid's house in his absence, they found his hand-written draft of Law 80. To his credit, the uncharacteristically enlightened Ba'thist officer commanding the unit warned his soldiers not to damage the draft, as it constituted a unique piece of Iraqi history.[10]

Perhaps Iraq's biggest loss after Qassem's death was the disappearance of the NDP from the national scene. The Iraqi people's valiant pursuit and struggle for democracy would come to be indelibly associated with al-'Ahali Group and the National Democratic Party and its leaders who, for twenty-seven years, had exhibited a spirit of extraordinary defiance and sacrifice as they sought to bring about the evolution of a parliamentary democracy. The NDP's cumulative impact on the Iraqi perception of what a democracy can bring to a country—in terms of economic benefits liberated from foreign exploitation; as well as freedom of action and thought brought about by a parliamentary system based on honest and fair elections—can never be exaggerated enough. The party played a critical role in every national Intifada that defied imperialist influence in Iraq, as well as the former regime's collusion with it. Such Herculean efforts by the party were crucial factors in rescinding the infamous Portsmouth Treaty, as well as in setting alight both the 1952 and 1956 Intifadas. The NDP, an architect and a partner in the National Front, took a vigorous stand against the Baghdad Pact, which led to Iraq's withdrawal from it after the 1958 Revolution. Instances such as these showed that the NDP's loss to Iraq in its forlorn quest for democracy was incalculable. Although the NDP leaders may now be dead and gone, the political heritage that they left behind is still very much alive and well-documented.

As for the other parties in Iraq's National United Front, the Independence Party (*al-Istiqlal*) also played a memorable role. But sadly, it too disappeared from the political scene under Qassem. The party had cooperated with the revolution, and came to be represented in the revolutionary government by its leader, Mohammed Mehdi Kubba, as a member of the Sovereignty Council, and by Siddiq Shanshal, as minister of guidance. But the party could not hold its line for long in supporting the government. In February 1959, Shanshal was one of the six cabinet ministers that staged a walk-out on Qassem. Kubba followed suit in March. The party sided with the Shawwaf Revolt, and from then on agitated strongly to bring Qassem down.

The Ba'th went from strength to strength. Having failed to dupe the army to carry out the 8 March coup, and take over the reins of government, it now returned strongly to power in July 1968, and continued to govern Iraq until 2003—as long as all other governments combined since the creation of the Iraqi state.

The Iraq Communist Party under the royal regime had more than its fair share of political persecution; its members underwent coercion, torture and imprisonment in the most inhumane conditions imaginable. Therefore, the 1958 Revolution was the actualization of an impossible dream for the ICP. The party and its members threw themselves fully behind Qassem, vigorously defending the revolution. The party enjoyed considerable sympathy amongst the intelligentsia, not only for what it stood for, but for its sheer capacity to take the brutal punishment meted out by the former regime. When it came to the Iraqi masses, the ICP enjoyed blanket sympathy and support, which it was to parlay into a Qassem support system, especially once the Ba'thist defections from Qassem began a few short weeks after 14 July. The ICP soldiered on after Qassem's purge and again after his demise but it, too, lost influence and appeal when the Ba'th took over in 1968.

Coming full circle, it may well be fitting to end this story, just as it started, with the British. Sam Falle in his book, *My Lucky Life*, gives one of the most accurate accounts of July 1958, as well as the British reaction to it, of any known Western writer. Falle was sent to Iraq as oriental counsellor (a euphemism for intelligence officer) at the British embassy in Baghdad and much against the wishes of the then ambassador Sir Michael Wright. The latter dismissed Falle sneeringly as a 'boy' (due perhaps to Falle's boyish looks) sent out to Iraq to do a man's job. In an illustration of the expression 'Indian not lost, Chief lost', it was Falle who would wind up getting it 'right' on Iraq, and Wright who would get it utterly wrong.

Soon after arriving in Baghdad, Falle immediately ingratiated himself socially with Baghdad's professional class, who took him into their confidence. Falle spoke fluent Arabic, unlike Wright who could not speak a word of it and quite often looked gauche as Falle chatted away in Arabic in Wright's presence, only sometimes remembering to translate for him. Falle developed a unique insight into the mind-set of the intellectual and mostly Western-educated class of lawyers, doctors, and architects who dined on *masguf*—the famous Tigris river fish that is grilled upright on the banks by local fishermen, and washed down with dousings of arak. The drinking of alcohol made a big impression on Falle, who found that he and his Iraqi hosts had this taste in common, and saw that they were free from the severe Islamic strictures on drinking. The group spoke openly about how Iraq was ruled by stooge governments taking their orders from the British embassy in Baghdad, giving as examples the unfolding Suez drama and the Baghdad Pact. Falle wrote that he had himself formulated the same opinion as his hosts by the time he left London, as a result of his work in the Middle East committee of the FCO and his own research in preparation for his new job.

Falle describes such evenings as the best introduction to political life in Iraq. They made him decide to try to meet the leaders of the opposition that his own embassy knew so very little about, in order to get a more balanced point of view. It was thus that he sought an introduction to Mohammed Hadid and to Kamil Chadirchi of the NDP. Chadirchi was in jail at the time for allegedly being too supportive of Egypt during the tripartite attack on her by England, France and Israel; added to this was the further flimsy charge of his being a communist. Falle had become convinced that Chadirchi was no more of a communist than he himself was, and that the NDP was merely a mild version of Britain's Labour Party. Falle did indeed meet with Hadid at this stage, though he omits this from his book, preferring instead to report on a post-revolution meeting that they later had.

Falle did not share his Iraqi friends' opinion of Nuri al-Sa'id as being a ruthlessly tyrannical British lackey. He found the accusation of tyranny to be somewhat exaggerated, despite Nuri's well-known penchant for leaving corpses hanging in public places as a lesson for those trying to subvert his regime. Falle concedes that Nuri was tough, and that he tolerated no serious opposition. His obsession with locking up Chadirchi at every twist and turn in order to scare off other opposition leaders was simply inept. Falle did, in a private conversation with the author, relate that he had been told by Nuri that Chadirchi had never been ill-treated or tortured in jail, as would certainly have been the case with other repressive regimes that followed. Mohammed Hadid, for one, did not get the relatively-mild treatment that Chadirchi received under Nuri when Hadid himself was incarcerated by the post-Qassem coup leaders. As far as Nuri being a 'British lackey' was concerned, Falle pooh-poohed such a suggestion, claiming that Nuri had the British ambassador 'in his back pocket, and not the other way round'. Falle exclaimed that every time he had tried to warn the ambassador of the gravity of the internal situation in Iraq, Wright would always counter with a plaintive 'but Nuri says...'.

During his posting to Baghdad, Falle continued his dialogue with Iraqis up and down the country, developing an insight into their mood leading up to and immediately after the 1958 Revolution. He did not realize, however, that even his own ambassador, let alone his superiors in London, had difficulty believing what Falle was actually reporting from the ground. Nevertheless, the remarkable accuracy of Falle's forecast—had it been taken on board—might have seen Iraq avoiding a revolution, with the monarchy continuing under Faisal II.[11]

Falle recounts that in April 1958, Sir Michael wrote a long and important memo to the Foreign Office—his last before the revolution. In certain parts, the memo did reflect much of what Falle had been telling his ambassador. In one section of it, Wright describes: 'the potentially explosive element of political frustration under an authoritarian regime, especially among the growing middle-class as well as the belief in Britain's dominant, and to some, sinister role'—guided in this by Falle's words. In another, Wright goes off on a tangent and says that 'the Army, although it has in the past erupted into politics, is at present showing no signs of doing so, and if it continues to receive good leadership and if the interests of the career officers as well as the Non Commissioned Officers continue to be watched, it is likely to go on supporting the regime'.

Wright's memo received only cursory attention in London and was generally discounted for its lack of hard intelligence. Even when, later, Qassem's name was passed on to Nuri as being the head of the Free Officers' movement, Nuri refused to believe it and is rumoured to have retorted: 'Karrumi [his pet name for Qassem]? Impossible! He's my friend'. Two months after Wright's memo, Falle told the ambassador that he had it on reliable sources that there was a group in the army that was planning to overthrow the government, but Wright did not bother even to pass on this information to the Foreign Office.

By the early summer of 1958, Falle was convinced that revolution could come at any moment. He constantly updated Wright on conversations he had had outside the embassy, recorded them in detail, and wrote assessments of the situation as he believed it was evolving. The ambassador breezily assured Falle that he had the balance wrong. In his book, Falle blames himself for not having pressed Wright hard enough to pass on his views to the F.O. But the latter, preferring to err on the side of caution, did not wish to appear 'alarmist' by relaying 'scare stories' to London. Falle wrote that as it turned out, it was Wright and Nuri who had the balance wrong. He added and that even after the passing of thirty-eight years, those events in Iraq still managed to keep kept him awake at night.

Falle had written a long minute to Wright based on his observations, and talks with Iraqis on both sides of the political spectrum. The majority believed that an army coup was imminent, and that it should be pre-empted by the regime with a palace coup of its own. Falle's minute is reproduced in full in Majid Khadduri's book, *Republican Iraq*. It concludes with the warning that if action were not taken soon, there would be a revolution, and probably a bloody one at that. Falle went on to profile what the revolutionary government might look like, and as things turned out, he was not far from right.

Falle recommended two courses of action open to the British:

1. That both Nuri and 'Abdulillah should be warned unequivocally—preferably by the British and the United States ambassadors acting in unison—that there was extreme danger of revolution, probably through an army coup. The government should immediately tighten up security in the army and, as a matter of urgency, set about a programme of social and economic reform. The power and influence of tribal sheikhs should be drastically reduced. As far as possible, a conciliatory policy should be adopted towards Egypt. The vast majority of the Iraqi people fiercely hated 'Abdulillah and despised Nuri. A revolutionary danger would continue to exist as long as these two men ruled Iraq. Nuri should be made to retire, and 'Abdulillah to leave the country, either as ambassador to Washington or, better still, as an exile living quietly somewhere abroad.

2. Falle thought that a palace revolution could have been engineered with a perfect candidate in the form of General Nurredin Mahmoud as prime minister of a new government. Falle thought Mahmoud was a political general with impeccable nationalist credentials, who was liked by both army and king. Falle believed that Faisal, though

regarded with some contempt and pity, was nevertheless not actively hated. The nationalists could certainly have tolerated him as a constitutional monarch. Such a government, Falle thought, would have been rid of the taint that clung to Nuri and 'Abdulillah for their subservience to the British. It also would have been free of the taunts then emanating from Nasser's UAR. It could have quit the Baghdad Pact, and asked the RAF to leave the Habbaniyya air base. It would have nevertheless been able to maintain the flow of oil through the IPC without the necessity of nationalization. Falle was convinced that the revolution would not have occurred if the scenario he had envisaged had taken place. Falle quotes his conversations with Mohammed Hadid and with 'Abd al-Rahman Bazzaz as illustration; each had intimated that had a proper introduction of democracy and freedom of political party life taken place, this would not have necessitated a revolution. Falle concluded that Iraqis were unusually difficult to govern, but under his scenario, Iraq would have stood a much better chance of avoiding the 14 July Revolution.

Falle regretted that Wright had not taken his recommendations seriously enough to send them to the F.O. He also felt that they had not been communicated properly to the royal family in Iraq. Majid Khadduri, however, writes that Falle's proposals were indeed communicated to the crown prince, 'Abdulillah, but he does not say by whom. Falle writes that he had formulated his proposals after discussions with Hadid, Bazzaz, and other leading nationalists. As far as he knew, only Ambassador Wright had seen them.

It transpired after the revolution and during the trial of General Ghazi Daghestani—deputy chief of the general staff before the revolution and a loyal Hashemite—that the general had been planning his own palace coup, very much in the style that Falle had envisaged. Apparently, and according to Falle, 'Abdulillah and Nuri, when faced with the idea of relinquishing power in order to save the monarchy, were not dead-set against doing so. In fact, 'Abdulillah went to Turkey for a 'holiday', but came back when Faisal begged him to return, since he had found the running of government too much to cope with. According to Falle's source, 'Abdulillah returned to Baghdad reluctantly, only to be killed by the rebels on 14 July. Nuri, too, would have retired from politics had 'Abdulillah relinquished power officially.

By July 1958, Falle was on the edge of utter frustration and had a keen sense of foreboding. He wrote a dispatch describing the situation in clear and unequivocal terms, which he followed up with a minute predicting imminent revolution. He says that 'to this day, I recall the exact wording of the red ink comment on the bottom of my minute dated 8 July: *"This does not accord with the facts"*.' He was further reminded by Wright that he had once again got the balance wrong. Indeed, Wright did not even bother to send this particular dispatch of Falle's to London.

Amazing as all the above may be, Falle had an interview on 9 July with the minister of interior, Sa'id Qazzaz, to whom he aired all his apprehensions. Qazzaz assured Falle that the political situation in Iraq was more stable than it had been since Suez, and that the regime was in no real danger. Falle found his statement to be highly complacent, if not outright smug. Qazzaz similarly ignored the warnings of his own chief of intelligence, Bahjat 'Atiyyah.

12 July 1958 was a date that would long remain in Falle's memory. Michael Wright had taken him to meet with the king, the crown prince and Nuri, so as to introduce him as the chargé d'affaires during Wright's holiday leave. Falle was struck by Nuri's remarkably bad English, when he had expected quite the opposite due to Nuri's long association with the British. In fact, Falle questioned how Nuri could have succeeded in communicating effectively with, say, someone like Sir Michael Wright. Falle describes the meeting as being 'like some crazy nightmare. I was convinced that the revolution could come at any moment; but if I had said so, Nuri would have laughed at me and Wright would have sacked me'. Falle found the king calm and polite, but 'Abdulillah in a high state of agitation, pacing up and down the room muttering, 'these dreadful things, these dreadful things!' When he had finally calmed down, he told Wright and Falle that he was expecting a Nasserist coup in Jordan, but mentioned no fears about anything similar happening in Iraq. Decades later in 1995, Falle received credible information that 'Abdulillah had indeed been very apprehensive about Iraq, which would have explained the hysterical state of anxiety he was in on that particular day in 1958. At the time, Falle expected Sir Michael to delay his leave in light of 'Abdulillah's unease, and thereby rob him of the chance to be the person who predicted the revolution, as the Foreign Office would have been then obliged to read his dispatches, since they would have come from a head of mission.

On the day of the revolution, an embassy official, Colonel Graham, was shot dead, probably mistaken for the ambassador. Embassy officials ran up to the roof and started firing above the heads of the mob. An Iraqi soldier shot himself in the foot by mistake, which enraged the crowd that believed he had been shot by the British. This precipitated an attack which resulted in the looting and burning down of the British embassy.

The success of the revolution was swift. After the declaration of a curfew, Baghdad was quiet and the number of casualties remained between twenty and thirty, which was surprisingly low for such an event. Falle and Wright went to see Qassem, the leader of the revolution, pondering that only twenty-four hours before, this very man had been responsible for the murder of the entire royal family, as well as their own colleague, Colonel Graham. Diplomatic immunity had been violated and the British ambassador's residence looted and burned down. Falle writes that in the days of empire, the British would have certainly sent an expeditionary force to avenge Colonel Graham, as well as the attack on the embassy. They would have 'strung up' Qassem and his men. But Suez had put an end to such British imperial acts in the Middle East. It must have been devastating for Wright to accept that British forces had no intention of intervening in Iraq. Falle saw that his fears had now been realized, that the British had been short-sighted and that somehow they would have to pick up the pieces.

On 15 July, the day following the revolution, Falle accompanied Sir Michael to meet with Qassem at his office which he had set up at the ministry of defence. They wished to protest the attack on the embassy. Falle writes that he immediately sensed the hostile atmosphere permeating the ministry and Qassem's office in particular. He recounted, with some irony, that he had had 'a friendlier welcome from the Japanese navy when they fished me out of the Java Sea' (he had been a naval officer who had fought the Japanese in World War II).

Following the meeting with Qassem, Falle asked to meet—and did actually meet—with Mohammed Hadid, now a senior civilian minister in the revolutionary government, whom he says welcomed 'him into his home with traditional Arab hospitality'. He writes that he was comforted at being in the presence of 'such a cultured gentleman who had studied at the LSE and had visited Britain many times in the past. We drank coffee and munched baklava as if I had just dropped in for a chat'. In fact, this was the first substantial conversation between the new government and a representative of the West. Hadid told Falle that he knew little about Qassem and 'Arif as people, though Qassem had made a good impression on him. Hadid was not so sure about 'Arif, who struck him as being too stiff and too military-like.

This meeting with Hadid was to prove a critical one for the British as far as their evaluation of the revolution was concerned. The British eventually recognized the new Iraqi Republic, and even set up a new style of political relation between the two countries. Falle had proven that he had not just predicted the revolution, but had understood Iraqi politics far better than anyone else in his British milieu, including his own ambassador. The meeting with Hadid had covered a wide spectrum of topics, dealing as it did with past, present and future British-Iraqi relations. Hadid must have sensed Falle's tacit sympathy for the nationalist cause and decided to speak to him candidly because of that. Falle made no secret of his agreement with many nationalist opinions. Hadid calmed British nerves by assuring Falle that the government was not communist, and had no plans to nationalize the oil industry. There were no immediate plans to join the UAR, or even to leave the Baghdad Pact. The new Iraqi government wanted good relations with the West, and very much hoped that Britain would soon recognize it. All this must have been music to Falle's ears, since he reported back very positively to the Foreign Office.

Falle writes that the 1958 coup changed Iraq for all time. It brought genuine popular jubilation, not just for the destruction of an old discredited order, but also for the birth of a new era. Finally, the alien Hashemites and their British masters were gone for good and freedom was at hand. For most Iraqis, this was a brief but wonderful moment when they could at long last express their political opinions. Falle tells that it is a strange quirk of history that revolutionary dreams are always so hard to realize. In the case of Iraq, those dreams ended in disaster, when the Iraqis were ruled by Saddam Hussein, who 'made Nuri and 'Abdulillah look like nursery-school children, and 'Abd al-Karim Qassem an angel of mercy'. He added:

My feelings were mixed. It was little satisfaction being proved right, but I, too, for a brief moment hoped that the new government, most of whose members I knew, would be good for Iraq and not too hostile to the West. In fact, this government was not unlike the one I had dreamt up before the revolution. It contained representatives of the main political movements and appeared moderate. While neither the Communist Party nor the Kurdish Democratic Party were invited to participate per se, Dr Ibrahim Kubba represented the communist point of view and there was an agreeable Kurd, Baba Ali Shaikh Mahmoud.

Falle got on with the job of making contact with all his old opposition friends, many of whom were now in government. He writes that he found them without exception accessible, frank and friendly. They were keen to receive recognition from the West, as well as to try and show a civilized face to the world, following the repulsive regicide that had just occurred. Britain's past was neither forgotten nor forgiven, but life had to go on and oil had to continue to flow. To the British, this revolutionary government had just brutally murdered their friends and allies, and an early recognition would have certainly appeared distasteful. But Falle writes that equally from the British side, a new relationship was now required and hard realism had to prevail. Although recognition from all Western countries had come relatively quickly, in Britain's case, Falle nevertheless thought, it had been given in a somewhat indecent and unnecessary hurry.

Falle's next call was on Kamel Chadirchi, who had been so often imprisoned by the old regime. Falle was more than familiar with Chadirchi's hugely-admired stance compared to the old regime, as well as his relentless struggle—along with his NDP colleagues—for democracy. Falle thought that if things had worked out differently, Chadirchi would have been president. At the meeting, Chadirchi was friendly and forthcoming, and told Falle that Iraq wanted good relations with the West based on mutual respect. But three weeks into the revolution, Chadirchi had become sceptical about democracy coming anytime soon to Iraq since he suspected that the army would never relinquish power. In October, Falle met with him again, and when asked about what made Qassem tick, Chadirchi replied tersely: 'He wants to remain leader'.

Falle made the following evaluation of Qassem: 'Qassem is in a way a tragic figure. To do him justice, I think he was inspired initially by a genuine desire to help his fellow countrymen, coming himself from humble origins. It is not clear to what extent he was responsible for the murders of the king, crown prince and Nuri. There are varying stories. The bottom line is that he was not up to the job, he may have been a tolerable brigadier and he was a good plotter but that was it'. Qassem came to power on a wave of popular enthusiasm. He really became the 'Beloved of the People'.

Again and again, Falle blames himself for not pressuring Sir Michael enough to report his findings back to the Foreign Office, since he felt in retrospect that he might well have prevented the revolution from occurring. He blames Sir Michael Wright for not having heeded vital intelligence and says that had Wright's replacement, Humphrey Trevelyan, been there in 1957, there would have been no tragedy for the British or the royal family in Iraq. But the British government had not listened to Trevelyan over Egypt; and having been foolish once, they might well have been so again over Iraq.

The author interviewed Falle on 11 June 2002, in Oxford. The author asked him what had gone wrong with the struggle for democracy in Iraq. His reply was that the Hashemites were not prepared to accept democracy and the country had been ruled by the unpopular crown prince and by Nuri: 'there had been a sort of phoney democracy with a parliament but everything was decided by Nuri and the crown prince. That certainly was the case when I was there and I am sure it was the same before. There was only a façade of democracy with parliament having nothing to say except to agree to everything that the palace or Nuri decreed. Nuri wanted absolute power'.

Asked why Nuri chose absolute power when constitutional power might certainly have been available to him, Falle replied that that was the way Nuri saw it; he believed that he was the one who knew best, and wasn't about to engage with what he referred to as those 'stupid' democrats. 'Nuri believed he knew what was good for Iraq and what was good for the Iraqis. He was going to do it his way and he wasn't going to tolerate any democracy'.

Told of the civilized relationship that Nuri al-Sa'id had nevertheless had with Mohammed Hadid—an avowed adversary—and of the episode in London when Nuri had asked Hadid to tea at Claridge's (both men happened to be in London at the time) in order to discuss a violent Intifada then taking place in Iraq, Sir Sam laughed heartily and said: 'Can you imagine Saddam sitting down to have tea at Claridge's with an adversary?'

Asked whether things had gone wrong for Iraq from the very outset when Faisal had been brought in to be imposed as king from the Hijaz—as opposed to electing a local candidate—Falle confessed that he himself had never understood this British manoeuvre: 'It's an odd quirk, you know; this whole idea of bringing someone from the Hijaz to rule Iraq has always beaten me. Our post World War I policy was to me absolutely crazy. Lawrence promised a united Arab state, and then the imperialists came back in and we agreed with the French, and went along with them. I think they were probably the leaders of it since they wanted Syria and Lebanon back…'

The author asked Falle how much he thought Nuri had been affected by Nasser. He replied 'Quite a lot, because Nasser was the real Arab leader who could unite the Arab world against the imperialists, and Nuri was the imperialist stooge. Suez just made things worse by pitching the Arab world against the British and embarrassing Nuri, because he had supported us. Nuri wanted Nasser to be clobbered. He repeated what Eden had told him that the British should take out Nasser, hit him *now* and hit him *hard*'.

Asked why the Iraqi regime had not come up with its own 'Nasser-like' Iraqi figure, who could represent a younger generation, since Nuri at that stage was already seventy-three or seventy-four; and why the crown prince, who was himself much younger, hadn't persuaded him to do so, Falle's response was that 'Nuri did not want to relinquish power and even when he stepped down from the premiership, he put his own stooge in. As for the crown prince, he wasn't a particularly courageous man and found comfort in an old stalwart like Nuri, who he knew supported the royal family and supported the status quo. They tried others, but there was nobody that really fitted the bill. Men like Chadirchi and Hadid were far too advanced and intellectual and liberal for them'.

After the death of Mohammed Hadid, the author found Sam Falle's book *My Lucky Life* among his possessions. Inside the cover he found a letter that Hadid had written to Falle, but the letter had never been sent, although his address in Sweden had been attached to it. When the author met Sam Falle at the Oxford seminar referred to above, he took his father's copy of the book and showed it to Falle along with the unsent letter. The letter read:

Dear Sir Sam,

Our mutual friend, Mr Alan Rush, was kind enough to supply me with a copy of your book *My Lucky Life*, of which I had not previously known.[12] What I have read of it in the last few days, I have found to be most interesting. It is particularly illuminating about the events that occurred in Iraq. I congratulate you for what you have written, and I specially wish to express my thanks for the comments and compliments which you kindly make about me in connection with the discussions we had before and after 14 July 1958.

It is a long time since we met. I have passed through many events, good and bad. I am now very old, and with two accidental falls and hip-joint replacements, I am almost disabled.

Presently, I am on a temporary visit to England and shall go back to Baghdad as soon as the means of transport become, to an invalid like myself, less painful.

With best regards

Mohammed Hadid

As the author sat next to Sam Falle in St Anthony's main lecture theatre, he watched him read the letter with a pained expression. Falle asked whether he could inscribe his book with a posthumous dedication to Mohammed Hadid. This read: 'This book is dedicated to the memory of my old friend Muhammad Hadid, a wise and humane Iraqi politician and a fine man'.

It was curiously touching that these two old adversaries were now communicating in this poignant way—Hadid through a letter that was never sent during his lifetime; and Falle by inscribing a posthumous dedication to his own book, which Hadid had been reading just before his death.

For the author, this mirrored an understanding that came too late, and a style of civilized behaviour between adversaries that has long since gone not only in Iraq, but in the entire Arab world. Things might well have been quite different had the British been able to communicate with the Iraqis in the humane way that Sir Sam Falle finally came to advocate towards the end of his life—when it was too late. It is also an ironic twist of history that Falle, representing the British in Iraq, should come round to advocating the very same opinions that the opposition parties had spent decades of struggle trying to persuade their own governments to accept.

14

THE LESSONS OF HISTORY

How much blood and treasure (measured in a million dead and trillions of dollars spent) could have been saved had the Americans learned the lessons of history about Iraq's complex past before embarking on their invasion of the country would probably never be known.

What is known is that the planners for the war had no post-war strategy for the country. George W. Bush, who two months prior to the war was still pronouncing 'Iraq' as the very American 'Eye-rak', was given a briefing by three Iraqi exiles living in Washington.[1] The meeting, which was supposed to last twenty minutes, went on for two hours, as the Iraqis soon realized that the president did not know the difference between a Sunni and a Shi'a—an integral piece of the Iraqi puzzle.[2] The Neo-Conservatives (Neo-Cons)—who for years had poured scorn on the idea of democracy in the Arab world—suddenly turned into its most zealous champions, without anyone questioning their U-turn. The Neo-Cons' motives were questionable since most of them were anti-Arab and quite possibly intent on Iraq's destruction, since it was the last Arab country that had the means to stand up to Israel. One Neo-Con, when argumentatively pushed against the wall, blurted out the truth that their plan was 'to get Iraq out of the Middle Eastern equation for at least a quarter century'. Many a Neo-Con had been in the direct employ of the Israeli government, including key figures such as Paul Wolfwoitz and Richard Perle.[3] In 1996 Perle, along with other Neo-Cons, had prepared a report for Benjamin Netanyahu—the then Israeli prime minister—that came to be known as the 'Clean Break' report. This advocated an aggressive policy towards Iraq that included the removal of Saddam Hussein.[4] Perle had worked for Israeli arms manufacturer Soltam, from whom he had received commissions for arms sales. Many Neo-Cons had dual Israeli-U.S. citizenships, including Henry Kissinger, Richard Perle, Paul Wolfowitz and Douglas Feith. Their pro-Israeli position made them agitate for the elimination of Iraq, which was still at war with Israel and which represented the last frontier of the Arab defence line.

The Neo-Cons had no excuse not to compile a detailed historical dossier on Iraq before advocating America to go to war there. Paul Wolfowitz, the lead Neo-Con planner, has been—prior to joining the Pentagon—dean of the Paul H. Nitze School of Advanced International Studies (SAIS) at Johns Hopkins University. As such, one would have expected him, at the very least, to have done some research on Iraq's history, given the vast archival resources at his disposal. Furthermore, SAIS and the American Enterprise Institute (AEI), the Neo-Con bastion, were only blocks from each other and enjoyed much intellectual cross-pollination, though of the right-wing and pro-Israeli kind. AEI was the intellectual home for Washington arch-conservatives such as Newt Gingrich and Lynne and Dick Cheney. Members such as Bernard Lewis, Fareed Zakaria, Fouad Ajami (director of The Middle East Studies Program at SAIS), and Donald Rumsfeld's aide, Steve Herbits (who became known as the 'Bletchley II' group), were all advising Wolfowitz, making it seem stranger still that no one bothered to read the history beforehand.[5] In actual fact, Bernard Lewis is even on record in a statement to *Newsweek Magazine* that Iraq never had a Western-style democracy prior to the US invasion—a clearly erroneous statement. Though an imperfect one, Iraq did have a Western-style democracy of sorts for thirty-eight years (1925–63) as the events recounted in this book make clear. Questions about Islamic history, the history of the Middle East, contemporary Middle East issues and issues particular to Iraq itself needed to be asked, but if they ever were, they received scant or faulty answers from Neo-Cons more expert on Israeli issues than Iraqi ones.

The Neo-Cons were both Arabophobes and Islamophobes. More seriously for Iraq, they also suffered from pronounced Sunniphobia. Americans blundered into Iraq with a total disregard for what the Sunni reaction to the destruction of the regime might be, complacent in the faulty idea that 80 per cent of the country's population was going to embrace them as liberators. This anti-Sunni culture, mainly pushed by the Neo-Cons, trickled down to the CPA (Coalition Provisional Authority) in Baghdad, with devastating effect on all class of Sunnis who, instead of becoming an asset to the coalition, now turned to join the resistance.

L. Paul 'Jerry' Bremer III, who was appointed the U.S. administrator to replace the hapless General Jay Garner, had a mere two weeks from the time he met George Bush in the Oval Office to learn about Iraq. Though a former state department official, he was no Middle East expert and spoke no Arabic. He nonetheless was tasked with putting together a hastily-improvised team to pick up the pieces from Garner's first sketchily-assembled group. The direction on the ground in Iraq and the advice given back to Washington—which influenced a strategy that was to define the Bush presidency and even American policy for a decade after—was being handled by a series of neophyte teams.[6]

On his first day in Baghdad, Bremer issued CPA Order Number One which called for the de-Ba'athification of Iraqi society. The top four ranks in the Ba'ath Party would be removed from their posts and banned from future government employment. One week later, Bremer issued Order Number Two, disbanding Iraq's ministries of defence and interior; the entire Iraqi military, and all of Saddam's special paramilitary organizations. These two orders will be singled out by future historians for their naiveté and political foolishness, which led to nine years—and still counting at the date of writing—of violence, destruction and death in Iraq. On hearing of Bremer's orders, the outgoing and lame-duck Jay Garner was stunned. He is reported to have exclaimed that 'Order Number One was dumb, but Order Number Two is a disaster!'[7]

John Sawers, then the U.K. representative to the CPA and presently the head of MI6, recalls that Bremer, upon his arrival in Baghdad, did not turn up at a dinner arranged by Garner to meet the Iraqi leadership, because he 'wanted to show everybody that he, not Garner, was now in charge'. Such hubris conveyed a sense that Iraqis were almost superfluous. Bremer even said to the Iraqi Governing Council: 'One thing you need to realize. You are not the government. We are. And we are in charge'. According to Garner, Bremer combined the worst faults of ignorance and arrogance. Garner, who liked to quote from Sun Tzu's 'The Art of War', believed that Bremer should have heeded the Chinese general's advice, 'not to go to bed at night with more enemies than you started with in the morning'. Bremer did just the opposite. He never tired of telling Iraqis that he was in charge and did not even bother to hide his disdain for them. 'Those people couldn't organise a parade, let alone run the country', he is reported to have told Wolfowitz. At the time of the invasion and afterwards, the media, both printed and electronic, was awash with ill-thought statements made by the top decision-making echelon of the U.S administration. 'Bring'em on!' declared President George W. Bush, referring to the insurgents in Iraq.[8] Not to be outdone, Vice President Dick Cheney weighed in with the statement (borrowed from General Frederick Stanley Maude upon the general's entry into Baghdad at the head of an occupying British army in 1917): 'We have not come as conquerors but as liberators'.[9] Defence secretary and one of the arch architects of the Iraq misadventure, Donald Rumsfeld pronounced his views that freedom was 'untidy' and that 'stuff happens' when Iraq's museum—one of the richest and most important in the world—was looted as American tanks stood idly by. Also at a meeting in the Oval Office on 21 December 2002, George Tenet, the director of the CIA, uttered the gaffe (which cost him his job) that the whole Iraq Weapons of Mass Destruction (WMD) programme and the legal case for war was 'a slam-dunk'.[10] The president himself was guilty of some rather unpresidential statements such as: 'Fuck Saddam, we're taking him out'—a statement made to three U.S. senators in March 2002, a year before the Iraq invasion took place. To General Jay Garner, just as the latter was about to embark on his Iraq mission on 28 February 2003, the president advised: 'Kick ass, Jay'. But in spite of these rousing words, Garner found himself suddenly replaced by Jerry Bremer without notice after barely a few weeks on the job.[11] This was not unlike what had happened in Iraq under the British in 1921 when the acting-civil commissioner, A. T. Wilson, was suddenly fired unceremoniously only to be replaced by Sir Percy Cox after the Iraqis had rebelled against the British occupation of the country.

Several similarities of cover-ups and lies existed between the American and British forays into Iraq. The Americans went to extraordinary lengths to hide the fact that no WMDs were ever found, since confessing to such truth would have vitiated their whole rationale for going to war. In this they were joined by their British allies in the present Iraq War. 'Major combat operations in Iraq have ended. In the battle of Iraq the U.S. and our allies have prevailed', trumpeted President Bush (the president later apologized for his hasty statement), as he stood under a banner that read 'Mission Accomplished' on the USS Lincoln aircraft carrier on 2 May 2003. Secretary of state Colin Powell's assurances to the United Nations that Iraq possessed nuclear, chemical and biological weapons were not any less embarrassing for their total inaccuracy, as he himself was forced to admit long after the destruction of Iraq had taken place.

The British, during their time in Iraq, had been equally economical with the truth. T. E. Lawrence prophetically wrote in *The Sunday Times* on 22 August 1920—almost a century earlier—that 'the people of England have been led into a trap in Mesopotamia (Iraq), from which it will be hard to escape with dignity and honour. They have been tricked into it by a steady withholding of information. Things are far worse than we have been told, and our administration is far more bloody and inefficient than the public knows'.

If one delves into Iraq's history for political lessons, certain decisions taken by the British early on were critical to the path the newly-created country was ultimately set on. The addition of Mosul province with its large Kurdish population to the Arab-dominated provinces of Baghdad and Basra, and the decision to perpetuate the Ottoman style of government through Sunni supremacy, were decisions that were to have grave consequences for the future of the new country. The Kurds never accepted their place in the new state, and conducted instead a sporadic guerrilla war from 1921 until 1991 when the Gulf War split off the Kurdish region from the rest of Iraq. In gaining this de facto separation the Kurds did not endear themselves to their Arab countrymen. The latter had believed that the Kurds had shown far too little loyalty to the Iraqi state in their readiness to ally themselves with any foreign power, however hostile. From the Kurdish point of view, it was inhumanly shocking that few Iraqi Arabs shed tears for the 5000 Kurds that Saddam killed in Halabja with chemical weapons. Where sympathy should have been proffered because of such brutality, many thought that the Kurds had got their just desserts for openly betraying Iraq and the Arab cause.[12]

Severe coercion was the tool which successive governments, beginning in 1921, used to quell dissent in the new state. Under Saddam, this coercion was taken to its extreme, making him Iraq's most durable if brutal leader. It is therefore no wonder that a whole school of thought is now gravitating around the long-held (if erroneous) view that Iraq can only be governed by a strong and ruthless leader, at the head of a powerful, highly-centralized and coercive state. Saddam Hussein al-Takriti used Iraq's vast oil revenues to penetrate and control Iraqi society by enriching his closest allies and depriving all others. He crushed any opposition to his regime, using the most horrific forms of torture and death to do so.

Furthermore, the elusive quest to forge an inclusive Iraqi national identity (a long-standing but forlorn dream) was harnessed by Saddam to promote his own legend. Existing ties of loyalty were shattered to be replaced by ties to Saddam himself via the Ba'ath Party. His goal was first to lobotomize the Iraqi people, then to construct a glorious example of 'Iraqi man', a being that somehow transcended sectarian and ethnic divisions, and who owed his primary allegiance to the great leader and the state of Iraq. This came to constitute an epic, if vainglorious, attempt to create a collective identity for the people of Iraq, using a combination of social engineering on a colossal scale with massive doses of violence when needed.

All such attempts were bound to fail, and eventually did fail, under Saddam as under previous Iraqi regimes. The task of creating an 'Iraqi' identity that would bind together Sunni and Shi'a, while simultaneously accommodating the Kurds in the north, has proved to be so far too daunting and unfulfillable. Iraq did, however, experience displays of national unity in the rebellion against the British in 1920 and in the defence of the homeland against Iran in the bloody war years 1980 to 1988. But these constituted major traumatic events; otherwise, such displays of national cohesion were few and far between. Constant foreign interference in Iraq's affairs was another reason why the state could never achieve any such national cohesion. Such interference has come in turns from Israel, Iran, the Soviet Union and the United States, which at various times supported Kurdish or Shi'a aspirations against the central authority.

Such a complex and traumatic legacy will almost certainly prove too difficult to overcome in the absence of a strong centralized state, willing to resort to coercion to impose internal stability. This begs the question of how future Iraqi governments might achieve stability and stop the fragmentation of the country without having to resort to the repressive measures of the past. America learned this to its detriment when it went to war in Iraq without the slightest notion of what to do once it had defeated Saddam Hussein. George Packer, in his book *The*

Assassins' Gate, writes: 'The Iraq war started as a war of ideas, and to understand how and why America came to be in Iraq one has to trace their origins. America, from the outset failed to understand the insurgency stating that it was made up of regime dead-enders and foreign terrorists who cannot possibly have the support of the 'sane element' of the populace. The British during the revolt of 1920, and the French in Vietnam suffered this same problem'.[13]

Just as the British had done in Iraq when they created and manipulated the state, the Americans courted the wrong Iraqi partners for the job of imposing their lofty aim of democracy after the 2003 war. The American ideological 'construct', if indeed it can be called that, was provided by the Neo-Cons, themselves an already tainted and dubiously-motivated lot, far more concerned with the protection and empowering of Israel than with Iraq. The pragmatic consequence of that ideological construct was the deployment of huge U.S. military power against a much weaker adversary. The idea was that by toppling Saddam, a domino effect would come into play, transforming the Middle East into a region of democratically governed countries.[14]

The American invasion of Iraq was nothing more than a replay of the events of the 1920 Iraqi Revolution, with the Americans in 2003 playing the role of the British in 1920. The sequence of events that led to the revolution; the similarity of the individuals tasked to deal with the Iraqis (e.g. substitute Bremer for A. T. Wilson), and even the very use of language by the protagonists, was quite uncanny. For example, both Winston Churchill and George W. Bush asked their respective underlings in Iraq to find words that would not reflect an image to the outside world that the Iraqis were putting up any resistance to their occupation. In the British case, A. T. Wilson and Gertrude Bell were made to pour over dictionaries to find a replacement for the word 'revolution'—finally coming up with 'insurrection' instead.[15]

In both situations, the occupying power committed a major error of judgment by deciding to exclude a major sect from government. The British neglected the Shi'a in 1921, out of vengeance, no doubt, because the Iraqi Revolution of 1920 had been valiantly fought by the Middle Euphrates Shi'a tribes who succeeded in inflicting on the British a significant dent in their armour. The Americans, perhaps foolishly, did not heed this British mistake, and decided, in their turn, to exclude the Sunnis and promote the Shi'a instead, thus creating an immediate sectarian division within the country. By also separating the Kurds from the rest of Iraq for several years, the Americans only added to their own self-inflicted difficulties following the invasion of 2003. How they ever imagined that a successful democracy might be established in Iraq by excluding and alienating the Sunnis and by actively encouraging Kurdish separatism has to be a serious error of judgement.

When it came to governance, the Americans should also have learned from the mistakes that the British committed almost a century earlier in Iraq. The British imported a foreign king to head a new monarchy in a country that had no monarchical tradition. The new king, in turn, brought with him the only Iraqis he knew—who happened to be the Ottoman army officers who had fought alongside him in the Arab Revolt against the Turks. These were a motley group of Sunni individuals, that even the British high commissioner of the time, Sir Henry Dobbs, dubbed as being no more than 'adventurers'.[16] When they were ejected from Syria along with King Faisal, they saw their opportunity for booty disappearing fast, and so were quick to follow him to Iraq, with the aim of collecting it there instead.

The Americans fared no better in their Iraqi incursion of 2003, preferring to deal and be guided by a group of exiles either living in London (and anywhere else except in Iraq) where they had not set foot for decades. This, it must be remembered, was when in-country Iraqis were eking out a pathetic existence under the harshest conditions brought about by American sanctions, which decimated an entire generation of children.[17] There was no attempt by the Americans to enlist the support of local groups (difficult though this may have been) that may have been more representative of Iraqi public sentiment. The 'exiles', for the most part, were well-intentioned groups of individuals that advocated a democratic and secular post-Saddam Iraq under a vaguely-defined American umbrella. After the invasion, most of these 'exiles' were categorically rejected by the public at the ballot box, in favour of groups that had stayed the course inside Iraq, and paying a very heavy price to do so. This experience was to be repeated in the Arab Spring upheavals of 2011 when mostly secular groups sparked change in the Arab World (e.g. Egypt, Tunisia, and Morocco up to the time of writing) only to lose at the elections to the far better prepared and experienced Islamic parties.

One matter that cannot be ignored in any topic regarding the Middle East is the racist attitude shown by Western powers towards the inhabitants of Iraq and the wider Middle East. This attitude is sinisterly wedded to a pervading sense of prejudice against and hatred of Islam.[18] It is doubtful indeed that the U.S. or the other Western powers will ever be able to resolve their differences with the peoples of the Middle East if they do not shake off this bigoted attitude. Patrick Seale, the noted journalist and author, delivered a key-note speech at the British Academy on 18 November 2010, with the title 'America's War against Islam', in which he stated—at the very outset—that as far as the people of the region are concerned America *is* at war with Islam. He argued that hostility to the West had spread well beyond the confines of extremist groups such as al-Qaida (representative of a minute percentage of Islamist thinking) to groups that reject al-Qaida's violent methods. This is because the overwhelming majority in the area is stirred by anger and humiliation at America's wars against Muslim countries; by America's one-sided policy in favour of Israel; and by the increasingly shabby way that Muslims and their religion are treated by the West.

George W. Bush, driven by the Neo-Cons, unwittingly became the father of the 'Freedom-for-Iraq' idea, using stirring language straight out of Woodrow Wilson's Fourteen Points. It is worth quoting part of a speech Bush delivered to the American Enterprise Institute on 26 February 2003, in illustration:

America has made and kept this kind of commitment before—in the peace that followed a world war. After defeating enemies, we did not leave behind occupying armies, we left constitutions and parliaments. We established an atmosphere of safety, in which responsible, reform-minded local leaders could build lasting institutions of freedom. In societies that once bred fascism and militarism, liberty found a permanent home.

There was a time when many said that the cultures of Japan and Germany were incapable of sustaining democratic values. Well, they were wrong. Some say the same of Iraq today. They are mistaken. The nation of Iraq—with its proud heritage, abundant resources and skilled and educated people—is fully capable of moving toward democracy and living in freedom.

The world has a clear interest in the spread of democratic values, because stable and free nations do not breed the ideologies of murder. They encourage the peaceful pursuit of a better life. And there are hopeful signs of a desire for freedom in the Middle East. Arab intellectuals have called on Arab governments to address the 'freedom gap' so their peoples can fully share in the progress of our times. Leaders in the region speak of a new Arab charter that champions internal reform, greater political participation, economic openness, and free trade. And from Morocco to Bahrain and beyond, nations are taking genuine steps toward political reform. A new regime in Iraq would serve as a dramatic and inspiring example of freedom for other nations in the region.

It is presumptuous and insulting to suggest that a whole region of the world—
or the one-fifth of humanity that is Muslim—is somehow untouched by the
most basic aspirations of life. Human cultures can be vastly different. Yet the
human heart desires the same good things, everywhere on Earth. In our desire
to be safe from brutal and bullying oppression, human beings are the same. In
our desire to care for our children and give them a better life, we are the same.
For these fundamental reasons, freedom and democracy will always and everywhere have greater appeal than the slogans of hatred and the tactics of terror.

Success in Iraq could also begin a new stage for Middle Eastern peace, and set
in motion progress towards a truly democratic Palestinian state. The passing
of Saddam Hussein's regime will deprive terrorist networks of a wealthy
patron that pays for terrorist training, and offers rewards to families of suicide
bombers. And other regimes will be given a clear warning that support for terror will not be tolerated.[19]

Stirring words, indeed, one might conclude, but as it was to prove,
more honoured in the breach than the fulfilment. If only the ideas of
freedom and democracy embodied in that speech had been uttered by
an Arab leader—any Arab leader from 1918 onwards—such a leader
would have been carried high on his peoples' shoulders and would have
attained historic greatness. Unfortunately for all concerned, George W.
Bush's words turned out to be no more than empty rhetoric. The American invasion itself turned out to be a catastrophe and the post-invasion
administration nothing but an exercise in gross greed and ill-planning.
It could and should have been considerably different.

The whole Iraq story from inception to aftermath has hinged on the
pressing question of freedom and the struggle to achieve it. The United
States could have played the role of facilitator rather than that of
destroyer and plunderer. Indeed, in an earlier role that America played
in the Middle East, its president, Woodrow Wilson, would not be satisfied with being the author of the Fourteen Points only; he actively
asked the Paris Peace Conference to agree to send a commission to
determine what the people of the Middle East wanted for themselves
as far as government. Howard Bliss, president of the American University of Beirut and a friend of President Wilson's, had persuaded the latter that a just and equitable settlement was badly needed in the Middle
East. The people there, Bliss argued, were 'earnestly and passionately'
depending on Wilson's Twelfth Point as well as on the Anglo-French
Declaration of November 1918, both of which promised a government
of the people's own free choice.[20] Bliss had stressed to Wilson that the
people of the area favoured the United States as guardian to guide

them towards eventual democratic rule, and not the British or the French that they detested because of their repressive colonialist record. It is an irony of history, that instead of enjoying an exalted position, America is presently at a nadir in its fortunes in the region.

The Paris conference was tied up in the Gordian knot that was the Middle East. Questions abounded on what to do with Arab lands; with the Jews and Palestine; with Armenians, Kurds, Assyrians and a host of other minorities; as well as all those problems inherited wholesale from the Ottomans. The conference accepted that a commission should indeed be sent to the area to investigate. The decision was music to Faisal's ears. He wrote to President Wilson saying that he could not find words to express his gratitude for such an opportunity provided to the Arabs to express 'their own purposes and ideas for their national future'.[21]

It is of interest, from a comparative history point of view at least, to list those recommendations that the commission advocated particularly for Iraq:

1. Iraq should not be colonized but governed by a mandate system. This was a pointed dismissal of the British plan in place for direct rule in Iraq.
2. Unity for Mesopotamia that included Basra, Baghdad and Mosul, with protection provided for the rights of Kurds and Assyrians.
3. The people should have choice in the form of government they wished to live under.
4. An acknowledgement that the people of Iraq wanted America as the mandate power with no second option.
5. An acknowledgement of the Iraqi fear that given the country's rich resources, it would be a difficult task stopping any mandatory power from exploiting the country's riches, or even importing huge numbers of Indian immigrant labourers to work there (even if they happened to be mainly Muslims), as this might eventually threaten or dilute Iraq's Arab culture.

As was made clear, the mandatory power that the people desired was the United States of America. It took this same U.S.A. another ninety years to assume a role akin to this in Iraq and, when it finally did so, it managed to leave behind only chaos and destruction. And what of the last recommendation, that warned against exploiting the country's riches? No exact figures have been released so far about the sums squandered by the occupying Americans and their Iraqi cohorts, but informed estimates easily run into a trillion dollar figure. If one were to factor in the actual cost of the war, the sum would run into more trillions. The tragic and incalculable cost in terms of the massive loss of life easily tops one million human beings.

Returning to the King-Crane Commission, their mission seems to have been an early prediction that the Americans would lose their way in 2003. To start with, Woodrow Wilson made the extraordinary remark that 'these two men (King and Crane) were particularly qualified to go to Syria precisely because... they knew *nothing* about it'—as indeed Bremer knew nothing about Iraq in 2003. Wilson's secretary of state, Robert Lansing, believed the directives given to King-Crane by President Wilson were shrouded in mystery; that no clear mission was outlined of what King-Crane were expected to do and that the 'spear of investigation' was left far too ambiguous.[22] Margaret MacMillan, a noted historian of the period, doubts that Wilson himself knew much about the Arab world. She suggests that his Twelfth Point was never meant by him to apply to that region.[23] Moreover, King and Crane were part of the zealous drive for a contemporary American missionary presence in the Arab world.[24] Indeed, Harry Howard notes throughout his authoritative book, *The King-Crane Commission*, that King-Crane and their support staff were more interested in protecting the rights of Christians in the area—especially Lebanon and Syria— rather than in any meaningful reading of Arab aspirations.

The King-Crane report when it was finally written ran to over 3000 pages. Despite its volume and the publicity surrounding it, it received scant attention by the French or the British. Georges Picot, the French foreign minister, told the Emir Faisal on 18 June 1919, that the commission 'had been sent out privately by President Wilson, and its findings would carry no weight at all with the [1919] Conference'. In the case of America, President Wilson's death just prior to the report's official publication also spelt the death of the report itself and it remains buried to this day. Crane had written to Wilson setting out the recommendations of the commission; in his letter, he assured Wilson that the area was ready for statehood, combining as it did three important elements: 'The rich and beautiful Arabic language, the presence of the Christian and Moslem faiths, and an ancient and interesting culture'.[25] Whatever went through Wilson's mind when he read Crane's letter, if indeed he ever did read it, will never be known. What is known, as reported above, is that the King-Crane report was shelved after Wilson's death and never again saw the light of day. Several commission members, such as Dr. George Montgomery and Captain William Yale, allowed afterwards that they were fearful that the Muslim majority would submerge the Christian community, with ominous consequences for the latter. It was striking that they had no such fears about Jewish designs on Palestine, since these were ones they ardently supported in the manner of today's evangelical Christians.

One strong theme of the shelved report was that Arab nationalism was very much alive at the time and would certainly play a role in any future ordained for the area. Faisal met with the commission and submitted documents to it which were signed by more than 300,000 Syrians, requesting him to put their hopes for an independent Arab nation before the King-Crane fact-finding commission. Though Faisal spoke eloquently when putting forth the Arab case, many members (led by the ubiquitous Captain Yale) remained convinced that Arab nationalism was an artificially-created phenomenon since in those Arab lands that the Turks did not govern, there was no discernible sentiment for it.

The sad part of the Iraq story is that it did produce men of calibre though regrettably they were unable to propel their country forward towards a free and democratic future. It is this author's contention that the period 1918–63 produced a plethora of men equal in stature to any nationalist leaders of that era. Some examples of these are the fifteen Mandubin that met at the Haydar Khana Mosque to demand the withdrawal of the British and the independence of the country in 1920. Those men represented a wide cross-section of Iraqi society: Shi'a, Sunni and Kurdish notables and intellectuals, religious leaders, and Iraqi officers returning from the war. All were eager to join the nascent nationalist movement. Names such as Baban, al-Sadr, Swaidi, Abul-Timman, Chadirchi, Naqshbandi, Daftari, and Fattah Pasha—representing all the sects of Iraq—all were to play a significant future role in a country that was yet to be invented by the British.

At the Haydar Khana meeting, the fifteen elected notables were asked to conduct talks with the British authorities. That was the first taste of democracy that Iraq experienced. The elected men met with A. T. Wilson to demand a parliament that would democratically appoint a government that the people wanted, in an environment of free speech and freedom of the press.

The British responded by shipping most of these early democrats into exile so as to banish their ideas of democracy in case they spread to the general population and upset Britain's imperial design for the direct rule of the country. However, this measure did not stop a tidal wave of dissent from spreading to the tribes of the Mid-Euphrates, with whom Ja'far Abul-Timman had been diligently liaising prior to his banishment by the British. The tribes stood up to the British and fought them for a full six months, bravely giving back as good as they got. They were the early national heroes of Iraq. Even today, their 1920 Revolution remains embedded in every Iraqi mind.

The hope of putting Iraq on a democratic path was lost right there and then. The people and their leaders could not have given more ample proof of their desire for freedom and democracy; nor of their willingness to pay the price in blood and treasure. Had their struggle for democracy been allowed to succeed, it certainly would have set a template for others in the region. In addition, the promises made to the Arabs and contained in the McMahon-Hussein correspondence, had they been fulfilled, could have been the basis upon which a free and united Arab world arose.[26] Wilson's Twelfth Point and the Anglo-French Declaration, had they been applied, would have further cemented such an entity. Had the recommendations of the King-Crane Commission been adopted and implemented, and had Britain and France not adhered to their sordid imperialist plans of exploiting the area both politically and commercially, the area today would have been a democratic one.

When the state of Iraq was finally concocted by the British in 1921, many of the nationalist elements were 'turned', so that practically all were represented in the new government. Talib al-Naqib (he of the famous Lady Cox tea party lore), for example, came back from his British-imposed exile in Ceylon to join a government whose British patrons he had initially opposed. Abdel-Rahman al-Naqib (no relation to Talib) who had once vowed never to serve under a Hashemite, had obviously changed his mind and accepted to become Iraq's first prime minister with Faisal as king. Yassin al-Hashemi finally returned to Iraq after having been ostracized by Faisal—then king of Syria—for having preferred to resign as minister of defence rather than go into battle against a much mightier French army at Maysalun, bent on ejecting Faisal from the throne.[27] Hashemi, who had correctly foreseen that his well outgunned army would be annihilated by the French in a matter of hours, was to go on to lead a benign opposition to several pro-British Iraqi governments.

The first decade of the new Iraq was dominated by the old-style politicians, many of whom were nationalists who had played a role in the 1920 Revolution. The rapprochement that had been forged between the leadership of the Sunnis and Shi'a during that revolution was the perfect environment for a new country like Iraq to flourish in. It brought cohesion amongst members of the intelligentsia, the local merchants, the landowners and notables; as well as the theologians and government officials. Unfortunately for the future of the country, this leadership lacked any long-term political, social or economic agenda outside the immediate aim of evicting the British forces from Iraq. It suffered from being ineffective because of its composition and the uneasy relations between its members. It lacked governing skills, and no one man ever emerged as its natural leader.

The army officers, who made up an important bloc in Iraq's new power structure, were equally bereft of any coherent ideology or beliefs. Their membership in *al-Ahd* secret society had not seemed to instil in them the lofty ideals of the leaders of the movement such as 'Aziz Ali Masri.[28] These officers found themselves in a serious dilemma. Since they did not show any great enthusiasm for fighting alongside the British or for Britain's protégé, Sharif Hussein, they stayed for the most part loyal to the Turks. However, confusion soon racked their ranks as the Turks suspected them of being traitors anyway and the British viewed them as enemies. In one episode, a group of 132 Iraqi prisoners of war were dispatched by the British to the Hijaz and told on arrival that they must fight with the Sharif against the Turks. To the surprise of the British and undoubtedly of the Sharif himself, 102 out of the 132 refused to do so. Only three officers joined the Sharif, and these were Ibrahim al-Rawi, Khalid al Madfa'i, and Sa'id al-Madfa'i.[29] When Baghdad fell in 1917, most of these Iraqi officers (with the exception of the members of *al-Ahd*, who were committed Arab nationalists rather than apolitical careerists), saw that the tide was turning against the Turks and that material and social benefits might accrue to them if they did join the Sharif's forces, and so they did.[30] The Sharif was not fooled by their motives and is reported to have told Colonel Wilson that he distrusted the whole lot of them.[31]

Many of the old-style politicians had also been members of *al-'Arabiyya al-Fatat*, sister society of *al-'Ahd*, but relations between the two groups soon lapsed as both had aspired to the same Arab nation-alist aims up until the creation of the new state. Once they decided on power-sharing, all their lofty aims of a joint ideology seem to have evaporated with an 'every man for himself' approach to their prag-matic political life. This soon became clear from the absurd number of political parties that appeared, each chasing some minor political aim to distinguish it from the next. This proliferation of parties played straight into the hands of the British—by way of the old 'divide and rule' policy. Britain simply toyed with these divergent groups, con-cerned only with assuring the protection of its own interests. One example of British dominance was the signature of the 1925 oil con-cession with its one-sided pro-British provisions that left a paltry share for the Iraqi people themselves. Another was the signature of the 1930 Anglo-Iraqi Treaty, an onerous 'agreement' that left Iraq seething with an anger that finally erupted years later in the Uprising of 1948 (al-Wathba). This uprising brought about the cancellation of the Portsmouth Treaty that had been designed to replace the discred-ited 1930 one.

Many of these Iraqi parties disappeared almost immediately after their formation and usually after their leaders' participation in govern-ment to implement a particular British demand. It will be remembered that one such person, 'Abdal-Muhsen al-Sa'dun, prime minister several times, killed himself, leaving a heart-breaking suicide note to his son that said that he could no longer bear to live with the public's percep-tion of him as a British stooge.

During this period, no leader of the new Iraq was able to stand up to the British and the palace; in fact, most leaders cooperated more than willingly with them. Yassin al-Hashimi, who led the National Ikha'a Party, was meant to represent the opposition. His party was twinned with that of Ja'far Abul-Timman's to form the National al-Ta'akhi Party. This was supposed to fight for citizens' constitutional rights for honest elections and representative government. Many of the nationalist elements in Iraq did join this party, including a young Kamil Chadirchi. In fact, he became the right-hand man of Hashemi, sat on the executive committee, and edited the party's paper. Yet despite such human assets, the union of these two parties nevertheless failed. Each disappeared shortly afterwards, having managed to offer only a token opposition to the system.

Collectively, the army officers-turned-politicians and the civilian pol-iticians failed during the decade of the twenties to bring any ideological content to their activities. Nor were they able to produce honestly-elected leaders who could have matured into national heroes in the eyes of the public. Devoid of any such ideology to guide their actions, the combined army-civilian nexus failed miserably in elevating the political life of the country into the democracy with which it supposedly started life. The British were not about to promote democracy in a country of their own invention, after they had become aware, as early as 1910, of Iraq's vast oil potential and its strategic importance in safeguarding the route to India. From an Iraqi democratic point of view, local British influence, an ever-compliant monarchy and a political system that emasculated all political opposition, left little chance to develop the necessary institutions essential to the creation of a democratic and modern state.[32]

The thirties brought new hope for reform. The advent of al-'Ahali Group, which rose meteorically in the public's esteem, culminated in the group's assumption of a lead role in the Bakr Sidqi coup of 1936 and in its subsequent government. Without doubt, the coup represented Iraq's second real opportunity to create the elusive democratic modern state that Iraqis hungered for. Yet again, it was another democratic moment lost. Why, one might ask, with so much going for the new government, were the leaders unable to get their act together? After all, every Iraqi sect was represented in the leadership line-up. Bakr Sidqi and Hikmat Sulaiman, ostensibly members of al-'Ahali, should have stuck to al-'Ahali's democratic agenda. Abul-Timman, leader of al-'Ahali, and Chadirchi, a cabinet minister in government, should have—together with Sidqi and Sulaiman—been able to implement the group's reformist programmes in which they strongly believed. The young generation al-'Ahali members such as Mohammed Hadid, Hussain Jamil and others, all brimming with hope and ideas for the democratic future the group envisaged, were solidly behind the government. The monarchy was alive, and doing well with a popular, young and nationalist king (Ghazi) rumoured to be himself in favour of the coup. The scenario was almost too perfect, noted the distinguished Iraqi writer Majid Khadduri.

The reasons the 1936 coup failed to develop into a functioning democracy, as was the intention of its two principal participants—the military and al-'Ahali—were to do with outlook. It transpired, to the detriment of Iraq, that the military did not truly subscribe to al-'Ahali's reformist credo. As in the aftermath of the 1920 Revolution, Iraqis

271

failed once more to follow up on a real opportunity for change. This was to happen yet again during the last and final opportunity presented by the 1958 Revolution. Once more, the military failed to honour its pledge to hand over the reins of government to a democratically-elected parliamentary government. Added to this, the military split amongst itself, thus leading to fissures in the ranks of the political parties that had previously agreed to cooperate with the revolution as a united front.

This book has been at pains to argue that the National Democratic Party was the party that held the most promise for a democratic regime in Iraq. The party had the vision, the ideology and the men to manage such a transformation. Kamel Chadirchi was the closest that Iraq ever got to having its own Nelson Mandela. Nevertheless, all was not plain sailing for the NDP. Again and again, Chadirchi suffered the indignity of imprisonment, which seems to be the lot of all great men in nations struggling for their freedom. His country was thus deprived of his most productive years, simply because of Nuri al-Said obsessing about Chadirchi and about communism. Nuri took an almost self-satisfying pleasure in intoning, as in the film 'Casablanca', the phrase 'Round up the usual suspects', whenever the slightest whiff of dissent appeared in the country.

Be this as it may, the NDP was not without its own internal problems. The group did not manage to escape the trait of 'Iraqi' divisiveness. Even at the start when it was still known as al-'Ahali, the fissures had started to appear. The group could not hold its members together firmly and lost Abd al-Fattah Ibrahim, a key founding member, because he viewed Chadirchi as an outsider who had taken over the leadership without ever having been elected to do so. Ibrahim viewed himself as the natural leader of the group, and wanted to author the ideology of al-Sha'biyya, which pitted him against Chadirchi. The latter ultimately won the argument to remain leader, though al-Sha'biyya principles were published eventually as written by Ibrahim.

Al-'Ahali's brand of soft socialism always constituted a bugbear for some in Iraq, as well as internally for some members of the group. Indeed, the group that later morphed into the NDP mistakenly carried the stigma of communism. This was engendered by the government's continued smear campaigns, which often put the party on the defensive. It must also be admitted that certain individuals in the group, though not communists themselves, held extreme left-wing views which were not shared by the mainstream membership. This played into the hands of the government and did their party no favours. Fear of the NDP's alleged communist sympathies was also anathema to another power block that was emerging in Iraq at the time, which was that of the tribes.[33] These tribes, prior to the 1920 Revolution and the creation of the state of Iraq, had lived a spartan, martial and impoverished existence punctuated by carrying out raids (*gharat*) against each other. Many adopted the nationalist sentiment that called for the ejection of the foreign occupier now in their midst and had valiantly fought the British whose presence had then permeated the country and its government. Successive cabinets had helped enrich their leaders who now sat in parliament leading newly-affluent lives that dampened their national fervour. Since many of them were illiterate, they proved easy prey for the government to 'turn' them against 'those communists' of the al-'Ahali who were supposedly about to deprive them of their lands. In 1937 in parliament, Mohammed Hadid had had a heated discussion with a fellow-parliamentarian tribal sheikh. This debate pitted the democratic bloc against the tribal one on the topic of feudalism and agrarian reform. Most attempts at democratic reform by the opposition were voted down by the tribal majority in parliament. This confrontational situation continued until the revolution of 14 July 1958 came to end tribal dominance and went on to pass the Agrarian Reform Act in September of that year.

When the NDP was licensed as a political party in 1946, it was greeted by strong support from a reform-minded public. Although the party became the voice of Iraq's muted call for parliamentary democracy, it was racked by internal strife. Yet again, the divisiveness and the inability to build the core of the party into a solid mass reared its ugly head. Without in any way detracting from Kamil Chadirchi's greatness as an Iraqi leader, he may have suffered from a personality disorder that led him to resign every time his way was not followed.[34] This oversensitive trait was reported by many of his friends (some of them from childhood) as well as by colleagues. It was one reason the party split among itself and disappeared altogether after the 1958 Revolution just as the big democracy prize was within its sights.

The 1958 Revolution was the last of Iraq's unrealized moments for democracy. Iraq might never see such a moment again. Brigadier 'Abdel-Karim Qassem, together with a group of patriotic army officers wishing to bring reform to their country, mounted a revolution that had unprecedented popularity amongst the people. All Iraq's sects were represented; the opposition united and with its members in the cabinet. Qassem himself leaned towards the NDP and as a result, for all intents and purposes, its members became the civilian government. They saw to it that a large number of their reformist policies were implemented. But again, Iraq's divisiveness tore at the core of the country. Only weeks after the revolution took place, 'Abdel-Salaam 'Arif split from Qassem and began pushing Iraq towards the Nasserist-nationalist camp. From this break in ranks, it was downhill all the way. 'Arif did not just split the government; he divided the military as well, and with woeful consequences. As in the past, the spectre rose of democrats fighting nationalists, and Pan-Arabists (*Qawmiyyin*) fighting Iraq First-ers (*Wataniyyin*), leaving Qassem unable to implement the revolution's original democratic aims on his own. Feeling isolated and betrayed, he soon went the way of all dictators. By the end of his rule, Iraq was more divided than ever.

After decades of Saddam Hussein's iron-fist rule, Iraqis became unable to act or think freely in their concentration camp of a country, cut off from the rest of the world. Iraq's per capita income went from US $7000 per annum prior to the Iraq-Iran war, to US $500 per annum in 2002. Saddam lobotomized the population, managing to suppress its endemic divisiveness but at a heavy price that came to destroy the country.

The same divisiveness—reflected in sectarian resentments, ethnic conflicts and tribal rivalries—that plagued Iraq in 1921 still tears at it today. Iraqis have not yet found the answer to the all-important question of national identity. Three decades of rule by the Ba'th, and by Saddam in particular, have served to increase hostilities between communities, as a minority Sunni regime sought to perpetuate its repressive rule over Iraq's disaffected Shi'a and Kurds. This pushed the country down the road of destruction and vengeance, more visible than ever today. The years under Saddam seem to have stripped Iraqis of their sense of common humanity. The continued absence of any civil society following Saddam's fall has led to more scenes of savagery perpetrated by Iraqis against each other. Today, the vacuum created by the lack of leadership—the erstwhile search for an Iraqi Mandela—has contributed to the inability of Iraqis to lead themselves out of the wilderness.[35]

Iraq's only way forward is to find a path that will take it out of the quicksand it has been stuck in since 1921. It has to begin to believe in and exploit its most important resource—which is not its oil, but its people.

Empowering its own people will not be easy to accomplish. It would certainly entail a leader emerging that can galvanize the country into union between its varied people. In its ninety-year history, no visionary, democratic or honestly-elected leader has been allowed to come to power in Iraq despite the availability of many capable men. The iron-fist style of rule favoured first by Nuri, then by Saddam, ensured that Iraq never had a chance to evolve into a democracy since seventy-seven years of its ninety years were ruled by these two men.

It is time that Iraqis underwent a severe critique of their role in the disastrous decline of their country into chaos. Always a fragmented country, which has grappled with the problem of national identity, Iraq's multi-ethnic, multi-sectarian, and multi-religious groups have never managed to blend together in the American 'melting pot' sense, or even in the Canadian 'mosaic' sense. St. John Philby, who knew the country well, quipped that Iraq was a 'boiling melting pot'!

Iraq is not unique in its struggle against national and sectarian divisiveness. Many countries have surmounted similar difficulties by calling on their people to bury their strife-ridden past and come together as a nation that they can look to with pride. In this forgiving spirit, Nelson Mandela said in his inaugural speech as president of the new South Africa on 10 May 1994: 'The time for the healing of wounds has come. The moment to bridge the chasms that divide us has come. We understand that there is no easy road to freedom. We must therefore act as a united people for national reconciliation, for nation building, for our country's renewal. Let there be justice for all. Let there be peace for all. Let freedom reign'. Iraqis might also do well to heed John F. Kennedy's famous exhortation to the American people: 'Ask not what your country can do for you, ask what you can do for your country' as they take responsibility for their own destiny.

The Iraqi 'federalists' who wrote the 2003 constitution attempted to appeal to the Iraqis' higher sense of nationalism. In the preamble to the constitution, they exhorted the people to unite, with rousing words about their common history. Unfortunately such words merely disguised what was a seriously flawed constitution, calculated to promote Iraq's divisiveness rather that its unity.

This is not to belittle in any way Iraq's rich and extraordinary past. This great country which gave the world the alphabet, law, agriculture, scholarship and intellectual endeavour, as well as science and poetry, must now find its future by looking back and drawing strength from its unique past.

The last word might well go to that Iraqi poet, whose stirring colloquial poem relays the words of a prospective bridegroom to the traditional question of, 'Who are you and who are your parents and uncles and tribe?' He speaks for all patriotic Iraqis when he answers thus:

I am the son of Hammurabi, raised on the bank of those two great rivers,
there I spoke the first speech, and fashioned the first letters.
My father's uncles they were Kurds from those wild mountains,
Who bravely fought in other lands, while longing for Iraq.
My mother was a Sunni from Baghdad,
So devout that to the five required prayers, she added yet another;
The brothers of my father, they were Shi'a,
Who battled all who would usurp this place.
From a Turkomanic tribe, came one cousin's wife;
Another cousin's children have a Yazidi for their mother.
My niece's handsome husband is Sabaen,
and my nephew's children speak Armenian, like their maternal clan.
In my blood, stream the rhythms of Syriac, Chaldean and Assyrian,
The sinuous shape of Iraq's mosques formed my proud features,
as did its ancient synagogues and churches–
All built by children of the first givers of the Law.
My tribe is generosity to the guest, and my creed is passion.
I am Iraq; Iraq is me,
who seeks your daughter's hand.

ANNEX

A NOTE ON IRAQ'S OIL

Although the story of Iraq's oil and the promulgation of the landmark Law 80, nationalizing it, is a theme in this book, this annex hopes to provide the reader with more detail about the critical role that oil has played in determining Iraq's modern history.

Two fundamental imperial aims of Britain towards Mesopotamia as it then was, and Iraq as it later became, were to secure the trade route to India and exploit the oil resources of the country.

The state of Iraq was created by the British in 1921. They strongly suspected that the country was rich in oil and were to be proven right when the resource was discovered in huge quantities in 1927. The existence of the mineral was not just known to the British, but to the Ottomans before them. In fact, its existence as a mysterious mineral was known to the Babylonians, and evidence of its use in the construction trade has been found amongst the ruins of Babel in Northern Iraq. In Kirkuk, and specifically in Baba Gurgur, natural gas has burnt its way up through the cracks in the earth's surface for millennia, its flames clearly visible to the area's inhabitants. In Giyara, a few miles from Mosul, tar (or *gair* in Iraqi) would similarly make its way to the surface with flickering flames, the object of amazement. This valued tar was mixed with other building materials in the building trade in Mosul as it was in Babel.

The period from 1901, the date of the first oil concession (known as the D'Arcy Agreement, later the Anglo-Persian Oil Company), until 1927 when oil was discovered in Iraq, was one that was fraught with systematic exploitation by the foreign partner and resentment by the local one. In the case of Iraq, this resentment was to taint its relations with Britain until 1958 when a revolution nationalized the oil industry in the country.[1]

British determination to establish a mandate over Iraq led them to use the pretext of adding the former Ottoman *vilayet* of Mosul to the new Iraqi state *only* if the Iraqis were to sign an oil concession before it could be debated, or approved by their own parliament. This stood in Iraqi historical memory as an example of imperialist greed. It caused the immediate resignation of several Iraqi ministers, who were appalled by the onerous terms of the concession. The Iraqi government itself first refused to sign, but was rail-roaded into doing so when Britain threatened to exclude Mosul from becoming a province of the country it had just created. Faisal I tried to oppose this hidden agenda of the Mandate from being used to twist the Iraqi government's arm, but was met with derisory remarks by Churchill and Cox (the High Commissioner). The latter wrote to Churchill: 'Faisal unmistakably displayed the cloven hoof. I have endeavoured to be absolutely straightforward and frank with him, and treat him like a brother, but there you are, when he is scratched deep enough the racial weakness displays itself'.[2] Churchill himself wrote to Cox: '…it should be explained to him (Faisal) that…it would be most foolish of him to cut himself off from the august authority of the Covenant of the League of Nations [which had recommended the Mandate] which gives him his status in the international circle and in the eyes of the whole world'.[3] Faisal had gone as far as preparing a resolution (it is said in consultation with Ja'far al-Askari, Nuri al-Said and others) opposing the Mandate, which was put to his government. In the end, however, all had to relent in order to have Mosul added to the new country of Iraq.

Mohammed Hadid writes in his memoir that negotiations between the Iraqi and British delegations were so weighted in Britain's favour, both in terms of technical capability and knowledge of the workings of the oil industry, that the Iraqi side found itself in the absurd situation of having to include *British* oil experts (suggested by the British delegation) to help their side.[4] The concession was first granted in 1925 for a limited number of locations, and with specific surface areas. This concession was based on a 'promise' that the Ottoman government prior to the First World War had given to the Turkish Petroleum Company.[5] The deal had included a 5 per cent share to an Ottoman national of Armenian descent, Calouste Gulbenkian, who came to be known universally as 'Mr. Five Percent'. Iraq, which had been promised a 20 per cent share, was unaware of the deception, which was in flagrant defiance of all post-WWI promises contained in President Wilson's new world vision, as spelt out in his Fourteen Points.[6]

On 15 October 1927 at three in the morning, one of the drilling sites erupted at Baba Gurgur (about 6 miles northwest of Kirkuk). A great roar resonated over a 10 square mile area, accompanied by a gusher that shot up 50 feet, drenching the entire area with oil and poisonous gas. Baba Gurgur Oil Well Number 1, as it was called, flowed at 95,000 barrels a day for an entire week before it could be capped. The questions surrounding Iraqi oil had been firmly answered. Oil existed and did so in bountiful quantities.

The race between Britain, France, Italy, Germany and America had already started for each to get a share of this then critical resource. Oil had already been discovered in western Pennsylvania in the 1860s, and been put to lucrative use.[7]

A German company had signed a contract with Ottoman Turkey to build the Berlin-Baghdad-Basra railway (the *Baghdadbahn*) which included a concession to explore the natural resources on either side of the railway line within an agreed distance.[8] At the same time, the Turkish Petroleum Company applied for a concession for the exploration of oil in the *vilayet* of Mosul, which in Ottoman times had included the provinces of Mosul, Kirkuk, Arbil and Slimaniyya. Calouste Gulbenkian obtained a 'promise' from the Ottoman state to grant the company an oil concession for Mosul Province and for the 'Arab' portion of that territory (inferring thereby that Mosul was still part of Turkey), to be divided between Britain and France. Following the First World War, the Turkish Petroleum Company applied to the new Iraqi state, which was under British tutelage, to grant the concession that the Ottomans had failed to give–based on the now outdated 'promise' that the defunct Empire had made to Gulbenkian. The latter now insisted that this was an 'obligation' that had to be honoured by Iraq's new government.[9]

The Turkish Oil Company by that time was composed of the Anglo-Persian Oil Company and the Royal Dutch Shell Company, with a percentage allocated to Gulbenkian for having brokered the deal. The United States and France watched the bartering for Iraqi oil closely and soon made their own move to receive their share of the spoils of war.[10]

Both the San Remo Agreement and the Versailles Conference had allocated a 25 per cent share of Iraqi oil to France and a 20 per cent share to the new Iraqi State. The French based their claim on these agreements. The United States then jumped into the fray, demanding *its* share under the 'Open Door' policy that stipulated that no one company could monopolize *any* natural resource *anywhere* in the world. The U.S., no doubt for its own purposes, challenged the legality of the concession demanded from the new Iraqi State as being merely based on a promise the Ottoman Sultan had granted the Turkish Oil Company. It stated that an issue of such importance should be decided by the government and the people of the country concerned.[11] This disingenuous U.S. tactic succeeded in stalling the negotiations for a new concession for a number of years. By then, the competing parties had decided to stop fending off each other's claims and to unite in joint exploration of Iraqi oil. It was agreed that Britain, France, Holland and the United States would each receive 23.75 per cent of the shares of a proposed new company, with the balance of 5 per cent to be allocated to Gulbenkian. This agreement flagrantly denied Iraq its agreed 20 per cent share in what must be counted as one of the biggest scams in corporate history. The new Iraqi government strongly opposed such outrageous unfairness, so much so that the British government interceded with the company to reach a fairer settlement with the Iraqis, perhaps foreseeing the pitfalls that such an agreement would create in any future dealings with the country. The company, however, categorically refused any change, even deciding to write a clause into the agreement, allowing itself to deny Iraq its rightful share![12] Considering that Gulbenkian's 5 per cent share grossed him millions of dollars in present-value money, Iraq's rightful 20 per cent share, had it been paid it, certainly would have gone a long way in accelerating the country's transformation into a viable modern state.

Negotiations dragged on until 1924, by which time several Iraqi ministers had resigned in protest at the unfairness of it all. As stated, the British government then deployed the 'Mosul' card to persuade the Iraqi government to sign the concession without submitting it to a vote in parliament or a referendum by the Iraqi people as the Iraqi Constitution stipulated it must do. The Mosul question revolved around the historical fact that when hostilities ended between Britain and the Ottoman Empire with a declaration of an armistice in 1918, it stopped both the British and Ottoman armies outside the Mosul territorial limits. This gave the province the status of one that was not part of the territories that had been split from the Ottoman Empire. Indeed, the fate of Mosul remained undecided until 1925, with both Britain and Turkey vying to add it to either the new Iraqi state or the new republic of Turkey. The British government, however, was not about to relinquish easily such an oil-rich territory, and certainly not to a defeated foe. Nevertheless, it decided to use the conflict as a ploy to threaten the new Iraqi government. If the Iraqis did not sign the concession, Britain told them, it was not prepared to support their claim to Mosul. The ploy worked, and Iraq signed the concession on the 14 March 1925. This signing predated the agreement that was later reached between competing Western countries for Iraq's oil.[13] This also preceded the signature of 'The Red Line Agreement', which effectively created a monopoly for the exploration of oil in the territories that had been carved out of the defeated Ottoman Empire.[14]

The discovery of oil in Iraq in such huge quantities following the eruption in Baba Gurgur in 1927 prompted oil companies to quickly finalize their agreements and reach a 'no-compete' clause. Shortly thereafter, the Iraq Petroleum Company (IPC) began to agitate to change the clauses in the 1925 Concession that it found no longer commercially viable. Most importantly among these was the clause that limited exploration to twenty-four specific areas of 8 square miles each—an area totaling 192 square miles. The company began by demanding the extension of the time period for exploration of those areas. Its pretext was that, due to the unresolved Mosul issue, it could not complete exploration work because the boundaries of the Iraqi state had yet to be finalized. Once Mosul joined Iraq, the company began to argue instead that the area limited by the concession was too small to justify the huge investment in infrastructure and equipment. It now insisted that the concession area be expanded to 32,000 square miles, running from the east of the Tigris up to the Iraqi-Turkish-Iranian border.

On 23 March 1931, a new oil concession was signed. This followed a three-year negotiation period between IPC and the Iraqi government, in which the latter asked the company to construct a railway from the oil sources in Iraq to Haifa on the Mediterranean. It also requested that the company pay a rental for the concession area, guarantee a minimum payment from the oil revenues, and subject the company to a similar tax as that imposed on other companies. This latter concession was signed for a period of seventy years. In it the company relinquished its exploration right to Iraqi land west of the Tigris, agreeing to build a pipeline from Kirkuk to the Mediterranean, with the line forking in two directions–one to Haifa, and the other to Tripoli in Lebanon. This pipeline would pump 3 million tons of oil per annum.

Despite the leniency shown by the Iraqi government to the IPC, which came at a considerable financial cost to the former, secret American congressional documents released years later reveal that the IPC deliberately delayed the work on the pipeline. It also ceased exploration work in the Kirkuk area, despite the recent discovery of oil there. The reason behind the IPC's actions was the discovery of oil in Qatar by the same group of companies. They wished to use this discovery as further leverage to increase their already highly advantageous position in Iraq. Economically speaking, this was a major setback for Iraq's development. Its weak position *vis-à-vis* the oil companies showed its vulnerability in not being able to defend itself against such a monopoly.

In the same period, a new company by the name of British Oil Development (BOD), which was later joined by Italian, German and French companies, attempted to break the monopoly of the IPC by applying for a concession in the area west of the Tigris. This was done in the name of a new company to be called the Mosul Oil Company. The concession, when it was granted, applied to an area north of latitude line thirty-three, as well as an area that covered 24,000 square miles. The Iraqi government was to receive a 20 per cent share of the crude oil extracted. However, this company too did not fulfill its obligations towards the Iraqi state. In addition, the crude oil extracted was of a lesser quality than that extracted by IPC. By 1927, the IPC was successful in buying up the shares of the Mosul Oil Company. It wound up in full possession of both concessions in Baghdad and Mosul. In 1938, the Iraqi government awarded a concession similar to that of BOD to yet another company named the Basra Oil Company.[15] This concession was added to those of the IPC and the Mosul Oil Company, which were now owned by the oil cartel that came about through the 'As Is' agreement and the Achnacarry Agreement (named after the castle in Scotland where it was signed).[16] This cartel now controlled international oil through the seven oil companies. These came to be known as 'the Seven Sisters', a derogatory name coined by the President of the Italian Oil Company (ENI), which had been excluded from the cartel. Thus it came to be that one cartel of international companies had taken over the entire territory of Iraq, east to west and north to south, under a new entity called the IPC Group, with the exception of a small oil field north of Khanaqeen on the Iraq-Iran border that belonged to British Petroleum (BP).[17] This latest IPC concession was awarded following the 1936 Bakr Sidqi Coup, when Nuri al-Sa'id had become Prime Minister following a pseudo-coup against the Jamil al-Madfa'i government. It is said that Nuri's own Minister of Defence, Taha al-Hashemi, and his Minister of Finance, Rustum Haidar, were vehemently opposed to such an onerous agreement, but both stopped short of resignation.

With the advent of the Second World War, the IPC asked the Iraqi government to postpone the company's commitments towards Iraq until two years had elapsed after the end of the war. The Iraqi government at first balked at the idea. It only agreed once an interest-free loan of half a million pounds, and a further loan of one million pounds were promised by the IPC after an armistice was signed.[18]

By the end of the war, the IPC and the Iraqi government had become entangled in a dispute, ostensibly over a formula the IPC had recommended for the payment of oil royalties to the Iraqi government. In reality, Iraq's intent was to use the negotiations with the IPC as a way of objecting to the manner in which Iraq was being exploited. The opposition parties were united in pressuring the government to do whatever was needed to redress the balance in its relationship with the IPC. They insisted that the concession had to be rid of the greed that favoured the oil companies while denying Iraq its legitimate rights. Furthermore, the monopoly that the IPC had enjoyed in the exploration of Iraq's oil barred other oil companies from operating in the country. This made competition that would certainly have benefited Iraq impossible.

Iraq's demands were soon given an important fillip when other oil producing countries were signing fifty-fifty concessions with oil companies operating in their territories (e.g. Venezuela and Saudi Arabia). Concurrently, Iran's nationalist leader Mohammed Mossadegh nationalized the Anglo-Persian Oil Company, thereby attaining hero-status not only in his own country, but in all other oil-rich countries where greedy foreign oil cartels operated. Iraq sprang up to ask for *its* oil to be nationalized. In fact, this would become a recurrent theme till the 1958 Revolution, which finally *did* nationalize Iraq's oil with the landmark Law 80. This law returned to Iraq its right to explore its own oil in 95 per cent of the country's surface area. This had previously been the exclusive right of foreign oil companies, according to the unfair concession they had extracted from its government. The 5 per cent remaining represented oil-producing territories already being operated by these oil companies. Law 80 allowed them to continue to operate under the existing concession. Indeed, Law 80 had global reverberations, as it was the first time that an oil-producing country had resorted to legislation in order to restore its sovereignty in the face of onerous concessions that favoured foreign interests. It has since been accepted that this law had a domino effect, as other countries soon began passing similar legislation.[19]

NOTES

PROLOGUE

1. When Sabounchi returned from his exile by the British to his hometown of Mosul, thousands were at the train station to welcome him back. As one observer noted, it was as if the entire town had turned out. Such was the public fervor for freedom and for anyone carrying its banner.
2. See Margaret MacMillan, *Peacemakers*, p. 401.
3. Al-Hajjaj ibn Yusuf, a controversial administrator of the Umayyad Empire known for his draconian—even savage—methods, was sent to govern (what is now) Iraq in 694 A.D. He, like Faisal after him, detected the divisive nature of the local inhabitants. His notorious 'O Iraq, O land of divisiveness' lives on in Arab schoolbooks. However, both the Hajjaj and Faisal failed to understand the Iraqis' phobia for foreign occupiers. Iraq soon saw the back of Hajjaj, when he gave up on dominating it and returned to Syria.

INTRODUCTION

1. Apart from agriculture, the land's other people, the Chaldeans and the Assyrians, gave the world the centralized state, division of labour, organized religion, monumental building, civil engineering, and mathematics and law, not to mention wheeled vehicles and a host of other inventions.
2. Ahmad Chalabi, a leading Iraqi politician in the post-Saddam era, told the author in an interview in London, in November 2010, that Ayatollah Sistani, Iraq's leading Shi'a cleric, had told Chalabi shortly after Saddam's fall, that this time the Shi'a leadership should not repeat the mistake of their predecessors but should fight for their democratic place in the country's government.
3. Karsh & Karsh, *Empires of the Sand*: A *Struggle for Mastery in the Middle East, 1789–1923*, (Cambridge, MA: Harvard University Press, 1999), p. 186. See also the same book (p. 194) for letter from Jamal Pasha to

Faisal warning him of British/French perfidy regarding the Sykes-Picot Agreement and the Balfour Declaration.

4. Abdal-Jabbar 'Abd Moustafa, *Tajribat al-'Amal al-Jabhawi fi al-Iraq*, pp. 85–6.

5. Hanna Batatu, *Old Social Classes and the Revolutionary Movements of Iraq*, (Princeton: University Press 1978), p. 323.

6. Tawfiq al-Swaidi, *Mudhkarati*, 2nd edition, Dar-al-Hikma, 1999.

7. T. E. Lawrence, *Seven Pillars of Wisdom: A Triumph*, (New York: Anchor Books, 1991), p. 45.

8. The anthem on Baghdad Radio announcing the 1958 Revolution was Amjad ya Arab Amjad.

9. Albert Hourani, *A Vision of History: A Triumph*, (New York: Anchor Books 1961), pp. 71–105.

10. Telegram published in the Turkish newspaper, *'al-Iqdam'*.

11. 'Abdallah Fayyad, *al-thawra al-'Iraqiyya al-Kubra*, 1920.

12. Wamidh Nadhmi, *al-Judhur al-Siyassiya wa al-Fikriya wa al-'Ijtima'iya fi al-Iraq*, p. 74.

13. Linguistic research has argued convincingly that Iraqi colloquial language is a distinct tongue from Arabic. Such research has identified a proliferation of Sumerian, Accadian, Syriac, Turkish and Persian words mixed with Arabic, with the latter very much taking a back seat. (Fahim Issa al-Salim, *Qawalib al-'Ammiyya al-'Iraqiyya*.)

14. The Lynch concession was a plan by the government to award a British company, Lynch Brothers, significant commercial advantages. This was in order to placate the British government so as to extract loans from them. Arab deputies opposed the idea, not only because it undermined local trade, but because it exposed the region to more Anglo-German rivalry. Iraqi and other Arab deputies abstained in the vote of confidence that the chamber granted to the Grand Vizier Abbas Hilmi Pasha, which resulted in his resignation. It can even be said that the Lynch affair revealed the power of participatory politics. An active campaign, backed by Iraqi and other Arab decentralist deputies, obstructed the concession and brought down a Grand Vizier.

15. George Antonius, *The Arab Awakening: The Story of the Arab National Moverment*, (New York: Capricorn Books, 1965), pp. 243–53.

16. Elie Kedourie, *England and the Middle East—The Destruction of the Ottoman Empire, 1914–1921*, (London: Bowes & Bowes, 1956), pp. 29–66.

17. David Hunter Miller, *My Diary of the Conference of Paris*, Vol.III; George Antonius, *The Arab Awakening*, p. 437 (for the full text of the agreement); Mohammed Hadid, *Mudhakarati*, p. 86–7; James Barr, *A Line in the Sand*, p. 62.

18. Mohammed Hadid, ibid, p. 86–7.

19. Zeine Zeine, *The Struggle for Arab Independence: Western Diplomacy and the Rise and Fall of Faisal's Kingdom in Syria*, (Beirut, Khayat 1966), pp. 151–4.

20. William Cleveland, *The Making of an Arab Nationalist: Ottomanism and Arabism in the Life and Thought of Sati 'al-'Husri*, (Princeton: Princeton University Press, 1971), p. 49.

21. Ibid, p. 52.

22. Hugh Foot, *A Start in Freedom*, (London: Hodder & Stoughton, 1964), p. 35.

23. Lawrence Graffty-Smith, *Bright Levant*, (London: J. Murray, 1970), pp. 151–4.

24. Ibid., pp. 151–4.

25. Lady Algernon Gordon-Lennox, *The Diary of Lord Bertie of Thame*, Volume 2, (London: Hodder & Stoughton, 1924), p. 123.

1. THE 1920 REVOLUTION (AND HOW IRAQ WAS INVENTED)

1. The San Remo Conference was an international meeting of the Allied Supreme Council attended by Britain, France, Italy and Japan. The resolutions of the conference were to ostensibly grant Syria and Mesopotamia provisional independence whilst 'reluctantly' imposing a system of mandates over those territories that was a flagrant denial of the promises made to the Arabs by those same allied powers for a united Arab country.

2. George Antonius, *The Arab Awakening: The Story of the Arab National Movement*, (New York: Capricorn Books, 1965), p. 305.

3. Margaret MacMillan, *Paris 1919: Six Months that Changed the World*, (New York: Random House, 2002), p. 376.

4. Rashid Khalidi, *Sowing Crisis: The Cold War and American Dominance in the Middle East*, (Boston: Boston Beacon Press, 2009), pp. 911–14.

5. Indeed, several cotton mills were erected in Baghdad at the time in preparation, one of which still exists today in Karrada, a suburb of Baghdad.

6. Ernest Main, *Iraq: From Mandate to Independence*, (London: G. Allen & Unwin Ltd., 1935), p. 63.

7. Ibid, p. 63.

8. For the period before 1921, and for the sake of convenience, the term Iraq will be used to designate the territory that came to represent the modern state. The territory's name always derived from its two rivers, hence, the names Mesopotamia, the Land of Two Rivers, al-Rafidain, etc. Early Muslims called the southern delta 'al-'Iraq', deriving from the Arabic word for 'vein' (*'irq*), possibly denoting its rivers.

9. Phillip Willard Ireland, *Iraq, A Study in Political Developments*, (London: The Macmillan Company, 1937), p. 273.

10. The Halabja poison attack (*Kimyabarana Helebce* in Kurdish), also known as Bloody Friday, was an incident that took place on 16 March 1988, during the closing days of the Iran-Iraq War, when chemical weapons were used by Iraqi forces in the Kurdish town of Halabja. Five thousand people were reported killed and 10,000 injured.

11. Churchill had famously proclaimed (about the use of mustard gas in war):

'I don't understand this squeamishness...I am strongly in favour of using poisoned gas against uncivilized tribes'. (See Violette Shamash, *Memories of Eden*, p. 239).

12. Mohammed Mehdi Kubba, *Mudhakarati*, p. 19: 'When it came to Iraq, the nationalist leaders were under no pretence that a massive treachery was about to take place, when they learned of the intent of the Sykes-Picot Agreement to divide up the Arab World, and subjugate it, thus rendering General Maude's statement that the British came to Iraq "not as conquerors but as liberators" as void'. (President George W. Bush and Vice President Dick Cheney made similar statements in 2003 when America invaded Iraq.)

13. Another day of infamy for the Arabs, enshrined in their collective memory as *Yaum Maysalun* (The Day of Maysalun).

14. Faisal's original minister of defence, Yassin Hashemi, had resigned rather than fight, correctly judging the impossible odds his army would face. See also footnote on p. 257 re: Faisal not forgetting Maysalun and cold-shouldering Hashemi as a result when he became king of Iraq.

15. Ronald Storrs, *The Memoirs of Sir Ronald Storrs*, (New York: Armo Press, 1972), pp. 455–6. See also Viscount Samuel, *Memoirs*, (London: Cresset Press, 1945), pp. 158–9.

16. 'The immediate question facing the British authorities in the spring of 1921 was the somewhat comic opera matter of Faisal's election'. Peter Sluglett, *Britain in Iraq 1914–1932*, (London: Ithaca Press, 1976), p. 67.

17. Adeed Dawisha, *Iraq: A Political History from Independence to Occupation*, (Princeton: Princeton University Press, 2009), p. 38.

18. Sir Henry Dobbs, Lecture to the Royal Empire Society, Near East and India, 23 February 1933, p. 148.

19. Sandra McKay, *The Reckoning: Iraq and the Legacy of Saddam Hussein*, (New York: W. W. Norton, 2002), p. 113.

20. The mandate called for a constitution, which was called 'a gift from the West', to be drawn. British advisors, who drew on the constitutions of Turkey, Persia, Australia and other countries, did this. This was then submitted to the colonial office before being submitted to a special committee in Iraq, who suggested some amendments.

Despite the name given to the constitution (this gift from the West), Mesopotamia (the then Iraq), nevertheless had parliamentary representation in the Ottoman parliament and, following the Young Turk restoration of the constitution in 1908, had deputies in parliament for six years. Hence the Iraqi constitutional experts injected a strong Turkish input (see Article 113) into the draft. Indeed, the final product took the rigid form of a Turkish constitution (which was based on Belgium's) rather than one embodying British parliamentary institutions.

From the outset, Britain ensured its colonial privileges contained in the Treaty of Alliance (aka The Anglo-Iraqi Treaty) (Article 3) by incorporating them in the language of the constitution. Two points are of significance:

1. That the Constitution shall contain nothing contrary to the provisions of the Treaty of Alliance.
2. That the Treaty prescribe the constitutional procedure, whether legislative or executive, by which decisions are to be taken on all matters of importance, including those involving questions of fiscal, financial and military policy.

Those two points were of paramount significance in shaping the political events that followed the assumption of the mandate by Great Britain. Of further significance, other articles (e.g. Article 26) confers upon the king the right of issuing ordinances while parliament is not sitting that have the force of law and, in matters relating to Iraq's treaty obligations, he need not submit them to parliament for ratification at all.

Articles 5–18 dealt with the Rights of the People:

1. Equality before the law.
2. The personal liberty of all inhabitants of Iraq is guaranteed.
3. Torture or deportation is absolutely forbidden.
4. The sanctity of private dwelling is recognized.
5. Freedom of access to the law courts.
6. Rights of ownership are guaranteed.
7. No illegal imposition of taxation.
8. Freedom of expression of opinion, liberty of publication, of meeting together and of forming and joining associations is guaranteed
9. Religious freedom and freedom of conscience is guaranteed.
10. All postal and telegraphic correspondence and telephonic communications are private and free from censorship.

Thus, the first prerogative accorded to the king, which is that of controlling the legislative system of Iraq, i.e. parliament, cannot display any of its functions without the concurrence of the king (Article 28), who is thus of great importance in the conduct of the affairs of a constitutional monarchy. It secures to the king wide and effective powers which are bound to have a large influence on the council of ministers. Thus, the king personally chooses the prime minster and appoints members of the senate. Consequently, both the prime minister and the senate soon fell under the long shadow of the king.

Most important of the prerogatives accorded is the power of the king to issue ordinances when parliament is not sitting that have the force of law. The tendency in constitutional monarchies is for the power of the king to diminish—but in Iraq, these powers (Article 26) gave a wide berth to the king to exercise influence on the conducts of affairs of state.

21. Matthew F. Jacobs, *Imagining the Middle East 1918–1967: The Building of an American Foreign Policy*, p. 143.
22. CO. 730/24/42297. (Sir Percy Cox was referring to Sassoon Heskiel, the then finance minister, and Abdul-Rahman al-Naqib, the then prime minister.)

23. Elizabeth Burgoyne, *Gertrude Bell to her Father*, from her personal papers, 2 Volumes, (London: E. Benn, 1958–61), p. 160.
24. Eugene Rogan, *The Arabs: A History*, (London: Allen Lane, 2009), p. 173.
25. It is of note that when Faisal appointed these Sharifian officers to positions of power in Syria, he provoked the ire of the local elites, who regarded them as upstarts.
26. American Legation, Baghdad to Washington, 3 February 1932, Diplomatic Series No. 119, Confidential, 890g. 00/176.
27. 20 August 1921, Telegram No. 336, C.O 730/4/41616.
28. Faisal may well have benefitted from the Caliph Mu'awiya's dying injunction to his son Yazid that, in order to keep the people of Iraq quiet, it was essential to give them a new governor every time they wanted one, however frequently that might be. Perhaps heeding Mu'awiya's advice, Faisal reshuffled his cabinets very frequently, developing skills akin to a juggler, thus creating new opportunities and recruiting new blood to tow the palace line, not to mention allowing side-lined older politicians to have another taste of power.

    Hikmat Sulaiman, a leading member of the Ikha'a Party, commented on this phenomenon in 1935 in an interview with Rufael Batti, editor of the newspaper *al-Bilad* (see *al-Bilad* 15, 16, and 17 December 1935) by writing that: 'In Iraq, the rise and fall of cabinets could be compared to a "joy wheel", with eight seats filled by eight ministers. Under the joy wheel, waited some twenty ex-ministers for it to stop so that another eight of their number could hasten to jump on. While in government, the ministers newly anointed spent their time fending off attacks from the ex-ministers, and no constructive work was ever done'.

2. THE ADVENT OF AL-'AHALI

1. Ayyubi, *Dhikriat Ali-Jaudat al-Ayyubi*, p. 196.
2. Al-Hassani, *Tarikh al-Wizarat al-'Iraqiyya*, Chapter 3, p. 7
3. Pachachi, a scion of a wealthy patrician Sunni family in Baghdad, was not normally known for his patronage of the palace or Nuri. He did not rely on a salary from the government for his upkeep and looked down with some disdain upon the coterie of Faisal's ex-Ottoman army officers. In what can only be viewed as an act of revenge, evidence emerged in May 1932 implicating Pachachi and other public figures as his accomplices, in writing four scurrilous and anonymous letters concerning Faisal's alleged immoral relations with the wife of a former Mayor of Baghdad. These letters alleged that the lady concerned, and certain women belonging to prominent Iraqi families, were allowed to become Faisal's mistresses in order to obtain royal favours. The typewritten letters referred to rampant acts of favouritism, nepotism, and misappropriation of land and public funds on the part of Faisal. In conclusion, the letters pronounced Faisal unfit to exercise regal prerogatives and called for the overthrow of his monarchical regime and the

establishment of a republic in Iraq (see C.O. 730/17088369). Faisal had throughout his reign never been averse to womanizing and was reported to disport himself with mistresses on his European jaunts, using the title of Prince Usama, yet he had pursued these activities with remarkable discretion. When the matter began to be widely discussed by the general public, the palace intervened and instructed the Kurdish minister of justice, Jamal Baban, to take legal action against Pachachi, suspending his parliamentary immunity and arresting him.

4. The Goodall, Nsouli and Mond incidents, briefly mentioned in the last chapter, are recounted more fully here for a better understanding of their significance in the development of civil dissent as part of the democratic movement in Iraq.
5. Hussain Jamil, *al-'Iraq: Shahada Siyasiyya 1908 ila 1930.*
6. Ibid., pp. 183–202.
7. Mohammed Hadid, *Mudhakarati: al-Sira 'min 'ajl al-demogratiyya fil,* p. 68.
8. Parker Thomas Moon (1892–1936) was a U.S. educator and political scientist who was born in New York City and educated at Columbia University. He became assistant professor there in 1919. In 1921, he became managing editor of the Political Science Quarterly. He was a member of the American Commission to Negotiate Peace in 1918–19. He was the author of *Imperialism and World Politics in the Nineteenth and Twentieth Centuries, the Latest Phase in the Expansion of Europe: A Preliminary Syllabus,* (New York: Columbia University Press, 1919), and *The Labor Problem and the Social Catholic Movement in France,* (New York: The Macmillan Company, 1921).
9. Fu'ad Hassan al-Wakil, *Jem'at al-'Ahali fi al'-Iraq,* p. 98.
10. Mohammed Hadid, *Mudhakarati,* p. 82.
11. The Bloomsbury Set was a group of writers, intellectuals and artists, and their friends and relatives, who worked and studied in London during the first half of the twentieth century. Their work influenced the literature, aesthetics, criticism, and economics of the period, as well as contemporary attitudes towards feminism, pacifism, and sexuality. Its best-known members were Virginia Woolf, Vanessa Bell, John Maynard Keynes, E. M. Forster, and Lytton Strachey.
12. Mohammed Hadid, *Mudhakarati,* p. 104.
13. Chadirchi resigned from the editorship of his party's newspaper in June 1933, and from the party proper in November 1933. This meant that he had already cooperated with al-'Ahali Group for almost a year.
14. Majid Khadduri, *Independent Iraq, 1932–1958: A Study in Iraqi Politics,* 2nd edition, (Oxford: Oxford University Press, 1960), p. 72. Also by the same author, *Political Trends in the Arab World: The Role of Ideas and the Ideals in Politics,* (Baltimore: Johns Hopkins Press, 1970), p. 133 and *Arab Contemporaries: The Role of Personalities in Politics,* (Baltimore, Johns Hopkins Press, 1973), p. 133.

15. Mohammed Hadid, *Mudhakarati*, p. 113. Hadid never shared this information with his colleagues, despite the continuing speculation about Chadirchi's reasons for joining al-'Ahali, revealing it only in his memoir, which was published in 2006.

16. Ibid., p. 113.

17. Fu'ad Hussain al-Wakil, *Jama'at al-'Ahall fil-Iraq*, p. 116. Wakil goes on to say that Chadirchi was hampered by his poor English in later life, when he headed the National Democratic Party and had to depend on Mohammed Hadid to stay abreast of British affairs. Britain's critical involvement in Iraqi affairs only heightened this deficit.

18. This opinion was shared by Sir Sam Falle in an interview with the author in June 2002, in Oxford. Falle was the British political counsellor at the embassy in Baghdad, a fluent Arabic speaker and well-versed in Iraqi affairs. He said that the biggest mistake the British made in Iraq was to have stuck with Nuri through thick and thin, allowing him to block the NDP's legitimate access to power by his use of election fraud.

19. Kamel Chadirchi, *Mudhakarat Kamel Chadirchi*, p. 27.

20. Ibid., pp. 27–8, also Mohammed Hadid, *Mudhakarati*. p. 140. It is a sad reflection on the state of politics in the Arab world today that the 'Arab Spring' of 2011 is clamouring for freedoms that were nascent in Arab countries like Iraq and elsewhere over eighty years ago.

21. Known in Iraqi lore as *Harakat al-Thani Mais*, or the Second of May Movement.

22. For a full narrative of the Assyrian tragedy, see Ronald Sempill Stafford, *The Tragedy of the Assyrians*, (London: G. Allen & Unwin Ltd., 1935).

23. Mohammed Hadid, *Mudhakarati*, p. 126. Also see Fu'ad Hussain al-Wakil, *Jama'at al-'Ahali fil-Iraq*, footnote p. 296.

24. See *al-'Ahali*, ref. 205, 25 June 1933, 'The Assyrians and their Ally'.

25. Majid Khaadduri, *Independent Iraq*, pp. 42–3

26. Before his death, Faisal must have despaired of ruling his new kingdom and its citizens. In a memorandum that he circulated to his confidantes, he had this to say: 'There is still—and I say this with a heart full of sorrow—no Iraqi people but unimaginable masses of human beings, devoid of any patriotic ideas, imbued with religious traditions and absurdities, connected by no common tie, giving ear to evil, prone to anarchy, and perpetually ready to rise against any government whatever'. The memorandum was dated January 1932, and appears in full in Ja'far al-Askari's memoir *A Soldier's Story: From Ottoman Rule to Independent Iraq: The Memoirs of Jafar al-Aksari*, (London: Arabian Publishing Ltd., 2003) in Arabic. Also Hanna Batatu, *Old Social Classes and Revolutionary Movements in Iraq*, p. 25.

27. Kamel Chadirchi, *Mudhakarat*, pp. 31–2

28. Mohammed Hadid, *Mudhakarati*, p. 126. Also see F'uad Hussain al-Wakil, *Jema'at al-'Ahali fi al-'Iraq*, p. 48. According to Mohammed Hadid, al-'Ahali Group was fully cognizant of Sulaiman's pro-British, pro-

palace background, but they believed overall that he held reformist views, which were in harmony with those of al-'Ahali.

3. AL-'AHALI AND THE 1936 BAKR SIDQI COUP

1. The Arabic for the meetings was 'mu'tamarat al-Sulaikh', i.e. the Sulaikh Conferences, although they had far less formality than the word 'conference' tends to imply.
2. Mohammed Hadid, *Mudhakarati*, pp. 138–9.
3. Older-generation politicians naively assumed that this would give Abul-Timman and his al-'Ahali Group an opportunity to spread their 'communist' ideas, probably not understanding the difference between al-'Ahali's mild socialism and what communism stood for, a misconception that was to plague al-'Ahali for much of its life-span. See Muhsin Abu-Tabikh, *al-Mabadi' wal Rijal*. Also, see Caractacus, *Revolution in Iraq: An Essay in Comparative Political Opinion*, (London: Gollancz, 1959), in which the author states that the regime was 'very apt to call any man of the most mildly liberal opinion a Communist', pp. 46–7.
4. Hashemi used the sentence: 'Uniting the word of the Nation'—a euphemism used at the time to signify one-party rule.
5. Kamel Chadirchi, writing under the pseudonym of 'Abdallah al-Basir, attacked Yassin and Rashid A'li for furthering their own interests at the expense of the nation, see *Fi 'Ahd al-Hashemi*, Rashid Press, 1936.
6. See *al-Bilad* newspaper dated 6 September 1936.
7. On the day of the coup, Hikmat was visiting his close friend Ra'uf Chadirchi, and heard the roar of the air force aeroplanes over Baghdad, dropping leaflets announcing the coup. He stated categorically: 'Yassin wanted to rule the country for ten years; but by God, he will not be able to rule for ten days or ten hours; not even for ten minutes!' See Majid Khadduri, *Independent Iraq*, p. 83.
8. Hikmat had returned from a summer holiday in Istanbul in 1935, totally imbued by what he had witnessed in terms of economic, industrial and social progress, as Turkish society was quickly modernizing along the Western model. He even came to sport a jaunty European hat as he strolled down Baghdad's Rashid Street. See Mohammed Hadid, *Mudhakarati*, p. 142 and Majid Khadduri, *Independent Iraq*, p. 75.
9. Kamel Chadirchi, *Mudhakarat Kamel al-Chadirchi*, p. 44.
10. Majid Khadduri, ibid., p. 79.
11. It could not have escaped Sidqi's attention that most of Faisal's prime ministers and ministers were ex-army officers who had fought with him (Faisal) in the Arab Revolt and who came from relatively humble stock, like Sidqi himself.
12. In 1936, Hashemi supported Fawzi al-Qawuqchi's venture to leave the Iraqi army and lead a group of volunteers to Palestine to fight alongside the Arab uprising there. This garnered much local kudos for Hashemi, but

he was forced to relent in the face of British pressure and withdraw his support.

13. Pronounced 'Kharalambo', 'Khara' unfortunately meaning excrement in Arabic.

14. Tawfiq al-Swaidi, *Mudhakarati*, p. 271.

15. In his memoir, ibid., p. 273, Tawfiq al-Sweidi, a prominent Iraqi statesman and former prime minister, confirms the view that Ja'far may have had his own thoughts about removing Hashemi. He states that Ja'far probably went to meet Sidqi's advancing army unit in order to join it and march back at its head to take Baghdad.

16. The British were aware of both 'Askari's possible coup and Hashemi's Republican plans. See F.O. 371/20795.E66. British embassy to Rendal, 5 January 1937. Also see Fouad Hussain al-Wakil, Jema'at al-'Ahali fi al-Iraq, p. 365.

17. Adnan al-Pachachi, *Muzahim al-Pachachi*, pp. 219–21. It should be noted that Muzahim had supported the Sidqi coup (despite his intimate friendship with Ja'far al'Askari) and thus had incurred the wrath of Nuri, who was set on exacting revenge from anybody who had been involved with or had supported Sidqi. According to the biography, relations between the two men seriously deteriorated from then on.

18. Safa'a Abd al-Wahhab Mubarak, *The 1936 Coup*, unpublished Masters thesis, Baghdad University, p. 114. Also, private interview by Mubarak with Hafdhi 'Aziz, ADC to King Ghazi, on 21 October 1971.

19. Sidqi did get the king's message, which he read angrily, before crumpling up the paper on which it was written and throwing it away. It was picked up by an army officer, who later gave it to Kamel Chadirchi. The latter made a copy available to Majid Khadduri and the text appears in his book, *Independent Iraq*, p. 89, although Khadduri arrives at a different conclusion as to why 'Askari went to meet Sidqi. Khadduri postulates that Askari was no fan of Hashemi or his policies. He saw no reason for the army to march on Baghdad now that Hashemi was prepared to resign together with his cabinet. He was confident that his own prestige within the army corps would carry the day if he went himself and explained the futility of the coup to Sidqi. He asked and got the king's permission for his scheme and got the latter to write a personal letter to Sidqi to stop the army's advance. It was a daring move and neither Askari nor the king foresaw its fatal consequences. Askari was determined however, to carry out his mission to hand the king's letter to Sidqi in person.

20. Both Mohammed Hadid in his memoir, *Mudhakarati*, p. 158, and Majid Khadduri in *Independent Iraq*, p. 91, confirm this fact, but do not shed further light on al-'Ahali's ultimate decision to partake in the government.

21. Mudhafar 'Abdallah' Amin, in his book *Jema'at al-'Ahali*, quotes C. J. Edmonds, a close acquaintance of Hikmat's and an advisor to the ministry of interior, confirming in writing that Hikmat had told him directly about these appointments.

22. As in fact he did do later, in the decade when he imprisoned Hikmat.

23. F.O. 371/20013, E6783/1419/93, No. 265 (R), op. cit. Also F.O. 371/20014, E7145/1419/93, No. 546 (Confidential), op. cit.
24. Mohammed Hadid, *Mudhakarati*, p. 158.
25. British intelligence officers, as well as regular army officers, were embedded with the Iraqi army around the country.

4. AL-'AHALI IN GOVERNMENT

1. Majid Khadduri, *Independent Iraq*, p. 93.
2. Hikmat's speech in full was: 'I want to thank His Majesty the King [for his confidence], and I have no other thing to say now except to ask the noble people of Iraq, who have given us their confidence, to return to normal life. I also want to ask public officials to fulfil their duties properly and I pray the Almighty to help us fulfil the objectives, for the attainment of which, I came to power'. Abul-Timman's speech outlining the government's programme is quoted later in the chapter.
3. The Society's programme was formally published on 9 December 1936, one day before the order to hold general elections was issued. A summary of its contents may be informative to the reader: (l) Friendly relations with Great Britain, Turkey, Persia, and Afghanistan were stressed and, in particular, the proposed pact of non-aggression with the three latter States was mentioned. Cooperation and friendly relations with the other Arab countries were emphasized, and a reference was made to the signing of a treaty of alliance with Saudi Arabia. (2) The programme promised more sweeping and extensive reforms to the internal affairs of Iraq. In government administration it aimed at raising the standard of efficiency by recruiting abler and better-educated young men, with due regard to their moral background and integrity. It also promised to apply the same principle in municipal administration, in public health, and in the courts. With regard to the tribal section of the population, the programme sought to hasten the settlement of the tribes by distributing land amongst them, settling the boundary disputes of their estates, and extending various other public services to them. (3) The programme also dealt with the economic and financial development of Iraq. It promised reforms to the taxation system, the encouragement of foreign trade, and the stimulation of nascent industries. It promised to pay attention to the condition of labour by founding trade unions as well as the development of agriculture, irrigation, transport, and other economic programmes. (4) The reorganization and the expansion of the army and air force and the encouragement of a martial spirit throughout the country. (5) The development of the educational system, popularization of culture, and improvement of rural and industrial education. Public education was to be free up to the secondary stages. (Majid Khadduri, *Independent Iraq*, p. 96).
4. Majid Khadduri, ibid., p. 94
5. See official text in *Program of the Sulaiman Cabinet (*Baghdad: Govt. Press, 1936).

6. See *Proc. Chamber of Deputies*, 1937, pp. 22–4.
7. He stated: 'Poverty, land disputes, feudalism, political strife, and many other problems, are all due to economic factors, which, in Iraq, are basically agricultural'. See Proc. Chamber of Deputies, 7th (Extraord. Sess., 1937, pp. 18–9). The speech, which resonated strongly in Iraq, is often quoted in academic and political works on the period.
8. The Muthana Club was a Pan-Arab Society formed in 1935 to promote the Arab nationalist movement.
9. A committee was formed of Sidqi's most loyalist supporters. Its mandate was to look into turning Iraq into a military dictatorship that would unite Arabs and Kurds under Sidqi's leadership—Sidqi himself being a Kurd.
10. F.O. 371/21865. op. cit., para 3. p. 3: 'His (Sidqi's) fatal attacks on his opponents and his wayward way of life, shook public opinion'. See also Gerald de Gaury, *Three Kings in Baghdad*, (London: Hutchinson, 1961), p. 87: 'I saw a singularly unattractive middle-aged Iraqi (Sidqi) sitting alone drinking whisky. The back of the head was flat, the neck thick, the lips sensuous, the face and expression vulgarly brutal. It was the face of a man born to be a criminal'. (de Gaury was reputed to have been homosexual, and later became very close to Regent 'Abdulillah, which may explain his pointed sense of physical observation of Sidqi.)
11. One of the resigning ministers, Saleh Jabr, who was not a reformist himself, recognizing an opportunity to weaken the government—in order perhaps to hasten its fall—resigned in the hope of a return to power of the former regime and its supporters.

5. THE ANGLO-IRAQI WAR OF 1941

1. Most memoirs (Hadid, Chadirchi, Jamil) skip this period with hardly a mention, advising readers to seek information about it from other sources.
2. Sir Maurice Peterson stated in his memoir, *Both Sides of the Curtain: An Autobiography*, (London: Constable, 1950), that 'I came to regard him (Madfa'i) as head and shoulders above other politicians of Iraq, not excluding Nuri Sa'id', p. 138.
3. Maurice Peterson, ibid., pp. 141–2.
4. The first four of those officers mentioned became known as 'The Golden Square'.
5. In his memoir, Mohammed Hadid recounts that on a visit to Kamel Chadirchi's house, he was introduced to Captain Hilmi 'Abd al-Karim. Chadirchi later intimated to Hadid that 'Abd al-Karim had told him of the existence of a plot engineered by a group of civilians and army officers opposed to the government, to assassinate King Ghazi and other government officials and place Prince 'Abdulillah on the throne. A few days later, on 6 March 1939, the government announced the discovery of the plot. See Mohammed Hadid, *Mudhakarati*, p. 172.
6. Maurice Peterson, *Both Sides of the Curtain*, p. 143.

7. Alan Rush, a noted chronicler of the Hashemites, believes that Ghazi died from a blow to the head delivered by one (or both) of the two servants riding in the back of his car. The very peculiar damage to the car has long been a source of mystery, as it could not logically explain the blow to the head that Ghazi had received. The two servants conveniently disappeared after the event. (Interview with the author.)
8. See Sinderson Pasha's unpublished memoir in St. Antony's College, Middle East Centre Archives.
9. Ghazi had suspected his own wife, 'Alia, of plotting to murder him. Warned by army officers of other plots to kill him, Ghazi had become quite paranoid, ever since a trusted servant of his was found shot dead inside the palace. He suspected that 'Alia was behind it. See Hanna Batatu, *Old Social Classes and Revolutionary Movements in Iraq*, pp. 342–4.
10. The Rosalind Ramirez Collection, St. Antony's College, Middle East Centre Archives. GB165–0408. (Faisal II conducted a fascinating and highly telling correspondence with his former governess, Rosalind Ramirez. Among her papers are first-hand accounts of witnesses of events surrounding King Ghazi's death.)
11. Hanna Batatu, *Old Social Classes and Revolutionary Movements in Iraq*, p. 344.
12. Maurice Patterson, *Both Sides of the Curtain*, p. 151.
13. Dr. Fritz Grobba was an erudite expert on the Middle East. He was multilingual, speaking several languages fluently which included Arabic and Turkish. He and his glamorous wife made the German Legation the hub of Baghdad social life, giving glittering parties at which King Ghazi was frequently the guest of honour.
14. Sinderson reports in *Glimpses of Royal and Political life in Iraq, 1920–1946*: 'Emir Abdullah is being much criticized in the local press for his present attitude. I hope there will be no family estrangement. Naturally he'd like the king job instead of his present, very impecunious and not very important office'. (p. 112.)
15. 'Abdulillah, who was somewhat effeminate, was obsessed with horses. The rumour mill in Baghdad had it that he had bestowed special favours on one particular Iraqi jockey, whom the British expat community had dubbed the 'Gordon Richards of Baghdad', a reference to a top English jockey at the time.
16. Salah al-Din Sabbagh, *Fursan al-Uruba*, p. 83.
17. Adeed Dawisha, *Iraq*, p. 93.
18. The Mufti, Haj Amin al-Husaini, was forced to flee Palestine for stirring opposition to British repression there. He came to Baghdad where there seemed to be relatively more political freedom coupled with a nationalist regime supportive of Palestine rights. The Iraqi government of the time housed him and gave him a generous salary.
19. Gerald de Gaury, *Three Kings in Baghdad*. De Gaury describes the Mufti as having 'watery blue eyes, a red beard and tight lips, with a cunning expression, hence he was nicknamed "The Red Fox"', p. 117.

20. The Assyrians were members of an ancient Nestorian Christian community in the upper valleys of the Tigris and the Euphrates.
21. When the choice of Faisal as king of Iraq was made by Churchill in Cairo in 1921, Faisal was in London. It was Cornwallis who was handed the task of informing him of that decision. He did this by waiting for Faisal in his hotel suite until the latter returned from the theatre late at night.
22. Sharif Sharaf was a Hashemite and a cousin of the king's. He may have had German-leaning tendencies, which might explain why he was paid a stipend by the Germans once he had fled after the defeat of Iraq.
23. Hanna Batatu, *Old Social Classes and Revolutionary Movements in Iraq*, p. 458.
24. It should be noted hat whilst 'Abdulillah had fled the country, the infant King Faisal II and his immediate family stayed in the country and were under no threat, and Iraq continued to be a monarchy.
25. It was said that 'even the thieves did not go out at night'.

6. AL-'AHALI BECOMES THE NDP

1. Translated from Arabic and summarized by the author from the much longer original version.
2. The coup d'état of 1936 culminated in the army finally deciding to rid the country of an unpopular government. This may have set a precedent that led to the military coup of 1941 and the revolution of 1958.
3. Al-'Ahali Group had lost a valuable member in Ja'far Abul-Timman, who had decided to retire from politics altogether. They had also lost Hikmat Sulaiman, who had moved to a different political place and who, in any case, was in jail for his role in Nuri's invented plot. Another member, 'Abd al-Qader Ism'ail, had left the country when he was stripped of his Iraqi nationality because of his alleged communist beliefs.
4. This first issue of *Sawt al-'Ahali* carried the number 76, which was meant to indicate the continuity of the newspaper, which had last appeared in the thirties, with an issue number 75.
5. FO, 371, 40042, E7251, Sir Kinahan Cornwallis, 16.11.44.
6. FO, 371, 35013, E7266, Sir K inahan Cornwallis, Baghdad, 6.11.45, *Internal situation in Iraq*.
7. Mathew Elliot, *Independent Iraq: The Monarchy and British Influence 1941–1958*, (London: Tauris Academic Studies, 1996), p. 24. See also FO 371, 40041, E1903, Sir Kinahan Cornwallis, Baghdad, 25 March 1944.
8. This was a continuing method of inflicting punitive measures on anything that hinted of 'communism', Nuri's *bête noire* throughout his political life.
9. See Article 3 of the 'Objectives of the Party' in the manifesto of the National Democratic Party.
10. For a fuller account of these, please see Kamel Chadirchi, *Mudhakarat Kamel al-Chadirchi*, p. 96.
11. 'Abd al-Wahhab Murjan went on to become prime minister in December

1957, by which time he had become a Nuri supporter. Sir Michael Wright, the British ambassador in Baghdad, wryly described Murjan's cabinet as 'a Cabinet of Nuri's supporters without Nuri'. (See Mathew Elliot, *Independent Iraq*, p. 129.)

12. Mohammed Hadid, *Mudhakarati*, p. 196. (Although Hussain Jamil was mostly absent from al-'Ahali Group's activities during the thirties due to his work commitments as a judge, he had been a founding member of *al-'Ahali* newspaper, as well as its managing editor for almost a year. In the forties, he once again assumed a leadership position in al-'Ahali Group.)

13. Daoud al-Sayigh was a member of the central committee of the Iraqi Communist Party. He later led a splinter group which failed to survive and soon after folded altogether.

14. Mohammed Hadid, *Mudhakarati*, p. 203. Also, see Khalil Kanna, *al-'Iraq': Amsuhu wa Ghaduhu*, p. 366: 'Nuri had insisted on the inclusion of Mohammed Hadid to represent the NDP in his government in 1946. Nuri continued to hold Hadid in high personal esteem until the very end and often said how unfortunate it was that membership of different parties had deprived the country of the services of such competent people'.

15. The reader can see the full text of the letter in Chadirchi's memoir, *Mudhakarat Kamel Chadirchi*, p. 145.

16. The group consisted of Kamil Qazanchi, Qadri 'Abd al-Rahman, William Yusuf, 'Abd al-Hussain Jawad and Hashim Jawad.

17. Kamel Chadirchi, *Mudhakarat Kamel Chadirchi*, p. 153.

18. Mohammed Hadid, *Mudhakarati*, p. 206.

19. It should be noted that the Liberal Party (*Hizb al-Ahrar*) also withdrew from the elections in protest.

20. Kamel Chadirchi, *Mudhakarat Kamel Chadirchi*, p. 163.

21. Chadirchi wrote: 'The NDP saw a danger to the Arab League resulting from this treaty and a barrier to Arab and Iraqi national aims. The NDP rejects the treaty and calls on all Iraqis to reject it as well'. Ibid., p. 164.

22. Mohammed Hadid, *Mudhakarati*, p. 208.

23. For a full text of Chadirchi's memorandum, see Chadirchi's memoirs, ibid., p. 193.

24. For transcripts of these meetings, see Chadirchi's memoir, ibid., pp. 185–92.

25. Mohammed Hadid, *Mudhakarati*, p. 213.

26. Ibid., p. 215.

7. THE PORTSMOUTH TREATY AND *AL-WATHBA*

1. The Saadabad Pact was a non-aggression pact signed by Turkey, Iran, Iraq and Afghanistan on 8 July 1937, in Teheran's Saadbad Palace, hence the name.

2. *Sawt al-'Ahali*, 27, 28, 29 and 30 May 1947.

3. The 'Fertile Crescent' and 'Greater Syria' plans for the division of the

regions of Iraq, Syria, Lebanon and geographical Palestine, received a great deal of attention from the politicians of the time, and were the focus of popular hopes that came to be represented by certain political parties and monarchies. The British were dead-set against the 'Greater Syria' idea (as were the French), but backed the 'Fertile Crescent' scenario, as they felt it would secure help for their own strategic interests.

4. Phebe Marr, *The Modern History of Iraq*, 2ⁿᵈ edition, (Boulder, CO: Westview Press, 2004), p. 101. Marr states that the regent's timing showed bad judgment, because it conflicted with Britain's support for a Jewish home in Palestine, and with growing anti-British sentiments in the bitter lead-up to war.

5. Majid Khadduri, *Independent Iraq*, p. 261.

6. Marr, ibid., p. 101.

7. The 1936 Anglo-Egyptian Treaty was successfully renegotiated in 1946 prior to its expiry.

8. The U.S. was equally irritated that its own representative was forcibly of a lesser rank than was his British counterpart.

9. 'Abd al-Razzaq al-Hassani, *Tarikh al-Wizzarat al-'Iraqiyya*, p. 215.

10. *Al-'Umma* newspaper, No. 974, 1 January 1948.

11. Mohammed Mehdi Kubba, *Mudhakarati fi Samim al-'Ahdath*, pp. 224–5.

12. Lord Birdwood, *Nuri Al-Said, A Study in Arab Leadership*, (London: Cassell, 1959), p. 213.

13. Ernest Bevin was holidaying in Portsmouth during the Iraqi delegation's visit, and asked that the entire delegation go down to Portsmouth for the signature of the treaty, rather than him going to London to see them. The significance of the name of the battleship on which the treaty was signed—Victory—would not have been lost on either Bevin or his mandarins at the Foreign Office.

14. Phebe Marr, ibid., pp. 102–3.

15. Majid Khadduri, ibid., p. 267.

16. Abd al-Razzaq al-Hassani, ibid., pp. 257–60.

17. S. H. Longrigg in his book, *Iraq, 1900 to 1950: A Political, Social and Economic History*, (Oxford: Oxford University Press, 1953), states that 'the Iraqi delegation (perhaps exhilarated by its perceived success in Portsmouth) decided to spend a few days of holiday in London. They felt no suspicion that their own countrymen would not accept an agreement which represented so obvious and advantageous an advance on the 1930 Treaty, and which seemed in no way calculated to offend national *amour propre*. They were rapidly undeceived', p. 345.

18. Abd al-Razzaq al-Hassani, ibid., p. 261.

19. House of Commons, Parliamentary Debates, Vol. 446, Col. 400.

20. 'Abd al-Razzaq al-Hassani, ibid., p. 265.

21. Majid Khadduri, ibid., pp. 269–70.

22. 'The restoration of order must, it appeared, devolve on the Army, if any-

one; and it was found by ministers and perhaps by the Regent imprudent not to invoke this force', S. H. Longigg, ibid., pp. 345–6.

23. The counsellor at the British embassy, Douglas Busk, concluded 'that parties do not at present provide a possible alternative to the "Old Gang" and that we must base our hopes of improvement of the Iraqi government rather on a continuous process of recruitment into the 'Old Gang' of more able and liberal members'. FO371, 75128, E74 Sir H. Mack, Baghdad, 17.12.48. (Mathew Elliot, *Independent Iraq*, p. 66).

24. *Al-'Ahali* returned to the stands on 8 February 1948, when the Sadr government finally allowed freedom of the press and the freedom to demonstrate.

25. 'The manner in which the parties were manoeuvred to acquiesce to this arrangement reflected the lack of agreement among party leaders who seem to have cooperated only to force the Jabr government to resign but were wholly unprepared to follow up their victory and achieve power'. Majid Khadduri, ibid., p. 270.

26. Mohammed Mehdi Kubba, *Mudhakarati fi Samim al-'Ahdath*, p. 248.

27. Majid Khadduri, ibid., p. 271.

28. In addition to its local political disturbances, the uproar in Iraq was intensified by the creation of the State of Israel.

8. THE YEARS 1948–1952

1. Liwa' al-'Istiqlal, no. 372, 13 May 1948.

2. National Centre of Archives: Memorandum of the National Democratic Party, no. 10/5, dated 23 May 1948. Also see Fadhil Hussain, *Tarikh al-hizb al-watani al-dimuqrati*, pp. 230–1.

3. *Sawt al-'Ahali*, no. 1510, 2 May 1948, and Al-Ahrar Publications: Communiqué by Ali Mumtaz al-Daftari, p. 12.

4. Communiqué by 'Ali Mumtaz al-Daftari, The Liberal Party Publications, pp. 13–14.

5. The regent even avoided the use of the word *Wathba* in his description of the uprising, woodenly preferring to describe this turbulent period of agitation as 'those public events and difficult circumstances'.

6. Fadhil al-Jamali, *Dhikrayat wa 'Ibar*, p. 15.

7. Shawkat was an extreme right-wing member of the Pan-Arab Muthana Club. He had written two books that touted his 'loony right' philosophy. He advocated a theory for 'The Art of Death' (*Sina'at al-Mawt*), which he expounded upon in a speech meant to inspire Iraqi youth to stand up and fight to the death for their ideas. His detractors commented that his 'art of death' could only be thought up by an ignorant doctor (since Shawkat was in actual fact a doctor of medicine). He spearheaded the Futuwwa (Youth) Organization which was based on Fascist principles, and meant to infuse Iraqi youth with Pan-Arab ideas. He went about Baghdad on horseback, wearing a black uniform. He was obsessively pro-Nuri, who rewarded his

loyalty by elevating Shawkat to cabinet rank. Nuri may have been unaware of the bizarre ideological havoc that his protégé had wreaked. Ironically enough, when the day came to fight the British in 1941, Shawkat
was the first to leave the sinking Futuwwa ship! (See Majid Khadduri,
Independent Iraq, pp. 166–7).

8. Kamel Chadirchi, *Mudhakarat Kamel Chadirchi*, p. 378.

9. Vol. 8, pp. 95–106. Also see Lord Birdwood, *Nuri As-Said, A Study in
Arab Leadership*, pp. 217–18.

10. Hanna Batatu, in *Old Social Classes and Revolutionary Movements in
Iraq*, (pp. 592 and 655–6) presented figures derived from actual police
department records, whilst the British embassy figures were nothing more
than amateur guesswork.

11. Chadirchi had a foreboding that Hussain Jamil might decide to pull a 'go-
it-alone' act. He wanted to confront him about it, but was dissuaded from
doing so by Mohammed Hadid, who felt that any such action might only
hurt the party. (See Mohammed Hadid, *Mudhakarati*, p. 239.)

12. See Mohammed Hadid, *Mudhakarati*, pp. 239–48, and Kamel Chadirchi,
Mudhakarat Kamel Chadirchi, pp. 345–66 and pp. 401–16.

13. Kamel Chadirchi, ibid., pp. 411 and 354.

14. Chadirchi had it on good authority that Jamil was consulting many friends
and acquaintances as to the pros and cons of leaving the party. He was
advised that such a move would destroy him politically. This may have
explained his obsessive desire to merge the party with another political
bloc, which would have resulted in the dissolution of the NDP and the creation of an entirely new entity that could back his joining the government
(so that it would not appear a decision he had taken on his own). Kamel
Chadirchi, ibid., p. 375.

15. 'Relations with Britain had deteriorated more over Palestine than over the
Treaty… visits were still paid by the Regent and by Nuri to London …
loans were gladly received and British experts recruited… but it remained
inconceivable that any younger politician, or indeed any party except
Nuri's, should not, by conviction or mere habit or "patriotic" duty, blame
Great Britain for all the evils of the State'. (S. H. Longrigg, *Iraq, 1900–
1950*, p. 356.)

16. Mohammed Hadid, ibid., p. 249. For the full text of Chadirchi's article,
see Chadirchi, ibid., pp. 431–3.

17. Hadid informed Chadirchi of Jamil's objection to the former's article at
that meeting, which may explain Jamil's pointed absence. (See Mohammed Hadid, ibid., p. 249.)

18. 'Iraqi Jews differed from those in Europe. They were educated and urbane
and were not victims of pogroms or state persecution. They enjoyed civic
freedom in Iraq and were courted as fellow Semites, Sons of Shem, and as
brothers by fellow-Iraqis who included them in their broad-based nationalist ideology. To Iraqi Jews, Zionism looked like an upstart foreign movement, irrelevant to their daily concerns'. See Marina Benjamin, *The Last*

Days in Babylon: The Story of the Jews of Baghdad, (London: Bloomsbury Publishing PLC, 2007), p. 111.

19. Iraqi Jews have always protested 'Adas's innocence of any Zionist affiliation and any connection to Israel. However, the last prime minister under the monarchy, Ahmad Mukhtar Babban, writes in his memoir that he was visited by a close Iraqi Jewish friend in the company of a foreign person who spoke English. The latter said that he was a European Jew and that he had come to speak officially to Babban on behalf of the International Zionist Organisation, which had authorized him to offer Babban a sum of eight million pounds sterling if Babban could use his position as chief of the Royal Court to persuade Prince 'Abdulillah (then the effective ruler of Iraq) to commute 'Adas's sentence from death to a lesser one. The foreign guest said that 'Adas was a highly-placed member of the World Zionist Organisation, and that the Organisation was prepared to bank the funds immediately at any bank of Babban's choosing. Babban said that he categorically turned both men down, and promptly asked them to leave. The following morning, Babban went to his office at the Royal Court and met with 'Abdulillah to tell him of this incident. 'Abdulillah asked for Adas's file to be brought over and signed the decree for his execution on the spot, stating to Babban that this was what the public and the government wished, and that he ('Abdulillah) had been convinced of 'Adas's Zionist affiliations, adding that Babban's recent experience was only further proof of this. (See Ahmad Mukhtar Babban, *Mudhakarat Ahmad Mukhtar Babban*, pp. 225–6).

20. As stated earlier, in a crackdown on the communists in 1949, NDP members were also included and Chadirchi was arrested and received a suspended prison sentence of four months.

21. Malek Saif, a founding member of the ICP, in a police testimony stated that Iraqi Jews had supplied arms and money to the 1948 Uprising on the orders of Yahuda Siddiq (a leading official of the party). (See Iraq Police Criminal Investigation Department J1, pp. 62–3.)

22. Irrespective of their motives for joining the Iraq Communist Party (ICP), Iraqi Jews' loyalty had not been in doubt when they stood shoulder-to-shoulder with other Iraqi compatriots on many an occasion, and never more so than during *al-Wathba*, where they suffered many casualties in dead and wounded, as they called for democratic freedom and an end to British influence. Marina Benjamin writes: 'It was a brief wonderful moment in which the Jews were welcomed by the rest of Iraq's people as allies, and they felt a sense of real equality'. Marina Benjamin, ibid., p. 170.

23. See Annex to the book for a brief history of Iraqi oil.

24. S. H. Longrigg, *Iraq, 1900 to 1950*, p. 365. (Longrigg criticized the Iraqi press, writing patronisingly that it was 'irresponsible and malicious as ever', when its newspapers pointed out that there was no noticeable rise in the standard of living in the country as a result of any of the Board's activities.)

25. '*Itila'at*, no. 7396, 18 April 1951.
26. Chadirchi, ibid., p. 543.
27. Abd al-Razzaq Hassani, ibid., pp. 697–8. (Hassani puts forth the interesting theory that their actual failure to stop the signing of the oil agreement was the reason why the opposition parties jelled so well together afterwards, as if united in defeat, and galvanized by it.)
28. The details of the meeting at the palace are recounted at length in letters that Chadirchi wrote to Mohammed Hadid, who happened to be in London at the time, accompanying a relative who was receiving treatment for cancer. Hadid included the full text of Chadirchi's letters in his own memoir. (See Kamel Chadirchi, ibid., pp. 551–71 and Mohammed Hadid, ibid., pp. 515–28).
29. Hashemi had tried to leave the room when the regent had started his rant against him, but the regent screamed at him: 'Sit down! Sit down! Do not leave the room until I have finished speaking to you'. Hashemi, being the military man that he was, obeyed the order. But when the rant continued and the regent accused him of being a liar, he did leave the room. Chadirchi, who was sitting next to Kubba, whispered to the latter while the rant was going on that he (Chadirchi) would support Hashemi if he replied in kind to the regent. If he decided to walk out, Chadirchi said he would walk out too.
30. The Peace Partisans were a Soviet-backed group that held to a different agenda than that of the ICP.

9. THE 1952 INTIFADA AND THE YEARS 1952–1954

1. Mathew Elliot in his book, *Independent Iraq*, writes that 'Abdulillah was a sycophant and would defer to the British as a pupil would to a house master. In one example Elliot gives, he describes how 'Abdulillah would pour his heart out to Ambassador Wright in 'melancholic outbursts so characteristic of him', p. 131.
2. 'Abd al Razzaq al-Hassani, in his *Intifadat Tishrin al-Thani*, says that General Mahmoud confessed to him, in a private interview, that the regent had told him (Mahmoud) that he wanted him to have all opposition leaders tried by Martial Court and that the general should start building hanging stands in public squares.
3. Kamel Chadirchi called it 'the rape of the sanctity of 1,000 homes', Chadirchi, ibid., p. 581.
4. *The Times* and the *New Statesman* published articles by Hadid. (See *The Times*, 26 November 1952.)
5. While Hadid was in London, Nuri al-Sa'id visited Britain after the disturbances were over and asked to meet with him. They met for tea in the civilized setting of Claridge's, and had a frank discussion about the events in Iraq. Nuri, true to form, put the blame for the Intifada on the communists, whilst Hadid explained that such a wide eruption of national sentiment

could not be attributed to any single source, and that the involvement of all political parties (except Nuri's) was proof enough of this.

6. Mohammed Mehdi Kubba, in his memoir, states that when firing over the heads of the demonstrators failed, the army turned their guns on them, killing eighteen and injuring scores of others in Bab al-Sheikh, a district of Baghdad. (See Mohammed Mehdi Kubba, *Mudhakarati fi samim al-ahdath*, p. 348.)

7. FO371, 98736, EQ1016/78, Sir J. Troutbeck, Baghdad, 28 November 1952.

8. Majid Khadduri, *Independent Iraq*, p. 283, as well as several other books on the same topic in Arabic.

9. Ibid., p. 283.

10. 'Troutbeck held a number of decided views on the causes and remedies of Iraq's problems and about Iraqi politicians, and in expounding his ideas he tended to give the impression that no other intelligent interpretation existed', Mathew Elliott, *Independent Iraq: The Monarchy and British Influence: 1941–1958*, p. 98.

11. Mathew Elliott, ibid., p. 103.

12. Muzahim Al-Pachachi, *Sira Siyassiyya*, p. 474.

13. For a detailed account of the new Electoral Law, see George Grassmusk, 'The Electoral Process in Iraq, 1952–1958', Middle East Journal, Vol. 14, 1960.

14. Khalil Kanna, *al-'Iraq Amsuhu wa Ghaduhu*, pp. 154–6.

15. Chadirchi, ibid., pp. 571–2.

16. The regent wanted to empower the Shi'a, but not under Jabr. He had plans to demonstrate to the Shi'a that they would gain far more by abandoning Jabr. (See Mathew Elliot, ibid., p. 103.)

17. Khadduri, ibid., p. 286.

18. 'Abdulillah had his eye on Syria as a possible kingdom for himself. He knew that if Faisal married and produced an heir, he ('Abdulillah) would no longer be crown prince. He had long schemed to rule Syria, and found in Fadhil al-Jamali a prime minister willing to try and actualize this scheme for him. Jamali formed his first cabinet on 17 September 1953, and secretly made of 'Abdulillah's Syrian scheme a priority. (See Phebe Marr, *The Modern History of Iraq*, p. 114, personal interview with Jamali.)

19. Tawfiq Swaidi, *Mudhakarati*, p. 520.

20. Mohammed Hadid, ibid., p. 268.

21. Phebe Marr, ibid., p. 113.

22. Atrocious measures were taken by guards in both Baghdad and Kut prisons, where the authorities opened fire on political prisoners, wounding many and even killing some. These incidents seem to have been a contributing factor to Madfa'i's resignation.

23. Mathew Elliot, ibid., p. 107.

24. FO371, 104666, EQ1016/49, Sir J. Troutbeck, Baghdad, 30 September 1953.

25. Mohammed Hadid, ibid., p. 273.
26. This was confirmed in a letter from Fadhil Jamali to 'Abdulillah dated 23 June 1954, in which Jamali relates a conversation he had with Nuri in which the latter lamented the entry of Chadirchi and his ilk into parliament, stating that they would make his job very difficult indeed. (Kamel Chadirchi, ibid., p. 637.)
27. Waldemar Gallman, *Iraq under General Nuri: My Recollections of Nuri al-Said, 1954–1958*, (Baltimore: John Hopkins Press, 1964), pp. 1–2.
28. Phebe Marr, ibid., p. 115.

10. THE BAGHDAD PACT AND THE YEARS 1954–1958

1. Iraq and Britain also concluded a private agreement which favoured the latter. The Iraqi Council of Ministers at the time was not made aware of this, and it only became known thirty years later, once the Official Secrets Act period had lapsed.
2. Technically, the 'Permanent Council of the Pact of Mutual Cooperation'.
3. At most meetings of the pact, Nuri belaboured the theme of the spread of communism and how communist propaganda should be stymied. In his view, no stability would ever come to the area unless the communist threat was eradicated completely.
4. Waldemar J. Gallman, *Iraq Under Nuri*, p. 54.
5. Ibid., p. 55.
6. Magnus Persson, *Great Britain, the United States, and the Security of the Middle East: The Formation of the Baghdad Pact*, (Lund: Lund University Press, 1998), p. 11.
7. George Lenczowski, *The Middle East in World Affairs*, (Ithaca, NY: Cornell University Press, 1962), p. 196.
8. Nuri pleaded with the American ambassador to secure for him more powerful transmitters (100 kilowatts) for both short and medium waves to match those of Cairo, but the Americans failed to deliver (with the ambassador claiming that his attempts to acquire them had come to nought). Nuri finally got the equipment from the British, but not before taking painful punishment from *Sawt al-Arab*, with its newly added 'Iraq Free Radio' station to intensify its anti-Nuri and anti-British invective. Ambassador Gallman commented wryly in his memoir that 'our treatment of Nuri was destined to be halting, and even bungling at times'. (Ibid., p. 50).
9. Gallman, ibid., p. 38.
10. Ibid., p. 39.
11. Mohammed Hadid, *Mudhakarati*, p. 291.
12. Muzahim al-Pachachi, *Sira Siyasiyya*, pp. 506–7.
13. Wilbur Crane Eveland, *Ropes of Sand: America's Failure in the Middle East*, (New York: W. W. Norton, 1980), pp. 162–71.
14. FO371, 128038, VQ 1011/1, Sir Michael Wright, 8 February 1957, and R. Hooper, Baghdad, 11 July 1956.

15. Mathew Elliot, *Independent Iraq*, p. 123.

16. FO371, 128038, VQ 1011/1, Sir Michael Wright, 8 February 1957.

17. Mathew Elliot, ibid., pp. 121–2.

18. FO 371, 128040, VQ 1015/2, *Chancedr*, Baghdad, 4 January 1957: FO 371, 134198, VQ 1015/36, Baghdad, 22 April 1958.

19. FO 371, 128040, VQ 1015/10, Sir Michael Wright, Baghdad 10 May 1957–24 May 1957. It is strangely amateurish that Wright did not see fit to dispatch an official from his embassy to check on the numbers of political prisoners in order to obtain an accurate figure with which he could counter Salih Jabr's dire but obviously more correct estimate.

20. FO 371, 128040, VQ 1015/9, Sir Michael Wright, Baghdad, 7 March 1957.

21. British accounts speak of Iraq and Jordan, unlike their rivals in Egypt, as respecting the niceties of constitutional proprieties by not wishing to announce the union before their parliaments had approved it. This was political self-delusion, of course, seeing that, in Iraq at least, parliament had been made nothing more than a rubberstamp for Nuri's exploits. (See Mathew Elliot, *Independent Iraq*, p. 131.)

11. IRAQ ON THE EVE OF REVOLUTION

1. The presence of numerous religious, sectarian or ethnic minorities, such as Kurds, Turcomans, Jews, Persians, Yazidis, Armenians, Assyrians, Chaldeans, Sabeans and various other Christian denominations, only added to the tapestry that was expected to become Iraq. Sitting astride all these, were two major Muslim sects, the Sunnis and the Shi'a, torn themselves by sectarian strife.

2. Talib al-Naqib had been invited (more likely duped) into taking tea with Lady Cox, the civil commissioner's (Sir Percy Cox) wife at home. When he left the Cox residence, he was forcibly escorted into a British tank and taken straight into exile!

3. David Fromkin's *The Peace to End All Peace: The Fall of the Ottoman Empire and the Creation of the Modern Middle East*, (New York: Henry Holt, 2001) is cited as a source by many historians including Margaret MacMillan and Davis Andelman, two noted experts on the terms of peace after World War I. Fromkin notes that Wilson's reply to the War Cabinet's request was that 'there was no way of ascertaining public opinion', citing H. V. F. Winstone's biography of Gertrude Bell (*Gertrude Bell*, London: Cape, 1978) as a reference. Winstone writes, regarding the plebiscite that 'there was no adequate means of establishing public opinion in Iraq at that time'. Winstone cites John Marlowe's biography of Arnold Wilson as a source of this conclusion.

4. Even after he was made king, the irritable Winston Churchill wrote of him contemptuously: 'I am getting tired of all these lengthy telegrams, about Faisal and his state of mind... Six months ago, we were paying his hotel bill

in London, and now I am forced to read day after day 800 word messages on questions of his status and his relations with foreign powers. Has he not got some wives to keep him quiet?' CO. 730/16/59435.

5. In the introduction to Gerald de Gaury's book, *Three Kings in Baghdad*, pp. 10–12, Alan de Lacy Rush paints a picture of 'Abdulillah as effeminate and shy, never popular and often arrogant. Freya Stark found him 'fawn-like, more often sinister and chinless'. Rush hints that 'Abdulillah, after divorcing his beautiful Egyptian wife, Malik, after a *marriage blanc*, was less interested in finding another wife than in having de Gaury introduce him to handsome young men in London.

6. 'Abdulillah may have continued to cherish the hope that he might go back to Arabia one day to be re-instated once more as royalty.

7. Private conversation with author, with Princess Fazilet and Princess Jah, the Nizam of Hyderabad's ex-wife. London, March 2010.

8. It seems that 'Abdulillah had a reputation for trying to secure a throne, any throne. Khalil Kanna in his book, *al-'Iraq': Amsuh wa Ghaduh*, p. 131, quotes a conversation he had in London soon after the assassination of King 'Abdallah of Jordan. 'Abdulillah had gone to Amman for the burial, but left abruptly soon afterwards. When asked by Kanna the reason for such haste, 'Abdulillah told him that the Jordanian royal family could hardly tolerate his presence, perceiving him as a vulture about to pounce on the Jordanian throne. He said he was made to feel obliged to leave that stifling atmosphere immediately.

9. Abd al-Razzaq al-Hassani, *Tarikh al-Wizarat al-'Iraqiyya*, vol. 10, pp. 162–3.

10. Ahmad Mukhtar Baban, *Mudhakarat Ahmad Mukhtar Babban*, p. 175. Babban is effusive in his praise for 'Abdulillah in his book, describing him as loyal to both Faisal II and to Iraq. (See Chapter 4 of Babban's book.)

11. For an extract of this memorandum, see footnote on p. 43.

12. Caractacus, *Revolution in Iraq: An Essay in Comparative Political Opinion*, (London: Gollancz, 1959), p. 20.

13. Caractacus, ibid., p. 46.

14. Khalil Kanna, *al-'Iraq: Amsuh wa Ghaduh*, pp. 317–19.

15. Caractacus, ibid., p. 123.

16. Mohammed Hadid, *Mudhakarati*, p. 301.

17. This episode is somewhat curious, in that neither Hadid nor Chadirchi in their memoirs mention any further initiative by Jamil other than this original meeting, when he informed them of the initial contact he had had. Why he should wait some twenty years after the 1958 Revolution to make this fact known, is indeed strange. (See Mohammed Hadid, ibid., pp. 281–2). (The curiousness goes further still in that when the revolution announced its cabinet of ministers, Jamil was not included.)

18. Chadirchi, it may be remembered, had been sentenced to three years in jail with hard labour by Nuri, for having sent a telegram to the president of the Iraqi senate while on a visit to Cairo following the tripartite attack on

Egypt, denouncing the Iraqi regime for having allowed Iraqi oil to be pumped to Haifa at that time. Hadid had intervened personally with the prison authorities to treat Chadirchi in a manner befitting a national leader according to internationally acceptable standards, i.e. not to be forced to wear prison clothes, and to have a private room where he could receive guests. The authorities had further allowed Chadirchi to receive his food from home, and to have his room water-cooled using a 'Kooler', a cooling system, locally manufactured, and well known to all Iraqis of that era. When Nuri heard of these arrangements, he allegedly said that Chadirchi was now in a 'luxury jail', where he could 'throw dinner parties if he wished inside the prison'. Chadirchi must have taken this 'cavalier' statement by Nuri to heart, because in his memoir, he lambasts Nuri for making it, adding bitterly that Nuri should try being in prison sometime. (See Mohammed Hadid, ibid., p. 282 and Chadirchi's *Mudhakarat Kamel Chadirchi*, p. 687.)

19. Fadhil Hussain, who wrote *The Fall of the Monarchy in Iraq* (*Suqoot al-Nidham al-Malaki fi al-'Iraq*), (and *The History of the National Democratic Party* (*Tarikh al-Hizb al-watani al-Demoqrati*), states in the former book (p. 71) that when Qassem offered the ministry of finance (via Mutlaq) to Hadid in early 1957, the latter accepted it. This is clearly erroneous, as Hadid and all other NUF leaders entrusted with portfolios did not accept them until just before the revolution—and, in the case of Hadid, not until the spring of 1958 at the earliest. Hadid and Chadirchi both point out several errors of fact made by this author. In one unlikely episode described on p. 70 of Hussain's book, he writes that Chadirchi, when asked about the fate of King Faisal II, who was murdered in the revolution, supposedly had replied that 45,000 sheep were slaughtered in Baghdad per day—so what if on the day of the revolution, that number had risen to 45,001! A callous and most unlikely statement to have been made by Chadirchi. Curiously, Majid Khadduri in his book, *Republican Iraq: A Study in Iraqi Politics Since the Revolution of 1958*, (Oxford: Oxford University Press, 1969), p. 46, makes the same 'cynical but cryptic' statement but attributes it rather to a civilian advisor of Qassem's, which Chadirchi was certainly not. Hussain's book was published in 1974, five years after Khadduri's. It contains several references to Khadduri's book, though his reference to the 'sheep' quote is made as his own, and not credited to Khadduri.

20. Khalil Kanna, ibid., p. 311.

21. Mohammed Hadid, ibid., pp. 312–13.

22. Majid Khadduri, *Republican Iraq*, pp. 36–7.

23. Khadduri, ibid., p. 36.

24. Interview with Sir Sam Falle by the author in June 2002, at the latter's home in Oxford.

25. King Hussain, *Uneasy Lies the Head: The Autobiography of His Majesty King Hussein I of the Hashemite Kingdom of Jordan*, (New York: B. Geis, 1962), pp. 159–61.

26. Precedent has shown that there was never any love lost between Iraqis and Kuwaitis, as demonstrated by the adversarial positions taken by King Ghazi, Nuri, Qassem and Saddam Hussain, which spanned a period of more than fifty years.
27. Mohammed Hadid, *Mudhakarati*, p. 315.
28. Testimony of General Ghazi al-Daghestani to the People's Court.
29. Quoted from an interview with 'Abd al-Majid by 'Ahmad Mukhtar Babban in the latter's memoir, ibid., p. 259.

12. THE 1958 REVOLUTION: THE BALANCE SHEET

1. The *abayya* is a black head-to-toe garment worn by conservative Iraqi women, which sometimes has a black veil, or *pushi*, to cover a woman's face.
2. These were Mohammed Mehdi Kubba, a Sh'ia former leader of the Independence Party and a member of the United National Front; Khalid Naqshbandi, a Kurd; and General Najib Rubay'i, a Sunni who was to head the council, in recognition of his support for the Free Officers' movement, and for the respect he enjoyed with the public and the army.
3. Phebe Marr, ibid., p. 158.
4. Uriel Dann, in his book *Iraq Under Qassem: A Political History, 1958–1963*, (New York: Praeger, 1969), p. 31, states that both Qassem and 'Arif later denied that Faisal's death was premeditated. When relations had been re-established with Jordan, Qassem blamed 'Arif for the murder. There is direct and credible evidence, he states, that orders by 'Arif were given to the party which penetrated the palace to kill both Faisal and 'Abdulillah. Dann attributes this information to two officers involved in the attack on the palace, though he concludes from the evidence that Qassem's own orders to 'Arif were deliberately vague.
5. Mohammed Hadid, ibid., pp. 316–17.
6. Uriel Dann, ibid., p. 34
7. The mayhem and massacres that followed the U.S. invasion of Iraq in 2003, and that lasted unabated for years, were dismissed contemptuously by the then U.S. secretary of defence, Donald Rumsfeld, churlishly as 'stuff happens'. This ill-thought phrase has since been the subject of a David Hare play of that name.
8. In hindsight, the NUF should have allowed the military to govern alone until a full assessment of their intentions and political leanings could have been ascertained. It may be remembered that this was Chadirchi's view when Hadid and Shanshal briefed him on the progress of the coup while he was still in jail.
9. There is a tendency to forget the fact that Nuri al-Sa'id, Ja'far al-'Askari, Yassin al-Hashemi, 'Ali Jawdat Ayyubi, Jamil al-Midfa'i, among many others, had all been Sharifian officers when they came to Iraq with Faisal I, only to become politicians afterwards.

10. Majid Khadduri, *Republican Iraq*, p. 62.
11. The Faylis were Shi'ia Kurds who had migrated to Iraq from Iran.
12. Mohammed Hadid, ibid., pp. 318–19.
13. U.S-Iraqi relations were not helped when two U.S. citizens were arrested on suspicion of involvement in a huge fire that occurred in an oil products depot in Baghdad. The two Americans were released after two days but only after immense pressure was applied to that effect by the U.S. embassy.
14. See Sam Falle, *My Lucky Life in War, Revolution, Peace and Diplomacy*, (Sussex: Book Guild, 1996). See also, 'Abd al-Latif Shawwaf, *'Abd al-Karim Qassem wa Iraqiyyun Akharun*, pp. 38–9.
15. It is said that when Nasser asked 'Arif what Qassem's reaction might be to 'Arif's idea of an immediate union of Iraq with the UAR, 'Arif is reported to have replied, to Nasser's clear astonishment: 'One bullet would take care of Qassem!' Apparently, Nasser continued to refer to 'Arif as *'al-Sabi'* (the boy) from that time onwards.
16. All three were descended from a higher social class than Qassem, and viewed themselves as rivals for the leadership position, and more fit for it than Qassem. In Talib's case, he was given a cabinet post in the new government in order to try and retain his loyalty. Talib was quoted as saying (by Dr 'Ali Karim Sa'id, *Min Hiwar al-Mafahim ila hiwar al-damm*) that word had reached him that 'Arif had said that he (and Qassem by inference) had 'dug a deep grave' for him, meaning that he was made minister to distance him from army affairs.
17. Qassem took pride at having emerged from a poor background, with a father who was a carpenter. He constantly referred to these origins in his speeches, hoping thus to carry with him the poor and the underprivileged. This endeared him to the vast majority of Iraqis throughout his life.
18. 'In the Iraqi Revolution, the contrast between the world of events, and the world of doctrines and ideas reached a high-water mark. There was no doubt of its popularity. Though the seizure of power was conducted by the military, it was immediately greeted with approval in conservative, radical, and communist circles. It is the only seizure of power in Iraqi history that can be called a "revolution"'. See Edith and E. F. Penrose: *Iraq: International Relations and National Development*, (London, E. Benn, 1978), p. 536.
19. W. J. Gallman, *Iraq Under Nuri*, p. 205.
20. Hanna Batatu, *Old Social Classes*, p. 806.
21. This bloc was composed of the National Democratic Party, the Independence Party, the Iraq Communist Party and the Ba'th Party.
22. According to the distinguished Iraqi statesman and former cabinet minister, 'Abd al-Latif Shawwaf, Mohammed Hadid became Qassem's 'brain'. 'In accepting to become Minister of Finance, Mohammed Hadid gave the revolution a certain stature that helped enormously in stabilising its position, both internally and internationally, in its early days ... He became Qassem's principal political and economic advisor, and played a critical

role in helping him remain steadfast against a powerful communist tidal wave'. 'Abdel-Latif Shawwaf, *'abdel-Karim Qassem wa Iraqiyyun Akharun*, pp. 38, 41.

23. Adnan al-Pachachi, *al-Sharq al-Awsat* newspaper, 29 March 2010.

24. Mohammed Hadid, *Mudhakarati*, pp. 468–9. See also Hanna Batatu, *Old Social Classes*, p. 981. Batatu says this of Qassem: 'Those who stood against him admit that the people had more genuine affection for him than for any other ruler in the modern history of Iraq'.

25. Uriel Dann, ibid., p. 54.

26. 'As befitted a student of Harold Laski', commented Uriel Dann, ibid., p. 59.

27. The complex that Qassem built, 'Madinat al-Thawra' (Revolution City), still stands to this day.

28. The Sterling Area included countries that were under the British sphere of influence. Countries could trade with each other in sterling but had to submit to British foreign exchange controls. The Iraqi Central Bank had to deposit all its foreign exchange assets (especially those accruing from oil sales) in the Bank of England, and had absolutely no say as to their management. During WWII, Britain benefitted enormously from this unjust arrangement. It paid for its own war expenditure out of Iraq's foreign assets, merely crediting it with the local and much-weakened currency equivalent, the dinar. This had a depressing effect on the dinar, which dropped in value when Britain deliberately forced down the value of sterling, to which the dinar was tied.

29. Edith and E. E. Penrose in their book, *Iraq, International Relations and National Development*, pp. 387–90 write that Mohammed Hadid's Law 80 in Iraq and the nationalization of oil by Mossadegh in Iran were the two foremost landmark oil events of the Middle East up to that period. In his book, *Asrar Thawrat 14 Tammuz*, Ism'ail 'Arif credits Law 80 as being the Qassem government's greatest achievement, p. 406.

30. Over 700 NGOs were licensed under the new law (see Hanna Batatu, *Old Social Classes*, p. 912. The Association Law was promulgated in 1960 to replace the old law of 1955, which gave sweeping powers to the executive (prime minister and minister of interior) to control party political life. The 1960 law was therefore a landmark law, as it abrogated those powers and invested them in the Court of Appeal's general committee, the highest legal entity in the land.

31. Agrarian reform was a principal tenet of the NDP, and axiomatic to Mohammed Hadid, the party's chief spokesman on the subject. Qassem may have been echoing Hadid's words when he declared in a speech: 'Agrarian reform will be the basis of the social reform program of this government'. (See Uri Dann, ibid, p.XX.) See also Hadid's speech to parliament in 1937.

32. This measure went to the very root of Iraq's society, which was still largely tribal. It went hand in hand with the Agrarian Reform Act, in an attempt

to destroy—once and for all—the legal basis for feudalism in Iraq. It sought to create a modern society, which owed its allegiance more to state benefits than to tribal ones, going as far as changing the tribal names of certain areas, to ones that did not carry the name of the tribe (e.g., Muntafiq was changed to Nasiriyya and Dulaim to Ramadi). Furthermore, civil and criminal laws were now to apply in these areas.

33. The Gender Equality Law met with stiff opposition from the reactionary elements of Iraq's society, particularly from religious sheikhs, as going against the tenets of Islam and the Qur'an especially when it gave women an equal share in inheritance. Unfortunately for Iraq, and after Qassem's demise, the governments that followed caved in to reactionary pressure. The law was vastly amended, but not in women's favour.

34. Iraq's economy boomed. Applications to register companies soared by 500 per cent. Businesses tripled or quadrupled their profits. Daoud Khalastchi, a scion of a prominent Jewish family from Shamia (in Iraq's south), and a typical successful businessman of his day, told the author that his companies, which dealt in autos, tyres, lubricant oils, combines and tractors, tripled their profits after the revolution. (Interview with Daoud and Evelyn Khalastchi at their home in London 22 November 2010. Evelyn Khalasatchi, nee Zilkha, hails from the Iraqi Jewish and internationally renowned Zilkha banking family.)

35. A phenomenon that continues to be true at the time of writing, reflected in the Iraqi elections of 2010.

36. Majid Khadduri, *Republican Iraq*, p. 132.

37. Isma'il 'Arif, *Asrar Thawrat 14 Tammuz*, pp. 369–70. The author was a Free Officer and became minister of education after the revolution. He describes 'Abd al Salam 'Arif as having taken the mantle of Nasser days after the revolution and would address the crowds by stating: 'I greet you in the name of our big brother Gamal (Nasser)', deliberately omitting any mention of Qassem in his speeches—a fact not lost on Qassem by any means. Isma'il 'Arif writes that 'Abd al Salam began to think of Qassem as the 'Mohammed Naguib of Egypt, who could be gotten rid of by a mere push'.

38. 'Ali Karim Sa'id, *From the Memories of Talib Shabib* (*Min hiwar al-mafahim ila hiwar al-damm*, pp. 112–13).

39. 'Arif, who never took up his post, returned to Baghdad unexpectedly and was summarily arrested. He was later brought before Mahdawi's Court for trial.

40. Isma'il 'Arif, *Asrar Thawrat 14 Tammuz*, p. 361. 'Arif confesses that Mahdawi was a constant source of embarrassment to Qassem who, on several occasions, threatened to move the proceedings to a proper law court. He finally suspended the Mahdawi Court in the summer of 1959, and moved the proceedings to a law court, only to reinstate it after an attempt on his (Qassem's) life'.

41. 'Ali Karim Sa'id, ibid., pp. 112–13.

42. Nasser's 'chronicler' and his leading Egyptian media voice trashed Qassem. Despite the availability of numerous books on the 14 July Revolution which were critical of Qassem for not establishing a Revolutionary Command Council (RCC), Mohammed Hassanein Haykal wrote in his book, *Nasser, The Cairo Documents*, (London: New English Library, 1972) that Qassem was chairman of the RCC and that 'Arif was his deputy. He makes further inaccurate comments such as pronouncing that Kirkuk was the capital of Mosul! (See 'Ala' al-Din al-Dhahir's article in *al-Mawsum*, vol. 32, p. 64.)

43. This may seem at variance with Nasser's avowed support for those pressing for union, including 'Arif. The circumstantial evidence would indicate that Nasser's assurance to Chadirchi was more in the way of a polite gesture which he (Nasser) did not actually believe in.

44. Mohammed Hadid, ibid., p. 448.

45. Hanna Batatu, ibid., p. 901.

46. Uriel Dann, in *Iraq Under Qassem*, writes that Chadirchi had relinquished the leadership in a fit of peevishness to the younger Hadid, and that the latter had now taken an independent line that Chadirchi wished to reverse, ibid., p. 291.

47. Hanna Batatu on p. 956 of *Old Social Classes*, refers to Chadirchi as 'old Chadirchi' and as out of touch. Also Uriel Dann ibid., p. 291: 'Chadirchi's… mind as a politician had been formed by the *Front Populaire* of the early 1930s which prevailed among the opposition until 1958. By then Chadirchi was an elderly man and very ill, and he could no longer adapt himself to a radically changed situation'.

48. Khalil Kanna, in his book *al-'Iraq', Amsuhu wa Ghaduhu*, pp. 366–7, attributes Chadirchi's 360 degree turn on Qassem and the revolution (after having accepted it at the beginning) to Chadirchi's so-called vanity, which Kanna claims he was famous for. 'Chadirchi dreamt of the leadership and the presidency of Iraq only to wake up and see another person robbing him of that role', Kanna writes. Kanna was a prominent figure of the former regime and often spoken of as Nuri's heir. See also *Mudhakarat Ahmad Mukhtar Baban*, p. 154.

49. Mohammed Hadid, ibid., pp. 325–6.

50. Uriel Dann, ibid., p. 62.

51. Ibid., p. 292.

52. Chadirchi has not left a record of this meeting, although at least four references exist of the conversation between the two men, according to *Le Monde*, 5 February 1963.

53. Isma'il 'Arif, ibid., p. 327.

54. Ibid., p. 198.

13. THE AFTERMATH

1. As indeed the fate that awaited many an Arab dictator in the Arab Spring of 2011.

2. 'Ali Karim Sa'id, *Min Hiwar al-Mafahim ila Hiwar al-Damm*, p. 110.
3. A gun was later found on Nuri's body under the woman's '*abaya* that he wore to flee.
4. Sam Falle, then retired and knighted, was interviewed by the author on 11 June 2000, at the latter's home in Oxford. Falle said 'there were people in Iraq who had tried to usher in democracy but had failed. Mohammed Hadid and Kamil Chadirchi were such people. They were the Nehru and Gandhi of Iraq'.
5. For the full text of Hadid's eulogy, see Mohammed Hadid, ibid., pp. 495–9.
6. Mohammed Hadid, ibid., pp. 322–3. Most of the memoirs written by the 8 March coup perpetrators decry the treatment of Hadid, who had rendered such invaluable services to his country.
7. The author, who was studying to be a chartered accountant in London at the time, was asked by his father, Mohammed Hadid, to research the topic with the Royal Mint, which had struck the coins in London. It was the Royal Mint that informed the author that the charge against his father would not stand, as the rise in the price of silver had more than covered the cost of the coins' minting, and that the meltdown value of the silver alone would show a neat profit to government coffers.
8. Majid Khadduri, *Republican Iraq*, p. 200.
9. Hanna Batatu, ibid., p. 24.
10. Mohammed Hadid, ibid., p. 474.
11. Falle found the young king a disappointment. True, he was manipulated from behind the scenes by his uncle 'Abdulillah, but he failed his subjects' expectation that he would emerge as his own man. Falle found him agreeable, courteous, intelligent and with the polish of a student at Harrow. He was not able, however, to assert himself and cut his uncle down to size, as had his 'tough little cousin' King Hussain of Jordan in the case of Glubb Pasha. Falle recounted that most liberal Iraqis right up to the revolution were still prepared to accept Faisal as a constitutional monarch provided that he ditched 'Abdulillah.
    Author's note: The Iraqi public seems to have had an innate sympathy for Faisal because of his well-respected nationalist father and the fact that he was raised as an orphan after his mother's premature death.
12. Alan Rush wrote a detailed obituary of Mohammed Hadid in *The Independent* newspaper, which was published on 6 August 1999.

14. THE LESSONS OF HISTORY

1. The three Iraqis were Kanaan Makiya, Hatem Mukhlis and Rend Rahim, the latter becoming Iraq's ambassador to the U.S. after the invasion.
2. Peter W. Galbraith, *The End of Iraq: How American Incompetence Created a War Without End*, (New York: Simon & Schuster, 2006), p. 83.
3. In the preface to his memoir, *At the Centre of the Storm: My Years at the*

CIA, (New York: Harper Collins, 2007), p. 1, George Tenet writes that on 12 September 2001—the day following the attack on the Twin Towers—he was stunned by Perle's statement that 'Iraq had a price to pay for what happened yesterday'. Tenet adds that there was absolutely no intelligence linking Saddam's Iraq to 9/11.

4. *A Clean Break: A New Strategy for Securing the Realm*, 1996.

5. The name 'Bletchley' derived from the British code-breaking and intelligence gathering outfit housed at Bletchley Park, the famous stately home in England.

6. Bob Woodward, *State of Denial, Bush at War, Part II*, (New York: Simon & Schuster, 2006), p. 190.

7. When asked at his farewell party from Baghdad what advice he would leave his Iraqi successor, Bremer replied to a bemused audience: 'de-Bremerfication'. At least the man had a sense of humour!

8. Bush later thought it politic to apologize for his statement in his own memoir, *Decision Points*, (New York: Crown Publishers, 2010).

9. Whether he meant it or not, George W. Bush, in his inaugural speech, had this to say to the world prior to 9/11: he told Americans that his presidency would radiate idealism to the world as a continuation of the American 'story'. This story, he said, is that of a new world that became a friend and liberator of the old, a story of a slave-holding society that became a servant of freedom, the story of a power that went into the world, to protect but not to possess, to defend but not to conquer. It is no small an irony how such ringing words were rendered hollow when measured against the reality of the Iraq War. Richard Hass, a frenzied supporter of the war and a former National Security Council official did an intellectual U-turn after the fact and changed his tune in his memoir, *War of Necessity, War of Choice: A Memoir of Two Iraq Wars*, (New York: Simon & Schuster, 2009) about the decision to go to war with Iraq: 'I will go to my grave not knowing how George Bush reached his decision. Maybe he wanted to destroy an established nemesis of the United States. Maybe he wanted to change the course of history by bringing democracy to an area that has resisted much of modernity. Maybe he wanted to accomplish what his father did not. The arguments put forward for going to war with Iraq—its non-compliance with UN resolutions, its possession of WMDs—turned out to be essentially window dressing, trotted out to build international support for a policy that had been forged mostly for other reasons'.

10. Having first claimed that he did not remember even saying those words, Tenet later confirmed before a crowd of 5000 people that 'those were the dumbest words I ever said'. See Bob Woodward, *State of Denial*, p. 304. See also George Tenet's own book, *Memoir*, p. 480.

11. Bob Woodward, in his book, quotes Garner as saying: (ibid., p. 181): 'Those sons of bitches! I busted my ass. I dropped everything I had… Suddenly Bremer appeared and it looked like they had fired me'.

12. Liam Anderson, *The Future of Iraq: Dictatorship, Democracy or Division?*, (New York: Palgrave Macmillan, 2004), pp. 186–7. The Kurdish question is obviously a very highly complex one, revolving around the unfulfilled promises made to the Kurds in the Treaty of Sevres for a homeland of their own. See Peter W. Galbraith, *The End of Iraq*, p. 148: 'In the aftermath of WWI, the Kurds believed that they had been promised an independent state drawing from President Woodrow Wilson's famous 14 Points. The Treaty of Sevres (article 64) gave credence to Kurdish aspirations for an independent Kurdistan'.

13. George Packer, *The Assassins' Gate: America in Iraq*, (New York: Farrar, Straus and Gigoux, 2005), p. 13.

14. The Arab Human Development Report (2003) identified a 'Freedom Deficit' in the Arab world and lamented the backwardness of Arab countries in lagging behind a world that was inexorably changing into a democratic one. This report was a wake-up call for the Arab world and it is not inconceivable that it was translated into action by the Arab Spring of 2011.

15. Hence, the British commanding officer in Iraq in 1920, Sir Aylmer Haldane's memoir was entitled *Insurrection in Mesopotamia, 1920*, (London: W. Blackwood & Sons, 1922).

16. Ja'far Pasha al-Askari, then Iraqi minister in London, answered Dobbs by retorting that they were not adventurers but had 'worked during the most difficult times and were, and are, animated by a sincere desire to work for their country to attain the glories of its ancient past'.

17. Iraq sanctions provides chilling statistics of hundreds of thousands of children dead, and the economic, social and cultural destruction of the country that it will never recover from, which may have been the reason for their cruel and vengeful imposition.

18. In an early example of British racism towards the Arabs, Winston Churchill, while attending the Cairo Conference of 1921 which created Iraq and appointed Faisal as its king, would summon the British group of Middle East experts (which included T. E. Lawrence, A. T. Wilson and Gertrude Bell among others) to the elegant Semiramis Hotel where he was staying to plot out British imperial designs for the would-be country. The future of Iraq was decided by Churchill and this British group without even consulting the only Iraqis (Ja'far al-Askari and Sasson Heskiel) that were included in the group, travelling to Cairo for that purpose. It seems Churchill did not approve of Arabs being allowed into the hotel, or even into its garden. (See Barry M. Lando, *Web of Deceit: The History of Western Complicity in Iraq, From Churchill to Kennedy to George W. Bush*, (New York: Other Press, 2007 p. 14.) More embarrassment was heaped on Askari and Heskiel in that their names were at the bottom of the delegates list, with junior British officers attached to the Iraqi army preceding Askari (who was a general) and minor ministry of finance British functionaries preceding Heskiel, the supposed minster. See Report on Middle East Conferences held in Cairo and Jerusalem, 12 to 13 March 1921. (F.O.371/6343.)

19. An address to the joint session of the two Houses of Congress in the United States by President Woodrow on 8 January 1918 formulated one of the most important documents for the propagation of democracy in the Middle East, which came to be known as the Fourteen Points, or 'Wilson's Principles'. In it, the president stated: 'We entered this war because violations of right had occurred, which touched us to the quick and made the life of our own people impossible until they were corrected and the world secured once and for all against their recurrence. What we demand in this war, therefore, is nothing peculiar to ourselves. It is that the world be made fit and safe to live in; and particularly that it be made safe for every peace-loving nation which, like our own, wishes to live its own life, determine its own institutions, and be assured of justice and fair dealing by the other peoples of the world against force and selfish aggression'.

20. Howard Bliss was described by Harry N. Howard as 'a distinguished looking American of the long, thin Yankee type'. See Howard's book, *The King-Crane Commission: An American Enquiry in the Middle East*, (Beirut: Khayats, 1963), p. 25.

21. Woodrow Wilson Papers. IX-A,33.

22. Harry N. Howard, ibid., p. 37.

23. Margaret MacMillan, *Paris 1919: Six Months that Changed the World*, (New York: Random House, 2002), p. 376.

24. Earlier, an American university was contemplated for Mosul because of its strong Christian population before deciding in favour of Beirut.

25. Harry N. Howard, ibid., p. 133. (Charles Crane was nicknamed Harun al-Rashid, the storied Abbasid caliph, by George Antonius for his love of all things Middle Eastern.)

26. The McMahon-Hussein Correspondence was a protracted exchange of letters (14 July 1915, to 30 January 1916) during World War I, between the Sharif of Mecca, Hussein bin Ali, and Sir Henry McMahon, British high commissioner in Egypt, concerning the future political status of the lands under the Ottoman Empire. In return for their role in assisting the British in defeating the Ottomans, the Arabs were promised a United Arabia under the leadership of Hussein as king. J. R. Colville, secretary to the MacMahon Committee, wrote: 'MacMahon had assured Hussein that when they were liberated from Ottoman rule, *all* Arabia, including Palestine which for two thousand years had been their home, should be theirs to inhabit and govern'. See J. R. Colville, *Man of Valour: The Life of Field Marshal, the Viscount Gort, VC, GCB, DSO, MVO, MC.*, (London: Collins, 1972), p. 259. The British promise had also been confirmed in the famous MacMahon 24 October 1915 letter, which Arnold Toynbee, who had been asked to scrutinize the correspondence, while affirming the promise, states may have been 'lost in translation' from Arabic into English by so-called British Arabists (in this case Hubert Young) thus confusing its meaning. This strikes the author of this book as constituting a most convenient cop-out!

27. Phebe Marr writes in *Modern History of Iraq* that when Hashemi fell on hard times, having stayed on in Syria after Faisal's ignominious departure, he became homesick to return to Iraq and join Faisal. He wrote to Faisal to request permission to return, but Faisal did not even acknowledge his letter. When he finally did reply, it was only to tell him that the time was not opportune for him to return. Faisal finally relented but not before he punished Hashemi by offering him the relatively lowly job of governor of a far flung province. Hashemi is reputed to have said to a friend: 'Two years ago, I was nominated to be prime minister in Syria. Now I am a humble governor of a remote province in my own country'.

28. Aziz 'Ali al-Masri (1880–1964) was among the most influential and brilliant Arab officers in the Ottoman army. He was the leader of the Arab nationalist movement among his fellow Arab officers, which led to the formation of the secret *al-Ahd* Society.

29. Ghassan Attiya, *Iraq—1908–1921, A Socio-Political Study*, (Beirut, 1973), p. 103. Also F.O. 371/2775/182183.

30. The reason that Iraqis came to predominate in the Sharifian forces was because they represented the majority among the students sent to the military academy in Istanbul.

31. F.O. 371/3381/146256.

32. 'Abd al-Karim Al-'Uzri, a former cabinet minister and staunch Nuri-supporter during the monarchy, told the author in a private interview on 21 February 2003: 'The British were the secret partner in the Iraqi Government, manipulating all decision-making through their men. Those men started with Faisal and 'Abd al-Rahman al-Naqib as prime minister in 1921, and finished with 'Abd al-Mohsen Al-Saadun and Nuri Al-Said by the end of the decade'. According to 'Uzri, the political order in Iraq was set by British high commissioners and by Miss Gertrude Bell, and not by the Iraqi government of the time.

33. The tribal leaders in Mesopotamia had always supported the Ottoman Empire in the belief that by serving the Caliphate, they were serving Islam. It finally dawned upon these leaders that the Turks had become only interested in advancing the cause of Turkish nationalism and had taken to showing arrogance and disdain for anyone not Turkish. The tribes withdrew into their own shell when they observed the callous behaviour of the Turks in governing them. They retained their strong will and their Arab identity. History of the last two centuries prior to 1918 has never recorded that the tribes were ever truly subjects of the Ottomans.

34. In fact, during the 1948 *Wathba* Uprising, demonstrators clamoured for him to become prime minister.

35. Andrew Kohut and Bruce Stokes, *America Against the World: How We Are Different and Why We Are Disliked*, (New York: Times Books, 2006), p. 3.

ANNEX: A NOTE ON IRAQ'S OIL

1. See Mohammed Hadid, *Mudhakarati*; Helmut Mejcher, *Imperial Quest for Oil*; Abdallah Isma'il, *Mufawadhat al-Iraq al-Naftiyya* and 'Abd al-Latif al-Shawwaf', *Hawla qadhiyat al-Naft fi al-Iraq*. All four books confirm this point.
2. Mejcher, *Imperial Quest for Oil*, p. 81.
3. CO 730/4/41616.
4. Mohammed Hadid, ibid, p. 403.
5. This was a British-Turkish company registered in England.
6. In August 1918, British Foreign Secretary Arthur Balfour worried that declaring the oil of Mesopotamia a booty of war would be 'too old-fashionably imperialistic'. He nevertheless went on to tell the Prime Ministers of the Dominions: 'I do not care under what system we keep the oil, but I am quite clear it is all-important for us that this oil be available'. To make sure this would happen, British forces captured Mosul *after* the Armistice was signed with Turkey. (See Daniel Yergin, *The Prize*, p. 189).
7. The control of this resource by British companies had become a strategic priority, as the British navy was converting its fleet from coal power to oil.
8. The Baghdadbahn was a 1,600-kilometre railway, built in 1903, that started in Konya and went on to Baghdad. The railway was an engineering masterpiece, one of the most ambitious projects of the Ottoman Empire and its successor states.
9. The Ottoman Sultan, Mohammed Rashad (Mohammed V), delegated negotiations with the Turkish Oil Company to his Prime Minister, Sa'id Hilmi Pasha, grandson of the Khedive Mohammed Ali of Egypt. It was Hilmi Pasha who was said to have promised the concession to Calouste Gulbenkian.
10. The United States had through Wilson's Fourteen Points championed the right of Arab countries to decide their fate of their own free will. When it came to its economic interests, however, it refused to play second fiddle to Britain, and insisted on receiving an equal share of Iraq's oil.
11. The British played along with the 'self-determination' card to humour the Americans. Robert Cecil, Junior Foreign Minister (1918) stated: 'We ought to play self-determination for all it is worth, knowing in the bottom of our hearts we are more likely to benefit from it than anybody else. It would be very important if we could produce an Arab who would back up our claims'. (CAB 23/42, Eastern Committee, Minutes, 20 December 1918). Faisal was to be that Arab, and Lawrence was the man dispatched to bring him in for talks in London.
12. 'There was no intent by the oil companies to place the oil in the hands of the Iraqi government nor of permitting the government to interfere in the management of what was to be a wholly-owned subsidiary'. See Edith & E.F. Penrose, *Iraq*, p. 60.
13. Thereafter, the company changed its name to the Iraq Petroleum Company (IPC).

14. Daniel Yergin, *The Prize*, pp. 204–5. Yergin writes about Gulbenkian's claim that, at one of the meetings during the negotiations, he asked for a large map of the Middle East, then took a thick red pencil and drew a line along the boundaries of the now defunct Ottoman Empire, which became the basis for the 'Red Line Agreement'. Yergin, however, pooh-poohs Gulbenkian's claim as 'over embellishment'. since several months earlier, the British, using Foreign Office maps, and the French, with maps from the Quai d' Orsay, had already established the boundaries of the monopoly. The agreement nevertheless created a monopoly for its signatories: the Anglo-Persian, Royal Dutch/Shell, the French and the Americans now operated under the Near East Development Company.

15. The Basra Concession soon bore fruit with the discovery in April 1938 of the abundant oilfield 'Burgan', a short distance from Basra.

16. The Soviet Union's stepping up of oil production in the 1920s instigated a global price war. This led to a meeting by the major Western oil companies in Scotland in 1928, which resulted in the Achnacarry Agreement. The heart of the document was the 'As-Is' understanding, in which the participants were allocated a quota in various markets based on their existing shares of 1928. A uniform selling price was thereby established, eliminating any fear about price competition amongst the adherents. (See Daniel Yergin, *The Prize*, pp. 263–4.)

17. Khanaqeen was a small area located on the Iran-Iraq border that formed part of the 'Transferred Territories'. The area came under Iranian sovereignty but was transferred to Iraqi sovereignty under a special agreement regarding the settlement of the Iran-Iraq borders. The exploration rights were granted to the Khanaqeen Petroleum Company, a subsidiary of the Anglo-Persian Oil Company (later to become BP). It produced 5000 bb a day.

18. Both loans had to be paid back from oil revenues after the war.

19. Abd al-Latif Shawwaf, ibid., pp. 10–11.

INDEX

Hadid, Hajj Hussain: family of, 42; Mayor of Mosul, 42

Hadid, Mohammed: 41, 44, 47, 58, 61, 70, 74–5, 77, 95–6, 99, 101, 105–8, 111, 116, 135, 139, 145–7, 149–50, 154–7, 159, 168–9, 186–7, 206, 214, 218, 220, 229, 233–4, 243, 246, 248–9, 252–3, 271, 273; adversarial relationship with Nuri al-Sa'id, 251; arrest of (1963), 239; background of, 42; death of, 252; economic policies of, 222, 241; family of, 42, 112; member of executive committee of NDP, 104; member of *Jam'iyat al-Sa'I li Mukafahat al'-Umiyya*, 52; member of NUF, 190; member of Sha'biyya Group, 40; memoir of, 9, 47, 104, 109, 116–17, 146, 152, 172, 176, 189, 203, 232; resignation (1958), 236; return to Iraq (1931), 45; speeches of, 151; Treasurer of The Young Iraqis Club, 43; withdrawal of resignation, 231; writings of, 56

Haidar, Rustum: Iraqi Minister of Finance, 283

al-Haidari, Daoud: resignation of (1948), 139

al-Haidary, Darwish: member of Sha'biyya Group, 40

Haikal, Mohammed Hussain Pasha: editor of *al-Siryassa*, 43

Haldane, General Ayimer: 17; *Insurrection in Mesopotamia*, 18

Hamandi, Ja'far: 156

Hammurabi, King: laws of, 2

Hanioglu, Sukru: 4

al-Hashemi, Taha: 9, 156, 162–3; family of, 60; Iraqi Minister of Defence, 283; leader of UPF, 161

al-Hashemi, Yassin: 9, 48, 55–6, 62, 64, 67, 83, 268–9; administration of, 29, 56–7, 66; death of, 81;

family of, 60; leader of al-Ikha'a al-Watani Party, 47, 52; speech in Basra (1936), 59

Hashemites: 20

Hassan, Qasim: 117, 156

al-Hassani, 'Abd al-Razzaq: 130, 132; *al-'Iraq fi Daurai al-'Ihtilal wal 'Intidab*, 19; *Tarikh al-Wizarat al-'Iraqiyya*, 144–5

Hassib, Khair al-Din: Governor of Iraqi Central Bank, 240

Haydar, Sa'id: 10

Herbits, Steve: member of AEI, 256

Heskial, Sassoon: first Iraqi Finance Minister, 5, 29

Hitler, Adolf: 91–2

Hitti, Philip: *History of the Arabs*, 2–3

Hmoud, Hudaib Hajj: 214, 233; withdrawal of resignation, 231

Hourani, Albert: 4

Howard, Harry: *The King-Crane Commission*, 266

al-Husri, Sati': 10; Director of Education at AUB, 38

Hussain of Jordan, King: 193, 210; family of, 173; *Uneasy Lies the Head*, 209–10

Hussain of the Hijaz, Sharif: 4, 20, 24, 269; family of, 20, 196; leader of Arab Revolt, 8–9, 37

al-Hussaini, 'Haj Amin: 140

Hussein, Saddam: 19, 195, 201, 237, 240, 249, 256, 260; family of, 200; political use of Iraqi oil reserves, 260; regime of, 3, 274–5; trial and execution of (2006), 238; use of chemical weapons against Kurdish population, 259

Ibrahim, 'Abd al-Fattah: 41, 44–5, 47, 60, 77–8, 81, 95–6, 99, 101, 107–8, 272; member of *Jam'iyat al-Sa'I li Mukafahat al'-Umiyya*, 52; member of National Unity